VALUE TRAP: THEORY OF UNIVERSAL VALUATION

From Academia and Money Managers

"*Value Trap* is terrific! It is full of immense wisdom and great stories. I loved it and I am confident that you will, too."

> Gary N. Smith, Ph.D.
> Fletcher Jones Professor of Economics, Pomona College
> Author of *Standard Deviations, The AI Delusion, Money Machine,* and *What the Luck?*

"Over 30 years as an investment advisor, I have been asked so many times to suggest "a book that teaches me how to do all this (investing) stuff?" My response has always been along the lines of, "Don't you realize that people spend $100,000 and more on MBA's in finance or go through the grueling process of getting their CFA certification--one of the hardest post-graduate exams out there? Many more have spent 20 or 30 years actually investing other people's money, and you really think you can read one book and match wits with these people?" Well, Brian, you did it. I can now honestly recommend this book to anyone, and confidently say, "If you read it, understand it, and (the hardest part) actually utilize it, you will have the tools to invest successfully on your own."

> William Deshurko
> Investment Advisor, 401 Advisor, LLC

"*Value Trap* addresses investing from a perspective that is so meaningful to today's investors and advisors. It offers so much wisdom and knowledge cementing Mr. Nelson's place in economic thought leadership."

> Deborah W. Ellis, CFP
> Investment Advisor Representative
> Author of *Your Money and You*

"*Value Trap* has a found a home on my bookshelf, nestled between Peter Lynch and Warren Buffett. The voluminous references compiled by Mr. Nelson in writing *Value Trap*--a 15-page bibliography; dozens of graphics; an index 16-pages in length; 21-pages of notes--reveal a man on a mission, sharing his passion, knowledge, and in-sights on how all investors can apply an equity valuation model grounded in analytical and behavioral finance. Serious students of the market need to read this book."

> Robert J. Kuehl, CFP
> Vice President, H.C. Denison Co.

"It doesn't matter if you are an individual investor, financial adviser, or chief investment officer for a family practice. You need to consume *Value Trap* as part of your foundation--in the way that reading a Berkshire annual letter, or revisiting Joel Greenblatt, or tossing back Peter Bernstein's *Against the Gods* resets your mind."

> Alexander Skabry
> Chief Investment Officer, Harvest Capital Assets

"*Value Trap* challenges the status quo offering alternatives to the pervasive groupthink mentality so common in the investing world today. With a focus on enterprise valuation, the book covers a lot of ground navigating through a minefield of contentious subjects like index investing, stock buybacks and market bubbles. Nelson provides loads of independent critical thinking. Astute analysis is paired with interesting anecdotes and Nelson's own experiences as a veteran equity analyst making the book an enjoyable read. Investors will find great value in *Value Trap*."

> Michael Euston, AAMS, AIF
> Managing Partner, Chief Investment Officer
> Heirloom Wealth Management, LLC

"As a Houston-based investor, the energy sector is very important to us. Brian's book clearly shows why many market participants, caught up in the thirst for yield, got the pipeline space wrong."

> Mark McMeans, CFA
> Chief Executive Officer, Brasada Capital Management

"As a student of investing and having read more books on investing than I can count, I think Brian Nelson has done a masterful job of presenting the more important concepts in an objective, truthful manner. The writing is excellent, and the academic rigor is as good as anyone might expect. He has addressed the facts head-on and dealt with them in a fair manner. I greatly appreciate his candor and all the references in the footnotes to support his points. This book contains a ton of helpful information, and while it is not an easy read, this is exactly what makes it worth one's time and effort. It should be read by all RIAs for their own benefit and because it will be helpful in communicating sound valuation insights to clients."

> David Phillips
> Former General Counsel and Investment Manager

"*Value Trap* is an excellent well written book that cogently articulates how critically important understanding enterprise value is to successful investing. There is much that either a seasoned professional or experienced individual investor can learn from Brian's in-depth and insightful analysis of enterprise value. I whole-heartedly recommend *Value Trap* to anyone interested in improving their investing skills and performance."

> Kevin Truitt
> Chief Investment Officer
> Director of Research, SDM Investments, LLC

"*Value Trap* is an informative book that provides great insight into enterprise valuation and how important it is to consider multiple factors when making an equity investment. It is a must read for any investor, from the professional to those who want to better understand the importance of valuation."

> David Homard, CFA
> President, Castellum Asset Management

"After 35 years in the business and having followed many great value analysts and investors, I've finally found a value formula that encompasses enterprise valuation and technical/momentum indicators that actually makes sense and works! Stock pickers in this business are a dying breed. With the tools provided in this fantastic book I can continue to provide great research and individual stock ideas for my clients."

> Thomas L. Judge, Jr.
> Managing Principal, Tiller Financial, LLC

"Brian Nelson is a man before his time. This book cuts through the weeds of modern investment theories and proves that investing is based on the future expectations of stocks, not the past performance. As a financial advisor, I can honestly admit that most folks in my profession do not know what they are doing any more than the average joe, any more than a car salesman knows if that car he just sold you is going to have engine trouble on the way home or not. Brian's system, Valuentum, inspects the ability of that car (stock) to pilot you home not just today, but years in the future. A 2005 Escalade might have been a nice car years ago, but before getting in a driving it home, shouldn't you know more than just what the price tag says? That's this book, and the amazing truths within its pages."

Brendan Messenger, CFP
Certified Financial Planner, Cornerstone Financial Southwest

"*Value Trap* is an amazing detailed framework of the science of universal valuation to bring research to a higher level toward better investing."

Craig Richman, CLU, ChFC, AIFA
Private Money Manager & Advisor, Richman Capital Management

"*Value Trap* is a brilliant encapsulation of the fallacy that underpins the very idea of valuation today and the pitfalls those fallacies create for investors. Brian does not stop at identifying the problem; he does what he does best; he lays out a hypothesis developed through experience and critical thinking and offers a better approach."

Curt R. Stauffer
President, Seven Summits Capital, LLC

"When I first met Brian, he was an officer of an investment group at Benedictine University. I was with a regional brokerage firm and was the rep of record for account held by Benedictine. From time to time, I would meet with the club, and from the first meeting with Brian, I could tell he had a passion for investments. I now utilize the Valuentum theory in selection of stocks and have been rewarded quite often through the process Brian and his group bring to the table."

Clint Bull
Financial Consultant, LPL Financial

From the Media and Financial Community

"I first heard of Brian Michael Nelson when he reached out to me in 2015 to pitch me on his bearish thesis on Kinder Morgan, a major energy pipeline stock with a big dividend yield that was then a darling of the income-seeking crowd. I decided to run his views on the Barron's website, along with rebuttal views from the Wall Street establishment. Bearish calls are often wrong, but when Kinder eventually cut its dividend sharply, sending the stock spiraling, I took notice. Suddenly, the bloom was off the rose of an entire sector and Brian was one of the first sounding a warning signal.

Brian has spent a career trying to answer the question of what moves stocks up and down. He's now written a book that discusses the evolution of his thinking, starting from his undergraduate days when he thought it all came down to P/E ratios and a "story." Inspired by economist John Keynes' early understanding that human behavior plays a major role in stock movement, Brian shares his complex but highly compelling "enterprise valuation" approach to analyzing stocks. This is not an Investing 101 book, but one designed for investors who want to get beyond the simple explanations and explore the myriad factors that impact stocks."

> John Kimelman
> Former Executive Editor
> Barrons.com

"Brian gives an insider's viewpoint of the way professionals analyze stocks. Both professional and individual investors will find this guide to be both insightful and a useful tool for judging which stocks have a greater potential to increase in price."

> Charles Rotblut, CFA
> Vice President and AAII Journal Editor
> American Association of Individual Investors
> Author of *Better Good than Lucky*

Value Trap

THEORY OF
UNIVERSAL VALUATION

BRIAN M NELSON

VALUENTUM SECURITIES, INC.

ILLINOIS

Library of Congress Control Number: 2018913533

ISBN 978-0-9980384-9-0

Book cover design by SelfPubBookCovers.com/JohnBellArt

First Published: December 19, 2018; This Version: May 20, 2019

Published by Valuentum Securities, Inc.
Woodstock, Illinois 60098
www.valuentum.com

To:

my son, Nathan, "my everything"

And to:

Leonard and Marilyn, my parents

And special thanks to:

My brother, for without him Valuentum would not have existed,

Chris and Kris, who made the time for this writing possible, and

Our loyal subscribers at Valuentum

CONTENTS

For time and the world do not stand still. Change is the law of life. And those who look only to the past or the present are certain to miss the future.

-- President John F. Kennedy, 1963

MARKET INEFFICIENCY AND ANALYTICAL FRICTION

Figure 1: Relative Underperformance of Kinder Morgan and Midstream Equities

Since June 11, 2015, an exchange traded fund (ETF) tracking the price performance of the S&P 500 (SPY), top, has advanced approximately 29%, while Kinder Morgan's (KMI) shares have fallen nearly 40%, middle, and shares of an ETF tracking midstream energy equities using the master limited partnership model, the Alerian MLP ETF (AMLP), have fallen more than 55%, bottom, through October 31, 2018. Image: TradingView.

The sweat was stinging my eyes as I leapt off the treadmill.

I didn't bother to hit the pause button. "Surely this didn't just happen," I thought as I struggled through the beads of sweat to read the news on my iPhone. I checked my inbox. Why wasn't anybody emailing? I walked away from the treadmill, or rather circled behind it, trying to verify the news. The unheard of *had* happened.

Kinder Morgan, one of the largest energy companies in North America, had cut its dividend 75%. I believed it, expected it, but I still couldn't believe it, if you know what I mean. It seemed as though everybody knew Valuentum had put its reputation on the line with this bearish call in June 2015 when we shared our work through numerous platforms, including most prominently with Barron's.com.

The treadmill was still racing.

At the time, I was still somewhat oblivious to just how pervasive indexing and factor-based investing[1] had become during the previous few years. Maybe nobody was paying attention, or nobody cared? Valuentum put its brand reputation on the line. Heck, I put my own reputation on the line. Years earlier, I oversaw a team that covered approximately 300 stocks at Morningstar, and never in my career did I come close to pounding the table on a call as I did in 2015. This was different.

In mid-June of that year, Valuentum explained a structural imbalance in the valuation framework for master limited partnerships (MLPs) and outlined 5 reasons why we expected a collapse in shares and why the dividend growth endeavors at the largest midstream equity, Kinder Morgan, would disappoint. Shortly thereafter, Credit Suisse issued a five-point rebuttal to our multi-faceted thesis. The research firm would say in its report that it "thought the valuation issues were settled," and the major point it "definitely" agreed with in our article was that the "Natural Reaction from Shareholders will be skepticism and disbelief to the points made."

---

[1] Since this is the first reference to factor-based investing in the text, it's worth some clarification. Technically, most anything can be considered factor-based investing. Even Valuentum investing, for example, can be considered a form of factor-based investing. In evaluating the merits of factor-based investing, this text applies the traditional definition of factor-based investing, which is mostly based on ambiguous data, lagged or otherwise, that only implies something with respect to the characteristics of a stock (e.g. a high B/M ratio is said to imply a value stock, or a low P/E ratio is said to imply a stock is undervalued). However, these characteristics cannot be supported without careful consideration of the enterprise valuation context, and therefore, ambiguous and impractical data can lead to incorrect interpretation, as stocks aren't necessarily bucketed or grouped appropriately, and potentially spurious correlations and results. See *The Data Dilemma and Valuentum Investing* that follows in this book's Preface.

Credit Suisse reiterated its $52 target price, which it based on a three-stage DDM, or dividend discount model,[2] one that reflected 10%+ annual distribution growth in the first five forecast years, more than 8% yearly expansion over the next five years, and 2.5% annual growth into perpetuity. This was good enough for an Outperform rating, implying a return of nearly 40%. Shares of Kinder Morgan were trading at approximately $39 each at the time.

I would end up sleeping at the Valuentum office in Dekalb, Illinois, that night, writing up five more reasons backing Valuentum's thesis, now ten in all, explaining in part how our thoughts were separate and distinct from an article that had been published in the print edition of Barron's, "Kinder Morgan: Trouble in the Pipelines?" The article Barron's ran as a cover story on February 22, 2014, had focused on Kinder Morgan as an MLP, questioning the measure of maintenance capital expenditures, something the company had already refuted, and something that was completely irrelevant to our take. Within an enterprise valuation framework, all capital spending, whether growth or maintenance, needs to be considered as a cash outflow to the business. It matters little whether that outflow is growth or maintenance capital spending.

But that wasn't all. In the context of enterprise valuation, distributable cash flow and by extension the distribution yield is merely arbitrary, and could be considered financially-engineered,[3] particularly if a company consistently (year after year) pays out significantly more as dividends than it generates as internal free cash flow, as measured by cash flow from operations less *all* capital spending. Valuations built around financially-engineered payouts, or those that aren't necessarily tied to the timing of all the net operating cash flows of the business (free cash flow), therefore, were of limited importance in the valuation context, meaning that the dividend discount model, as used by Credit Suisse to derive its $52 price target for Kinder Morgan, was a largely impractical valuation tool. Many others may have been valuing the equity in this fashion, too.

---

[2] The dividend discount model is a method of stock valuation that views a company as the sum of all its future dividends, discounted back to their present value. The most popular version of the model is the Gordon growth model. Credit Suisse was using a three-stage dividend discount model in its valuation of Kinder Morgan. In this text, there is substantial criticism of the dividend discount model, and its application both in intrinsic value estimation and with respect to key assumptions in quantitative finance.

[3] A financially-engineered dividend is one that is supported by the financing section of the cash flow statement, and not one supported consistently by the net of a company's operating cash flow and capital expenditures.

I would share my counter analysis to Credit Suisse's rebuttal with Barron's.com. It, too, was published, but it may not have helped clarify how our perspective was original. On Kinder Morgan's second-quarter conference call July 15, investors continued to confuse our 10 reasons with the previous thesis on the MLP regarding maintenance and growth capital spending, as outlined by Barron's in February 2014, with a person on the conference call proclaiming that Kinder Morgan's shares were being punished, in part, by "the timely or untimely resurrection of what I thought was a wholly discredited bear attack by a tabloid claiming that your investment grade debt is not serviceable."

Our thesis had been new, genuine and unique, however, and we didn't disagree that the work published February 2014 by Barron's had largely become extraneous once Kinder Morgan had rolled up its MLP structure. After all, the security KMP had been retired by mid-2015. In November 2014, Kinder Morgan had pursued a C-Corp conversion, and it offered KMP unitholders a 12% premium for the KMP units at the time. In February 2014, KMP had been trading in the low-$40s, and the newly-established corporate KMI had peaked at nearly $45 per share in April 2015.

In July, Kinder Morgan's executive chairman and director would purchase 100,000 shares and 500,000 shares, respectively, at prices in the mid-$30s. The next month, Credit Suisse would upgrade the MLP sector to an Overweight rating, saying "reversion to the mean yield ranges suggest total return outlook of over 40%." A few days later, Goldman Sachs would add the company to its Conviction Buy list, with a $48 price target, *implying the company had ~50% upside.* Goldman would say: "In an uncertain macro, commodity-price and volume environment, we see KMI as a safe haven due to its diverse portfolio of assets with a high percentage of fee-based, take-or-pay contracts." It seemed like the industry didn't want to deal with its valuation quandary, and that was that. Little did I know that the inertia of thinking, or just assuming something is correct regardless of new ways of looking at it, was even more prevalent than just in midstream energy valuations, that such thinking even had roots in modern quantitative finance.

In late September 2015, we would share an extension of our work on MLPs with Barron's.com, reiterating, in part, our prior views.[4] Barron's.com would title the article that referenced our work, "Why the MLP Business Model May Be a

---

[4] See Notes at the back of this text for an excerpt.

Goner." A few days later, on October 1, Barron's.com would follow up that piece with a rebuttal from CBRE Clarion Securities, describing Valuentum's thesis as "sensationalism."[5] Why didn't it seem like anybody was agreeing with us? It wasn't until sometime in 2018, however, that I found out just how bad my analysis was being smeared. S&P Global Market Intelligence would say on October 5, 2015: "…numerous analysts responded to Nelson's comments, telling investors to disregard them as inflammatory assertions lacking rigorous analysis. The analysts said Nelson conflated midstream MLPs with non-traditional MLP entities and ignored the fact that most traditional MLPs own assets that were built on the back of long-term, fee-based contracts."

Of course, my *exact* point was that MLPs shouldn't be looked at differently in the valuation context. Janney Montgomery Scott would say the following:

> Reasons we disagree with [Valuentum's] article: 1) the article lacked any rigorous analysis or facts to back it up (no numbers that we have seen) and 2) inappropriately assumed the maintenance capital demands of E&Ps/Upstream MLPs were applicable to the midstream/downstream space. We would argue that if there was an impending collapse of the MLPs business model, there would be some evidence of it in history. But in fact, history shows just the opposite. The reliable, predictable cash flows of MLPs/Energy Infrastructure companies are just that.

Our analysis had data backing it, and lots of it, a complete enterprise valuation model, in fact. But how many analysts and researchers still think this way: If something is to happen in the future, "there would be some *evidence* of it in history." Or that something can't happen in the future because "*history* shows just the opposite." Or that something will just bounce back because "*reversion to the mean*…ranges suggest" that it will. How many analysts are still using the dividend discount model?

---

[5] On October 4, we would post a response to the rebuttal that had been written in Barron's, and we would title it: "In the Name of Our Independence and Integrity…For Goodness Sake."

I had no idea at the time how much backward-looking analysis[6] had been permeating the investment decision-making landscape, and I was disappointed to find out later how many investors may have been confusing the meaning of "empirical" and "evidence" with "causal" and "predictive" in some quantitative applications and other studies.

Our concerns about Kinder Morgan's stock and the broader energy MLP space would only grow in the coming weeks, and it wasn't long before our thesis was validated. On October 21, more than four months after we published our call, Kinder Morgan revised its dividend growth plans lower, to the range of 6%-10% expansion over 2015 numbers (expectations had been for a 10% increase each year through 2020), and the company announced a sophisticated financing plan in the form of $1.6 billion in mandatory convertible preferred equity.

Credit Suisse would downgrade its rating of Kinder Morgan to Neutral from Outperform and reduce its target price to $39 per share. The research shop would say at the time: "We don't think investors should be too surprised by the reduction. Nonetheless, in the 13 years of following KMI, we don't recall management having to reduce guidance...ever." SunTrust, which had only just initiated the company as a Buy a few months earlier, would cut its price target to $38 from $48, still maintaining its Buy rating. On November 10, another research shop, Argus, would cut its price target to $35 from $50, it, too, maintaining its Buy rating. Shares of Kinder Morgan would close at $25.45 that day.

On December 1, some of the biggest news would hit the wire. Moody's would downgrade Kinder Morgan's credit rating outlook.[7] An integral part of our thesis had been based on what we described as "a circular flow of unsubstantiated support" for Kinder Morgan's shares. The company's dividends, which were not

---

[6] As this is the first reference to backward-looking analysis in the book, it is worth explaining it here. Backward-looking analysis can involve ambiguous or impractical data that can, at best, only *imply* something with respect to the characteristics of a stock. Ambiguous or impractical data, lagged or otherwise, should not be considered causal or predictive in most cases. Backward-looking analysis can include data mining, data dredging, data snooping or other means of drawing conclusions from in-sample data. Backward-looking analysis may also suffer from model or parameter risk, where researchers may set the parameters of a study, but may not consider conditions that may be likely to occur in walk-forward testing but are lacking within in-sample data. See *The Data Dilemma and Valuentum Investing* that follows in this book's Preface.

[7] See Notes at back of this text for a short block quote of the credit-outlook downgrade.

covered by internal free cash flow generation, or rather not tied to the operating economics of the company, were being applied in dividend discount models to value the equity, thereby offering unsubstantiated support for a lofty share price. Kinder Morgan's market capitalization, of which price is a function, could then support its credit quality, as in most market cap-to-debt-related metrics, and then both a strong equity price and credit health could be used to continue to drive dividend growth, and so on and so forth.

By December 2015, this "circular flow of unsubstantiated support" seemed to be coming to an end, particularly as energy resources prices swooned, serving in our view to merely expose the circular flow than act as the main reason for weakness across the midstream sector, which many had wrongly argued was immune to energy resource pricing. Midstream equities are inextricably tied to the health of their upstream customers, which are directly impacted by energy resource pricing. On December 3, Argus would pull its Buy rating, and Fitch Ratings would say:

> Five-year credit default swap (CDS) spreads on Kinder Morgan widened out 28% over the past week and nearly 400% since the start of 2015. Kinder Morgan's CDS are now at their widest level in seven years. After pricing consistently at 'BBB/BBB-' levels for much of the past year, credit protection on Kinder Morgan's debt is now pricing in 'B+' territory.

While some analysts maintained the view that Kinder Morgan would be able to continue to grow its dividend, others started to factor in a greater probability of a dividend cut, some more explicitly than others. On December 4, Kinder Morgan said its 2016 distributable cash flow per share would be "consistent with previous guidance of 6 to 10 percent above the 2015 dividend," a pace of expansion that "would be sufficient to support dividend growth in the range discussed in the third quarter call," or in the 6%-10% range. Shortly following news Kinder Morgan was reviewing its financial expectations and dividend policy, on December 7, Credit Suisse dropped its target price to $25, and research firm Jefferies would say at the time that the company should cut its dividend all the way to $0.01 per quarter (was $0.51). Morgan Stanley reportedly would remove Kinder Morgan from its model portfolio. Then, perhaps impossible to believe only a few short months earlier, on December 8, Kinder Morgan cut its dividend 75%. The move would prompt Moody's to rescind the credit outlook downgrade, and Credit Suisse would eventually lower its target price to $18.

On June 11, 2015, Valuentum wrote that "Kinder Morgan may turn into one of the worst-performing companies [in 2015] and into 2016." That day, Kinder Morgan's shares would close at $39.78. By January 20, 2016, however, they would hit an intra-day low of $11.20. By February 11, 2016, the Alerian MLP ETF, which tracks the performance of a basket of midstream energy equities, had hit a low of $7.77 per share, down from a close of $16.15 per share on June 11, 2015. As of 2018, some 40% of energy infrastructure is comprised of C-Corps, with midstream company after midstream company transitioning away from the MLP business model, a percentage that's up from practically nothing in 2013 and just 15% at the end of 2014, a trend we predicted.

On January 21, 2016, Valuentum would author another piece that would be shared with Barron's.com, this time painting a more optimistic tone on Kinder Morgan's prospects, in part because shares had fallen so much relative to our estimate of their intrinsic value. Enterprise valuation[8] is our window to the markets. If the share price is well below an estimate of intrinsic value, it could represent a bargain. If the share price is well above an estimate of intrinsic value, it could be too expensive. Our fair value estimate for Kinder Morgan would stand at $20 in December 2015 and remain there for years after.

Traditional free cash flow analysis is how we evaluate the health of a company's dividend or distribution. Focusing on accounting measures such as earnings per share in the dividend payout ratio or distribution coverage ratios, as presented by the midstream energy complex, can leave income investors sorely disappointed. Dividends are paid out of cash, not accounting earnings or measures that only capture part of cash flows. Kinder Morgan had raised its payout October 21 by 16%, and just a few short months later, it slashed it. The safest dividend is clearly not always the one that's just been raised.

I jumped back on the treadmill.

For analysts, it really doesn't get better than making a stock call like this one, one that runs counter to almost every other opinion out there, and then is proven correct in time, or in a relatively short time, as in this case. In 2015, Kinder Morgan and most of the MLP universe were clearly *value traps,*[9] artificially

---

[8] This text goes into great deal about the enterprise valuation process, or the free cash flow to the firm method in estimating stock values.
[9] As this is the first reference to the term "value trap" in the book, it's worth defining it here. A value trap is a stock that appears cheap based on certain measures (earnings multiples, dividend

supported by inadequate valuation techniques (and financially-engineered dividends). Stock calls like this aren't supposed to happen in the world of finance where there are hundreds of thousands of CFA charterholders and PhDs, and probably even more brokers and advisors with other letters after their names, all watching the market's every move. It's not easy to go against popular opinion. Why is our take so unique that thousands or millions before us, equally qualified and looking at the same information, haven't thought through? It takes a high degree of conviction and sometimes a lot of career risk.

Kinder Morgan wasn't some small company, and this wasn't some small-time obscure call in the blogosphere or on the message boards or chat rooms. Kinder Morgan was the largest energy infrastructure company in the United States, owning or operating some 80,000 miles of pipelines transporting oil and natural gas. In 2014, the master limited partnership sector totaled $500 billion in market capitalization. That was the size of Apple's market capitalization in the summer of 2016, before the iPhone-maker ballooned into a trillion-dollar behemoth. In September 2018, despite all the fanfare and media coverage, the entire cryptocurrency market was just $186 billion. The call on Kinder Morgan and the MLPs was absolutely huge.

Some of my University of Chicago friends might say markets are near-efficient.[10] Surely, something like this cannot possibly happen, they may argue, a call where almost everybody else is wrong, and we were right. How arrogant does this sound, but things like this do happen, and it would imply market inefficiencies *do* exist (and they can be identified). In this particular instance, there wasn't "new" information in the traditional sense. What made this stock call unique was that it was based purely on a fresh look at the valuation and a credit assessment of the corporate. We were looking at the same information as everyone else, and when we showed another way of looking at it, the market adjusted. Mispricings can and do happen.

---

yield, and the like, traditionally used in quantitative analysis), but that really isn't cheap in the context of enterprise valuation. Value traps are often commonly called "falling knives," as when investors keep trying to catch a stock that keeps falling in price, it hurts as if one is trying to catch the blade of a falling knife.

[10] This is a reference to the efficient markets hypothesis, which stipulates that stocks are priced correctly, and even if they are not, investors still won't be able to recognize whether stocks are fairly-valued, undervalued or overvalued.

But maybe I was just lucky. Energy resource prices were swooning at the time, and there were certainly areas of fundamental deterioration at Kinder Morgan that happened during those several months that I simply couldn't have predicted. "Hmmm…" I was running faster now.

It didn't matter to me.

It felt good to help people, to make a difference, to provide the variant opinion that may have saved investors tons of money. It felt good to eventually be proven right when seemingly everybody was telling us that we were wrong in no uncertain terms, and it really seemed like it was everybody. I didn't know at the time that few may truly have known what I was talking about, the in's and out's of enterprise valuation, or rather *universal value*, something that I view as a critical lens to view both individual stocks and market activity as a whole. What became clear to me, however, was there should be more talk about enterprise valuation and evaluating dividend safety.

It's been several years since the Kinder Morgan call, and shares may eventually recover from the high-teens mark. Many have since forgotten the details, and others continue to say that we were wrong, or rather right for the wrong reasons. That's okay. During the past few years, Kinder Morgan has paid its common dividends out of traditional free cash flow[11], and what happened to the company may continue to happen to other MLPs in the future, in addition to the dozens that have already cut their payouts and rolled up their complex MLP structures.[12] What many may not appreciate is that the job of an analyst is not to pump a stock, or to focus only on the good aspects of the company. This is generally how some bubbles can be formed.

Instead, the job of an analyst is to provide a balanced perspective, both in writing and in valuation. It's the job of an analyst to share their genuine thoughts about companies, and when things don't add up, an analyst must pound the table -- and not lightly. This is what the world read in our work on Kinder Morgan and the MLPs in 2015, an analyst team that covered over one thousand stocks

---

[11] Kinder Morgan's traditional free cash flow coverage of the dividend (as measured by cash flow from operations less all capital spending, the difference divided by cash dividends for common shares) for the fiscal years ended 2015, 2016, and 2017 was 0.34, 1.71, and 1.26, respectively.
[12] According to research from CBRE Clarion Securities, as of October 2017, entities that were included in the Alerian MLP Index have reduced distributions 56 times, including 45 cuts that were explicit and 11 cuts that occurred through business-model simplification efforts in the past three years. There would be many more explicit and stealth cuts after October 2017.

emphatically writing that something wasn't quite adding up with this particular subset of companies. The job is never easy, but doing it right takes a tremendous amount of grit as well as a willingness to be able to change one's mind when the facts change, all the while trying to anticipate what may happen in the future.

I founded Valuentum in 2011 to help investors, to put investors first. It was all I knew. It was more than an extension of my principles as a CFA charterholder or my experiences at independent research giant Morningstar, however. There was something else to it. The research industry seemed to be flailing. The Global Analyst Research Settlement of 2003 helped to highlight the issues of conflict of interest in relation to securities analyst recommendations, but it only went so far. These ideals have not made it to the mainstream public, social media or blogosphere. In some ways, now 15 years after the research settlement, some investors may seem to be favoring the exact opposite of independent, objective analysis of stocks, confusing credibility and expertise with having "skin in the game."[13]

Hardly anyone talks about the lessons of analyst research from the dot-com bubble anymore, where analysts were pumping "hot IPOs." While the abuses by the investment banks have been lassoed in, I feel investors still need something better, and not just more ambiguous data or more stock screeners. The conversation about investing for most investors seems to be limited to these types of topics or on financial advising, in general, such as saving for retirement, maxing out one's 401k, staying disciplined, and avoiding behavioral biases. There are blogs and websites that talk about stocks, of course, but access to high-quality financial analysis backed by iron-clad methods such as enterprise valuation just aren't as prevalent as they should be. Without enterprise valuation, an

---

[13] "Skin in the game" is typically a phrase used to describe someone taking on risk to achieve a goal, and the person is directly impacted by the consequences. The phrase was made even more popular recently with Nassim Taleb's 2018 book titled *Skin in the Game: Hidden Asymmetries in Daily Life*. For example, executives that own a large stake in their companies have "skin in the game." Their interests are generally aligned with shareholders. Valuentum has "skin in the game" because our customers decide if we succeed or fail as a company. We have contact with the "real world." There are situations, however, where having "skin in the game" is not ideal. With respect to writing stock analysis or opinion on the web, being an owner of the stock might be viewed more as having conflicted opinion. Quite simply, having an ownership stake in the stock doesn't automatically make that author a more knowledgeable authority on the stock's investment merits. In many ways, the ownership stake may present misaligned incentives for the author to be overly optimistic about a company's investment prospects. When it comes to stock analysis, the independent opinion may often be the best one.

understanding of universal valuation cannot be attained. They are one and the same.

This book, in some ways, is a reflection on my career experiences as an analyst and entrepreneur, a lens into how I view the stock market, but it is also a response to many worrisome trends and processes in the investment management business today. The text strives to answer the question: what is the appropriate *empirical evidence* in evidence-based finance? Surely, not just any empirical evidence will do. The book is not meant to be controversial, but a discussion of the great contradiction of "explaining" stock return behavior between factor-based investing (which is based mostly on ambiguous, realized data within in-sample[14] sets) and the efficient markets hypothesis (which is based on expectations of future data, *realized or not*) may make it so. The text is heavy in behavioral thinking and puts forth enterprise valuation as a behavioral framework in which to view stock prices and their movements. This book also shows how enterprise valuation is much more than a simple stock valuation tool, but rather that enterprise valuation is truly universal valuation, resting at the intersection of behavioral economics, quantitative theory, equity valuation, and therefore finance, itself.

I'd like to issue a roadmap to this book before you begin. A reading of *The Data Dilemma and Valuentum Investing* in the Preface is necessary to understand the various types of data I refer to frequently in this text: ambiguous, causal and impractical. Also emphasized in this book is the difference between in-sample,

---

[14] In-sample tests include statistical analysis of historical data and may be exposed to the pitfalls of data mining, data dredging or data snooping. Such tests are also subject to model or parameter risks, and the results should generally not be extrapolated in the future. Out-of-sample tests occur when a hypothesis is pre-defined, data is then observed and collected, and statistical work is then performed on the observed and collected data. It's important to further differentiate out-of-sample tests (e.g. tests of theory or strategy on historical data from another country or asset class) from walk-forward tests, a subset of out-of-sample tests. With a walk-forward study, tests are performed on data that has not yet occurred as of the time of the in-sample hypothesis, therefore making it impossible for a researcher to turn out-of-sample tests into in-sample ones. Something that troubles many quant strategists is the application of in-sample theories or strategies across many *historical* out-of-sample sets. This is believed to enhance the robustness of a theory or strategy, but really in doing so, the use of historical out-of-sample data just makes the process a larger in-sample test. On the other hand, a walk-forward test on a brand new data set, one that has yet to happen and can only be collected in the future, solves this issue. A backtest or a regression model such as that of the Fama-French three-factor model is an example of an in-sample test, and an example of a walk-forward test is that applied to the Valuentum Buying Index, as described later in this text.

out-of-sample and walk-forward studies, the latter I believe to be the most robust and authentic of processes.

In the first section of this book (chapters 1 through 3), I welcome you on a journey through the early lessons of my career and introduce some of the major shortcomings of traditional quant factor-based analysis, while building up the importance of a common theme in this text: the information contained in share prices. In the second section of this book (chapters 4 through 6), the causal nature of enterprise valuation to stock prices is explained, culminating in the Theory of Universal Valuation, which offers enterprise valuation as the central theme to quantitative value studies, efficient markets hypothesis testing and beyond. If at any time, it gets too theoretical, please feel free to skip ahead.

In the final section of the book (chapters 7 through 10), I talk about practical application of the principles explained in this text: how enterprise valuation can be used to identify bubbles and mispricings, how it's valuable to dividend-growth and income frameworks, how it's connected to economic moat and economic castle theory, and how it can be applied practically in an equity portfolio setting, as in Valuentum investing. The conclusion of this text backs enterprise valuation as the most socially-responsible form of investing and offers my opinion of the consequences of a marketplace where the proliferation of price-agnostic trading continues into the coming decade and beyond.

This book is not a how-to manual on how to perform enterprise valuation, or a get-rich-quick investment program, but rather a text that I feel lays the foundation for a genuine conversation about stock investing, a conversation about price versus estimated intrinsic value. The book is chock-full of footnotes, too, offering greater depth in areas that may require it. If I have written this book in the fashion as I endeavor, I want every sentence, every paragraph to be worth your while. I hope this text stands the test of time and even shapes the future.

THE DATA DILEMMA AND VALUENTUM INVESTING

Through the course of this text, there will be references to different kinds of data. It is worth clarifying as precisely as possible at the beginning of this text the difference between what will be labeled as *ambiguous* data, *causal* data, and *impractical* data. Impractical data can be considered a subset of ambiguous data.

Ambiguous data, as that traditionally used in today's quantitative factor-based analysis, can be backward-looking data or forward-looking data (lagged or otherwise). Put simply, it is data that, at best, can only imply something with respect to the characteristics of a stock (e.g. "value" or "growth"). Any valuation multiple (ratio), except those that *actually* measure price versus estimated value, as in the price-to-estimated-fair value estimate ratio (P/FV), for example, can be considered ambiguous data. A company's current book-to-market (B/M) ratio, price-to-earnings (P/E) ratio, and EV/EBITDA multiple (or a company's B/M ratio, P/E ratio, and EV/EBITDA multiple forecasted five years hence) may be believed to imply something with respect to the characteristics of a stock (e.g. "value" or "growth"), but whether a stock with such a multiple should fit those characteristics cannot be discerned by only looking at the ratios, themselves. The characteristics can only be supported with careful consideration of the enterprise valuation context, and therefore, ambiguous data can lead to incorrect interpretation and potentially spurious correlations and results. With the application of ambiguous data, stocks aren't necessarily bucketed or grouped appropriately (e.g. "value" or "growth"), even if they have similar ratios.

Causal data, on the other hand, is what can be considered a fair value estimate of a company's stock, an estimate that includes the present value of a company's future expected free cash flow stream (which has explicit forecasts of revenue or earnings growth within it). Enterprise valuation, the process by which fair value estimates are derived, is presented in this book as the primary causal, explanatory driver of stock prices through the influence of public-to-private arbitrage on investors' buying and selling activity. While forward looking and subjective in nature, an estimate of intrinsic value could then be measured against stock prices contemporaneously, lagged or otherwise. With causal data, expectations aren't implied to represent some characteristic of a stock (e.g. "value" or "growth"), as in past or even future multiples (ambiguous data), but rather expectations are explicitly captured within the forward-looking analysis of the fair value estimate, itself. Unlike ambiguous data, where there is no clear indication of what the data should imply, embedded within a fair value estimate are literally thousands of explicit forward-looking assumptions, and what is implied by ambiguous data can be deciphered through reasonable forecasting within the enterprise valuation process. A P/FV ratio measures the actual difference between price and estimated fair value (e.g. value-derived P/E ratio versus price-observed P/E ratio). Unlike ambiguous data, causal data does not use another fundamental item (e.g. book equity, EBITDA, EPS, and the like) as a proxy of an estimate of intrinsic value, itself.

Whether enterprise valuation or its output, the fair value estimate, is subjective or analyst-driven is not fair criticism. **Index investors rely on the subjective view that stock values will advance over time, though enterprise valuation suggests this doesn't always have to be the case. The efficient markets hypothesis relies on the subjective, non-falsifiable assumption that all assets are priced "correctly," give or take some unrecognizable error. Where it is believed that historical valuation multiples avoid forecasts, they have implied and opaque future forecasts embedded within them.** Using ambiguous or impractical data because it may appear objective does not make that data more meaningful or useful. To measure the concept of value, it comes down to the simple takeaway that one must *actually* attempt to measure price versus estimated value, not use a proxy of value as in B/M, the P/E ratio, or EV/EBITDA, as examples. That stock values are in part a function of future expectations and not future reality, which is unknowable, is also more consistent with a framework that applies forward-looking enterprise valuation as the explanatory variable for stock returns than any other framework that is based on realized data alone.

Impractical data can be considered a subset of ambiguous data and can best be defined as data that lacks a convincing logical basis for its use to explain stock returns, offering limited analytical insight. For example, two of the risk factors of Eugene Fama and Kenneth R. French's famous three-factor model believed to "explain" stock returns, can be described as impractical. With the size factor, there may be little logical basis to believe small stocks should outperform large stocks just because they are small.[15] Further, the arbitrary nature of book equity, as this text will demonstrate in detail, makes the application of the B/M ratio, as in the traditional quant value factor, illogical. Impractical data might also represent certain data within logical approaches, with one such example being beta within the Capital Asset Pricing Model (CAPM). Though it has largely failed to predict returns in real-world testing, the CAPM may logically tie risk and reward, but the application of beta as a measure of risk within it becomes a shortcoming. Impractical data may be surfaced through data mining, data dredging, data snooping measures or other means of drawing conclusions from in-sample data and generally embodies data that lacks an iron-clad rationale for its application.

This text explains in depth how the outcome of the enterprise valuation process, the fair value estimate, is the independent variable that influences valuation multiples, which are dependent on enterprise valuation.[16] Such an observation therefore makes most valuation multiples ambiguous within quantitative statistical applications. Enterprise valuation acts as the confounding, lurking variable that reveals correlations between most valuation multiples and stock returns, or traditional factor-based investing, to be unreliable. The Theory of Universal Valuation shows how enterprise valuation derives other valuation multiples, and by swapping equity value with price, it explains how enterprise valuation is the primary causal, explanatory driver of stock prices through the influence of public-to-private arbitrage on buying and selling activity on the marketplace.

As I write this text in 2018, most of quantitative finance is using either ambiguous data or impractical (realized) data within processes that may not be backed by walk-forward studies, and almost all are not implementing actual measures of price versus estimated intrinsic value, as in what has been defined

---

[15] McKinsey found that from 1963-1973 and from 1984-2000, small stocks were outperformed by large stocks. The research firm noted that large companies have outperformed small companies since the premium's discovery in 1982. According to AQR's Cliff Asness, "The size effect paper is the easier one to discuss in a short blog. There isn't one. That is, there isn't a pure size effect (there is a paper). In fact, there never was a size effect. Among other issues, the data used to discover it was flawed (though no fault of the author, that was the data back then) in a way that favored small stocks." -- *It Ain't What You Don't Know That Gets You Into Trouble*, 20 June 2018.

[16] There are literally thousands of assumptions within the enterprise valuation process. Each one of those assumptions drives the fair value estimate, but it is the fair value estimate that derives a company's valuation multiple, as this text shows. This makes enterprise valuation the confounding, lurking variable in many traditional quantitative factor applications.

in this book as causal data. Ambiguous data, as in valuation multiples, are short cuts to calculations of enterprise value and fair value estimates, and therefore such multiples do not offer clear value signals and become unreliable in statistical processes (e.g. not all low P/Es should be value stocks). Impractical data, as in book equity, for example, does not capture a logical component, and therefore, the conclusions drawn by the application of such data should not be extrapolated in any case. Almost every other factor used as a method of evaluating stocks, absent a distinct measure of price versus estimated intrinsic value as in enterprise valuation, may be potentially spurious or illogical, lacking potential causal or predictive capability.

We won't cover Valuentum investing until Chapter 10 in this text, but some clarification of how the process is differentiated from traditional quantitative finance is required up front. Quantitative finance may focus almost entirely on the concept of "value" and momentum in a portfolio setting but *separately* across stocks. For example, a quantitative combination of "value" and momentum in a portfolio might have 50% of the portfolio long "value" stocks and short "growth" stocks, while the other half of the portfolio might be long stocks that recently performed well and short stocks that recently performed poorly. Another method of portfolio construction might hold 40 "value" stocks and 40 momentum stocks. Generally speaking, variations of quantitative portfolio construction view stocks as either having "value" or momentum qualities, but not both.

Valuentum investing, on the other hand, applies the concepts of value and momentum *within* stocks, using enterprise valuation as the primary value-signal, bolstered by relative (behavioral) valuation considerations, and augmented by technical and momentum assessments. In applying enterprise valuation techniques, Valuentum investing uses what the author describes as predictive or causal data in its processes. Tests of the Valuentum process have been based on walk-forward studies, which the author believes are more robust than in-sample or multiple historical out-of-sample tests on theories or strategies developed primarily by in-sample methods.

CHAPTER SUMMARIES

One: Stock Prices

A billionaire's laugh. How to think about what price movements imply. A newspaper beauty contest analogy. Guesswork and speculation. Some ambiguous and impractical data use. Some "fuzzy thinking." Changing correlations and LTCM. Backfilled data. The empirical Zodiac quantitative factor. The rise of price-agnostic trading. The pitfalls of book equity, as representative. Planes, burgers, and pizza. Not the dividend discount model again! The field of finance is still young. The stock market as a reflection of us. Some guy named Babson. "Blue Skies."

Two: Once the Mind Is Stretched

Empirical evidence-based analysis is a misnomer. The gift. Keynes was dead. Apologetic works. What are predictive or causal factors of stock prices? Future expected data that is realized or not. Letter B. What's in a name? Betting at the Derby. H2O. Importance of walk-forward performance. Reality becomes the anomaly, and the backtest remains truth! The randomness of factor returns. Never-ending empirical asset pricing model iterations. Don't bet on ambiguous or impractical data.

Three: Lessons from the Financial Crisis

A huge Ponzi scheme. Banks are driven by pure confidence, seemingly nothing more, nothing less. *It's a Wonderful Life*. Capital market dependence can be a wrecking ball to equity prices. Equity and credit analysis are inseparable. Stock prices contain valuable information that can't be found in historical GAAP fundamentals. When things go bad, they really go bad. General Electric and value traps. Correlations often break down at the exact time that you need them the most. Moral hazard is often not punished, and sometimes it can be rewarded.

Four: The Right Mental Model

Classical art, fine wine, and vintage baseball cards. Stock value is not always in the eye of the beholder. Enterprise valuation as the causal framework to view the markets. The influence of public-to-private arbitrage on the price-setting function. The consistencies of enterprise valuation and the efficient markets hypothesis. The end game for prices. The importance of value sensitivity in understanding price volatility. Precision is folly and the margin of safety. Reverse engineering. True intrinsic value may not matter. The stock market doesn't care what you think. Long-duration value arbitrage. Nice quarter. Long-term expectations impact prices today. "The future ain't what it used to be." The mirage of the long term.

Five: The Enterprise Valuation Framework

The Theory of Universal Valuation states that value cannot exist in separate vacuums depending on which investment strategy one pursues, whether it is a quantitative strategy or whether it is a fundamentally-based, enterprise-value oriented strategy, or other. The enterprise valuation model transcends styles into quantitative factor-based methods and establishes universal value. Enterprise value is the confounding, lurking variable behind many statistical studies. Also, shortcomings of the P/E ratio, as representative. Introduction to behavioral valuation. How key drivers impact share prices. Peculiarities of some quantitative observations explained. On residual income and economic-profit models and their relevance to banking enterprises. Buybacks and wealth destruction.

Six: The Greatest Contradiction of All?

The biggest commonality of stock market bubbles. Some ridiculous valuations. The two separate components of a non-falsifiable hypothesis. Is the market getting its own expectations correct? Getting to know the joint hypothesis problem. Introducing the next best alternative: The Price-to-Estimated-Fair Value Test. Thoughts on the CAPE ratio. *If all information is supposedly factored into prices, as in efficient markets theory (and arguably the most critical information in setting prices is forward looking in nature), how can backward-looking factors based on realized ambiguous data be considered logical explanatory drivers behind stock returns?* Another perspective on market arithmetic, and an overreliance on mutual fund data. How index investing drives market inefficiencies.

Seven: The Latest Bubble to Pop

"Bogle's folly" and the resistance to change. A 10-point thesis on Kinder Morgan. Some quality financial analysis. The market reacts quickly to correct structural mispricings. The role that falling energy resource prices played. Distribution cuts and MLP business-model rollups. Traditional free cash flow analysis and assessing capital-market dependence risk. A plea to retire a controversial non-GAAP measure. Thinking about maintenance versus growth capital spending. How to tie price-to-distributable cash flow to enterprise valuation. A unique way to look at financial leverage.

Eight: The Dividend Misunderstanding

Monopoly. The role of the market specialist. The dividend as a possible symptom of value, not a driver of it. Dividend irrelevance and enterprise valuation. A Yogi-ism. An ex-post construct of enterprise present value? Ask why a lot, and then some more. Why have stocks that continue to pay and grow their dividends do well? Thinking about total return the right way. The "free dividends fallacy." Overheated consumer staples stocks. Price versus value is paramount. The Dividend Cushion ratio demystified. A warning on the implications of share price declines on high-yield stocks.

Nine: Economic Moats and Economic Castles

Some medieval nomenclature. How to think about the concept of economic value. Pitfalls of some common return metrics. Negative invested capital, and why it could signal a fantastic business. Good companies, but bad stocks. The Oracle of Omaha. The competitive-advantage period. Thinking about mispriced moats, not moats themselves. Magnitude and duration of economic profit. Not a wooden palisade, but a royal castle. Airlines and garbage: which is the better oligopoly? The wider the moat, the lower the stock return?

Ten: Putting It All Together: Valuentum Investing

Not the Woodstock you're thinking of. Building a hypothesis. Moving mountains to build the infrastructure. Introducing the Valuentum Buying Index. Running a marathon to calculate meaningful data. Forward-looking expected data and walk-forward testing. No data mining, data snooping or data dredging. Putting the logic first. The Valuentum way. Best ideas and dividend growth. The importance of diversification.

I.

WHAT A MESS

1

Stock Prices

A billionaire's laugh. How to think about what price movements imply. A newspaper beauty contest analogy. Guesswork and speculation. Some ambiguous and impractical data use. Some "fuzzy thinking." Changing correlations and LTCM. Backfilled data. The empirical Zodiac quantitative factor. The rise of price-agnostic trading. The pitfalls of book equity, as representative. Planes, burgers, and pizza. Not the dividend discount model again! The field of finance is still young. The stock market as a reflection of us. Some guy named Babson. "Blue Skies."

I n 2004, I was fresh out of undergrad.

Benedictine University in Lisle, Illinois, was good to me. I'm still proud of being second all-time in career homeruns (26) in a school with a 100 years of baseball history, and I even met my wife there. Some of my best memories happened on that campus.

Midway Airport on the southwest side of Chicago is where you can hop on the Orange Line to head into the city. Right after graduation, I landed a new job at Driehaus Capital Management. Every day on the "L," I'd read *Investors' Business Daily* on the way to work. I had a subscription to the *Wall Street Journal* and *Financial Times*, of course, but *IBD* had a lot of overlap with the Small Cap Growth strategy that our team used at Driehaus to manage a few hundred million dollars. At the time, I think Driehaus held $2-$3 billion in assets under management, most of it Richard Driehaus' money, as I understood.

Some months prior, Richard Driehaus had pulled me aside downstairs as part of my interview in the Driehaus offices, the Ransom Cable House at 25 E. Erie St.

in Chicago, and I pitched him one of my favorite ideas at the time.[17] I don't think I ever saw him without a suit and tie. He always made an excellent impression.

"Do you know what the best thing about being 63?," I think I remember Richard saying at his office birthday party one year.

"You can drink 3 times as much as when you were 21!" He would break out into an infectious laugh that was uniquely his. If you ever want to hear what a billionaire's laugh sounds like, you need to hear Richard's. I don't think Richard ever used email. He would travel often and send faxes to the office from the St. Regis Hotel in New York. In 2005, he took the entire Driehaus research staff to Saint Thomas, U.S. Virgin Islands. There, I learned how much he loved wine, and it turns out, so did I. Richard and I both attended Chicago Catholic League schools, him Saint Ignatius and me Saint Laurence.

"Yes. I think you might be right," Richard said, carrying my work up the switchback staircase of the Driehaus mansion. I felt I could have done a better job with the pitch during the interview, but I was prepared. I sat in the lobby downstairs waiting for what was next.

The Driehaus office was truly exquisite. The Ransom Cable House, itself, was of Richardsonian Romanesque style, with peach-pink façade, and every now and then you might see one of Richard's antique cars in front. Inside, the office was immaculate, decked out in some of the most luxurious furniture and décor. The house had once been used for a funeral business during most of the 20th century, and analyst lore would say the lower level had all the signs of an embalming room. That's where all the tough questions from visiting management teams would be asked, one might joke.

It couldn't have been but a few weeks after the interview that I was offered the Research Assistant job at Driehaus Capital Management. Life was good. My first real job. Looking back, I think my parents even drove me to that job interview. I was as green as it gets. Sometimes I forget how far I had come already, even at 22 years of age. My dad was a stationery engineer at a local hospital, and my mom was a housewife. Both did a great job putting me and my brother on the right path in life. We were the first ones in our family to graduate from college.

---

[17] I can't remember exactly which idea it was, but I think it was Cognex, a company that makes image-based products that utilize artificial intelligence.

What Price Movements Actually Imply

I learned a lot at Driehaus, from technical analysis (evaluating charts) to assessing quarterly beats and long-term earnings growth potential. Richard's investment philosophy centered, in part, on buying high and selling higher and stood in stark contrast to traditional value techniques that bought stocks on their way down, hoping for a turnaround. Selling losers and letting the winners run was a core part of the Driehaus philosophy.

Sometime later, I would conceptualize such market movements in the valuation context. Wall Street tends to want to buy low and sell high, but it may pay no mind to what a declining stock price may actually imply, a declining value, too. Many believe that just because a stock is falling in price, the stock is cheaper, but that doesn't have to be the case. The stock's value could have fallen even more. Stock prices that are going up, on the other hand, imply market backing and the belief that their intrinsic values were also higher. Investors should therefore prefer appreciating stocks because it means that the market believes they should be valued higher, it stands to reason.

But why is thinking about the direction of prices, as perhaps an indication of the market's opinion about future business value, so important? Well, since its inception in 1980 through the end of September 2018, Driehaus Small Cap Growth strategy has generated an annual return of ~17.5% versus approximately 9% for the Russell 2000 Growth Index, and this return is net of fees. Most active fund managers, on the other hand, tend to trail their respective benchmarks. An estimated 84%-92% of large-cap managers, mid-cap managers, and small-cap managers lagged their respective benchmarks over a 5-year period ending 2017, while 92%+ of managers lagged their respective benchmarks over a 15-year period ending 2017.

At Driehaus, I learned what drives stocks, and I think the firm's trading desk, which was but a few feet from my corner desk, may have left its impression. Fundamentals may influence buying and selling behavior, of course, but it is still that buying and selling behavior that *actually* drives prices. For me, knowing the very basic construct of the market was critical, and it eventually became the catalyst to understand the drivers behind investors' buy and sell decisions in evaluating prices, as in pure Keynesian[18] beauty contest fashion. Little did I know that this basic concept would lay the methodological framework for the behavioral aspects behind the Valuentum process some years later. John Maynard Keynes would write in the *General Theory of Employment, Interest and Money*:

> Professional investment may be likened to those newspaper competitions in which the competitors have to pick out the six prettiest faces from a hundred photographs, the prize being awarded to the competitor whose choice most nearly corresponds to the average preferences of the competitors as a whole; so that each competitor has to pick not those faces which he himself finds prettiest, but those which he thinks likeliest to catch the fancy of the other competitors, all of whom are looking at the problem from the same point of view. It is not a case of choosing those which, to the best of one's judgement are really the prettiest, nor even those which average opinion genuinely thinks the prettiest. We have reached the third degree where we devote our intelligences to anticipating what average opinion expects the average opinion to be. And there are some, I believe, who practice the fourth, fifth and higher degrees.

What Keynes meant is that it's not about what I prefer in a stock investment, per se, or even what you may prefer in a stock investment, but rather what you and I think other investors may prefer in a stock investment and so on. So, for example, if you and I (and the market) believe that the market is seeking to price equities on the basis of an intrinsic value estimate, it is likely that the Nash equilibrium[19] might eventually center on the market's estimate of what it thinks is intrinsic value, or the price that you and I believe others will value it, and so on (not true intrinsic value, itself). In such a case, to predict future prices, it then becomes critical to assess how the marketplace may evaluate intrinsic value to predict changes therein, more so than any personal investment preference.

---

[18] John Maynard Keynes was a British economist whose ideas are best known within the practice of macroeconomics. However, his thinking regarding stock prices may have laid the foundation for what we know today as behavioral economics.

[19] The Nash equilibrium is named after mathematician John Forbes Nash, whose life inspired the popular movie, *A Beautiful Mind* (2001). Nash would win the Nobel Prize for his work in explaining non-cooperative games, commonly called game theory. In the stock market, the Nash equilibrium might center on what others think others think is the best estimate of a company's intrinsic value.

In the case of Valuentum's bearish call on Kinder Morgan and the MLP sector in 2015, for example, the market worked to correct what had been a long-time systematic overpricing based on the company's and sector's externally-supported dividends (distributions),[20] as in the dividend discount model, by incorporating the enterprise valuation framework. The Nash equilibrium had been reset. In enterprise valuation, the dividend is a symptom of value, not a driver, and therefore, in most cases, it is largely irrelevant to a company's intrinsic-value calculation, meaning that a dividend cut should not, by itself, impact the true intrinsic value of the equity, or by extension, its stock price. Had Kinder Morgan's equity been valued based on its intrinsic value, as in enterprise valuation, a dividend cut simply wouldn't, or rather shouldn't, have mattered.

Unlike its share price, Kinder Morgan's distributable cash flow wasn't cut in half. In fact, the measure that was widely-followed by other analysts held in the range of \$4.48-\$4.7 billion during 2015 and even the two years following, up significantly from \$2.6 billion in 2014. What had happened, however, is that conditions in the equity and credit markets, in part driven by falling energy resource prices, made external capital prohibitive, and because the company's dividend at the time was not internally-supported via free cash flow, it had to cut it. Kinder Morgan's share price shouldn't have budged, but since many investors were valuing the company via a dividend discount model based on a dividend that was not internally-supported, its share price suffered immensely.

If the market had applied the enterprise valuation framework from the beginning, Kinder Morgan's equity likely would never have reached bubble levels as those in 2015, and such a large mispricing may never have occurred.[21]

---

[20] There are two types of dividends, a stock dividend and a cash dividend. A stock dividend can be viewed as similar to that of a stock split and generally inconsequential to the enterprise value of an entity. In this text, cash dividends and cash distributions are used interchangeably, as they have the same impact in the enterprise valuation context, even though both have different tax consequences to the investor when they are paid.

[21] There are several techniques or models to value a company. This text explains how many of them eventually revert to enterprise valuation as the inevitable price-setting mechanism in the marketplace via public-to-private arbitrage discussed at length in this book.

Getting Lucky

There are many ways to think about investing, but one of them seems to be the most common. During most of my undergraduate studies and into my early days at Driehaus, I primarily evaluated a company's price-to-earnings (P/E) ratio and whether there was a "story" behind the stock (later, earnings momentum and technical analysis would be added). I guess you can say I looked for stocks that had a firm valuation foundation, as I knew it then, and ones that had interesting "stories" or otherwise had "castles in the air." I must have read Burton Malkiel's *A Random Walk Down Wall Street*, which made famous Firm-Foundation Theory and Castle-in-the-Air Theory, in college, and I'm sure I read a few other investment classics in undergrad, too. Enterprise valuation, however, was not a course topic at my alma mater, unfortunately.

In any case, at some point during 2004, I found a little company called Synaptics that made interesting touch technology for handheld gadgets. The winter of that year, I think Richard Driehaus ended up buying the entire research staff an Apple iPod in part because of that call on Synaptics, or at least that's how it seemed to me. "No, I was lucky that Apple created the iPod and that it had chosen Synaptics' click wheel technology," I remember telling my boss after the fact. It's truly how I felt. "You identified that technology. You really did a great job," he said nodding. I even remember walking into the neighboring room of the Driehaus mansion, "Is this guidance right… for the next sequential quarter?" Perhaps the other team thought I was bragging. "Ah… tech," I can still hear the words echoing through the Driehaus mansion now.

But picking the next "Synaptics" seemed too much like guessing. Trying to understand which technology might be adopted by the next tech behemoth in the next fancy gadget involves too much luck, even to those skilled in engineering, or highly knowledgeable about the technology itself. There are too many things that can go wrong, too many unknown unknowns,[22] and some of the uncertainty can simply be based on subjective managerial or strategic preference. The best products or the best ideas don't always win. I think many investors today think about investing in the way I thought about Synaptics back then. Will this company become the next "big thing," or sell the next "big thing" to another company? It

---

[22] Former Secretary of Defense Donald Rumsfeld popularized the term "unknown unknowns," which generally means that there are things that we don't know that we don't know. It differs from "known unknowns," which are things that we know we don't know.

seems such a line of thinking jives well with the concept of holding stocks for a long time, but that's not necessarily investing to me (at least not anymore).

To me, investing in this fashion borders more on speculation and almost always involves a high degree of luck. Even if you identify a good "story" stock, consumer behavior and competition can change on a dime. Look at the rise and fall of Palm Pilot, the Moto Razr, and BlackBerry[23], for example. Even if you were to predict that technology would be leapfrogged, it would be very difficult to pick the company that would be doing the leapfrogging. The near term, in any case, seems much more predictable than the long term, even though both time horizons are difficult to size up. In buying "story" stocks or in chasing the next "big thing," even if your time horizon is long term in nature, you're not really an investor, per se, but rather a speculator on the future adoption of some new technology. Investing, on the other hand, involves a deep dive into the differences between the market price of the company and the estimate of the intrinsic value of the company.[24]

That is not to say investing doesn't consider a fundamental evaluation of the long term. It does. But investing focuses more on the value part of the conversation, while speculation focuses more on the price aspect. Investing involves comparing the share price to an estimated value that has a reasonable chance of being close to the company's true value, with the assumption that the price may eventually converge to the estimate of intrinsic value, regardless of the length of the holding-period. Investing involves evaluating the business at hand and its *reasonable* future enterprise free cash flows in the long run, not chasing ideas with fancy new technologies, or justifying the price paid for a stock by building in expectations of low probability, or ones that may never come to fruition even with a long-term focus.[25] Part of this line of thinking would eventually lead to work that separates

---

[23] Very few investors could have predicted the magnitude of Apple's meteoric rise prior to the launch of the iPod, and even prior to the launch of the subsequent iPhone. The popularity of handheld devices such as the PalmPilot (1997), the Moto Razr (2004), and even the BlackBerry (1999) have since faded. Technology changes fast.

[24] In *Security Analysis*, Benjamin Graham and David Dodd drew a distinction between investing and speculation. This book defines investing as a process that seeks to understand the difference between a company's share price and an informed estimate of a company's intrinsic value based on future expected enterprise free cash flows. Indexing and most quantitative investing (price-agnostic trading) do not fit this definition and can be viewed closer to speculative activity.

[25] How many of you might have invested in flying-car technology, hoverboards, and self-lacing sneakers during the mid-1980s? These technologies are far from mainstream today compared to how the movie *Back to the Future* portrayed them in the year 2015.

the frameworks of economic moats[26] and economic castles, or the difference between the magnitude and duration of economic profit creation, respectively.[27]

The idea of a company generating economic profits for a long time sounds great, but there may be greater risk to a small, long-term economic profit stream due to its duration (a moat), than a large economic profit stream generated in the near future (a castle). Investors of all types, all else equal (including price), should generally prefer the highest risk-adjusted economic profit stream, regardless of its composition, whether cyclical, fleeting or other. In a real-world setting, the confidence of predicting whether an economic profit stream will still exist 20 or 30 years in the future may be rather difficult.[28] Quite simply, if you have two equivalent economic profit streams, in aggregate, one of them generated within five years and one of them generated within 30 years, the rational investor should prefer the shorter-duration economic profit stream. Not only is the short term more "predictable," in most cases, but the time value of money provides a reasonable basis to prefer the shorter-duration economic profit stream, too.

As my understanding of enterprise valuation and identifying mispriced securities has advanced, I no longer try to seek out the next "big thing," chase 'stories" or pursue ideas with fancy new technologies, even if I like those technologies. Long-duration equity analysis can be fraught with significant overpayment risk, particularly if the market's expectations of the magnitude and duration of a company's economic profit stream can be truncated rather easily. This means that

---

[26] The first reference to the term "moat" in the investment world is credited to Warren Buffett in a November 22, 1999, Fortune article titled *Mr. Buffett on the Stock Market*: "The key to investing is not assessing how much an industry is going to affect society, or how much it will grow, but rather determining the competitive advantage of any given company and, above all, the durability of that advantage. The products or services that have wide, sustainable *moats* around them are the ones that deliver rewards to investors."

[27] Economic value or economic profit considers the economic costs or the opportunity costs of a company, not just its accounting costs. It represents the difference between a company's return on its investments and the financing costs of its investments, or the cost of capital. It is not the same as market price or market value, but rather a measure of how well a business allocates its capital to endeavors relative to the capital costs of such endeavors.

[28] If we think back 30 years ago to the late 1980s, for example, when Eastman Kodak, Sears and Montgomery Ward ruled the day, when Bear Stearns and Lehman Brothers were still around, and portable VHS recorders and arcade games were all the rage, it becomes obvious that predicting the long term is not easy. The convergence of digital-camera technologies within cell phones, Amazon's founding in 1994 and the proliferation of e-commerce, and the release of Windows 95 and the heyday of the PC were still many years away. Bear Stearns and Lehman Brothers would eventually be challenged during the Financial Crisis, the latter going completely belly up.

you won't find me getting excited about many of the stocks you might hear about in the news, and I'm perfectly fine if others make money on these considerations. To me, trying to size up the long-term market opportunity and then divvying up potential industry earnings among participants for relatively unproven technologies, or even some products evolving from regulatory change, for example, is mostly speculation, even if some level of an informed probability can be attached after extensive research efforts.

The range of probable fair outcomes[29] for these types of stocks, and by extension their implied pricing volatility, is so large that anxious, optimistic speculators might talk themselves into paying any price for shares and still feel good about it. As an investor, it is paramount to control your emotions and view analysis through a skeptical, yet objective lens. These types of securities may come with a lot of hype, but they involve too much guesswork and arriving at a reasonable fair value estimate range to truly bank on may simply not be achievable. When it comes to one-trick ponies, exotic securities that will never generate enterprise free cash flows, or betting on the upside scenario of some new technology, count me out.[30]

Factor-Based Investing and Astrologists

At no time in history has factor-based investing been more popular. Factor-based investing may trace its roots indirectly to Benjamin Graham's and David Dodd's text, *Security Analysis*, when investors first started to focus on the concept of value via public-to-private arbitrage. In Graham's and Dodd's case, however, the focus was on stocks that were *actually* trading below net current asset value (NCAV), stocks that could be taken private to exploit a cash mispricing between the share price and the company's net current assets alone. Graham would write

---

[29] It is informative to think of a company's intrinsic value estimate as a probability distribution, with the fair value estimate being the most likely outcome of what the market should think is true intrinsic value, not necessarily what is true intrinsic value.

[30] It's worth noting that the enterprise valuation framework is not necessarily inconsistent with estimating value for high-growth stocks (e.g. biotech entities), but rather the uncertainty embedded within estimated enterprise free cash flows, in some cases, is so large and long-dated that a reasonable estimate of fair value may simply be elusive. Many may opt for different valuation methods but doing so won't change the uncertain nature of the company's forward prospects (and intrinsic value).

in the *Intelligent Investor*: "A good part of our own operations on Wall Street had been concentrated on the purchase of *bargain issues* easily identified as such by the fact that they were selling at less than their share in the net current assets (working capital) alone, not counting the plant account and other assets, and after deducting all liabilities ahead of the stock."

Today, factor-based investing is much more arbitrary in nature and can simply be viewed as another name for style investing. Some factor anomalies, or those revealing what many describe as "empirical evidence[31] of *historical* positive risk-adjusted excess returns associated with them," can come with labels such as value, size, momentum, low volatility, and income. Investors that like to hold stocks with low price-to-book (P/B) ratios,[32] may have exposure to what is called a value factor, while a momentum factor might be broadly defined as stocks with strong recent share-price performance. There is no comprehensive and definitive list of what is or isn't a factor, so there could be as many factors as there are ways to analyze a stock. As of July 2016, there were more than 600 factor-based exchange-traded funds (ETFs) on the market, up from just 20 in 2001 (an incredible 550+ of those have been added since 2005).[33] In late 2017, it was estimated that factor-based funds amounted to more than $1 trillion in assets.

Nobel laureate Eugene Fama and Kenneth R. French's five-factor asset pricing model, released in 2014, which built on their original three-factor asset pricing model, released in the early 1990s, is a popular instance of well-known factor-based research, adding the factors of profitability (stocks with high operating profitability may have better returns) and investment (stocks with higher total asset growth may have lower returns) to the original three: market (stocks with high betas may have better returns), size (small-cap stocks may have better returns), and value (stocks with high book-to-market ratios may have better returns). Even within the strict confines of *in-sample*, backward-looking analysis,

---

[31] In this text, there is substantial criticism of the use of the terms "empirical" and "evidence" in financial applications, particularly with respect to ambiguous and impractical data in factor-based methods and conclusions drawn from data mining, data dredging, data snooping or other means of drawing conclusions from in-sample data. There is nothing wrong with making decisions based on empirical evidence, but it is a matter of finding the appropriate evidence, not just any evidence. See *The Data Dilemma and Valuentum Investing* in this book's Preface.

[32] In academic works, the price-to-book ratio is inverted to become the book-to-market ratio. Within quantitative finance, companies with high book-to-market ratios are believed to be value stocks, while companies with low book-to-market ratios are believed to be growth stocks.

[33] Through February 2018, it is estimated that quantitative researchers have identified 316 factors.

however, Fama and French's latest "five-factor model can leave lots of the cross-section of expected[34] stock returns unexplained." What this means is that, even over a historical measurement period, stock returns still cannot be fully "explained" with the data available.

The pitfalls embedded in the assumptions behind the analysis may be worse than any shortcomings of the conclusion, however. This analysis, and most factor-based analysis like it, assumes stock returns can be explained by ambiguous and impractical data,[35] which, given variables such as buying and selling based on forward-looking enterprise valuation, they simply cannot be. Not only this, but that such factors, or even anomalies[36] as they are called, are then used to build expectations about future returns becomes a stretch.[37] More recently, the components of the three-factor asset pricing model haven't been performing in *walk-forward* tests[38] as one might have expected, and others continue to reaffirm that the bedrock of modern finance, the Capital Asset Pricing Model (CAPM) and beta[39] "do not explain anything about expected or required returns." However, instead of new "empirical" studies based on any "evidence" (e.g. the

---

[34] It is important to clarify what is meant by "expected" in this instance. "Expected" in most traditional factor-based methods is based on backward-looking analysis without consideration of walk-forward future expectations. It is somewhat of a misnomer, as the word "expected," in this case, assumes the best estimate of the future is the past, which is often not the case.

[35] Please refer to *The Data Dilemma and Valuentum Investing* in the Preface for an extended definition of ambiguous and impractical data. For how traditional factor-based investing is defined, please see footnote 1 in the Preface.

[36] Quantitative finance draws a distinction between a factor, which technically can be considered any way in which to invest, and an anomaly, which based on in-sample and sometimes ambiguous and impractical data, has been shown to offer excess return without corresponding risk. Though quantitative finance assumes anomalies are expected to continue in walk-forward conditions, this text makes the case that this view may be misguided for anomalies that are uncovered by the application of in-sample studies using ambiguous and impractical data.

[37] Ibbotson studied the differences between the cost of equity distributions of the CAPM and Fama-French three-factor model, with both models failing to produce "logical results for a large number of entities (Ibbotson 2009)." In the Fama-French three-factor model, the research firm noted that there was a meaningful number of companies whose cost of equity estimates unreasonably exceeded 30%. With the CAPM, there is not a pure linear relationship between risk and return, and the performance of traditional quant size and value factors suggests deficiencies in the ambiguous and impractical data used within the Fama-French three-factor model.

[38] This text emphasizes the distinction between in-sample and out-of-sample tests, but also walk-forward tests (a subset of out-of-sample tests). The author believes walk-forward tests are the most robust and authentic. Please see footnote 14 in the Preface for more detail.

[39] Quantitative beta measures the volatility of a stock versus the overall market. If a stock's quantitative beta is above 1, the stock is more volatile than the market. If a stock's quantitative beta is less than 1, it is less volatile than the stock market.

Fama-French five-factor asset pricing model) being met with a greater degree of skepticism, finance seemingly has only attracted more and more miners looking for factor "gold," and investors have only become more eager to embrace the findings.

Though I admit, like Mr. Buffett, that I entertained a form of this type of "fuzzy thinking"[40] some years ago, the stock market doesn't quite work that way. Excess returns or "premia" cannot be "mined" from past data, and stocks aren't some chemical composition or secret potion that can be decomposed into various elements. Finance is mostly a behavioral science where asset prices are based on future expectations, and where no complete answer to some of its greatest questions may exist. Empirical asset pricing models[41] that are based on ambiguous and impractical data may only offer false hope the future may look like the past. In some ways, investing based on arbitrary factors may be among the purest forms of speculation, even in the context of modern portfolio theory[42] or a diversified portfolio. In the future, it may become important to differentiate between factors based on ambiguous and impractical data such as those that are prevalent today (factors that can only imply something with respect to the stock) and causal factors[43] such as that of forward-looking enterprise valuation, which while subjective can more accurately define the characteristics of a stock.

---

[40] In his 1992 Letter to Berkshire Hathaway Shareholders, Warren Buffett explained how he had once thought of stocks within "value" and "growth" buckets, to at least some degree. He viewed that as "fuzzy thinking." I may have fallen into a similar trap years ago in trying to explain "Valuentum investing" within the framework of factor investing, itself. Key components of the process were lost in translation, given stark differences in the forward-looking nature of Valuentum investing, which embraces enterprise valuation, and the ambiguous nature of traditional quant factors.

[41] It's important to explain "empirical asset pricing model" a bit more. For example, the CAPM or the Fama-French three-factor model are empirical asset pricing models, largely because they are based on objective inputs observed on the marketplace. The enterprise valuation framework is a model that prices assets, too, but because it is based on forward-looking assumptions, which are subjective, it is generally not viewed as empirical. Results emanating from studies on the performance of enterprise valuation models should be considered empirical, however.

[42] Modern portfolio theory suffers from two major shortcomings. Risk is generally not adequately measured by standard deviation, r-squared, or tracking error. A stock, for example, is not riskier because it is more volatile at a lower price; it could actually be less risky at that lower price. Modern portfolio theory also assumes that the correlations of the past will hold in the future, which is often not the case.

[43] This text explains how enterprise valuation is the independent variable that drives valuation multiples, which are used in most traditional quant factor-based analysis.

Though I believe this distinction to be paramount, it doesn't appear to be a prime consideration today given the proliferation of quantitative strategies, some perhaps only supported by a backtest and others arguably lacking satisfactory logic. Factor-based investing has a lot going for it during the sales process, particularly because of the widely-held view that the "empirical" nature of the work makes it somehow more valid, more meaningful, or more objective. As the old saying goes, "there are lies, damn lies, and statistics." Every day I challenge myself to be open to new viewpoints but interpretations of what some data means can be flawed, making many conclusions in quantitative finance misleading, at best. Correlating the movements of celestial bodies against stock market returns is *empirical* work, for example, but is it meaningful? I certainly don't think so. Many newcomers to the field of finance take empirical to mean causal or predictive, but it may be far from it.

Time and time again, we see quantitative models molded by statistical data fail in the real world, and sometimes badly. The story of Long-Term Capital Management (LTCM) is one cautionary tale. Founded in 1994, LTCM was a hedge fund run by some of finance's elite--veteran bond trading experience, PhDs, Harvard, MIT, and Stanford all graced the resumes of its partners. Two of them, Robert C. Merton and Myron Scholes, would even win the Nobel Prize in 1997, and by 1998, the fund would control assets well over $100 billion (if you consider off-balance sheet positions, it had exposure well over $1 trillion). That same year, however, the hedge fund would fail, almost bringing down the global financial system with it.

The lessons from the collapse in LTCM are well-documented. Leverage is a double-edged sword, and liquidity risk can be fatal, but there's more: Statistical models can sometimes fail horribly, and historical correlations between assets can change rapidly, right when you need them to hold the most. Through most of LTCM's existence, the correlation between corporate and Treasury yields estimated with a two-year moving average remained above 0.94. However, the correlation dropped to 0.80 in 1998. Had LTCM performed more stress-testing, it may not have made such big bets that ultimate led to its demise.[44] Overconfidence may have had something to do with it, too.

---

[44] An interesting "what if" about LTCM is that the correlation between corporate and Treasury yields estimated with a two-year moving average had reached a low of 0.75 in 1992, two years

Today, according to a study by the Index Industry Association, there are now more than 70 times as many stock indexes as there are stocks, and many of these stock indexes have been created by somewhat suspect methods and backtests. Hypothetically speaking, an index can be created with the best performing stocks in history, showcasing significant outperformance relative to any benchmark or peer group, but what does pre-selected past performance imply with respect to the future performance of the index? Not much, if you ask me. "There's never a backtest a researcher didn't like," some industry veterans might say. Unlike walk-forward studies, where a methodology is tested in real-world conditions (not just in other historical out-of-sample data sets), some indexes today seem to be backfilled from scratch. When these stock indexes are converted to products such as ETFs and go live, future actual performance may be far different than the substance of the in-sample backtest used to originally support the product.

The PowerShares Multi-Strategy Alternative Portfolio Fund is one such example. According to WealthManagement, the fund was marketed with backfilled[45] data that showed enviable returns. The backfilled returns were so good that if the index had been live, it would have achieved "90 percent of the returns of the S&P 500 with 20 percent of the volatility and a maximum drawdown only 2.4 percent." This would put it among the top 1% of hedge funds during the past 10-year stretch. Since the fund went live in 2014, however, it lost money through 2018, while the S&P 500 advanced. What's worse is that its maximum drawdown was over 15%, more than six times that of how the strategy performed during the worst of times in the backtest, which even included the Financial Crisis. Think about the marketing muscle of having pre-selected data in backtests though.

In some ways, it may explain, why passive investing and quantitative strategies have become popular relative to active management, and it may be caused by how performance is marketed to and interpreted by the investor. For starters, it may be impossible for an active manager to theoretically outperform pre-selected backtests (how could they?). If you could imagine an investor deciding between two funds in which to invest. If the investor is presented with backfilled data of

---

prior to the start of the fund. If LTCM considered this, it's possible it may have avoided catastrophe altogether.

[45] The idea of indexes using backfilled data may in some ways be related to instant history bias, or when "an index contains histories of returns that predate the entry date of the corresponding funds into a database and thereby cause the index to disproportionately reflect the characteristics of funds that are added to the database."

one fund versus actual data of another fund, that investor may not know that those comparisons aren't apples-to-apples. In such a case, it's not as simple as selecting the best-performing, risk-adjusted fund based on past data (in fact, you should never do this, as past is not prologue). The attractive characteristics revealed in past backfilled data could be far from predictive of what may happen in the future, perhaps more so than the track record of an active fund with actual results.

The markets may truly have gone full circle over the past century. During the flapper years of the "Roaring '20s," many investors followed the advice of Evangeline Adams. Ms. Adams was an American astrologist during the early 20th century who called New York her home. She owned a burgeoning astrological consulting business at the time, and her stock-market prediction newsletter had one of the largest followings, even by today's standards (estimated at 100,000 subscribers). She called Charlie Chaplin, Mary Pickford, Groucho Marx, and even J.P. Morgan her clients. Some say Ms. Adams could predict prices so accurately that it was no different than having read the market activity in the newspaper. For months, Ms. Adams would look at the stars and predict ever-higher stock prices. She taught her subscribers how the Zodiac could influence the ticker tape.

To me, reading the stars or using ambiguous and impractical data to try to explain stock returns may be one and the same. There simply is no good reason for the relationship, in most cases, to be causal. Movements of celestial bodies do not cause stock price movements, no more than fuzzy data does. This line of thinking is primarily why some quantitative models fail in the real world: The researcher lets the empirical results tell them what matters, and they seem to leave logical thinking out of it.[46] If the signs of the Zodiac implied something statistically significant with respect to stock returns, researchers might just add the Zodiac factor to their *empirical* asset pricing models.

---

[46] In *Fooled By Randomness*, Nassim Taleb would joke, "I am convinced that there exists a tradable security in the Western world that would be 100% correlated with the changes in the temperature in Oulan Bator, Mongolia." Tyler Vigen, author of *Spurious Correlations*, offers a few real examples: "US spending on science, space and technology" is highly correlated with "suicides by hanging, strangulation and suffocation," and the "number of people who drowned by falling in a pool" is correlated with "films Nicholas Cage appeared in." My personal favorite is the 0.9926 correlation coefficient between the "divorce rate in Maine" and the "per capital consumption of margarine" from 2000-2009, though the 0.9524 correlation coefficient between "people who drowned after falling out of a fishing boat" and the "marriage rate in Kentucky" from 1999-2010 comes close to topping my list of favorites. Correlation does not imply causation.

If you think I am joking, please refer to the *Journal of Empirical Finance* from January 2006, "Are investors moonstruck? Lunar phases and stock returns." The paper analyzed the relationship between phases of the moon and stock returns and "discovered" something called a "lunar effect," where stock returns were lower around the days of a full moon. The effect couldn't be explained away by other variables. It's interesting reading, but I wouldn't consider developing a trading strategy around it. I'm not trying to build a straw man argument, but rather, given the likelihood of spurious correlations and confounding lurking variables, "empirical" may simply not mean what investors think it means in the field of finance. Many believe the word goes beyond data and observation to also mean causal and predictive. In many cases, it is far from it.

"This is an Orange Line train to Midway," the familiar announcement rung out.

I was still getting used to the 5am trips to Chicago and the late nights while working at Driehaus. My journey at the University of Chicago Booth School of Business also began at Driehaus. I enjoyed my experience there, but as Nobel laureate Richard Thaler may have felt, I was somehow misbehaving[47] if I didn't agree with the latest quantitative research, even if I didn't know it then.

Just How Bad Is Data Interpretation?

Passive strategies and quantitative investing may seem like they are on the fringe, that investors aren't paying a lot of attention to them, but this could not be further from reality. According to a study by J.P. Morgan in 2017, "fundamental discretionary traders," or those trading on firm-specific fundamentals, account for just 10% of all trading in stocks. By the research firm's estimates, roughly 60% of stock trading now comes from passive and quantitative investing, or price-agnostic trading,[48] more than double that of just 10 years ago.

---

[47] Richard Thaler may have coined the term "misbehaving" in the financial world. For example, a researcher may be "misbehaving" if they write an economics paper that reflects how people actually behave in real life, which may not fit nicely into a statistical model.

[48] This is the first use of the term "price-agnostic trading" in the body of the text. This term refers to trading that influences share prices but is not based on the consideration of a company's intrinsic value estimate. If everyone pursued price-agnostic trading or buying and selling regardless of the absolute price level, the markets could theoretically become nonsensical and entirely irrational.

Much of the growth of passive strategies and some areas of quantitative investing, however, may be based on little more than fuzzy logic, the failed statistical models of yesteryear, and a thirst by investors just to keep costs low.

Big data is, nonetheless, upon the financial world--whether the data makes sense or whether the data actually measures what researchers believe it measures. Don't get me wrong: There's nothing inherently wrong with big data, itself. Running a regression on last year's book-to-market (B/M) ratio or last year's P/E ratio may be a valuable learning exercise. There's also nothing inherently biased with the researchers either. I hold a tremendous amount of respect for their skills and talents, and I think many may believe that what they are "finding" may be causal or predictive, in some cases.

Significant problems arise, however, from the assumptions behind what researchers think the data measures (e.g. "value" versus "growth"), and more importantly, the conclusions drawn from those assumptions (e.g. "value" outperforms "growth"). In particular, researchers may say they are measuring value in an observed B/M ratio, as in the Fama-French three-factor model, and they may say, *or rather conclude*,[49] that "value" has outperformed "growth" over a certain time period. These types of conclusions are misleading,[50] but very few seem to be taking the data-interpretation issues seriously.

---

[49] To get a sense for how many in quantitative finance may be thinking about "value" and "growth," we have the following from *Quantitative Momentum*: "Great minds can disagree on the explanation, but nobody can dispute the empirical fact that value stocks have outperformed growth stocks by a wide margin." This text will explain how "value" and "growth" stocks may not only be misclassified due to arbitrary book equity, but also that most of the analysis of ambiguous and impractical B/M (that which separates "value" and "growth") is in-sample analysis, not of the walk-forward variety. The "value" and "growth" conversation in quantitative finance today may be similar to the conversation about the efficient markets hypothesis in the 1960s and 1970s, where most researchers are simply accepting the conclusions as fact or having been proven when they aren't.

[50] McKinsey performed a study, using the S&P 500/Barra Growth Index and the S&P 500/Barra Value Index during the period 2002-2005 and found that those labeled as growth stocks with respect to B/M ratios had revenue growth rates that were "virtually indistinguishable from those labeled as value stocks." The research firm found that ROIC was a somewhat better indicator of whether a company was labeled a "growth" stock, which might make sense definitionally, as these entities generally might have lower accounting book values (bolstering ROIC). However, the takeaway was not that ROIC is a better way to sort value versus growth, but rather that the concepts of value versus growth "are just not meaningful." Such simple classifications between value and growth may be misleading to investors, the research firm added.

There are instances, for example, where book value can be negligible or negative for important and widely-known companies that have tremendous intrinsic or market value. Boeing and McDonald's have been two of the highest-profile examples. In 2008, Boeing's total shareholders' equity was -$1.14 billion (negative $1.14 billion), while at the end of the third quarter of 2018, McDonald's total shareholders' equity was -$6.79 billion (negative $6.79 billion). That there are documented high-profile B/M outliers, suggesting book equity is meaningless as a measure of value *in just a few instances*, is not necessarily the point though.[51]

Instead, it is the very understanding behind the existence of these high-profile outliers where problems with drawing any conclusions about "value" or "growth" from the B/M ratio arise. In Boeing's case, the company incurred an increased pension liability due to the market turmoil of the Financial Crisis that caused an equity adjustment, driving book equity into negative territory. The negative equity at McDonald's was driven by share buybacks funded with increased borrowings. To be fair, these items impact the intrinsic-value calculation for both firms, but the absolute or relative level of book equity to market value is still arbitrary for most operating, non-financial companies.[52]

Situations like Boeing and McDonald's are not merely outliers to be thrown out of quantitative studies, as they are often done when book equity is being studied. One might as well throw out all the other companies, too. Almost every company's book equity is impacted one way or another by one-time items, their capital structure, and their dividend policy. This means that *for a large number of companies*, not just the ones that have negative or negligible measures, accounting book equity[53] for operating, non-financial entities can be considered mostly

---

[51] According to a study in 2007, the researchers estimated that approximately 5% of all listed stocks had negative book equity (Brown 2007). There were an estimated 118 companies in the US market with negative equity as of April 2018. One of the best performing stocks of this century, Domino's, has had negative book equity since it went public in 2004. Other high-profile companies that had negative book equity in April 2018 were HP, Motorola, Denny's, AutoZone, Wayfair, H&R Block, and Yum Brands (Fairchild 2018).

[52] This text will cover situations with respect to financial entities, where book equity may offer an alternative basis for valuation, even if it may not be as robust as enterprise valuation for non-financial operating companies. See Chapter 5.

[53] Accounting principles may change over time and a company has the option to choose among various methods to account for items, but this only changes the appearance of the company on paper. The cash flows, themselves, do not change, and therefore neither does business value under different accounting treatments. Book equity, or shareholders' equity, is one such accounting item.

arbitrary and largely unreliable when it comes to any measure of "value" or "growth." Book equity may, indeed, depend more on one-time adjustments, a company's capital structure, or its dividend policies than truly anything else.

A study performed by Ching-Lih Jan and Jane A. Ou and published in 2012 in *Accounting Horizons*, for example, found that over a period of 1996-2005, the market even priced negative-book-equity companies higher than positive-book-equity companies. The study also found that the correlation between market value and book equity for negative-equity companies was negative. Another study by O'Shaughnessy Asset Management estimated that negative-equity companies outperformed the market in approximately 57% of rolling 3-year periods from 1993-2007. The arbitrary nature of book equity when it comes to assessing its importance to market value may be even more apparent in the case of Domino's. The company has had negative equity for as long as it has been public, and its returns have trounced the market by more than 5,000 percentage points since 2009.

Figure 2: Domino's Negative Equity and Stock Outperformance

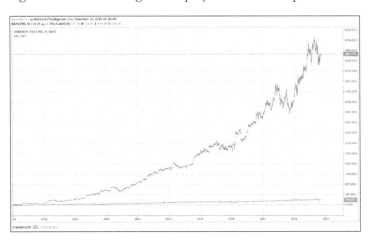

Figure 2 shows the performance of Domino's (DPZ), which has had negative equity since going public in 2004. Shares of the company have outperformed the market by more than 5,000 percentage points since 2009. The line that runs almost parallel to the x-axis is the comparable market return, as measured by an ETF that tracks the S&P 500 (SPY).

Widely-read pieces of statistical work often tie the B/M ratio to the dividend discount model to defend its use, but this creates an even bigger problem.[54] Not only is the meaning behind book equity and the B/M ratio undefined in most cases, but the logic behind the use of a dividend discount model is hugely problematic. First, we witnessed how detached from operating conditions dividend-discount valuations can become with Kinder Morgan and the MLPs with respect to their financially-engineered dividends and distributions in 2015 (see Preface). Second, though it may be reasonable that the value of a company may theoretically be a function of all "dividends (cash)" returned to shareholders (such that the company eventually ceases to exist, has nothing left), the dividend discount model often may not be practical, or logical, given the concept of the time value of money.

Berkshire Hathaway hasn't paid a dividend in 50 years,[55] and even if we assume that it will, the value of Berkshire Hathaway in 1970 could not practically or logically have been a function of its speculated, expected future dividends in 2025 (if Berkshire Hathaway begins paying dividends at that time, or decides to liquidate and provide a one-time dividend at that time). The market wasn't pricing Berkshire in 1970 on what it thought it would pay shareholders in dividends at some point in the coming century. The same might be said of Apple, where the estimated value of its equity in 1990 can be reasoned, practically and logically, to have little to do with its speculated, expected dividend profile today.

Researchers understand that Boeing and McDonald's are not trading near $0 per share, and they shouldn't just because their book equity is negligible. Researchers also know that companies have value even if they don't pay a dividend, or never will. So what gives? The simple reality is that ambiguous and impractical data is being used because it's there, because it's available. While empirically, there may have been some observation of a link between book equity and market value in the past, correlations between the two have since deteriorated. According to Oakmark, "for companies in the S&P 500 today, the correlation between stock

---

[54] Fama and French's paper on their new five-factor model, for example, suggests the logic behind B/M is tied to the dividend discount model. However, book equity is largely arbitrary for most operating companies. Dividends aren't always tied to the operating economics of the business, and the timing of the final dividend (when a company "dividends itself out") make the dividend discount model too impractical. The correlation that once tied B/M heavily to share prices has declined considerably in recent decades, too.

[55] Berkshire Hathaway paid one dividend in 1967. Warren Buffett has joked that he must have been in the bathroom when it was authorized. He prefers reinvesting capital into new businesses.

price and tangible book value has become quite small, just 0.14. This is a very big change from 25 years ago, when that correlation was 0.71."[56]

The changing correlation over time exposes the pitfalls of letting the empirical data tell the story and not logic. Some researchers believe "something" is meaningful, for no better reason sometimes, than the results that led to its generation were "empirical," or in most cases of reference, backward-looking within in-sample sets. According to Nobel laureate Richard Thaler, Fama and French have all but conceded "that they did not have any theory to explain why size and value should be risk factors." It seems that the interpretation of the three-factor or five-factor models may be built on the assumption of predictability,[57] at least perhaps with respect to estimating the cost of equity, but there seems to be a limited logical basis for it.[58]

Unlike the field of physics, the field of finance is comparatively much younger. Where it has taken hundreds of years from Copernicus to Einstein to better our understanding of the field of physics, by comparison there have only been a few decades of research in finance. Even the collection of financial data doesn't stretch back that far. For example, "the first systematic collection of stock market prices, was compiled under the auspices of the Alfred Cowles Foundation in the 1930s," and there is substantial criticism of studies that use centuries old data to draw any sort of conclusions, namely some of Jeremy Siegel's findings in *Stocks for the Long Run*. The *Wall Street Journal's* Jason Zweig would write: "There is just one problem with tracing stock performance all the way back to 1802: it isn't really valid."

---

[56] Correlation coefficients in the range of 0-0.25 can generally be considered very weak. Those between 0.5-0.75 may have a moderate to strong positive relationship. Causality is not considered in such a coefficient, however.

[57] Looking at how literature is generally interpreting the Fama-French three-factor model with respect to the cost of equity calculation, in particular, the following from Ibbotson can be considered: "This finding suggests a predictive model in which these variables--size and book-to-market ratio—are used (in conjunction with beta) to estimate the expected return or cost of equity capital (Ibbotson 2009)." Note the term "predictive."

[58] Firms with higher book-to-market ratios perhaps may have been hypothesized to be more financially-distressed, and therefore require a higher return, but that may not be the case at all, given the many exogenous factors that can impact book equity in an accounting context. It may be reasonable to believe that investors should require higher returns for smaller firms, but being small, itself, should not necessarily be considered causal to returns. It was found out later that the data used to develop the size factor was flawed (Asness 2018).

It is much more than this, however. Even if we had financial market data going back thousands of years, it would still not address the crux of the issue: Most efforts with data analysis in trying to explain stock returns are based on ambiguous and impractical data that have incorrect interpretations, instead of being based on causal data that captures future expectations. I believe that if the financial industry had data on calculated enterprise values of stocks dating back to the 1930s or earlier, as derived by enterprise free cash flow models, value factor assessments in a quantitative setting might be more appropriately measured on an enterprise valuation basis, or pure metrics of the difference between market price and estimates of intrinsic value, instead of B/M ratios or even EV/EBITDA or P/E ratios, which suffer from the same shortcomings as the B/M ratio (stocks with high P/E ratios[59] can still be undervalued, for example).

How the Market Functions

The Great Crash of 1929 serves as an important reminder of how the stock market itself functions. Often lost in this digital, sometimes impersonal, world of the 21st century is that the stock market will always be made up of people, their actions, if not their thoughts and ideas, whether it is the financial mathematician writing the algorithm for a high-frequency trading strategy, or the trader placing an order for 1,000 shares or 100,000 shares. Those that were buying stocks on Ms. Adams' astrology advice and those that were selling stocks as a result of margin calls during the Great Crash of 1929 acted together as the structural backbone of the stock market--no different than those buying on chart patterns and selling based on valuation considerations today.

If a stock is in demand, its shares will be bought, and it will go up in price (the demand curve is shifted outward). If there is no demand for the stock, the price

---

[59] Throughout this text, I will make several references to various price-to-earnings (P/E) ratios. The quantitative P/E ratio is one that you may be most familiar with. It is observed on the marketplace and calculated as the price of the stock divided by annual earnings. The quantitative P/E, or price-observed P/E, differs from the value-derived P/E, which is derived through the process of enterprise valuation. The quantitative P/E, or price-observed P/E, is compared to the value-derived P/E to determine if a company may be fairly-valued, undervalued or overvalued. The absolute level of the quantitative P/E, or price-observed P/E, may offer limited information to the investor, if not also compared to the value-derived P/E. The quantitative P/E is ambiguous.

will go down as those looking to sell the stock can't find enough buyers at the current price (the supply curve is shifted outward). Wall Street knows the game well enough: Price in the form of a stock quote is what you pay for a share of stock; value in the form of a fair value estimate is what you get as a share of a company's future free cash flow stream, its business. Price and value are two separate concepts, often used interchangeably, but incorrectly so.

When they are first introduced to the stock market, investors sometimes want to believe that investing is an exact science--that it must be as precise as accounting or physics or mathematics, for example, disciplines with well-defined rules and outcomes. As humans, we don't want to admit that something that is so fragile and fickle and so entirely "random" to the untrained eye as the stock market can be responsible for the preservation of so many jobs, for the savings and pensions of so many retirees, for the growth of organizations both public and private, for the stability of our families, and for funding behind the education of our very own children. To many, the stock market must be "explainable" with vast amounts of realized data.

New investors want to believe that if a company has a tried-and-true business concept its stock will do well, too, oftentimes regardless of the price at purchase. We don't like to see the stock prices of tried-and-true companies such as Chevron, IBM, Exxon Mobil, United Technologies, Intel, Procter & Gamble, and Walmart fall 20% in any one year. Surely these businesses aren't worth 20% less than they were just a year ago? We want the link between good companies and good stocks to be firmly established, with complete disregard to timing, just like when we mix red and blue, we get purple. Unlike the defined outcomes of mixing colors, however, even great companies can sometimes make for bad stocks, and vice-versa, over certain periods of time, sometimes during the most important periods of our life, our daughter's wedding or our son's first year of college.

The human mind wants the stock price of a company to track the company's reported earnings and free cash flow in lock step over time, with predictable certainly, regardless of a time lag, or even with one. But it won't. It never will. It can't. If the earnings and free cash flow of a company advance over time, it is perhaps equally plausible that the same company's stock price may have gone up, or down, or stayed flat during that time. MIT-educated Roger Babson, of

"Babson Break"[60] fame, who warned about the impending Crash of 1929, knew the importance of forward-looking information--not historical earnings or dividends, unless of course, the historical information influences future buyer/seller behavior--as the only type of analysis that matters in the stock market:

> When I want to know what the temperature in this room is going to be an hour or two from now I don't consult the thermometer on the wall. I go to the boiler room and see what is going on down there. I go to the factor that causes the future temperature. You men were looking at bank clearings, retail sales, wholesale indexes, stock car loadings and trends–the thermometers on the wall.

But it is not enough to be ahead of the curve as a forward-looking investor. Even if the astute forecaster predicts accurately that earnings will advance over a period of time in the future, stock prices could still be disappointingly lower than they were at the start of that period. Earnings for companies in the Dow Jones Industrial Average soared more than 50% during the period April 1929 through July 1930 as the stock market crashed during that time. Shares of Microsoft peaked at nearly $60 each in 1999 on operating income of $11-$12 billion for June fiscal year ends 2000 and 2001, but the software giant traded for as little as $26 per share as recently as 2012 on operating income of $26-$28 billion in June fiscal year ends 2013 and 2014. Even a rosy outlook today may not be good enough to support a stock price that had been backed by even rosier expectations in years prior.

The idea that buying and selling activity moves the stock price, the emotional ups and downs of greed and fear and not historical earnings and dividends that we can objectively and confidently measure in statistical models, leaves us completely unsatisfied, thirsty for the order that is innate to other disciplines that must somehow also be present in the financial discipline, too. But it is not. That there's not a "wizard behind the curtain"[61] that changes the market from a discounting, probability-weighting mechanism of future earnings and free cash flow into a precise mechanism in the future that translates earnings and free cash flow one-to-one from the company to the shareholder may leave many unsatisfied. As humans, we find the stock market completely inconsistent with

---

[60] See Notes at the back of this text.
[61] This wouldn't be a book without a reference to *"The Wizard of Oz."*

our quest for security, which we hold dear, which we've fought for, that we continue to fight for.

Watching a small or micro-cap company's share price move after a large buy order is simply unsatisfying in a world that has applied the laws of science and physics to put a man on the moon. Witnessing a company "break out of a base" or surge due to a "cup and handle" pattern as technical investors pile into the stock with purchase orders fails to offer the degree of comfort that a tried-and-true chemical reaction may provide to help treat a disease. We want something tangible, something we can measure and understand easily, even if we must use those dreaded numbers--not something based on fear and greed.

What investors are reminded of time and time again throughout history, however, is that the stock market is nothing like we want it to be; it is without precision, structure and defined outcomes, and it is not as easy of a path to wealth and riches as many may make it out to be. If the stock market is then a reflection of our human behaviors, all the good and all the bad, does this then mean that we are nothing like we want to be either, or does it mean something completely different? By studying the stock market, are we in fact learning more about ourselves than anything else? Do we not like what we see? Surely others wiser than I am have pondered these questions.

But just as we embrace our very own children for who they are and will be, investors should embrace the stock market for what it is, too--not try to "explain" its inner workings through ambiguous and impractical data, not seek to present it only through rose-colored glasses, but instead show it for all its good and all its bad. Then, and only then, in accepting the superficial, unsatisfying foundation of the stock market--the laws of supply and demand, that some people are greedy, that some people are fearful, that people make mistakes, and that hidden biases lie beneath some conventional wisdom[62]--can investors tear off the shackles of precision and structure to therefore learn that it is those very "perfect" imperfections that themselves are solely responsible for outsize profit opportunities that many seek to exploit.

From those that lived through the Crash of 1929 and the Great Depression, to those that lived through the Crash of 1987, to those that bore witness to the dot-com bust, to those that navigated the Financial Crisis of 2008-2009 and

---

[62] See Notes at the back of this text.

Great Recession, to those that experienced the Flash Crash of 2010[63], and to those not yet embracing the August 2015 crash[64] in the Dow Jones Industrial Average as a modern-day iteration of such a dynamic, the stock market will always be a reflection of ourselves, our lives, a reflection of our invincible and arrogant youth, reborn with each new generation. Like those before us, the generations of tomorrow will forget the lessons taught by the generations of the past, ad infinitum, and each new generation will believe that there will only be blue skies[65] ahead, failing to remember that the skies are sometimes the bluest right before the storm.

---

[63] The Flash Crash occurred on May 6, 2010. The Dow Jones Industrial Average fell almost 1,000 points in less than an hour during afternoon trading, or approximately 9%, before recovering a large part of the loss.

[64] Within minutes of the S&P 500 opening on August 24, 2015, the index fell nearly 5% before the market gained back most of its losses.

[65] The mood just years before the Crash of 1929 could be best summed up by Irving Berlin's "Blue Skies," a popular song written in 1926: "Blue skies, smiling at me. Nothing but blue skies, do I see."

2

Once the Mind Is Stretched

Empirical evidence-based analysis is a misnomer. The gift. Keynes was dead. Apologetic works. What are predictive or causal factors of stock prices? Future expected data that is realized or not. Letter B. What's in a name? Betting at the Derby. H2O. Importance of walk-forward performance. Reality becomes the anomaly, and the backtest remains truth! The randomness of factor returns. Never-ending empirical asset pricing model iterations. Don't bet on ambiguous or impractical data.

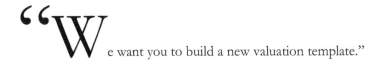

e want you to build a new valuation template."

I was sitting at a table in a small room at the old Morningstar headquarters at 225 West Wacker Drive in Chicago. It must have been in either 2007 or 2008, before the brunt of the Financial Crisis hit. "Sounds great. What are we looking to do?" I said, glad to be of help to the organization. I was proud to be a part of Morningstar. The people were great, and the company stood for something. "We want to make the model simpler."

At the time, I don't think I knew exactly what that meant, and I'm not sure my triumvirate of bosses sitting at the table knew either. Indexing and factor-based investing had been budding in the background of the industry for years, but these investment approaches had zero impact on the daily life of an equity analyst that was focused on evaluating the investment merits of a company. Perhaps that was why. After all, the job of a stock analyst, to a degree, is to identify mispriced stocks, which generally flies in the face of buying everything at any price, as in index investing, and factor-based investing in its present-day form seemed so simplistic that it might be hard to believe that most would be, or could be, betting billions on backward-looking B/M ratios, for example.

But there was a disconnect. The views of equity analysts are not always the views of the investor, as I found out later, and the investor allocates capital to strategies and methodologies where they wish. It's difficult to explain that researchers may be obfuscating the meaning of the term "empirical evidence" in hopes that investors may interpret the term similarly to how it is viewed in other fields of study.[66] In finance, if the data applied is not causal or predictive, betting on the future based solely on empirical backtests that use ambiguous or impractical data may be among the worst forms of speculation, particularly given the track record of prior empirical asset pricing models.

How times have changed in the past couple decades. Looking back to when I had only some basic knowledge of finance and investing, the P/E ratio and "story" stocks seemed like a plausible approach to investing, even a sophisticated one. The average fundamental investor may still invest in this manner, but I have changed. There's something far more substantial to look at.

Hello Enterprise Valuation

It is experience that influences the thinker, not what is or what isn't, it seems. Had I not been asked to rebuild Morningstar's enterprise discounted cash-flow model used by dozens of analysts to estimate the intrinsic values of companies, would I ever have truly understood the shortcomings of the P/E ratio? Would I still be interested in chasing earnings beats, or looking for "story" stocks? I honestly don't know. But once the mind is stretched, it can never go back. What Morningstar provided me was a gift. The firm provided me with an opportunity to learn enterprise valuation. Those six months or so that I spent rebuilding Morningstar's valuation model template, working with each and every sector head

---

[66] It may even be simpler than this, however. Data may just be used to back up the strategies some investment managers are selling. It doesn't matter whether the data is ambiguous or impractical, or if the data results in spurious correlations. If retail investors are "buying it," some will sell it. It may be another way to reduce responsibility or accountability. If last year's realized B/M ratio implies this or implies that, the B/M is just cyclical, or the traditional quant value factor is just out of favor. The investment manager that uses ambiguous or impractical data can never be wrong in this sense. It's just the nature of the data, they may say. The situation is very similar to the non-falsifiable component of the efficient markets hypothesis.

to make it happen, and the years spent optimizing it, is an experience that few others can or will ever have.

I embraced it.

I wasn't the best in Excel, far from it, and I required help with some of the VBA programming, but the model was solid. Granted, it was just a model, but it was a window to view the world. It put together all the key facets to understanding a business. How do interest rates impact value? What about tax implications? How does one quantify the value of the company's competitive advantages? From revenue to net income and earnings before interest, after taxes, to invested capital, it had it all. To me, it just made sense. Enterprise valuation wasn't some lucky bet on some future technology. Enterprise valuation was far more meaningful than valuing stocks on a P/E ratio or B/M ratio, as in some factor-based considerations. Enterprise valuation showed how value advances over time via the time value of money, forming what I would consider to be the primary reason anyone would even consider indexing: stock values generally advance over time.[67]

Enterprise valuation puts Vanguard's Jack Bogle, Berkshire's Warren Buffett, and University of Chicago's Eugene Fama all at the same table. Even the top behavioral economists have a seat. Enterprise valuation is universal.

The Coup d'etat of Modern Finance

What I didn't know at the time, and probably Warren Buffett knows all too well,[68] is that quantitative finance, or what I describe to be the outgrowth of modern portfolio theory and variations of the CAPM, had changed the conversation, not in the 2000s, but in the 1950s and 1960s. Harry Markowitz's

---

[67] This book characterizes the merits of index investing as an investment process that is built mostly on speculation and chance. However, index investing holds a basket of stocks, and because the value of a basket of equities generally increases over time within the enterprise valuation context, share prices may loosely follow, all else equal. The proliferation of indexing and quantitative trading, however, brings up a key question this book raises: Will share prices continue to loosely follow values in the event price-agnostic trading completely overwhelms value-conscious buying, or the means by which prices track value?

[68] In an article titled the *Superinvestors of Graham-and-Doddsville*, published in 1984, Warren Buffett noted that the academic world has migrated away from the teachings of value investing principles during the past 30 years.

mean-variance framework in modern portfolio theory in the early 1950s was followed up by Jack Treynor's development in the early 1960s of the CAPM, which paid no mind to the fundamentals of an individual equity at all, but merely used the risk-free rate, an estimate of expected market return scaled by beta, or a measure of the volatility of the price of the asset.

The CAPM, or a one-factor model (beta), had largely been shown to be less useful even by the late 1970s, but it had become the authoritative "perceived truth" in the academic community. Even today, the CAPM forms the foundation for the publishing of various other multi-factor models, including Fama and French's three-factor model and five-factor model. Though these models suffer from the same structural shortcomings of the original CAPM (stock returns are, in part, a function of future expectations), they were developed decades later, and only after the coup d'état of modern finance had already happened in the 1960s and 1970s. Millions of investors have been influenced by the studies in the 1960s and 1970s, even though many of those studies have now been overturned, or significantly modified. The 1970s changed the course of finance, and there was nobody like Keynes, who had passed in 1946, to balance the conversation.

But there is more to this story.

There may have been no true channel to actually challenge the efficient markets hypothesis during most of the 1970s and 1980s. There's some evidence that investors actually believed that efficient markets theory to have been proven in the 1970s,[69] and papers that refuted its findings had to be apologetic, it seemed, just to get published. According to Nobel laureate Richard Thaler in his work *Misbehaving*, these papers would say things like, "the behavior of security prices…is, perhaps, not completely described by the efficient markets hypothesis," and "given its longevity, it is not likely that it is due to a market inefficiency, but it is rather evidence of a pricing model misspecification." Thaler would add: "In other words, there must be something left out of the model because market efficiency cannot be wrong."

When reputations are on the line and the network of source material could unravel, causing a cascade effect on decades of prior conclusions in the world of

---

[69] "I believe there is no other proposition in economics which has more solid empirical evidence supporting it than the Efficient Market Hypothesis." -- Michael C. Jensen (1978)

finance, the opposition to change is understandable.[70] It seems well-entrenched ideas and inertia-based thinking are very difficult to challenge, even in the case of the confines of in-sample, backward-looking analysis (as it relates to quant anomalies debunking the efficient markets hypothesis), but also in the idea that stock returns are driven in part by future expectations (as it relates to the implausibility of using realized data to develop quant factors to explain returns), the latter the efficient markets hypothesis itself does not dispute (see Chapter 6). The second observation is important.

Researchers may point to anomalies uncovered via in-sample statistical analysis, suggesting that because these anomalies exist, the market is therefore inefficient.[71] However, the existence of anomalies derived by applying ambiguous realized data in in-sample tests says nothing about whether markets are efficient or not. There may be no logical reason to believe such anomalies uncovered in backtests will continue in real-world conditions. The efficient markets hypothesis assumes, too, that all information, including the forward-looking variety,[72] is reflected in stock prices. Therefore, market efficiency can only truly be tested in a forward-looking manner based on future expected data, *realized or not*. In-sample data has already been realized and may not reflect future expectations, which influence returns.

Quantitative statistical models, broadly defined as price-observed models (e.g. the CAPM or the Fama-French three-factor model), are limited by the ambiguous and impractical nature of data that is readily available. The definition of predictive may be built on the foundation of what I learned in my buyside experience, but it is also something that is generally understood by the marketplace. For something to be a predictive factor, or a causal factor,[73] it must influence future

---

[70] There may be more to it than just reputations on the line. It could be a systemic issue. Journals choose what they publish, people are interested in specific topics, and specific types of research get funded. Independence and objectivity may not be as prevalent as one might believe.

[71] It's important to draw a distinction between statistical factor-based anomalies, as in risk factors, and those of behavioral nature. Where most statistical factor-based anomalies are based on ambiguous data, behavioral anomalies may not be. Where quantitative finance is merely young, behavioral finance may be in its infancy, so a distinction may be required as new research pushes forward.

[72] This refers more directly to the idea that, to explain any price movement, whether such prices make sense or not, efficient markets theorists may say that the market is just factoring in new expectations. There is another part of this, too. Even under weak-form efficiency, however, because the current observed price, as in a price multiple, implies expectations about the future, tests for efficiency must always be forward looking in scope.

[73] Two variables that may be highly correlated does not mean that one variable is the cause of the change in the other variable. When two or more variables are not causally related to each other, it

buying and selling activity because it is the future buying and selling activity that drives future prices.[74] It may be easiest to understand what data may not be predictive. Running a best-fit regression model based on the first letter of company names could result in a statistically-significant output, but is the data or model predictive? Not really. One wouldn't say that a company with the letter A is any more likely to outperform than a company with the letter B based on the first letter of the company name alone.[75]

But what if the model suggests a high probability of companies with the letter A outperforming companies with the letter B based on historical data? What if the results were even statistically significant? Let's now replace 'companies with the letter A' and 'companies with the letter B' with 'companies with high B/M ratios' and 'companies with low B/M ratios.' After this change, is the study any more meaningful, implying causality? Just like it may seem obvious to any observer that the first letter of the name of the company shouldn't matter in the first case, it is equally obvious to me that B/M ratios shouldn't matter in the second. It is market value that matters to returns, and market value is based in part on buying and selling influenced by future expectations of enterprise free cash flows, not last year's accounting book equity, which itself, is arbitrary for most non-financial operating firms.

That is not to say that companies with the letter 'A' can't outperform in the future, of course, but if they do, it won't be because their names start with the letter 'A,' no matter what history implies. Apple has not been the stock that it has been because its first letter starts with 'A.' Boeing has not been the stock it has been because its first letter starts with 'B.' There have been instances where companies

---

reflects a spurious (false) relationship. The Super Bowl indicator, which suggests that a win by an NFC predicts a rise in the market, and the skirt length theory, which suggests skirt lengths are predictive of market movements, are two widely-accepted examples of spurious correlations. There are many more spurious relationships in quantitative finance as this text indicates.

[74] This is an important point that forms one of the key takeaways of this text. The end game for prices, as in public-to-private arbitrage, rests in an estimate of intrinsic value (enterprise valuation) for the company, an estimate that the market must accept for the company to be taken private (and the price that shares trade to before being delisting). It's equally important to note that indexers and quantitative investors are becoming a larger part of the Keynesian "beauty contest," and they are not necessarily trading based on intrinsic value estimates. The conclusion of this text covers the consequences of the proliferation of price-agnostic trading.

[75] Some businesses may change their names to be listed higher up in the phone book, and that may lead to more business, but when it comes to listings on the stock exchange, it's a completely different situation.

have pursued name changes to catch the favor of the markets, perhaps best exemplified in the early 1960s when companies used some "garbled version of the world 'electronics' in their title" (even if their businesses had nothing to do with electronics), or during the dot-com bubble during the late 1990s and early 2000s,[76] or even perhaps more recently with companies adding "blockchain" or "crypto" to their company names, but any statistical insights gained from evaluating pricing performance based on the first letter of a company name should be viewed by any reasonable investor as rather silly.

You may be surprised how prevalent this type of thinking has become in the markets, perhaps as popular as it is in other areas. In prepping to wager on the Kentucky Derby, "the most exciting two minutes in sports," there's always some fun past data to consider. Check out this statistic that was shared regarding the 2018 Kentucky Derby, for example: "Horses with the first initial 'A' have won the race 11 times from 96 tries, including Always Dreaming's win last year. The 11.5 percent success rate is higher than any other initial, good news for fans of Audible." Doesn't this sound a lot like the conclusions of some quantitative financial analysis? A lot of good such work would do for the average bettor on Derby day, however, as Justify would end up taking home the Triple Crown that year. It's fun to bet on your favorite horse, of course, for whatever reason, but logically, it simply doesn't matter what letter the horse's name begins with. It's not predictive, or causal, to the outcome of the race. The same could be said about most conclusions drawn from ambiguous or impractical measures, of which most of quantitative finance draws upon.[77]

They're Digging in the Wrong Place

Empirical asset pricing models, as in the CAPM or multi-factor models, of which ambiguous valuation multiples (ratios) can be a part, are based mostly on

---

[76] Pets.com is a notorious flop from the dot-com era. Launched in November 1998, the company would see its stock price rise to $14 per share by February 2000. Later that year, in November, Pets.com would be liquidated. Other "dot-bombs" include Webvan.com, eToys.com, theGlobe.com, and Garden.com, all failed endeavors, costing investors millions. eToys.com shares once hit high of $84.35 in October 1999.

[77] It may be worth a reminder that this text draws on three labels of data: ambiguous, causal, and impractical. They are defined in *The Data Dilemma and Valuentum Investing* in the Preface of this text.

a fundamental factor's relationship to price observations, not necessarily on the rational or logical drivers behind those prices or whether those factors do, in fact, drive the prices. Such correlations say nothing about whether the relationship between the correlated variables is meaningful, or causal. An examination of what might be causal, or predictive, becomes necessary before arriving at any conclusions. There may be confounding, lurking variables.

But where one might look for causal or predictive data? Because it is future expectations that drive buying and selling activity, and therefore prices, it is within the realm of future expectations where predictive data should therefore be expected to be found. Ironically, and most dishearteningly, it may be in the very search for empirical *realized* data, which is almost a prerequisite of most "evidence-based" analysis, where efforts to explain share prices ultimately fall short. Here's why: If prices are based on future expectations, and future expectations are either *realized or not*, the idea of mining empirical data, which is realized, is more than just theoretically off the mark. It may be completely wrong.

This is worth emphasizing: Even if researchers could predict into the future with precision the very fundamental ambiguous data that they are using, it may not match with today's market expectations of that data, or the data that drives prices. Put another way, when it comes to data and its causal ties to prices or returns, future expectations, *realized or not*, may be the only data that matters. Quantitative finance shouldn't necessarily be using ambiguous or realized data to explain prices or returns, but rather it should be trying to systematically capture future expectations within empirical asset pricing models to explain prices. Future expectations may be the most important consideration when it comes to explaining prices.[78]

Let's provide a comparison between the interpretation of "empirical" in another field such as the physical sciences, and the interpretation of "empirical" in the field of finance, as in the traditional value factor. For example, another name for water is dihydrogen monoxide, and the molecule is produced from a synthesis reaction of hydrogen and oxygen. This chemical reaction is empirical, and its observation is also predictive. The experiment of mixing hydrogen and oxygen with heat will always result in water, in the past *and in the future*. The findings of

---

[78] This is worth clarifying a bit. Future expectations of enterprise free cash flows are a large part of the value construct, but so is the company's present-day balance sheet. Each company's composition of value will be different. See *The Duration of Value Composition* in Chapter 4.

empirical finance are none of the sort, however. The Fama and French quant model that observed the traditional quant value factor was published in the early 1990s, but it pulls in data for decades and decades before that. The observation up through its publish date was that "value" outperforms "growth" based on the two arbitrary assignments of stocks with respect to the B/M ratio.

But how has the model performed in real world, walk-forward studies? The rolling 10-year annualized return of the Fama-French value factor has underperformed terribly since the Financial Crisis, to the point where trailing 10-year annualized returns of "growth" have been exceeding those of "value," since the middle part of this decade, or starting with the time period 2005-2015, or thereabouts. The Fama-French three-factor model wasn't developed until the early 1990s, so basically if we assume that "live" 10-year annualized returns start in 2004, where 2004 data is the first 10-year annualized period, the model has underperformed more in its "live" life over the past 15-20 rolling 10-year periods than it did during the *entire backtest* from 1926-1993.[79]

Yet, instead of concluding that the model doesn't work live, reality becomes the anomaly, and the backtest remains truth! It's not just this model either, where arbitrary measures of "value" are failing. As published in a May 2018 article in Investment News, "if we look at the past 30 years--certainly the long term by anyone's definition--large-company growth funds have gained an average 9.23% a year, while large-company value funds have gained 9.01% a year. In fact, growth has topped value the past 25, 20, 15, 10 and five years." So, why do some quantitative models miss the mark when it matters?

In this case, a discussion of what constitutes a "value" stock and what constitutes a "growth" stock cannot be definitively categorized with *ambiguous* valuation multiples. Growth is a component of value, and growth stocks can be undervalued (see Chapter 5). Furthermore, *impractical* data is applied with respect to book equity, which is effectively an arbitrary accounting measure. Finally, there is very little reason to expect a backward-looking quantitative "value premium"

---

[79] Ibbotson says that the Fama-French three-factor model can only be tested going back to 1962 given Compustat data (Ibbotson 2009). The information I am referring to with respect to this analysis comes from an image showing the Fama-French value factor going back to 1926. In any case, the conclusions are the same. The Fama-French value factor performed well in the past backtest, but it did not perform as well when it went "live."

based on ambiguous multiple analysis and applying impractical data to continue to perform in the real world as it did in a past backtest. Why would it?

When valuation multiples are the same for different companies, it could be for a whole host of different forward-looking reasons that may be completely unrelated to the company's growth prospects or even a determination of its value. So how can stocks even be categorized by value based on B/M or P/E ratios, for example? Is there meaning behind it? Well, not as much as what one might think, unfortunately. However, instead of retiring the conversation between "value" and "growth" permanently, researchers now merely say that the factors are cyclical and move in and out of favor. I don't agree with this view.

Figure 3: The Randomness of Factor Returns in Walk-Forward Tests

Equity Factor Returns Appear Random In Out-of-Sample Tests				
USA **2008**	**2009**	**2010**	**2011**	**2012**
Highest Low vol, 89.5%	SIZE, 28.5%	SIZE, 13.6%	Low vol, 40.4%	**Value, 11.5%**
Income, 20.6%	**Value, -7.9%**	Momentum, 8.6%	Income, 29.5%	SIZE, 7.8%
Momentum, -2.3%	Income, -17.2%	Income, 7.1%	Momentum, 1.3%	Momentum, -1%
SIZE, -4.3%	Low vol, -30.7%	**Value, -4.6%**	SIZE, -3.7%	Low vol, -1.9%
Lowest **Value, -6.3%**	Momentum, -50.7%	Low vol, -15.5%	**Value, -12.7%**	Income, -7.6%
2013	**2014**	**2015**	**2016**	**2017**
Highest SIZE, 5.3%	Low vol, 11.1%	Momentum, 42.4%	**Value, 17%**	Low vol, 6.3%
Momentum, 4.5%	Income, 1.6%	Low vol, 13.5%	Income, 15.1%	Momentum, 5.2%
Value, 4.5%	**Value, -2.1%**	Income, 2.1%	SIZE, 9.6%	SIZE, -6.8%
Income, -8.3%	Momentum, -5%	SIZE, -9.3%	Low vol, -1.9%	**Value, -9.7%**
Lowest Low vol, -9.3%	SIZE, -6.7%	**Value, -11.9%**	Momentum, -22.4%	Income, -13.6%

Sources: Elroy Dimson, Paul Marsh, and Mike Staunton (UK premiums and US momentum); Professor Ken French, Tuck School of Business, Dartmouth (website) (other US data). Credit Suisse (2018).

A look at the *walk-forward* performance in the US of five most widely-accepted factor anomalies reveals a dynamic that may best be described as random. Quantitative "value" has underperformed its "growth" counterpart in seven of the past ten years, and the anomaly's performance relative to other anomalies, including momentum, has been all over the map. The story with the low volatility anomaly may even border on irony. Low volatility was the best performing factor in 2008, up nearly 90%, but then it was among the worst performing factors in the subsequent two years, down more than 30% and nearly 16% in 2009 and 2010, respectively, only then to rally back as the best-performing factor in 2011, up 40%, only to the underperform again in the next couple years.

Instead of anomalies being considered cyclical or moving in and out of favor, don't researchers mean that most, if not all, backward-looking factors based on ambiguous or impractical data may just be spurious?[80] "They are digging in the wrong place,"[81] I often say referring to the idea that explaining returns *must* fall in part within the subset of future expected data, realized or not. This is more than just a segment of a field of study that may be off track, however, and walk-forward studies may only confirm what many fundamental-based investors have known for so long: There may be insufficient logical substance supporting most factors derived with ambiguous or impractical data, meaning they cannot be causal or predictive, almost by definition.

That said, there may be several anomalies derived through in-sample testing using ambiguous or impractical data, and such anomalies may have even continued into walk-forward tests. If we stick with the B/M ratio, for example, following the release of the Fama-French three-factor model, the traditional quant value factor did perform as expected for some time after launch. The rolling 10-year annualized data didn't start to invert ("growth" outperforms "value") until the Financial Crisis, but it never came back despite what can be considered a "normal" bull market.[82] To bet that it will ever come back, however, is a bet on ambiguous and impractical data, and that may be nothing more than gambling. When it comes to factors, the moral of the story is that, even if some anomalies continue into walk-forward tests, it's important to make sure they are backed by causal and logical data, or correlations may not last.

But let's say that these widely-known factor anomalies aren't necessarily targeting excess-return potential but rather risk-mitigation techniques. The problem may be the same, however. Certainly, one wouldn't consider the low-volatility factor in the US "low volatility" given the performance of walk-forward testing. If someone had levered up to bet on the low-volatility factor being "low volatility," prior to the performance in the table, it's more than likely such a hedge fund and many like it would have "blown up." Perhaps the financial industry has already been warned. For example, in February 2018, the markets may have gotten a little

---

[80] This text suggests that even many anomalies, or those with empirical evidence of historical positive risk-adjusted excess returns, may not be causal. The enterprise valuation context may be the confounding, lurking variable.

[81] A reference to the 1981 film *Raiders of the Lost Ark*.

[82] According to First Trust, the average bull market lasts about 9 years with an average cumulative total return of 480%. As of the writing of this text, the bull market that began in 2009 has lasted 9.6 years, with a cumulative total return of approximately 385% through September 2018.

taste of what happens when leveraged bets against market volatility go bad, when the VelocityShares Daily Inverse VIX Short-Term ETN, a $2 billion exchange traded note, fell 93% in just one trading session (the ETN would be liquidated a few weeks later). February 2018 turned out to be one of the most volatile months since the Financial Crisis, and some "short-vol" traders didn't stay solvent long.

Figure 4: Heightened Market Volatility Following ETN Failure

But what about using several of these widely-known quantitative factors together to hedge risk? Where one may have expected quantitative "value" and momentum to be negatively correlated as they have been in some studies, a walk-forward test in the US suggests a less clear relationship for long-term investors. During the period of 2008-2017, for example, quantitative "value" (-2.7%) and momentum (-4.9%) were the two worst performing factors in the US of the five major factors listed in the table in Figure 3, according to Credit Suisse. From 2008-2017, quantitative "value" and momentum have either been both positive or both negative in four out of the past ten years, for example. On the other hand, data from the UK speaks of a highly negative correlation between quantitative "value" (-2.6%) and momentum (13.5%) over the same time period. At best, walk-forward studies are mixed, perhaps as one might expect with ambiguous or impractical data.

Here's the reality when it comes to factors backed with fuzzy data:

> Individual factors are likely to experience lengthy and severe drawdowns, and diversification across factors cannot be expected to eliminate all the risks of factor investing--even though frequently cited low historical correlations, especially derived from backtests, can be very impressive. The reality is that correlations between factors are not constant over time and multiple factors may be exposed to the same underlying risk drivers. Thus, investors with exposure to multiple factors may still experience severe drawdowns and decade-long periods of underperformance (Research Affiliates).

In this context, it becomes paramount to clarify the difference between what quantitative "value" implies and what fundamental intrinsic value implies, as determined through enterprise valuation, particularly in light of the factor returns in Figure 3. The cumulative return of quantitative "value" was negative from 2008-2017, both in the US and UK (cumulative data and UK data not shown). In fact, out of these five factors, quantitative "value" was the second worst-performing factor in the US (after momentum) and the worst-performing factor in the UK. This, however, says nothing about the returns of processes that apply enterprise valuation, or actual measures of price versus estimated value (not just short cuts of "value"). Combining share-price momentum with a forward-looking enterprise valuation process is something that creates an entirely unique investment process compared to traditional factor-based investing (more on this later). This distinction is critical and should not be misconstrued.

Data Is Comforting and That's the Problem

Financial advisors tend to guard their clients against emotional or behavioral mistakes (e.g. too much trading, becoming overconfident in their investment beliefs and the like), which is great, but the behavioral and forward-looking dynamics of stock-price discovery[83] are not something to guard against, but rather something to be embraced if one wants to understand stock market returns. Each

---

[83] "Stock-price discovery" is a term used to explain the function of market participants trading on estimates of intrinsic value, a dynamic which then drives prices to arrive at the market's estimate of intrinsic value. Estimates of intrinsic value are forward-looking.

data point in history is a function of expectations of the future at any point in time. Prices, therefore, cannot simply be mapped or lagged against ambiguous or impractical data to explain them. There's much more to it than that. Behavioral economists may argue that there is no such thing as an empirical asset pricing model, and quantitative researchers may say that the latest multi-factor model is just missing something (or that it is misspecified), that the model just needs more risk factors to explain returns (it doesn't matter whether these risk factors make logical sense, or whether they are based on ambiguous data). This line of thinking seems off the mark, however.[84]

Regardless, finance now has a "zoo of new factors,"[85] and the field of quantitative research, instead of backtracking on some of its questionable conclusions that, it, itself has proven inaccurate based on its own parameters, continues to come up with new ways to defend prior inferences. In real-world testing, much like the CAPM or the traditional "value" factor that is based on the B/M ratio, prior models aren't performing as expected, and very few researchers seem to believe that it is the application of ambiguous and impractical data in methods that may be the source of disappointment. Over time, it can only be assumed that there will be new and more sophisticated empirical asset pricing models, but these, too, if based on ambiguous or impractical data, may only have to be revised again and again in the future to incorporate new and more updated return information, and they still may fail at being predictive, which is what matters.

Many are already suggesting that a six-factor model could be next up in line, adding momentum as a risk factor.[86] How long these factor-model iterations will

---

[84] Even the concept of identifying statistical anomalies from backtests that may be used to "disprove" the efficient markets hypothesis is wrong-minded, as there may be no reason for such anomalies to continue on a go-forward basis in the real world.

[85] John H. Cochrane coined the phrase "zoo of new factors" in his work, "Presidential Address: Discount Rates," *Journal of Finance*, August 2011.

[86] There may be nothing entirely wrong with adding momentum to the Fama-French five-factor model, or multi-factor models more generally. Momentum is neither ambiguous nor impractical, in my view. Momentum is consistent with capturing the market's expectations of changes in intrinsic value and the buying and selling behavior of portfolio managers as positions are built and sold over time. However, in continuing to add more and more risk factors to "fix" other ambiguous or impractical data, therein rests the concern. **As more and more factors are added to empirical asset pricing models, quantitative finance may inevitably converge to enterprise valuation, eventually incorporating forward-looking data that captures the future expectations that drive share prices and returns. See Notes, page 269: Rf + factor(1) + factor(2) + factor(3)... = Rf + (estimated fair value/price – 1).**

continue before quantitative researchers conclude there simply cannot be an empirical asset pricing model based purely on *realized* ambiguous and impractical data--because stocks are based in part on future expectations, *realized or not*--is anyone's guess. But "perceived truths," as in the 1960s and 1970s (e.g. the non-falsifiable efficient markets theory) have in some ways stymied new innovative research in the field of finance, and we could be witnessing some of that today when it comes to the current state of quantitative equity investing.

As the declining correlation between stock returns and tangible book value has shown, observation alone should not indicate which factors may matter. Correlations can, do, *and should* change over time, thus making many backward-looking empirical observations of ambiguous or impractical data largely meaningless when it comes to explaining stock market returns. The word "empirical"[87] in finance, if based solely on ambiguous or impractical data, as I've defined in this text, should be viewed closer to the word "spurious" than "predictive," even if it is not so in the dictionary. Causality should be the prime consideration of any factor.[88]

What quantitative researchers were doing couldn't have been further away from my thoughts during my days at Morningstar, however. I remember the walk from the Ogilvie train station to Morningstar headquarters. It was mandatory exercise, and when I was late for the last express train out of the city, it offered a nice reason for an evening jog, or sprint in some cases. The morning coffee at Caffé Baci was one of my favorites, and I visited Chipotle far too often for lunch. Across the Chicago River, the *Sun Times* building rested as an inspiration for those seeking truth in print, and the history behind the newspaper is enough to motivate anyone to make a difference.

It was nice to be a small part of a large company like Morningstar, but I felt that there was more to finance than just being a part of it. I wanted to influence it, make it better. "The market is too small for a valuation model product," I was

---

[87] This may be worth clarifying. Investors should always base decisions on evidence or empirical data, but not just any evidence or empirical data. Forward-looking fair value estimates, as derived by enterprise valuation, might be considered empirical data, even if the measures themselves may be subjectively derived by analysts. Empirical, in this case of fair value estimates, can be considered predictive. However, with ambiguous or impractical data, empirical is closer to spurious than predictive.

[88] The text will go into the causal nature of enterprise valuation on valuation multiples, and it has yet to explain the causal nature of enterprise valuation on prices via the concept of public-to-private arbitrage.

told. Sometime later, I had pitched the idea of developing an enterprise valuation model for the individual investor. It seemed like a good idea, and from where I stood, it seemed to make a lot of sense, but it wouldn't have moved the needle even a little bit at the company. Still, I found it hard to believe that the average investor didn't seem to be thirsting to learn about enterprise valuation. How could this be?

I didn't know at the time that the lure of data, seemingly any data, remained all too great. EPS estimates and screeners with tons of ambiguous and impractical data could be easily retrieved, too, and data is comforting. It makes us feel like we are in control, but the conclusions can be misleading if the data isn't used in the right way. Enterprise valuation, on the other hand, required an in-depth knowledge of not only the company and its outlook, but also expertise in accounting, financial theory, and broad-based economic conditions. I couldn't unlearn what I had spent years mastering. No matter if I wanted to, I couldn't go back to being that kid fresh out of undergrad that loved finding stocks with low P/E ratios, exciting technology, and stories that could be "sold." I didn't notice how much this experience had changed me at the time.

I still may not know how much it changed me today, but I do know that it changed me.

3

Lessons from the Financial Crisis

A huge Ponzi scheme. Banks are driven by pure confidence, seemingly nothing more, nothing less. It's a Wonderful Life. Capital market dependence can be a wrecking ball to equity prices. Equity and credit analysis are inseparable. Stock prices contain valuable information that can't be found in historical GAAP fundamentals. When things go bad, they really go bad. General Electric and value traps. Correlations often break down at the exact time that you need them the most. Moral hazard is often not punished, and sometimes it can be rewarded.

id you hear about that Madoff guy?"

Jim was puffing a smoke. We were standing outside the new office headquarters of Morningstar, now at 22 West Washington. The traffic was busy most mornings outside Block 37, a mixed-use project in the Chicago Loop. Morningstar was the largest tenant in the building and the company's sleek logo could be seen outside on Washington St. WBBM-Channel 2 was also a tenant, and it stood across the street from the Daley Center. The open office layout was a hit, but I still preferred the convenience of Caffé Baci at the previous location. My guess is that many others did, too.

"No, who?" I hadn't yet heard the news, my back leaning against the building.

"A huge Ponzi scheme," Jim mumbled in his friendly voice, as he extinguished his smoke.

Bernie Madoff hadn't yet become a household name in 2008, but had he been around before Mr. Ponzi, himself, they may have named it a Madoff scheme. When it was all said and done, some estimate Madoff had ripped off some 4,800 clients, to the tune of about $65 billion, one of the largest frauds in financial history.

"Whoa," I said as we began walking back into the office, filtering in through the crowds and up the elevators.

Staring Into the Abyss

The global financial system was still in dire straits at the time, and it wouldn't be until March 2009 that the S&P 500 would finally hit bottom. None of that mattered, however. The lessons of the Financial Crisis had already been taught to those willing to learn. September 2008 may have been the crisis' worst month, and I even framed the front page of the *Wall Street Journal* from September 15, 2008, to remind me of how close the global financial system was to crumbling upon itself during those dark days.

> The American financial system was shaken to its core on Sunday. Lehman Brothers Holdings Inc. faced the prospect of liquidation, and Merrill Lynch & Co. agreed to be sold to Bank of America Corp. The U.S. government, which bailed out Fannie Mae and Freddie Mac a week ago and orchestrated the sale of Bear Stearns Cos. to J.P. Morgan Chase & Co. in March, played much tougher with Lehman. It refused to provide a financial backstop to potential buyers. Without such support, Barclays PLC and Bank of America, the two most interested buyers, walked away. On Sunday night, Bank of America struck a deal to buy Merrill Lynch for $29 a share, or about $44 billion. Lehman was working on a possible bankruptcy filing that would allow most of its subsidiaries to continue operating as the firm is wound down. – *The Wall Street Journal*, September 15, 2008

At the time, I wasn't yet 30 years old, but I feel like I aged a few decades during the tumultuous days of late 2008 and early 2009. There are lessons taught by the Financial Crisis that I will never forget. During the toughest of times, 1) banks are driven by pure confidence, seemingly nothing more, nothing less, 2) capital-market dependence[89] can be a wrecking ball to equity prices, 3) stock prices

---

[89] This is the first use of the term "capital market dependence" in the text, and it is worth defining here. If a company cannot consistently cover the sum of both its future expected capital expenditures and its future expected cash dividends or distributions with cash flow from operations (operating cash flow), the company can be considered capital-market dependent.

contain valuable information that can't be found in historical GAAP fundamentals, 4) when things go bad, they really go bad, and correlations often break down at the exact time that you need them most, and 5) moral hazard is often not punished, and sometimes it can be rewarded.

It's easy to say that people overreacted to the events of the credit crunch of the late 2000s, but the global financial system truly was staring into the abyss. US gross domestic product was plummeting (not just falling), unemployment was skyrocketing (it hit 10%), and banks seemingly weren't lending to anybody, or at least not on a sufficient scale. Everybody was afraid that everybody else held toxic (non-performing) assets, and they couldn't even be confident that their own financials were sound. Many a book has been written about the causes and the aftermath of the Financial Crisis, but it truly was a mess.

Banks and Confidence

The financials sector, and the underlying banking industry, in particular, is distinctly different than other sectors such as industrials, retail, or healthcare, for example. Unlike the latter industries, banks use money to make money (net interest income), instead of using operating assets like property, plant and equipment (PP&E) and raw materials to drive revenue and resulting free cash flow. This means that continued access to money and credit is the primary source of banks' economic returns and more specifically their survival.

The "5 Cs of credit" -- character, capacity, capital, collateral, and conditions -- is a widely-followed framework and generally-accepted guideline for lending to consumers, but for corporate banking entities, another C is much more important: confidence. In almost every situation where a bank has encountered trouble, it seems it has resulted from a loss of confidence in the sustainability of the entity as a going-concern. The loss of confidence could originate from counterparties, intermediaries, depositors or clients, or from any other core stakeholder.

Lack of confidence typically spreads quickly, too. Lehman Brothers' bankruptcy filing in 2008, for example, was accelerated by clients leaving the firm and worries over credit rating downgrades that obliterated market confidence in the sustainability of the entity. Barclays now owns Lehman, which had been a staple in American society since its founding in 1850. Washington Mutual, one of the largest savings and loans in US history, had its foundation rocked that same year when its customers, over a period of just 9 days, withdrew approximately $17 billion in deposits, or about 10% of its total deposits, in the modern-day equivalent of a bank run. The Federal Deposit Insurance Corporation seized Washington Mutual and sold the 120-year-old company to J.P. Morgan shortly thereafter. In both cases, the loss of confidence prompted disaster, leaving shareholders with only a fraction of their invested capital.

It seems like the markets experience a new financial crisis every decade or so. During the past few decades alone, there have been three significant banking crises: the savings and loan crisis of the late 1980s/early 1990s; the fall of Long-Term Capital Management and the Russian/Asian financial crisis of the late 1990s; and the Great Recession of the last decade that not only toppled Lehman Brothers, Bear Stearns, Washington Mutual, and Wachovia but also caused the seizure of Indy Mac, Fannie Mae and Freddie Mac. Incredibly, at the time Fannie Mac and Freddie Mac were taken into conservatorship, their total assets-to-capital ratios stood at 20-to-1 and 70-to-1, respectively, astronomical leverage figures, and ones that didn't include all the mortgage-backed assets they guaranteed. According to some estimates, at the time of the Financial Crisis, Morgan Stanley was leveraged 34-to-1 while Goldman Sachs was leveraged 27-to-1.

It's likely we will have another financial crisis at some point in the future, the magnitude and duration of which are the only questions. My primary reason for this view is not to be a doomsayer, but rests on the human emotions of greed and fear and the nature of a banking entity's business model, which does not hold a 100% reserve against deposits. Our good friend George Bailey, played by actor Jimmy Stewart, in the movie *It's a Wonderful Life* knew this very well when he tried to discourage Bedford Falls residents from making a "run" on the beloved Building and Loan. It's a movie that some of us have watched a dozen times or never at all, but it's a scene, to me, that's unforgettable. We attribute such a run-on-the-bank dynamic to the Great Depression, but WaMu fell prey to this very situation in 2008. If the market does not have confidence in a banking entity, that banking entity will likely cease to exist.

Though other business models depend on continuous access to the equity and credit markets and incremental capital, a run-on the-bank dynamic is a risk that is almost entirely unique to banks. FDIC insurance does not cover the financial products that a bank offers, including stocks, bonds, mutual funds, and life insurance, and the standard FDIC insurance amount is $250,000 per depositor, per insured bank. Because the government cannot insure everything and plan for all risks, traditional run-on the bank dynamics can never be completely hedged away, no matter how advanced or regulated the banking system becomes. An insufficient capital position brought about by excessive risk-taking (leverage), poor lending standards, and under-water loans as a result of asset declines may be more tangible operating reasons for a bank's failure, but without confidence, even strong banks cannot survive.

Equity and Credit Analysis Inherently Linked

The banking sector was not the only sector that faced considerable selling pressure during the Financial Crisis of the late 2000s, of course. Other companies that required funding to maintain their business operations faced severe liquidity risk, or a situation where refinancing, or rolling over debt, might be difficult to do on fair terms, making such financing prohibitive in some cases. Those that faced outsize debt maturities during the most severe months of the credit crunch faced a real threat of Chapter 11 restructuring[90] had the lending environment completely seized. In thinking about share prices as a range of probable fair value outcomes, equity prices tend to face pressure as downside probabilities such as a liquidity event are baked into the market price and at a higher probability. Because debtholders are higher up on the capital structure than equity holders, shareholders can sometimes get nothing in the event of a bankruptcy filing. Entities that are extremely capital-market dependent, or those that require ongoing access to new capital to fund operations, often face the greatest risk of the worst equity price declines during deteriorating credit market conditions.

The meltdown during the Financial Crisis reaffirmed the inseparable link between equity and credit analysis, something I did not lose sight of as Director of Global

---

[90] I learned a lot about the bankruptcy code covering the airline industry, which has notoriously been a bad business. Chapter 11, a form of bankruptcy named after U.S. bankruptcy code 11, allows a company time to restructure debts while continuing to operate. Chapter 11 has been used successfully in the airline industry to consolidate and rationalize excess seat capacity (supply), countering a condition that has largely contributed to declining real ticket prices and the boom-and-bust cycle innate to the airline business.

Equity and Credit Research (Training and Methodology). The concept of matching future cumulative expected traditional free cash flows with cash, debt-like commitments as time passes was intuitive to me. During times of tight liquidity, traditional leverage metrics matter little if the company doesn't have the cumulative internally-generated resources to meet debt maturities as they come due, as in the case of actually having to repay debt instead of just refinancing it (rolling it forward). My work in this area evolved into what has now become known as the Cash Flow Cushion, a proprietary metric at Morningstar that measures how many times a company's future internal cash generation plus liquid cash will cover debt-like contractual commitments over a future five-year period. The measure also helps to pinpoint the period at which the company is exposed to liquidity or refinancing risk.

Without an in-depth background in enterprise valuation, I don't think such a metric would have been top of mind during the credit crunch of late last decade. These were some of the most difficult times the country had faced since the Great Depression, and I had to develop tools for equity and credit analysts that depended on my experience and expertise. The banking system was under attack and assessing capital-market dependence risk within equities became the cornerstone of my equity risk assessments later in life. When times get tough, equities with severe capital-market dependence risk can see their equity prices obliterated, regardless of their historical track records. By extension, a need for ongoing external capital to support a dividend only makes that dividend riskier, almost impossible to sustain during times of tight credit.

The Financial Crisis may have only reminded the world how important credit analysis is to equity investing, and baptism by fire led to the creation of Morningstar's Cash Flow Cushion, which indirectly led to some of the thinking behind Valuentum's Dividend Cushion ratio (see Chapter 8), one of the most important tools that any income or dividend-growth investor can harness. The Dividend Cushion ratio sums up a company's future expected free cash flows over a forward five-year period and adds that to its net balance sheet net cash (subtracts it if there is a net debt position), and divides that sum by future expected dividend payments over the same five-year period. In combining information held on both the balance sheet and cash flow statement, the measure is useful in ranking the health of dividend payers based on future expectations and is a step forward in assessing dividend strength relative to the accounting-based payout ratio.

Backward-Looking Data Not the Answer

But the Financial Crisis taught more than just the importance of assessing capital-market dependence risk. For starters, there was really nothing in Lehman Brothers' historical GAAP financial statements that would have warned you about what was to come. There was really nothing in WaMu's SEC filings that could have put you ahead of the run-on-the-bank dynamic. Both companies had been operating the way they had for years, and during the go-go years prior to the bust, their share prices kept marching higher. The historic GAAP financials didn't help investors in these cases. *The technicals told the real story.* The markets were factoring in future liquidity events at financial institutions around the world, and both the Fed and Treasury needed to provide a huge backstop to prevent the global financial system from unraveling.

The value of the information contained in prices (technical analysis), however, is not limited to the banks or during times of economic stress, as in the Financial Crisis, however. Stock prices can fall for good reasons, and it may not always show up in near-term fundamentals. A share price decline, for example, could be attributed to worsening long-term structural characteristics of the industry that may truncate the market's expectations of the company's economic profit stream or secular declines in demand for a company's services or products. One might view Gilead Sciences as an example of the first case, where the value of finding a cure for hepatitis C was further truncated as rivals entered the fray. One might think of GameStop as an example of the second case, where digital video gaming has shifted consumer preferences away from pre-owned game sales and traditional consoles. Both companies may look cheap with respect to traditional valuation multiples, but their seemingly low prices relative to last year's GAAP earnings are telling a different story, one about long-term risk.

The type of information contained in prices is not always easy to discern, however, and one of the greatest challenges of any investor is to try to differentiate stocks that are truly undervalued, or ones that the market should believe are undervalued, from stocks that may just look undervalued, as in value traps. But there are ways to tilt the odds in your favor. Where a declining share price, for example, may imply an increasing likelihood that the market believes the company's intrinsic value is lower, on the other hand, an appreciating price on a stock that one already thinks is undervalued may only reinforce the under-valuation assessment. It is in this light that the investor may consider adding a technical and momentum element to a valuation framework, as it may increase the likelihood of price-to-estimated fair value convergence, while minimizing downside risks and exposure to "falling knives" or value traps.

The story of General Electric may be a great example of how to think about the context of "falling knives" and value traps. Once a sprawling conglomerate with a seemingly impenetrable moat, GE has cut its dividend three times during the 10-year period ending 2018, after decades of raising it each and every year. This speaks to the idea that history is only material to the investment decision-making process if it informs the future, but that is not necessarily the point with GE in this example. Many believed that GE's true intrinsic value had been greater than its share price during much of 2017 and 2018. However, there was something lurking in its financials that suggested the dividend was not healthy, and the enterprise valuation model brought it clearly to light in May 2017, when shares were trading at ~$28. Valuentum wrote:

> We're as surprised as you are by this alert, but we're removing GE from both newsletter portfolios. After rolling our discounted cash flow model forward (2017 first forecast year) and in light of GE's release of its 10-Q late April, which showed surprisingly poor cash flow from operations conversion (negative $1.6 billion in industrial cash flow from operations) and only modest capital spending reductions (two key components of the Dividend Cushion ratio), we no longer have the confidence in shares as we did before. But why the change and why now? New information in the 10-Q, and new forecasts in our newly rolled-forward discounted cash flow model…

> …Looking toward the end of this decade as GE transitions to a purely-industrial entity (and support from non-core asset sales and its financials operations wane), our expectations for normalized industrial operating cash flow of about $12-$14 billion and industrial gross capital spending of ~$6 billion will put traditional industrial free cash flow generation (FCF) at $6-$8 billion, which is lower than current annual run-rate cash dividend obligations ($8+ billion). For context, GE's adjusted industrial cash flow from operations came in at $12.2 billion in 2015 and $11.6 billion in 2016 against gross capital spending north of $7 billion for both years.

> In light of the most recent update to our discounted cash-flow model, we've lost our appetite for shares.

GE's stock kept falling, and shares hit the mid $20s in July 2017. Then, they hit ~$20 in October 2017, and then the low teens in March 2018. At Valuentum, we still considered GE to be cheap, but we sat back and watched the company's share price keep falling. Shares of GE would eventually fall all the way to the high-single-digits by late 2018. Enterprise valuation and traditional free cash flow analysis certainly flagged the risk of a dividend cut in time, but had one not considered share-price action in an investment framework, and only acted upon a valuation assessment, one might still be holding shares of GE, which inevitably turned into a financially painful proposition.

Combining enterprise valuation with share price momentum can help avoid value traps. Perhaps, instead of thinking that a stock is cheaper because its share price has fallen, think that in the event of a share price decline, the market believes that the true intrinsic value of the company is lower than it was before. The idea of momentum fits nicely into this framework, too. As the market adjusts the price of the company to reflect what it believes is its intrinsic value, stocks can exhibit both positive and negative momentum for sustained periods of time (as portfolio managers build positions).

In this light, it may become much more acceptable to like stocks that the market believes are undervalued (stocks that are increasing in price) than stocks that the market believes are overvalued (stocks that are decreasing in price). Said another way, it may make sense for long investors[91] to not only like stocks that they believe are undervalued, as calculated by the enterprise valuation framework, but also stocks that the market believes are undervalued, too, as evidenced by an appreciating equity price (in true Keynes' beauty contest fashion).

That the market may know more than any one investor is a humbling way of saying that pricing action should always matter to the fundamental investor, but another reason is much more straightforward. For ideas to work out, share prices

---

[91] The opposite may be appropriate for short-idea considerations, or ideas to consider selling or generally avoid. Short investors may consider stocks that not only are believed to be overvalued on an enterprise valuation basis, but also are exhibiting a falling share price, which may be a sign of deteriorating underlying fundamentals. Combining overvaluation and negative momentum with short investing helps address situations where, to paraphrase John Maynard Keynes, share prices can stay irrational (in its estimates of value) longer than one can stay solvent.

generally must advance from the purchase price, and this price appreciation comes from support by the market. So, if an investor is truly long-term focused, why not just wait for such support first, right?

The stock market, after all, is a forward-looking mechanism, and price usually leads fundamentals. Quite simply, without a turnaround in the share price, the risk that the fundamentals of an undervalued stock have not turned for the positive is higher. **Buying undervalued stocks on the way up won't guarantee that the investor will avoid every "falling knife" or value trap, but it may help the investor stay away from companies that may never turn upwards, or eventually present the investor with an even better (lower) price for consideration.** An evaluation of backward-looking data at GE was not the way to anticipate a share-price decline or predict its many dividend cuts, and ignoring the technicals would have left the investor with major losses.

Share prices simply convey important information, a key lesson from the Financial Crisis that is still relevant today, and this would eventually form one of the most important methodological tenets of the Valuentum process, which wasn't yet a glint in my eye prior to the Financial Crisis. The idea of blending an in-depth enterprise valuation framework with the information contained in prices, or an appreciating equity, hadn't yet been explored in modern finance. In such equities, not only would there exist substantial intrinsic-value support, but the market would be standing behind it as well. I didn't know it at the time, but the idea of what might constitute the definition of a Valuentum stock had started to form, bolstered both by my experience at Driehaus and during the credit crunch while I worked at Morningstar.

Another lesson from the Financial Crisis may be the most important, however. Much of modern portfolio theory rests on the concept that asset price correlations will generally remain somewhat static over time, even during times of economic stress. During the dark days of 2008 and 2009, however, where widespread and indiscriminate selling was prevalent, correlations among stock sectors rose considerably. According to data from Morningstar, average daily correlation over the trailing six months between individual stocks increased to 0.66 at the end of 2011 from just 0.10 in 1994. The average sector correlation for monthly returns on the S&P 500 index was 0.84 during the Financial Crisis period 2008-2012, up from 0.69 between 1994-2008. The rise in the correlation between US (S&P 500 index) and non-US stocks (the MSCI EAFE Index) increased to 0.95 during the period 2000-2011, up from 0.48 during the period 1970-2000.

There may be a lot of truth to the saying that stock correlations approach one during times of economic crisis.[92]

The point is not that diversification isn't good for you. It is. For example, a hypothetical portfolio that held 50% US stocks, 40% bonds, and 10% cash only lost 16% of its value during 2008, much better than US stocks, which lost nearly half of their value during the year. The takeaway, nonetheless, remains: Statistical correlations between any two variables can, do, *and should* change over time, during good times, during bad times, and regardless of their asset classes. The credit crunch showed, to some varying degree, that even widely-diversified portfolios across various asset classes may still not be diversified enough.

After all, a flight to cash prior to 2008 would have outperformed a hypothetical portfolio of 50% US stocks, 40% bonds, and 10% cash by 16% during the year. Is assuming that correlations will hold in the future to stave off big portfolio declines during the next crisis any different than the assumption that investors cannot time the market by going to cash prior to the collapse? Building portfolios based primarily on historical correlations, augmented by sophisticated backtests, as in modern portfolio theory, may not fully protect you when the going gets tough. It didn't protect Long-Term Capital Management, and they were stacked with statistical talent.

During the depths of the credit crunch late last decade, I thought the stock market would never be the same, probably as much as I thought that we may never see another Republican President elected for at least a half dozen terms or more following the bad rap given to the second Bush administration as a result of bailout. But it's incredible how easily things are forgotten. On the 10-year anniversary of September 15, 2008, the Dow Jones Industrial Average stood at 26,154.67, up from 11,421.99 on that dreadful day. Donald Trump is President of the United States. The moral hazard pursued by the global financial system of last decade has been rewarded, not punished. Many of the banks that were "saved," are now reaping huge fees from Main Street. People are now indexing

---

[92] In a paper titled, *Correlation of Financial Markets in Times of Crisis*, Leonidas Sandoval Junior and Italo De Paula Franca showed through the tools of random matrix theory (eigenvalues and eigenvectors of correlation matrices) that "markets tend to behave as one during great crashes." In popular finance parlance, this means that correlations approach one during times of global financial crisis. When the outlook is bleak, assets tend to trade together.

as if the stock market only goes up in the long run (and stock selection doesn't matter), and cryptocurrencies and cannabis stocks are all the rage.

I remember the depths of the Financial Crisis like yesterday, but the markets sure seem like they don't.

II.

FINANCIAL THEORY

4

The Right Mental Model

Classical art, fine wine, and vintage baseball cards. Stock value is not always in the eye of the beholder. Enterprise valuation as the causal framework to view the markets. The influence of public-to-private arbitrage on the price-setting function. The consistencies of enterprise valuation and the efficient markets hypothesis. The end game for prices. The importance of value sensitivity in understanding price volatility. Precision is folly and the margin of safety. Reverse engineering. True intrinsic value may not matter. The stock market doesn't care what you think. Long-duration value arbitrage. Nice quarter. Long-term expectations impact prices today. "The future ain't what it used to be." The mirage of the long term.

A stock is unique.

Unlike other investments such as classical art, fine wine, or vintage baseball cards, for example, stocks represent a claim on all the assets of the company, particularly their future enterprise free cash flows. Whereas the prices of a rare Picasso, the best Bordeaux money can buy, or an authentic, gem-mint Cracker Jack "Shoeless" Joe Jackson may be almost entirely based on what someone else will pay for them, stocks are different, and it is in this difference that enterprise valuation is distinguished from speculative, illogical frenzy. Stocks can *actually* have intrinsic monetary value, in addition to what someone will pay to take it off your hands.

Now that is not to say that intrinsic value estimation is not part art and part science--both arguably of equal importance--but it is the very idea that a share of stock is not just a piece of canvas or cardboard or a fermented grape that very much matters. For one, a fine Picasso cannot intrinsically generate enterprise free cash flows, a Bordeaux cannot either, nor can one of the most sought-after treasures of the 1914/1915 Cracker Jack baseball card collection. Because a stock is an ownership claim on a company's assets (and, by definition, those very assets' future enterprise free cash flow stream), a stock has tangible monetary value, regardless of one's opinion of the company.

In the case of stocks, intrinsic value--not to be confused with price--is therefore not always in the eye of the beholder. A dollar of enterprise free cash flow generated by the company rightly belongs to the shareholders, and it is because of this that stocks are not, in substance, just pieces of paper, even as this truism may be obscured during manias or in times of panic, when ranks of the greedy or fearful grow, respectively. Rather, stocks have intrinsic, monetary and foundational worth. Stocks generate cash (i.e. free cash flow), and this is a huge difference between them and other investments that do not.

Surely no logical person, for example, would say that a dollar generated by a company is not a dollar. After all, a dollar is what it is, a dollar. Where there exists a disconnect in translating what a Picasso, Bordeaux, "Shoeless Joe," or even what the price of gold is "worth" in terms of dollars,[93] there is not one in the case of stocks, which are conveniently priced in dollars and generate enterprise free cash flows in dollars (which can be discounted back to today to arrive at an intrinsic value estimate), or the currency of your choice. When I use the term 'dollar,' I mean some form of a store of value.[94]

Enterprise valuation establishes the view that price and value are two different considerations. A stock's estimated intrinsic value, not to be confused with its price, must always be a function of the present value of all future free cash flows the company will generate for shareholders, including the cash emanating from the balance sheet such as a large net cash position or arising from the monetization of "hidden assets" (e.g. an overfunded pension or a stake in another entity where its holding value on the books is less than its market capitalization). It is only in the struggle to "correctly" estimate the magnitude and duration of future enterprise free cash flows and commensurately the "proper" rate to

---

[93] In his 2011 Letter to Berkshire Hathaway Shareholders, Warren Buffett speaks about the shortcomings of gold as an investment class, namely about how gold is essentially incapable of producing much besides some "industrial and decorative ability." Gold cannot generate enterprise free cash flows, and therefore, its pricing behavior is based more on speculative activity.
[94] Cryptocurrency has started to become incrementally more mainstream, at least as it relates to the presence of price movements of cryptocurrencies such as Bitcoin on the major financial news networks and across the financial media, and it would not be surprising to see exchanges in the decades ahead become further intertwined with digital assets.

discount such future enterprise free cash flows where art (subjective forecasting) collides with science (financial statement analysis) within the valuation context, and the determination of whether price actually differs from *estimated* intrinsic value (not true intrinsic value, itself) is made.

What is important to understand is the concept of enterprise valuation, not necessarily its intricacies, though that can give you an upper hand, too.[95] I'm not saying the application of enterprise valuation is the secret to success for everyone. Instead, what I want you to understand is that, definitionally, stocks have intrinsic worth, and this intrinsic worth makes them unique. Investors act on these estimates of intrinsic worth, and this drives stock returns through the influence of public-to-private arbitrage. The idea that stocks generate free cash flow makes enterprise valuation a prime consideration, even if prices may detach greatly from estimates of intrinsic value. Knowing what constitutes value as in future enterprise free cash flows lays the foundation for determining whether shares of stocks can be considered fairly-valued, undervalued or overvalued.

Establishing Causality: A Critical Framework to View the Markets

Enterprise valuation sets up a critical framework in which to view the markets, and this framework inevitably makes enterprise valuation the primary causal driver to share prices.[96] Because an investor can take a company private if the company may be trading for far less than what the investor believes is the future expected risk-adjusted discounted cash flow stream (its estimated intrinsic worth), the price of that company's equity is generally "pushed" to intrinsic value through buying and selling. If that company's market price stays artificially depressed relative to an estimate of its free-cash-flow based intrinsic value, then the investor can take the company private and reap the benefits of those mispriced future free cash flows, making a profit along the way (i.e. public-to-private arbitrage).[97]

---

[95] I cover the details of the enterprise valuation process in Chapter 5.

[96] Later in this text, I explain how enterprise valuation is causal in determining traditional valuation multiples, which are defined in this book as ambiguous data. This is a different concept than enterprise valuation being causal to stock prices.

[97] Nobel laureate Richard Thaler notes that there will sometimes be limits to arbitrage. One example occurred in March 2000 when 3Com carved out Palm by floating 5% of its subsidiary.

Viewing the markets in this way, as a function of ever-changing expected future enterprise free cash flows, helps to frame what drives market prices. If prices get out of whack, companies are either driven closer to a better value estimate or are simply taken private at a more reasonable price that better reflects estimated value.

Backward-looking analysis in the form of ambiguous or impractical data,[98] even under the guise of "empirical evidence," cannot explicitly capture the drivers behind this embedded phenomenon of ongoing price-setting by market participants. In other words, the application of ambiguous and impractical data cannot explicitly capture the forward-looking nature of estimated intrinsic value, which influences buying and selling activity *caused* by the prospect of public-to-private arbitrage. The observation of prices tells one only what has happened in the past relative to some other observed metric, not that the relationship is causal or predictive. Said another way, the observation of prices alone cannot tell one why those prices are changing, how future prices will react (even in the presence of past momentum), whether a stock is fairly-valued, undervalued or overvalued, or whether markets are either efficient or inefficient.

In establishing the enterprise valuation framework as the lens in which to view the markets, enterprise valuation is not fully inconsistent with the thought processes behind the efficient markets hypothesis. Both frameworks believe that markets are forward-looking pricing mechanisms that discount future expectations. However, where enterprise valuation assumes that markets are inefficient and mispricings can and do exist, the efficient markets hypothesis may say that prices are correctly established on the marketplace, and if they are not, the market's errors are random and cannot be exploited by the investor.[99] Neither

---

Such a small float, which restricted arbitrage, caused the market capitalization of Palm to grow larger than that of 3Com, suggesting that 3Com's other highly-profitable businesses had negative value, which made little sense. There are other instances of the limits of arbitrage, too. For example, HNC Software/Retek and Daisytek/PFSWeb in 1999 and Methode Electronics/Stratos Lightware in 2000 were three more instances where the parent's market capitalization was less than the owned value of the spin off. Flowers Industries/Keebler Foods and Limited/Intimate Brands are two additional examples that occurred in 1999, where the value of the ownership stake in a key asset was greater than the total market capitalization of the parent that owned the stake (Nofsinger 2002). The law of one price sometimes does not hold.

[98] For a refresher on what this text defines as ambiguous or impractical data, please see *The Data Dilemma and Valuentum Investing* in the Preface.

[99] It's probably worth clarifying a bit here. Random walkers may say that market efficiency does not necessarily require the market price to be equal to true value at every point in time as long as

framework, however, suggests that returns can be explained by backward-looking ambiguous or impractical data, and the leap of logic from the CAPM to multi-factor empirical models that attempt to explain stock returns with ambiguous or impractical data has created a misunderstanding of the very concept of what drives prices at all, including the concept of public-to-private arbitrage.

As with the efficient markets hypothesis, the enterprise valuation framework provides a fundamental context for understanding market price movements, even those that may be viewed as irrational bubbles. Proponents of efficient markets may say that prices reflect new expectations of the future, whatever those expectations may be, and therefore bubble prices are reasonable. Within enterprise valuation, an analyst can sometimes extrapolate growth rates and operating leverage that may not come to fruition, resulting in a firm-specific overestimation, which could create bubble valuations and prices, too. The big difference, however, rests in how the enterprise valuation process forces the analyst to think through a great many explicit assumptions, as opposed to implied future expectations in the efficient markets hypothesis. The enterprise valuation process also prevents an overreliance on just one output such as the dividend (as in dividend discount valuation models), which incidentally happens to be independent to intrinsic value itself.

John Maynard Keynes' "beauty contest" is also an important reference in interpreting price movements through the enterprise valuation process. Whereas Keynes may have believed that it may not make much sense to pay $25 for a stock that one values at $30 but expects the market to price at $20 in three months, viewing market price changes as the market adjusting its implicit modeling expectations to arrive at expectations that would imply a value of $20 is one good example of viewing the markets through the lens of enterprise valuation.

The drivers behind the enterprise valuation model therefore become the drivers of prices, and market price movements can be conceptualized as such. Understanding this is critical. If market prices can be explained, or rather conceptualized, through changes in the assumptions of the forward-looking enterprise valuation framework, and public-to-private arbitrage is critical in price-

---

the market's errors are random. Efficient markets theory suffers from the joint hypothesis problem, where it requires an equilibrium model for testing, but in the test, one cannot be sure if it is the equilibrium model or the theory that is wrong. The efficient markets hypothesis is non-falsifiable in this respect.

setting behavior based on mispriced future expected free cash flows, then how can prices or returns possibly be explained by factors derived on backward-looking ambiguous or impractical data?

They really can't.

The overlay of enterprise valuation with market price activity, or the information contained in prices, further builds on an important idea. If one believes a stock trading at $25 to be worth $30 but that it will trade down to $20 in three months, as Keynes may have described, a logical investor may only be interested in such a stock after it starts moving higher from $20 on the way to $30 (think: buying undervalued stocks that are "going up," as in the Valuentum process).[100] This seems like common sense.

Keynes may simply not have focused on the idea that stock-selection methodologies do not have to be either fundamental, behavioral, or quantitative, but they can blend all three and more (not to mention that valuation also influences crowd behavior). In waiting for an undervalued stock to first start to appreciate, one logically combines Firm-Foundation Theory and Castle-in-the-Air Theory, the former suggesting investments are anchored to intrinsic value and the latter based on the understanding of how the crowd may behave in the future.

The End Game for Stock Prices

We may only know when the share price of a stock equals its "value," as in the final cash payment to shareholders, in one instance on the marketplace. Price will equal "value" of the company *to public shareholders* when companies are taken private. This doesn't imply that the price paid is "correct," or that this is the "true" intrinsic value, however. In a 2018 study by the American Investment Council, which assessed the returns of over 160 U.S. public pension funds, private equity outperformed considerably, leading all asset classes. According to the report, private equity's median 10-year annualized return of 8.6% was materially higher than public equity's 6.1%, fixed income's 5.3% and real estate's 4.7%.

Another test for public market inefficiency therefore may counterintuitively rest in evaluating private equity returns, as the efficient markets hypothesis suggests

---

[100] The Valuentum process is talked about at length in Chapter 10.

any outsize opportunity in public-to-private arbitrage would be very unlikely, as prices always should generally reflect intrinsic value, give or take some random unexploitable error. Though private equity returns are generated in many more ways than just taking public companies private,[101] the data is interesting nonetheless, as it may imply a large number of deals are *actually* completed at a bargain price for the acquirer (not just at a price the acquirer thinks is a bargain).

That said, significant changes can be made to the business when a company is taken private, and this may account for a material portion of private equity outperformance in such public-to-private arbitrage situations, outperformance that otherwise might not have been achieved had the company stayed public. However, it's important to think of Berkshire Hathaway as a public-to-private arbitrageur, too, or a firm that strives to capture the dynamic explained in this text as public-to-private arbitrage. Unlike most deals in private equity, Berkshire Hathaway has a hands-off management approach,[102] in which the strategic direction of the company is not generally influenced.

Since 1965, Berkshire Hathaway's per-share book value and per-share market value have advanced at a compound annual rate of approximately 19% and 21% through the end of 2017, respectively, while the S&P 500 (with dividends included) has advanced at a compound annual pace of approximately 10%. Part of the reason for the outperformance of private equity more recently and Berkshire Hathaway over a much longer time horizon may come from a deep understanding of how to estimate intrinsic value coupled with the opportunities to capitalize on mispriced expected future enterprise free-cash-flow streams.

Another takeaway may even be more important, however. In situations of public-to-private arbitrage, had the markets priced public companies' enterprise free cash flows correctly, or even close to correctly, with some degree of random error, such outsize returns should not have been achieved, particularly in the case of Berkshire Hathaway. The company's performance speaks heavily to generally

---

[101] Though we make note that there are other areas of focus within private equity, according to McKinsey, buyout funds represent the largest asset class within the group at just under one third of total private equity assets under management.

[102] Warren Buffett tends to give executives of the companies acquired by Berkshire Hathaway autonomy in running their businesses. Even when things tend to go badly for certain companies, Buffett doesn't really get involved. He generally believes it would be foolish for him to tell CEOs how to run their businesses.

inefficient markets and situations of mispriced future enterprise free-cash-flow streams in public equity. However, that may not be the most important takeaway.

The connection between price and the "value" accruing to the public shareholder is paramount. It shows that, when a company is bought out (as its price converges to the takeout price), statistical measures such as the historical B/M ratio and the stock's prior correlation with other assets, for example, may be completely irrelevant to the end game. *These items are not causal.* What mattered was how the price compared to an estimate of intrinsic value.

Value Is Sensitive = Prices Are Volatile

An analyst may never know, or rather can never know, with precision the exact intrinsic value of a stock because of the forward-looking nature of forecasts and the subjective substance of estimating discount rates, among other future considerations. To be successful, the analyst, however, does not have to know the true intrinsic value with precision. The goal of enterprise valuation in stock analysis, or valuation approaches in equity investing, more generally, is not to pinpoint precisely what a company's stock is worth. This is impossible. Where most criticisms of enterprise valuation rest is that the output of the process, the fair value estimate, is very sensitive to several key future assumptions and forecasts.

However, the very idea that those future forecasts are difficult to predict is consistent with the concept of pricing volatility, as future market expectations iterate over and over again, and logically defines enterprise valuation as an important causal pricing framework. Market volatility can be explained in part by changes in expected growth rates, interest rates, tax rates and other key drivers of the enterprise process. That these assumptions are ever-changing and that prices are ever-changing is an important logical link. If, on the other hand, everybody knew the future, and therefore, the exact intrinsic value of stocks, we wouldn't see much volatility in the markets at all. Stocks would, or rather should, trade at their "known" fair values. The fair value estimate sets the anchor for prices.

In some ways, it is the imprecision and sensitivity of enterprise valuation that may offer a core analytical advantage. In evaluating the sensitivities of certain drivers behind the company to changes in forward assumptions, one gets a feel for the valuation impact of a change in a particular driver. For example, a one percentage point change in the mid-cycle operating-margin assumption for a company such as Amazon could have widespread implications on an intrinsic value estimate given the company's significant earnings leverage and sensitivity to small changes in its operating margin. The same one-percentage point change in the mid-cycle operating-margin assumption for a company such as Microsoft, however, could be immaterial. The analytical inferences of assessing such sensitivities not only explains how changes in value occur, their drivers, but also why the share prices of some stocks are more volatile than others as a result.

To focus on precision in value estimation is folly, and it is neither the goal nor even the endeavor to pursue precise value estimation, as it is unreasonable to believe that even the most talented analysts can get every future assumption "correct" within the enterprise framework. Even if the analyst did get everything "correct," the stock price may still not fully converge to that estimated intrinsic value if the market simply disagrees. Incidentally, this is why paying attention to the information contained in share prices matters, even for value-focused investors (more on this later). In instances where price-to-estimated fair value convergence may never occur, however, it still is helpful to use the enterprise valuation framework to understand the drivers behind security pricing, and to arrive at a better understanding of the behavior of a subset of active management, or those that apply extensive discounted cash-flow modeling as a key driver of buying and selling activity, which causes price changes.

It should not reduce the utility of enterprise valuation even if one fully embraces the criticism that the future enterprise free cash flows of an entity will always be unpredictable to varying degrees. The future enterprise free cash flows of consumer staples stocks such as Coca-Cola or Kimberly-Clark may be steadily growing, and analysts may be able to estimate such future enterprise free cash flows with only a very slight margin of error when they are reported. On the other hand, the future enterprise free cash flows of a fast-growing Internet-darling such as Facebook or Alphabet may result in a much larger disparity between future projections and actual results when they come in. Therefore, it is only reasonable to assume that the analyst may require a much larger share-price discount to estimated intrinsic value in considering an investment in Facebook or Alphabet than for Coca-Cola or Kimberly-Clark.

The concept of a margin of safety is well-documented in the writings of Benjamin Graham and the works of his student Warren Buffett.[103] A stock trading at $50 per share, for example, but estimated to be worth $100 per share may offer the investor an adequate margin of safety because, even if the true intrinsic value of the company is $75, the large difference between price and the estimated fair value offers the investor a very important safety-net against losses. Whether the market ever comes to price the stock at $75, however, is another thing altogether, and a consideration that makes observing price activity and the information contained in prices all the more relevant. Graham and Buffett's margin-of-safety framework can be further extrapolated to view equity valuation in the context of a range of fair value outcomes or a cone of fair value possibilities, with the fair value estimate being the most likely probability along a fair-value distribution function.[104]

For example, it may not necessarily be accurate to say that a company is worth precisely $25 per share, when the stock is likely worth somewhere between $20-$30 per share, and it may not be truly undervalued or overvalued, respectively, until it breaches these bounds around the fair value estimate. But why? Well, an analyst can only estimate what a company's future enterprise free cash flow stream will look like. Certain factors will hurt that enterprise free cash flow stream relative to forecasts, while other factors will boost performance relative to expectations. That's how a downside fair value estimate and an upside fair value estimate could be generated to form a fair value estimate range of $20-$30 in this

---

[103] The originations of the concept of a margin of safety is credited to the works of Benjamin Graham, who dedicated an entire chapter to the topic in his text *The Intelligent Investor*. "Here the function of the margin of safety is, in essence, that of rendering unnecessary an accurate estimate of the future. If the margin is a large one, then it is enough to assume that future earnings will not fall far below those of the past in order for an investor to feel sufficiently protected against the vicissitudes of time (Graham 2003)."

[104] Fair value estimates or intrinsic value estimates for companies, which differ from price targets, generally mirror what the analyst might describe as a base-case scenario reflecting base-case expectations of the company. Even though the analyst may pursue sensitivity analysis, base-case assumptions generally do not represent optimistic cases or pessimistic cases, but rather the scenario that may have the highest probability of occurring. In valuation, however, because it is forward-looking in nature, and therefore not a precise exercise, the theoretical upside and downside cases of forecasts result in what can be described as a fair value estimate range for each company (encapsulating the concept of a margin of safety). True intrinsic value can only be estimated and explained as a function of the probabilities of a variety of potential estimated fair value outcomes. When the probability is significantly tilted in investors' favor, as in a very large mispricing, opportunity may present itself.

instance. Value can never be a precise point fair value estimate because the future cannot be predicted with precision.

Figure 5: A Stock's Fair Value Estimate Range

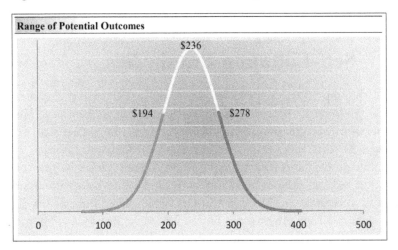

The image is a hypothetical illustration of a probability distribution of a fair value estimate of a stock, where the most likely true fair value for the stock is $236 per share in this example, with a reasonable fair value range between $194-$278 per share. This stock may be considered undervalued if its share price fell below $194 or overvalued if its share price rose above $278.

Another good use of the enterprise valuation model is to triangulate assumptions to recreate the stock price, or to reverse engineer the stock price with the best reasonable assumptions within the model, itself. Such an exercise helps to assess what the market may be assuming, and over time, as the price of the stock changes, the model can be used to further triangulate on the market's implied assumptions, and so on and so forth. The analyst gains experience identifying when price moves are reasonable compared to the market's implied assumptions, and when they may not be, as in the occurrence of a price-to-estimated-fair value mismatch or a market mispricing. Perhaps the enterprise valuation model's greatest benefit occurs over years of its use across the same companies, not necessarily as a construct to take snap-shot estimates of value at one point in time.

Whether it was Keynes or British philosopher Carveth Read that said it first, "it is better to be roughly right than exactly wrong," and it is in the spirit of this quote that valuation approaches, whether the enterprise valuation or another, are attempted, or rather should be attempted, in earnest. Underlying all of this, however, is that the sensitivity of value estimation is completely consistent with the concept of share price volatility. As is often the case, the most volatile companies are the ones whose values are most sensitive within the enterprise valuation context.

Self-Fulfilling Prophecies

Embracing the unpredictable, probabilistic nature of the valuation context may not be enough to justify the utility of enterprise valuation in the eyes of pure momentum investors, technicians, and behavioral "beauty-contest" enthusiasts, which may even go so far as to posit that all fundamental analysis (perhaps the field in its entirety, including valuation) is of doubtful importance. Keynes, for one, may have argued that nobody knows for sure what will influence the future fundamentals of a company, and by extension, intrinsic value estimates may be of doubtful value.[105] This progression of thought may overlook who may constitute the crowd, however. As long as active management is influenced by estimates of intrinsic value, the inherent link between enterprise valuation and other processes is firmly established.

Neither the behavioralist, nor the technician, nor the momentum investor that rely on information in prices, can fully cut ties, on a practical basis, to enterprise valuation--even if they wanted to. Behavioral investors know that pure value investors want to scoop up stocks that are perceived to be undervalued, so the "behavioralist" must practically, if not directly or willingly, embrace the concept of intrinsic value estimation for no other reason than because intrinsic value estimation is impacting the behavior of value investors, their investment-decision making process, and their resulting influence on market prices.

---

[105] Keynes' *General Theory of Employment, Interest and Money* is known for likening the conditions of the stock market to that of British newspaper beauty contest, but he also offers the view of its similarities to a game of musical chairs. "Nor is it necessary that anyone should keep his simple faith in the conventional basis of valuation having any genuine long-term validity. For it is, so to speak, a game of Snap, of Old Maid, of Musical Chairs—a pastime in which he is victor who says Snap neither too soon nor too late, who passes the Old Maid to his neighbor before the game is over, who secures a chair for himself when the music stops. These games can be played with zest and enjoyment, though all players know that it is the Old Maid which is circulating, or that when the music stops some of the players will find themselves unseated (Keynes 1936)."

Likewise, if technicians and momentum investors, in conducting their trading activity, apply the information contained in prices, which is driven in part by the behavior of fundamental investors that apply valuation techniques, then they, too, must be bound in part to valuation principles. One may posit that behavioral economics doesn't make value investing, or the enterprise valuation process, or fundamental analysis less significant. In some ways, it can be argued that the very concept of behavioral economics makes the study of how investors use valuation to make investment decisions even more important.

Keynes' "beauty contest" analogy of the stock market also offers context as to why investors shouldn't necessarily care about not being able to calculate the true intrinsic value of a company *with precision*. Quite simply, it is the market's interpretation of the true intrinsic value of the company that will drive pricing, and even if the analyst happens to calculate the true intrinsic value of the company, the share price may still never converge to the true intrinsic value, if the market never factors in expectations that eventually agree with the view. Whether estimated fair value ever equals true intrinsic value may, for all intents and purposes, not entirely matter in investing. Prices can only reflect future expectations at any given time, not future reality.[106]

Theoretically, stock prices converge to the market's estimate of intrinsic value because investors collectively think the stock is worth that estimate of its intrinsic value and vote with their capital to drive the stock price to that estimate of intrinsic value, but if nobody thinks a stock is worth that estimate of true intrinsic value, its share price will never come to reflect it. On the other hand, if everybody happens to think a stock is worth its true intrinsic value, it would trade to its true intrinsic value, or more likely, already be trading there. If you believe a stock is worth your calculation of intrinsic value, no matter if it is the true intrinsic value or not, and nobody else agrees with you or ever will, then you will likely have an

---

[106] Whether the market's long-term expectations truly come to fruition may not matter within the pricing framework, per se, as long as the market continues to believe the long-term expectations will come to fruition. It is only when the market comes around to building in new long-term expectations that pricing activity will start to change. Efforts to predict pricing activity should therefore center on efforts to predict expectations revisions in the future, whether within the enterprise value framework or a reversion back to it via anchoring to public-to-private arbitrage, for example. In the case of Kinder Morgan and most MLPs in 2015, falling energy resource pricing and difficult market conditions caused the market to reevaluate expectations in a new equilibrium framework, enterprise valuation.

underperformer on your hands, as there is no market activity to drive the share price to your estimate of intrinsic value.

It is this self-fulfilling mechanism that makes the stock market what it is and shows how some methodologies can be viewed somewhat equivalently in this respect. Technical analysis, or chart reading, for example, may be a self-fulfilling prophecy because it is driven by the actions of buyers and sellers reacting to or anticipating patterns in a chart. Technical analysis works if people buy and sell based on technical analysis, driving a stock price higher or lower respectively. But the same self-fulfilling dynamic is present with a value approach. Value investing works sometimes because people buy and sell based on value principles, driving a stock higher or lower, respectively. The same can be said about growth investing or other widely-followed methodologies.

There are a few nuances to consider, however. In the event of the application of widely-available backward-looking ambiguous or impractical data, the self-fulfilling nature driving such strategies tends to act as an arbitraging mechanism reducing the potential for excess return as these strategies are more broadly used. For example, one may hypothesize that, because last year's B/M ratio is widely-observed, investors trading on this information may very well be responsible for the traditional quant value factor's underperformance in walk-forward studies, if it wasn't mostly arbitrary in the first place.

On the other hand, because enterprise valuation is an ever-iterative function of future expectations, arbitrage opportunities are continuous. Additionally, the concept of momentum, which may be logically explained as the market resetting its estimate of intrinsic value (i.e. money managers building positions or eliminating positions over time) may only be augmented as more investors jump into appreciating shares, not arbitraged away. The merits of combining enterprise valuation and momentum *within* stocks may represent a sustainable investment proposition, which is what the Valuentum style is based on.[107]

Strictly speaking, the more investors that think a stock is truly undervalued, the more it will be bought and the higher the likelihood its share price will be driven higher, to the market's estimate of its intrinsic value. The more investors think that a stock is truly overvalued, the more it will be sold and the higher the

---

[107] Building a foundation is far more important in these early chapters, so we will not get into the specific topic of Valuentum investing until later in the book (Chapter 10).

likelihood its price will be driven lower, to the market's estimate of its intrinsic value. If all investors think the same about one thing in the stock market, it will likely already be the present reality, driven by the collective actions of market participants.

In other words, it doesn't matter if you think a stock is undervalued or overvalued. It matters if others (after you) think a stock is undervalued or overvalued, and then they buy or sell that stock driving it higher or lower, respectively. Only then will it converge to your estimated intrinsic value. The market is not magic. Other people must eventually agree with you (and vote with their money) for your ideas to work out. As an investor, you are highly dependent on what other people think. You must hope that they eventually come around to what you believe, or else your stock may never be a winner.

The psychological concepts that link fundamental and valuation approaches to technical, momentum and behavioral approaches, in part, form the backbone of multi-faceted processes that may focus on which stocks the majority of investors might consider buying or selling in the future by analyzing the most widely-known tools available to those investors. This may include: fundamental as in enterprise valuation, a mix of fundamental and behavioral as in relative valuation (as in the forward P/E ratio and PEG ratio[108]), and behavioral as in technical and momentum dynamics, collectively the three pillars of the Valuentum Buying Index rating system (more on this later). To a very large degree, the concepts of enterprise valuation and behavioral economics are intertwined in the stock market, and it is largely because of one that the other matters, and vice versa.[109]

All things considered, the paramount objective of enterprise valuation becomes three-fold: 1) it can be used as a lens to interpret price movements as changes in the market's expectations within the modeling framework, 2) it helps the investor understand what may influence crowd behavior and the buying and selling activity by investors (the causal nature of prices), given the widespread application of the enterprise valuation framework, as in general equity valuation, M&A

---

[108] The PEG ratio was popularized in Peter Lynch's book, *One Up on Wall Street*. It gets at the heart of the idea that not all P/E ratios are created equal, by dividing the price-observed P/E ratio by a company's expected growth rate in earnings. However, as this text shows, there is much more embedded in the P/E ratio than future expected growth in earnings.

[109] Many may believe that enterprise valuation is the antithesis of behavioral finance, but they are inextricably linked in assessing the valuation tools used by the "crowd." The concept of behavioral valuation will be introduced later in this text.

considerations or private equity and 3) it can be used to identify gaps between price and estimated value that are so large that even after considering a margin of safety the analyst can still reasonably and comfortably say with a rather high degree of confidence that there is a price-to-true fair value[110] disconnect in the equity of question.

The Duration of Value Composition

In Warren Buffett's 1992 Letter to Berkshire Hathaway Shareholders, perhaps his best letter ever written, the Oracle of Omaha referred to John Burr Williams' *The Theory of Investment Value*. Burr's text was written in 1938 and laid the groundwork for the equation of value, which for any investment, whether stock or bond, is based on the cash inflows and outflows, discounted at an appropriate rate,[111] for the remainder of the asset's life. As Buffett noted in the letter, the formula is the same for stocks *as it for bonds*, but with one critical difference. A bond has both a coupon and maturity date, where future cash flows are defined, while the future "coupons" (i.e. free cash flows) of a stock can only be estimated.

Within an enterprise valuation model, one might expect that the forecasts for enterprise free cash flows for the next couple years generally won't vary much from consensus estimates or management's provided guidance. The long-duration composition of intrinsic value is the primary reason why analysts should generally be comfortable with this, and because dozens of analysts are studying expectations in the next quarter or year, it literally becomes hit or miss when differentiating from consensus earnings estimates. I generally believe the markets should be relatively efficient in estimating quarterly earnings, meaning that the "wisdom of crowds" makes it very difficult to identify beats and misses

---

[110] In this reference, we make a distinction between price-to-estimated fair value and price-to-true fair value. We can never know the true fair value of a company because its value is based on the future. However, when there are sufficiently large gaps between price and estimated fair value, the likelihood that there is also a large gap between price and true fair value is enhanced.

[111] Though John Burr Williams' framework helped to validate the concept of discounted cash flow valuation, he relied too heavily on the concept of stock value being based on future dividends and a future selling price. As this text discusses, there are considerable shortcomings in relying on dividends alone in estimating intrinsic worth (e.g. they could poorly reflect the operating economics of the business, and the timing of when a company "dividends itself out" is too theoretical for practical application). See Chapter 1 regarding major criticisms of the dividend discount model.

systematically, and to profit from it.[112] On the other hand, I don't think the markets are efficient in estimating long-duration value at all.

In any case, it may not even matter if you could consistently predict next quarter's earnings with precision. Even if an analyst could determine an earnings beat or miss was on the horizon for the quarter, what management issues as forward guidance and what they say on the conference call about the company's outlook, more important drivers behind the stock value and price movements, could pretty much negate the analyst's entire effort during the quarter, counter-intuitively sending the stock in a completely different direction that what was thought prior to the report, despite the analyst being correct in predicting the beat or miss.[113] If the analyst could predict what management would do with forward guidance, adjusted for quarterly results, and what they say about the outlook on the call, now that would be a different story.

However, playing the Wall Street earnings "game" is far too difficult, and most are focusing on this analytical area of the marketplace where the benefits are questionable. Let's ask two logical questions to hit this point home: What if a company continues to miss earnings expectations every quarter into infinity? Will its stock price keep going down forever until it reaches 0? The answer simply is no. Stock prices are determined by expectations of future enterprise free cash flow, and a company will still have value even if it continues to miss earnings estimates. If a company that has exceeded earnings estimates in the past has been a strong performer, it has more to do with the idea that expectations for future enterprise free cash flows have increased, not because the company has exceeded historical earnings estimates. In a healthy-functioning market, the anchor for stocks should always be the market's estimate of intrinsic value.[114]

---

[112] When saying the markets should be relatively efficient in estimating quarterly earnings, it implies the consensus earnings estimate (including "whisper" numbers) is likely the best one. The phrase "wisdom of crowds" became more popular from a 2004 book written by James Surowiecki called *The Wisdom of Crowds: Why the Many Are Smarter Than the Few and How Collective Wisdom Shapes Business, Economics, Societies and Nations*.

[113] In a January 2013 article, "Avoiding the Consensus Earnings Trap," McKinsey noted that as much as 40% of the time, companies saw their share price, adjusted for market activity, advance despite the consensus earnings miss. McKinsey studied 266 companies in the Fortune 500 during 2010. The forward outlook matters much more than how a company performed in the most recently-completed quarter in almost all cases.

[114] In the same January 2013 article by McKinsey (see prior footnote), across the subset of Fortune 500 companies it analyzed over a period of seven years from 2005-2012, the research firm found that it didn't much matter if companies meet or beat consensus earnings estimates,

In any case, the arguably meritless efforts to predict quarterly earnings per share hasn't shifted Wall Street's focus away from the near term, even if management teams are looking more long term. On Wall Street, there may be more resources allocated to evaluating what the company will do in the next quarter or year than anything else, and sadly, once the quarter is over, those efforts are largely wasted, as a new quarter or year is already upon the analyst. Where the "wisdom of crowds" may make sense with respect to arriving at financial forecasts in the near term within the enterprise value framework, the intermediate- and long-term horizon is more important to the derivation and substance of a fair value estimate, and therefore price activity, and where most of the differentiated analysis should occur.

Figure 6: Sample Distribution of Equity Value Composition

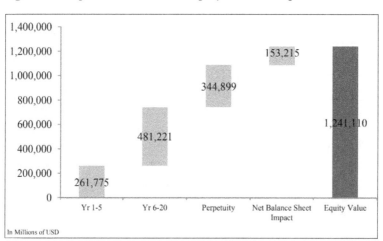

This figure shows the composition of a sample company's equity value. The majority of value is generally ascribed to a period beyond year 5, making an evaluation of mid-cycle revenue and mid-cycle margin assessments generally more important than near-term forecasts within the enterprise cash flow process. Source: Valuentum's 16-page equity report of Apple, September 2018.

---

after accounting for differences in growth and operating performance (key drivers within enterprise valuation). The research firm noted that falling short of consensus estimates was "seldom catastrophic." McKinsey said that missing consensus earnings estimates repeatedly over several years mattered, but such weak earnings (and stock) performance may be better explained by operating failures at the company (and a reset of its enterprise valuation lower), not necessarily that the cause of its pricing action was driven by continuously missing earnings estimates.

In the sample company's equity breakdown in Figure 6 on the prior page, approximately $262 billion (21%) of the company's estimated value comes from value ascribed over the next five years, $481 billion (39%) from years 6-20, $345 billion (28%) from perpetuity (year 20 into infinity), and the remainder from the company's balance sheet position (namely net cash). For the sample company, one that generates copious amounts of enterprise free cash flow annually, an intense focus on the drivers behind long-term enterprise free cash flow generation, or mid-cycle operating assumption, is much more important than an assessment of how fundamentals may perform in the coming quarter or year.[115] The enterprise valuation framework helps to conceptualize the idea of long-duration value arbitrage, or that which impacts estimated value, and therefore expected near-term prices, on the basis of long-term expectations.

Long-duration value arbitrage differs from what can be characterized as Wall Street's focus, or identifying near-term expectations differentials in earnings estimates, or near-term value arbitrage, which based on a company's value composition, shouldn't have as much of an outsize impact on the company's value or price movements, provided that fundamental changes in the near term aren't expected to be more structural or long term in nature. Where Wall Street is focusing on identifying value differentials corresponding to the next couple years, a smaller component of the value composition, the enterprise valuation framework showcases that there is far more to work with in striving to identify mispricings. If the analyst can *anticipate* changes in the market's estimate of long-duration value "correctly," a focus that matters much more to intrinsic value calculations, the near-term earnings game becomes significantly less important.

The terminal value, or the "perpetuity" value, of a company's value composition is another one of the major criticisms of enterprise valuation. However, this should not be viewed as much as a criticism of enterprise valuation as it should be viewed as a lens into the rather sensitive nature of the value construct and stock prices, themselves. It should not be the goal to change one's valuation processes such that they are less dependent on long-term considerations, especially if it is the long term that is most important to valuation and prices.

---

[115] The term "mid-cycle" may be worth defining. For example, if peak or trough conditions are modeled during the latter stages of the enterprise valuation framework, unrealistic distortions with respect to value estimation can occur. It's important when thinking about latter stages of the enterprise-valuation process to use mid-cycle estimates of revenue growth, operating margin, and net new investment, as just a few examples.

Valuation *should be* long duration, and it *should be* sensitive to the inputs, much like prices are highly volatile as expectations change. For example, it can only be reasonably assumed that, if a company's share price advances and falls 15% within the course of a few years (a rather conservative pricing range), a fundamentally-driven fair value estimate range of 30%, which may appear superficially large, should not be considered inappropriate. The idea that the company's value, and corresponding price, may change significantly because of changes in long-term expectations is theoretically sound and may be an accurate representation of reality.

In any case, there are a few ways to overcome the major shortcomings of an over-concentration of value in the terminal value, without resorting to residual income methods that may be built on the arbitrary nature of accounting book value for non-financial operating companies (e.g. Boeing and McDonald's).[116] For starters, a three-stage forecast horizon that extends to year 20 by the end of stage two of an enterprise valuation model will facilitate a normalization of major drivers, ensuring long-term expected growth rates and discount rates are reasonable within the terminal value function. Second, the fading of the EBI (NOPLAT)[117] growth rate and a normalization of net capital spending by the end of stage two of the model should generate a reasonable enterprise free cash flow measure to use in the numerator of the perpetuity ratio.

Most market observers may attribute changes in price movements around quarterly reporting as a result of the company beating or missing the most recently-reported consensus forecast. It is not that simple, however, particularly given that, in most cases, when forward-looking guidance is issued above expectations, it often trumps the poor earnings performance in the already-completed quarter, sending the stock higher. Large price movements around quarterly earnings reports can instead be generally viewed, in part, as driven by

---

[116] Some may prefer the residual income or economic-profit model because it is generally believed that the residual income model recognizes value "earlier," something implied by the construct, where book equity or Invested Capital is grossed up by the discounted future economic profit stream. However, the idea that value is recognized "earlier" in residual income or economic-profit models may not be a correct perspective. For example, in the case of entities with negative book equity such as in the instances of McDonald's or Boeing, one generally wouldn't believe that value-destruction is recognized "earlier," or that book equity as a component of the value equation, itself, should be considered meaningful, other than it can be used as a driver to achieve expected EBI (NOPLAT), that which drives enterprise valuation.

[117] Earnings before interest after taxes (EBI) or net operating profit less adjusted taxes (NOPLAT) is a core driver of enterprise free cash flow.

the market's resetting of long-term expectations of the company and its estimate of intrinsic value through buying and selling activity. The changes shouldn't necessarily be attributed to whether the company beat or missed last quarter's consensus EPS estimates, something largely irrelevant to intrinsic value estimation (provided it may have no bearing on future expectations). Quite simply, the quarterly report matters mostly because it impacts intermediate- to long-term expectations.

"Why do I care what is going to happen five years from now? I'm already retired, and I need to know what will happen this year and next," an attendee from the American Association of Individual Investors (AAII) meeting in Cleveland asked me some years ago. It was a good question, without a doubt, and it hit on just how confusing the markets (particularly how the time horizon of forecasts impact values and prices today) can be to investors, even to ones that are putting in the time to understand it.

I walked back and forth in front of the room, raising and lowering my arm to explain how changes in the trajectory of future long-term expectations had an impact on intrinsic value and the share price today. "If the market's long-term expectations are higher than before, it impacts the estimated value and share price today." I raised my arm, trying to simulate the trajectory of expected enterprise free cash flows. "If the market's long-term expectations are lower than before, it impacts the estimated value and share price today." I lowered my arm. I paced back and forth, trying to draw a distinction between the two points in time by stopping abruptly on either side of the room, emphasizing how the near-term price and long-term expectations are separate concepts, but inherently connected.

In most texts, the concept of duration is used within fixed-income analysis, but stocks are long-duration financial instruments, too. Enterprise valuation establishes this framework, where changes in long-term expectations can have a greater impact on the value and corresponding share price of the equity *today*, even more so than changes in near-term expectations that may even occur over a near-term holding period. The enterprise valuation model's outsize value composition in the long term explains why most enterprise valuation frameworks are sensitive to the discounting mechanism behind interest rates. Adjustments in the market's long-term expectations of benchmark interest rates, for example, may matter more to driving near-term equity value and price changes than any news that may actually impact near-term results during any near-term holding period.

To sum up, the enterprise valuation framework, in my opinion, is the right mental model in which to interpret share price movements. The estimated value ascribed to a company beyond the next five years, as in the example in Figure 6 on page 76, theoretically becomes much more important to evaluate than that which impacts near-term fundamental performance, provided that fundamental changes in the near term do not alter intermediate and long-term expectations. The enterprise valuation framework makes it clear that it is most important to *anticipate* the market's expectations of a company's mid-cycle and corresponding long-term assumptions "correctly," a time frame that has more influence in determining a company's fair value estimate *today*, and by extension a stock's pricing activity *today*. Ironically, given the general emphasis on quarterly earnings results and revisions by Wall Street, market participants may not be making the connection.

The Long Term Is Elusive

Many may describe long-term investors as those holding stocks for a long time. The concept of the long term, as I see it, however, is much more complicated than a time horizon, and similar perhaps to thinking about how short-term-oriented news may not necessarily impact near-term prices as much as long-term considerations. Long-term investing, in my opinion, is not necessarily leaving your assets in one place for a long time, just because the market has gone up in the past or that you'd like to reinvest dividends and experience compounding. Instead, long-term investing, to me, involves a consideration of the long-term fundamentals and future free cash flows of a company in the investment analysis, which could impact decisions at any time. Where the long term to some may imply simply a holding period, the long term to me *also* implies an analytical period that impacts pricing activity via long-duration value composition.

But this thinking has other important implications. At any point in time, the stock price of a company can be hypothesized to be based on (or rather, imputed from) the expectations of future free cash flows, as in enterprise valuation. In 10 years, the stock price of the company will still be based on expectations of future enterprise free cash flows at that time. Investors will never reach the long term, and when it comes to the view that share prices are based on future expectations, there may very well be no such thing as a true long term, even as one may say that all of the value of any asset today is based on expectations of its future free cash flows over the long term.

Let's try this hypothetical. Many investors may consider 2050 to be the long term, as in a long-term holding period, one that's about 30 years from now. But the value of a stock on January 1, 2050, will in part still be based on the market's expectations of the company's future free cash flows in 2050 and over a new long term, not from today through 2050, though accumulated net cash from today through 2050 will still have some impact on the price, as it does with value. In any case, a brand new long-term will have been "created," of which the stock price in 2050 is then based on. The long term of today was never reached. It remained elusive.

Let's try this now in a real-world context. Apple has been a great performing stock because its future today has a larger free cash flow stream expected in it (and perhaps lower risk ascribed to it) than that of the future of its past, and therefore its future value today (and price) is larger than what it was in the past. The present value of expectations of its long term, a "new" long term, have changed over time, driving the price higher over time in this instance. In some ways, the long term is psychological, based on expectations, not chronological.

Because expectations of the future are always changing, and the future is inherently unpredictable, there can theoretically never be a definitive "long term." In fact, there is only a series of iterative expectations of the long term that drive the stock prices of *today* and stock prices *as time passes*. It is not necessarily the passing of time (chronologically), per se, that causes stock prices to advance or decline, but instead it is the change in the market's future forecasts of the company (free cash flow and the like) plus net cash (or less net debt) on the books at any point in the future that causes the stock price change (driven by buying and selling activity based on these changing expectations).

I'm not saying that a long-term *holding period* may not matter,[118] nor am I saying that saying that buy and hold can't work,[119] nor am I saying that dividend reinvestment and compounding isn't important (see Chapter 8). What I'm saying, however, is that stock prices will always be based on current expectations of future enterprise free cash flows over the long term (at any point in time in the future). As Yogi Berra has been credited in saying, "The future ain't what it used to be." Future expectations are always changing, and that's what's driving price moves. There is no magic switch 10 years from now that will change the market from a discount mechanism of expected future enterprise free cash flows to a precise mechanism that translates earnings one-to-one from the company to the shareholder. If this does happen, the stock market will no longer be a market (it will be some pass-through entity).

Long-term investing, to me, is based on analyzing the long-term dynamics of a business and making a stand that at some point other investors will drive the stock toward one's intrinsic value estimate (over the long haul). Long-term investing does not mean that, all of a sudden, the company will be valued differently because we're now 10 years into the future, or even that the stock price will be higher 10 years from now because earnings have expanded, or fundamentals have improved. If you're willing to hold a stock for 10 years, your total return will be a function of the dividends paid over time and how the market

---

[118] Jeremy Siegel wrote in *Stocks for the Long Run* that, since 1802, there has never been "a negative real holding period return yield over periods of 17 years or more." This observation backs the idea of holding stocks for a long time, as a potential cure for all stock-market ills, but there are other instances, of course, where a long-term holding period may still have left investors sorely disappointed. In December 1989, for example, the Nikkei 225 Index hit 38,000+, but through 2012, the index was still struggling to stay above 10,000. In March 2000, the NASDAQ soared to 5,000+, but some ten years later, it was still laboring under 2,750, despite recovering from the devastation of the Financial Crisis that sent the index's value to sub-1,500 levels. Dividend reinvestment, or that which contributes to holding-period returns, wouldn't have offset much of these steep losses.

[119] In the *Future for Investors*, Siegel would say that, if investors bought the original S&P 500 firms in 1957 (and never bought another company added to the index), they would have outperformed just about every mutual fund for the past half century. Further, a study by Sanford Bernstein & Company that spanned 1926-1993 showed that returns from the best 60 months, or about 7% of the time, averaged about 11%, while the returns of the remaining months, or about 93% of the time, were flat, on average. Timing the market is never easy, and some of the biggest portions over investment returns happen over short periods of time. That said, it's important not to forget that it took the Dow Jones Industrial Average until 1954 to recover to its price level in prior to the Crash of 1929. Though this price comparison excludes collected dividends, it still speaks to the idea that a long-term holding period can sometimes be a very, very long time, sometimes just to break even.

reacts to expectations of future enterprise free cash flows at a time 10 years in the future, which will, in part, along with net cash accumulation during the past 10 years, influence the share price (and its P/E ratio). The interaction of these factors determines the total return of the investment, and whether the investment was a winner or loser.[120] We'll talk more about the concept of total return in Chapter 8.

---

[120] Changes in future expectations can matter tremendously. The August 2000 edition of *Fortune*, for example, offered a "buy-and-forget" portfolio of 10 stocks: Enron, Nortel Networks, Nokia, Univision, Viacom, Genentech, Morgan Stanley, Broadcom, Charles Schwab, and Oracle. By the end of 2002, this group of equities would suffer a decline of about 80%, on average. Certainly, the fraud at Enron was an unusual situation, but most of the pricing declines of these stocks over such a short period of time was caused by changes in future expectations.

5

The Enterprise Valuation Framework

The Theory of Universal Valuation states that value cannot exist in separate vacuums depending on which investment strategy one pursues, whether it is a quantitative strategy or whether it is a fundamentally-based, enterprise-value oriented strategy, or other. The enterprise valuation model transcends styles into quantitative factor-based methods and establishes universal value. Enterprise value is the confounding, lurking variable behind many statistical studies. Also, shortcomings of the P/E ratio, as representative. Introduction to behavioral valuation. How key drivers impact share prices. Peculiarities of some quantitative observations explained. On residual income and economic-profit models and their relevance to banking enterprises. Buybacks and wealth destruction.

V aluation shouldn't be complicated.

Though there may be an infinite number of variables to consider in assessing qualitative aspects of an investment opportunity, there are generally three primary cash-based sources of intrinsic value of a company,[121] or that which makes stocks different than most other asset classes. First, the company's operating activities are a source of value, as measured by the present value of all future enterprise free cash flows (A in Figure 7 on next page) that are generated for all investors of the business (debt holders, equity holders, other non-equity investors, etc.).

---

[121] The emphasis on "cash-based" is key in this instance. If a characteristic of a company does not translate itself, directly or indirectly, to either balance sheet cash or future enterprise cash flows, it generally cannot be considered a source of value. Enterprise valuation measures material worth, not sentimental considerations. McKinsey generally describes this concept as the conservation of value, or "anything that doesn't increase cash flows doesn't create value (assuming no change in the risk profile)."

Figure 7: Major Components of the Enterprise Valuation Framework

$$\text{Fair Value} = \left[\sum_{t=0}^{\infty} \frac{A(t)}{(1+d)^t} - B(0) - C(0) + D(0) \right]$$

where A (t) is an Enterprise Free Cash Flow (1) at year t,

B (0) is a Total Debt at time 0,

C (0) is a Preferred Stock at time 0,

D (0) is a Total Cash at time 0,

d is Weighted Average Cost of Capital (WACC).

This figure defines the basic structure of the enterprise free cash flow model in deriving enterprise value, which is then divided by shares outstanding, to arrive at a fair value estimate per share. The company's share price is then compared to a fair value estimate to determine a price-to-estimated-fair value (P/FV) ratio. A price-to-estimated-fair value ratio, which includes enterprise valuation, differs from other valuation multiples, including enterprise value-to-EBITDA (EV/EBITDA), or EBITDA to total enterprise value (EBITDA/TEV), which do not directly compare a company's share price with estimates of its intrinsic value, and therefore are not true measures of price versus estimated value. The price-to-estimated-fair value ratio, augmented by a margin of safety, is the first component of the Valuentum Buying Index (more on this later).

Second, the company's balance sheet is a source of value. For example, if a company has $1 billion in total cash and $500 million in total debt and no preferred stock outstanding, and if the company's board should decide to shut down today, shareholders would be entitled to the net cash position, or $500 million ($1 billion less $500 million), adjusted for closing and unwinding expenses.[122] Incidentally, the very idea that a company can have intrinsic value

---

[122] The goal is to identify all non-equity claims implied in the capital structure, with the net impact either subtracted or added to the present value of future enterprise cash flows. Depending on one's modeling methods, there can be a variety of non-equity claims. Off-balance sheet debt is one potential example that is dependent on whether operating leases are capitalized or rent expense is allowed to flow into the model as a deduction of EBI (NOPLAT). Balance is important in such adjustments. If the analyst capitalizes operating leases, for example, rent expense should no longer be a deduction within EBI. Another less obvious non-equity claim may capture the probability of the firm having to pay damages as a result of a lawsuit, something not explicitly captured in future enterprise free cash flows.

with no earnings almost precludes the systematic application of the P/E ratio as a measure of value in a quantitative setting, further supporting its ambiguous nature. Third, a company's "hidden assets"[123] such as an overfunded pension or an equity stake in another company that may not be accurately reflected in GAAP accounting statements can have value (this aspect is not included in formula above, but an expanded definition might include it).

Enterprise free cash flow, unlevered free cash flow, or free cash flow to the firm (FCFF) are three labels that mean the same thing, and the measure is generally calculated by tax-effecting earnings before interest and taxes (EBIT) to arrive at earnings before interest, after taxes. This is called EBI or net operating profit less adjusted taxes (NOPLAT). In this sense, the enterprise valuation framework assumes that the company has an all-equity capital structure in the calculation of future enterprise free cash flows, as the interest tax-shield is captured within the discount rate.

Net working capital changes, excluding balance-sheet cash, and net capital spending (all capital spending less depreciation) are then subtracted from EBI or NOPLAT to arrive at the measure, enterprise free cash flow. Future financial forecasts are made within the model,[124] and the present value of future enterprise free cash flows is summed up to arrive at the first component of value. The second component of value is lifted straight from the balance sheet, total cash less total debt less total preferred, while the third may take some digging within a company's SEC filings to uncover any hidden assets or liabilities.

---

[123] "Hidden assets" is a term used to describe non-operating assets or non-operating liabilities. Another example of this might be a company's equity stake in another company, in which the accounting method does not impact the consolidated cash flows of the business. The value of this stake is "hidden."

[124] Because the historical data is entered into the model on a nominal basis, future forecasts should be nominal, as well. Explicit forecasts are made on the income statement, balance sheet, and cash flow statement, and enterprise free cash flow is then derived.

Figure 8: Basic Calculation of Enterprise Free Cash Flow[125]

	EBIT x (1 - cash tax rate)
+	Depreciation
--	Capital Expenditures
--	Change in Net Working Capital (excluding cash)
-----	---
=	Enterprise Free Cash Flow

These three components (present value of discounted enterprise free cash flows, addition of net cash or subtraction of net debt, and "hidden" assets or liabilities) are then summed up to arrive at equity value, which is then divided by a company's shares outstanding to arrive at equity value per share.

Another way of explaining enterprise valuation may be through the perspective of someone's personal financial situation. Hypothetically, think about one component of the valuation framework as a person's salary less expenses for every year in the future, with some risk adjustment such that the person's net future income is discounted back to today. Another component might be the person's net cash in the bank, his or her total cash less all total debt. The third might be the person's non-income generating assets such as most durable items such as a car, equity in a home, or most anything that can be sold.

Thinking about corporate valuation in this personal setting helps to conceptualize some of the important drivers of the enterprise valuation equation. It is much more important to think of value, in part, as a future stream of long-term income payments, than in what a person may make next year, the latter equivalent in corporate finance to perhaps next year's earnings per share. The importance of the balance sheet in corporate valuation also becomes obvious within the

---

[125] There are a few peculiarities to be aware of. First, to tax-effect EBIT, the construct uses an estimated cash tax rate, not an effective tax rate. Therefore, future projections will hardly ever match GAAP representation. Also, embedded within EBIT, but not explicitly labeled, is the add-back of any non-cash operating items, including amortization. The price paid for acquisitions is generally a deduction in the calculation, but the framework should generally not assume future, unannounced acquisitions. Net working capital breaks down into the difference between the sum of inventories, accounts receivable and other current operating assets less the sum of accounts payable, accrued liabilities (including deferred revenue) and other current operating liabilities. Note that these are current operating items, and that it is the positive change in net working capital that is subtracted (if the change is negative, it is a positive contribution to the calculation). All capital expenditures, whether maintenance or growth, are deducted in the enterprise valuation framework, and all contributions from these investments are factored into future EBI. This concept is a source of confusion within midstream equity valuations (see Chapter 7).

personal financial framework. A person with a $1 billion in the bank and no debt is much better off than a person with very little cash and a $1 billion in debt owed to the bank, all else equal. The value emanating from the balance sheet may be one of the most overlooked sources of intrinsic value given Wall Street's emphasis on earnings per share, which may only capture a sliver of the valuation impact from interest income, particularly in a low interest rate environment.

With perhaps a few exceptions, most all other sources of "cash-based" intrinsic value should be implicitly captured within the intrinsic value calculation in the formulaic calculation in Figure 7 (e.g. dividends are paid out of cash from the balance sheet, including newly-raised debt, or accumulated future free cash flow generation). As for competitive considerations such as a company's low-cost position, its network effect, its brand strength, or any intangible asset (management, culture, and the like), such items can effectively be valued by summing up the company's ability to translate those strengths into future enterprise free cash flows. These items already form a key component of the enterprise value equation and are not incremental to it.

The takeaway of this consideration is important with respect to the discussions of qualitative competitive-advantage analysis, or moat analysis (see Chapter 9). It can be reasoned that if such competitive advantages do not translate into future value, as measured specifically by future enterprise free cash flows, as expressed as a spread between return on invested capital and the discount rate, then those competitive advantages may not be valuable competitive advantages, or even worse, they may not be competitive advantages at all. There are always exceptions to any generalizations, of course, as a company's buying back stock at attractive prices and pursuing value-creating acquisitions can augment intrinsic worth, but the enterprise valuation model is one of the best tools to help quantify the qualitative subjective context.

If enterprise free cash flow is the key driver when it comes to intrinsic value estimation, why is there such an emphasis on underlying metrics seemingly everywhere? For example, why does the market pay so much attention to net additions to subscribers, as in Netflix, or on a company's gross margin, as in Cisco? In short, these items are internals of the company and may shed some light on the quality of fundamental performance to determine future sustainability of earnings and free cash flows. If net additions to subscribers are better than expected in any one quarter, analysts may expect the company to generate more enterprise free cash flows in the future from the now-higher subscriber count. In the case of a gross margin, it may reveal how well the company is managing its costs and how competition is impacting pricing, both of which could have ramifications on future operating income, a core part of the enterprise valuation framework.

Sometimes, metrics can be more distracting than informative, however, and it's important for investors to differentiate between 1) things that matter significantly such as expectations of future enterprise free cash flows or net balance sheet health, 2) things that may matter because they influence expectations of future enterprise free cash flow such as net subscriber additions or gross margin, and 3) things that seem to only distract investors from the underlying performance. One metric that may fit in the latter category could include Instagram followers of new stars before and after a web television series is launched on Netflix. That Millie Bobby Brown's Instagram followers, for example, surged to 17.6 million from practically nil following the release of *Stranger Things* on Netflix doesn't matter nearly as much as Netflix's burgeoning content costs on the value of the equity.

Knowing what matters and what doesn't is critical. Some investors may have little difficulty comparing the value of objects when given their monetary worth. However, when the similar comparison is done with stocks, where values are also provided, it becomes increasingly more challenging for investors to identify which stock may be the better investment. Investors tend to place additional value on items that already are embedded in the derivation of a company's intrinsic value estimate, sometimes more so than the intrinsic value estimate itself, which already considers all factors of an investment within it.

In May 2018, I conducted a very informal survey where I asked the following:[126] "You have three buckets: the first is filled with $100 worth of ice, the second is filled with $100 worth of worms, and the third is filled with $100 worth of shampoo. Which one is worth more, assuming each bucket is identical?" More than half of the respondents said that all the buckets were worth the same, an outcome that I believe was expected. However, I then asked the following question: "You have three companies. One beats earnings estimates, and the enterprise valuation suggests it is worth $70. The second company has a "moat," and enterprise valuation suggests it is worth $70. The third company pays a hefty

---

[126] The survey was conducted on Twitter and should be viewed more anecdotally. Out of my thousands of Twitter followers, 46 responded to the first series of questions and 39 to the second series of questions.

dividend, and enterprise valuation says it is worth $70. Which company is more valuable? In this example, nearly two thirds of respondents said the companies were not all worth the same, despite each being listed as worth $70!

Though the topic deserves further study, this dynamic might be called the "composition of value" versus "value" behavioral pitfall. Intrinsic value analysis, as in the enterprise valuation framework, represents the conclusion to any and all stock research: What is the company worth? Enterprise valuation captures the expectations of a company's competitive advantages, growth prospects, strategic endeavors, and any other qualitative factor. No other process does this. Putting to numbers a plethora of fundamental, and sometimes very qualitative, items in arriving at a fair value estimate is the cornerstone, and the most critical component, of any stock research analysis. Without an in-depth intrinsic-value assessment, research is but a story that has no ending.

Don't Sweat the WACC

The discount rate used in enterprise valuation, or the weighted average cost of capital (WACC) assumption, is one of its most important variables. Whether it's the 30-year bond rate, or 10% because it's a good round number,[127] or the Capital Asset Pricing Model (CAPM) or other multi-factor models that are used to estimate the discount rate, the measure is very subjective. Subjectivity doesn't mean, however, the enterprise valuation process, itself, is not of considerable utility to investors. Part of finance and intrinsic value estimation will always rest on the reality that the future is unpredictable, whether it is future expected interest rates (a driver behind the discount rate) or future expected revenue and operating earnings (a driver behind enterprise free cash flows).

The theoretical component of the WACC is based on what an investor's required return might be, that which ties future expected enterprise free cash flows back to today, or the time value of money. A dollar generated today is worth more than a dollar generated tomorrow because it can be reinvested to generate an incremental return. Though perhaps optimistic, investors today may have

---

[127] In response to a question during the Berkshire Hathaway 2017 annual meeting, Warren Buffett talked about return expectations of about 10% for Berkshire Hathaway, which may imply required returns or a baseline discount rate of about 10% for a large, diversified US-based company.

expected annual stock returns anywhere between 8%-12%[128] over the long run, and from a top down standpoint, a distribution of WACC assumptions (or required stock returns) across companies, one that mirrors those expectations, seems most appropriate--the least fundamentally risky at the lower end, the most fundamentally risky at the higher end. The mean (average) WACC assumption across equities in Valuentum's coverage universe, for a point of reference, was approximately 9.5% during 2018.

The framework of the WACC does not have to fit within the confines of quantitative methods. In some ways, maybe it shouldn't, given real world testing. The WACC, for example, could also be derived completely independent of the quantitative CAPM,[129] or three-, five-, and other multi-factor models, instead of sharing their major criticisms. For those inclined to ignore most quantitative theory on this topic, using a discount rate, or WACC of ~9.5% may be a good shortcut in today's relatively low interest-rate environment (3%-5% on the 10-year Treasury), provided that the analyst runs sensitivity analysis and compares outcomes across a broad swath of companies to identify outliers (whose underlying risk and therefore share prices may be mispriced). In this context, the WACC should be viewed as a "hurdle rate" for new projects, far removed from the structure of quantitative theory and its shortcomings (e.g. data may not be representative of what it measures, as in the B/M ratio and value; data may not capture future expectations as in how the efficient markets hypothesis explains bubbles, for example; and data may not be causal or predictive).

In the enterprise valuation framework, a fundamental CAPM can be considered. The fundamental CAPM attempts to "correct" for the quantitative shortcomings of beta, not the least of which is that quantitative beta is backward-looking and really doesn't have a standard measurement period.[130] That a stock has been more

---

[128] According to Aswath Damodaran, professor at the Stern School of Business and widely-recognized for his work on the equity risk premium (ERP), the average T-bill rate (4.73%) plus implied ERP (4.16%) has averaged 8.9% for S&P 500 companies from 1961-2017. Under this framework, applying the CAPM, for one of the strongest companies, on average, one with a quantitative beta of 1 and one with no debt, its cost of equity and its weighted average cost of capital assumption would be 8.9%.

[129] It's important to make a distinction between the quantitative CAPM, which is derived from quantitative beta within the original CAPM framework, as this text discusses a fundamental CAPM as well as an adjusted fundamental CAPM.

[130] There is no standard time period to measure quantitative beta. For example, a stock's quantitative beta during the past year could be greater than 1, and its quantitative beta during the past five years could be less than 1. The quantitative beta that may be more representative of what

or less volatile in the past does not make it riskier, as in what quantitative beta may imply. In some respects, a falling share price that becomes more volatile could spell opportunity for the long-term value investor (i.e. it offers a bigger bargain or a wider margin of safety to guard against further losses), not necessarily that the analyst should use a higher discount rate in the modeling framework, or that the company is worth less. Warren Buffett may have said it best "...volatility is almost universally used as a proxy for risk. Though this pedagogic assumption makes for easy teaching, it is dead wrong: Volatility is far from synonymous with risk."

A fundamental beta ranking scale (below 1 = below-average fundamental risk; above 1 = above-average fundamental risk) can be used to replace quantitative beta, but even this fundamental CAPM framework may still need an adjustment. For example, within even a fundamental CAPM framework, a financially-leveraged entity with material bankruptcy risk may end up with a lower WACC assumption than a financially-sound, net-cash-rich operation with negligible bankruptcy risk. This happens because the after-tax cost of debt[131] is definitionally lower than the cost of equity, creating a situation where stocks with high levels of debt end up with lower cost of capital assumptions (given the higher weight of debt in the WACC equation).

This situation may not make sense practically. Debt-free companies should probably receive a benefit to their cost of equity assumptions,[132] a component of the weighted average cost of capital, given their lower financial risk, which is not measured in the structure of the CAPM, itself. In any case, when reviewing valuations, it is valuable to ask whether the WACC assumption makes sense relative to that of the average of the coverage universe. Is this company's fundamental risk to an estimate of its future expected cash flows below-average

---

to expect for the company's future share-price volatility then becomes highly debatable. This debate, however, is limited to expected share-price volatility, which is separate than what might be the true investment risk of a company, as measured by investment losses, not share-price volatility.

[131] If you may recall, in enterprise valuation, we tax-effect EBIT in the calculation of enterprise free cash flow (as if the company has an all-equity structure). However, companies with debt benefit from an interest tax shield. This shield is captured by using the after-tax cost of debt in the WACC.

[132] As another data point for triangulation, McKinsey noted that the average cost of equity capital for most large firms was in the range of 8%-10% in late 2009.

risk (<9.5%), about average risk (~9.5%), or above-average risk (>9.5%), for example?

Though such a framework still suffers from estimation risk, in a fundamental-adjusted CAPM, the way to possibly think about how to calculate the WACC generally might distill into the following (using round numbers): ~4.3% long-term expected 10-year Treasury rate (perhaps a function of the spot rate and the historical average of the 10-year) and the long-term equity risk premium of 6.5%[133] and then the after-tax cost of debt, where synthetic credit spreads above the 10-year Treasury on the basis of the firm's credit quality may be applied (implied spreads based on corporate credit quality).

In short, the mean (average) weighted average cost of capital assumption of ~9.5%, as that reflective of Valuentum's equity coverage universe, might be viewed as what investors may demand as a required annual return on an average stock investment (given a risk-free rate assumption in the low-to-mid single-digits), that which ties future enterprise free cash flows back to today. Regardless of which approach to determine the discount rate is pursued, analysts should perform extensive sensitivity analysis around the measure and seek to identify outliers, which could indicate where risk may be mispriced.

---

[133] Using data from the Center for Research in Security Prices (CRSP) from 1926-2008, Ibbotson estimated that the long-horizon equity risk premium was approximately 6.5%. The difference from the 4.16% figure, as put forth by Aswath Damodaran from 1961-2017, speaks to the subjectivity in selecting which quantitative measures may be most appropriate, even if they may be statistically and objectively derived.

Figure 9: Illustration of WACC Calculation[134]

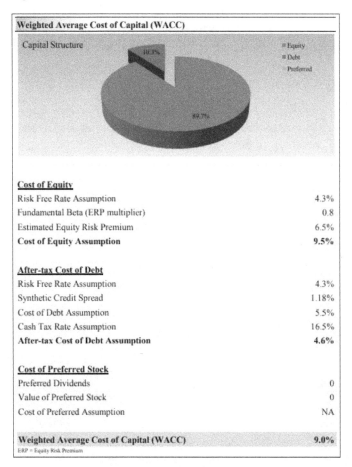

Weighted Average Cost of Capital (WACC)	
Cost of Equity	
Risk Free Rate Assumption	4.3%
Fundamental Beta (ERP multiplier)	0.8
Estimated Equity Risk Premium	6.5%
Cost of Equity Assumption	**9.5%**
After-tax Cost of Debt	
Risk Free Rate Assumption	4.3%
Synthetic Credit Spread	1.18%
Cost of Debt Assumption	5.5%
Cash Tax Rate Assumption	16.5%
After-tax Cost of Debt Assumption	**4.6%**
Cost of Preferred Stock	
Preferred Dividends	0
Value of Preferred Stock	0
Cost of Preferred Assumption	NA
Weighted Average Cost of Capital (WACC)	**9.0%**
ERP = Equity Risk Premium	

There are various other ways to interpret the enterprise valuation framework with respect to the WACC. The traditional application of enterprise valuation may be to calculate the best fair value estimate for the equity, but in a more general sense, any output can be calculated implicitly given other parameters. For example, plugging the current share price into an enterprise framework to replace the traditional output, the fair value estimate, can solve for what the market may be implicitly assuming within the share price with respect to other assumptions such as interest rates, growth rates, or the cost of equity and the WACC, itself, for

---

[134] WACC = [(E/(D+E)] x Cost of Equity + [(D/(D+E)] x Cost of Debt x (1-tax rate)

example. The analyst can then evaluate whether those parameters are reasonable in making an overall value determination of the equity. The exchanging (swapping) of estimated intrinsic value with price within the model is an important focus when it comes to using enterprise valuation to not only explain price movements, but also to identify when underlying assumptions, as implied in the price, make little sense.

Let's pull some of these thoughts together. In February 2015, Kinder Morgan, for example, had generally guided the analyst community to a weighted average "hurdle rate" of 3.3%, consisting of 50% equity at a 4.1% yield and 50% debt at a 2.4% cost of debt. Practitioners of enterprise valuation, however, would immediately recognize that such a WACC, or hurdle rate, is far too low to be reasonably applied in enterprise valuation, or really any valuation context (especially for companies with long-duration projects). Situations within the valuation construct where discount rates approach zero can have an abnormally-large impact on the output, causing fair value estimates to be largely disconnected from reason. Think of the WACC, in this example, as x in $f(x)$ as the fraction $1/x$. As x becomes smaller and smaller, the values of $f(x)$ become ever larger. Whereas the impact on the fair value estimate may not be as large with a change in the WACC assumption to 9% from 10%, the impact could be considerable with a change to 3% or 4% from 10%. Eventually, the limit approaches infinity as x approaches zero.

In enterprise valuation, matching the duration of future enterprise free cash flows (from year 1 to perpetuity) with expectations of the average discount rate, or WACC, over the forecast horizon (from year 1 to perpetuity) is important to achieve consistency and balance within the valuation framework. Hypothetically, discounting a cash flow in Year 20 at the current spot rate or an ultra-low "hurdle rate" may not make much sense. One of the better ways to achieve expectations of the long-term future average rate of the 10-year Treasury (risk free rate) may be to use the weighted average of the historical 10-year Treasury and the current spot rate, as outlined in the example in this section. Other methods may consider the yield curve in arriving at a WACC to discount future enterprise free cash flows, while others may use a long-term average of the risk-free rate without considering near-term changes in the 10-year Treasury rate.

Like quantitative beta, however, using the spot rate of the 10-year Treasury as the risk-free-rate in any valuation framework would not only cause significant fair-value volatility, [135] but also may result in a systematic "misvaluation" of companies relative to their long-term estimated intrinsic worth (if the spot rate falls materially below reasonable long-run averages). Valuation is more about logic and balance than plugging and chugging numbers. Thinking about how everything fits together, and how one variable may impact another variable is simply par for the course. As in the real world, the term "all else equal" generally does not exist in enterprise valuation either, even if such an assumption, when changed, can provide insight into the direction of how one particular driver impacts estimated fair value.

Value Is Not Static

Share prices, which are driven by the buying and selling of stock, are not static, and neither are fair value estimates. When important drivers within the enterprise cash flow model change or when new information comes to light, fair value estimates can *and should* change, much like the prices themselves. Though there are perhaps an infinite number of reasons why a fair value estimate can change, there are generally two primary reasons that account for most fair value estimate revisions: 1) "rolling the model forward,"[136] and 2) significant changes in expectations or transformative acquisitions.

Modest tweaks in fair value estimates within the enterprise valuation process may occur when an analyst rolls a company's model forward one year. This occurs when Year 1 of the model changes from, say, 2019 to 2020. The timing of this revision generally occurs after a company issues its fiscal annual report (form 10-K or form 20-F). For most companies, this would occur late in the first quarter, as audited new information for the last fiscal year (which is released in the form 10-K or form 20-F) is entered into the model.

---

[135] In the case of quantitative beta, for example, the process may not only result in unreasonably high cost of equity assumptions, as in the Fama-French three-factor model, but the volatility of quantitative beta, itself, would cause value estimates that would be far too volatile to be meaningful. The same dynamic may happen with spot rates of the 10-year Treasury applied within the WACC calculation given the measure's volatility.

[136] The phrase refers to the action analysts take to move the projected current year's numbers to reflect realized last year's actuals within the modeling infrastructure, most commonly done within Microsoft Excel, or other spreadsheet software.

Generally speaking, if forecasts have been relatively accurate in setting the original fair value estimate, the fair value estimate should theoretically increase by its discount rate less the dividend yield each year, all else equal, through the course of the year. This phenomenon is caused by what is called the time value of money (as companies collect cash through the year, their value increases, net of cash going out the door, the dividend payment), and because of the steady advancement in value through the course of the year, there may actually only be modest tweaks to an estimate of intrinsic value when rolling the model forward, in most cases.

It's important to note, however, that as future expectations are always changing, so is the iterative value estimate of the company through the year, with the passing of time providing an upward bias (e.g. larger cash flows are brought closer to the present with the passing of time, assuming the company is growing).[137] The time value of money nonetheless forms the backbone of why equity values generally advance over time, consistent with stock prices having drifted upward through the course of history (or the market factor). If you recall, Fama and French's three-factor model included the B/M ratio for value, size, *and a market factor* to try to explain the cross-section of stock returns, but both the B/M ratio and the size factor have since become less important considerations.

It's possible at times that the trajectory of the company's future free cash flow stream and its capital structure can experience more material changes as they are refined with the new information in the 10-K or 20-F. For example, if a company has engaged in value-destructive activities during the previous year (e.g. it has overpaid for acquisitions or bought back its own stock at egregious prices), this may show up more vividly in the new fair value estimate. On the other hand, if a company is a wise capital allocator, the company's balance sheet and future cash flow trajectory may have been enhanced from the previous year. This may cause an upward revision in the fair value estimate (sometimes by 10% or more), all else equal, once these value-creating buybacks are incorporated.

When rolling the model forward, there are a near-infinite number of drivers (factors) that could influence a fair value estimate of a stock, though changes in

---

[137] This point is worth emphasizing. Though the company is collecting cash as time passes, bringing future larger enterprise free cash flows closer to the present (they are then worth more), value and prices will always be an iterative function of future expectations. The time value of money only provides an upward bias to the iterative process, all else equal.

the balance sheet (specifically the net cash or net debt position) and revisions in the future enterprise free cash flow stream (revenue, earnings before interest, capital spending, working capital and other components) are among the greatest causes of change. However, most of the drivers behind a change in a fair value estimate resulting from rolling the model, should be operational (e.g. updating the cash flow trajectory and accounting for cash generated during the previous year as reflected in the updated balance sheet and/or lower share count).

It may not be wise to adjust a firm's cost of equity often or to adjust the risk-free rate frequently, even if such adjustments may happen in some cases, as these more subjective considerations could muddy a cleaner operating assessment of value. Though the fundamental-adjusted CAPM still has shortcomings, the very idea of a pure application of quantitative beta, which may be ever-changing with prices, almost precludes its use under any reasonable valuation framework.[138] Fair value estimates and, by relation, the enterprise valuation process is forward looking, meaning that when expectations of a company's future free cash flow stream are revised because of forward guidance revisions, or when a company pursues a transformative acquisition that will materially change its capital structure in the future, the fair value estimate should change accordingly.

The variables that may cause the biggest changes in the fair value estimate on an operating level are generally forecasts of a company's mid-cycle operating margin (year 5) expectations, mid-cycle revenue growth rate (year 5), and capital spending over the 5-year discrete forecast period (or what can be described as the first phase of the model). That is not to say that, if a company comes out with substantially lower revenue and earnings guidance for the current year than what the analyst had been modeling, there shouldn't be a downward revision in the company's fair value estimate.

The early years of the forecasts within an enterprise valuation model, however, generally do not impact the fair value estimate materially in most cases, but the information behind the revised guidance could influence the intermediate-term and even the long-term forecasts of the model (think "ripple" or "cascade" effect), and this would cause an even larger fair value estimate revision (in some

---

[138] According to Ibbotson, using a 60-month rolling cost of equity measure, the volatility of quantitative beta caused as much as a 10 percentage-point range in the cost of equity for small companies during the period September 30, 1970, through September 30, 2008, across the CAPM, CAPM with size premium, and Fama-French three-factor methods.

cases). Whenever the trajectory of the future enterprise free cash flow stream changes, the fair value estimate, which is based on the future enterprise free cash flows, changes, and generally so should the price of the equity.

Shortcomings of the P/E Ratio

Why the continued emphasis on cash flow in this work, and not earnings or widely-publicized EPS, the denominator of the P/E ratio? For starters, earnings or net income is just one component of cash flow from operations, which itself is one component of free cash flow, and the variations between earnings and cash flow not only arise in working capital changes over time (their influence on a company's cash flow from operations), but also in the timing of the cost of replacing those assets that generate earnings (capital expenditures versus depreciation). Earnings are too smooth and may disguise important cash movements of the company.

Varying levels of interest rates paid on debt can also muddy the water on earnings, not to mention that there are various analytical ways to account for rent expense (whether to capitalize such assets or to allow the expense to flow through the operating line).[139] Because earnings quality (are earnings being converted to cash flow?) and capital efficiency (how much capital needs to be plowed back into the firm to maintain earnings) are critical to assessing the health of a company and its valuation, using cash flow to evaluate companies is a much more comprehensive process, even if precision is not necessarily the goal. The denominator of the P/E ratio, itself, has significant shortcomings, but this isn't the emphasis in my highlighting the pitfalls of the P/E ratio.

An examination of the P/E ratio in how it is tied to enterprise valuation is critical to understanding the universal aspects of the enterprise valuation process. The P/E ratio is generally presented to investors in simplistic fashion as a price-

---

[139] To adjust rent expense of an operating lease to reflect an owned asset and its corresponding debt, rent expense (an item on the income statement) is typically capitalized at an 8x rent factor, a back-of-the-envelope adjustment that generally reflects an interest rate of 6% and a useful life of the asset of 15 years. This adjustment to capitalize operating leases in arriving at rent-adjusted leverage, for example, is similar in thinking to the dividend-adjusted leverage ratio (see Chapter 8), which "capitalizes" the dividend as a component of cash obligations to the dividend growth and income investor. (Hi Nathan--I know you wanted your name on page 100, so here you go buddy!)

observed ratio, but this view is incomplete. On a price-observed basis, the trailing P/E is calculated as the price per share of the stock divided by the annual net diluted earnings per share the company generated in its last fiscal (or calendar) year (or the trailing 12-month period). The forward P/E is the price per share of the stock divided by next fiscal (or calendar) year's annual net diluted earnings per share of the firm (or the forward 12-month period).

The P/E has probably become the most common measure to help investors compare how cheap or expensive a company's shares are, as stock prices, for lack of a better term, can be considered arbitrary, depending on share count. For example, firms like Warren Buffett's Berkshire Hathaway, which has never split its stock, have traded over $300,000 per share (it does offer B shares, however), while other well-known companies like Sprint can trade for just a few bucks per share. Citigroup was once a penny stock before its 10-to-1 reverse split in 2011, and Apple effected a 7:1 stock split June 2014.

It's only when investors compare a company's share price to its annual net diluted earnings per share that they can get some sense for whether a company's shares may be expensive (overvalued, overpriced) or cheap (undervalued, underpriced). The higher the P/E, it is believed the more expensive the company's stock, all else equal. The lower the P/E, it is believed the cheaper the company's stock, all else equal. The definition seems way too simple, so why the emphasis? Well, the truth is that the P/E ratio is not as simple as one might think (and even some of the most seasoned investors may be thinking about this valuation multiple incorrectly).

Some investors may evaluate a company's forward P/E ratio by comparing the measure to that of its industry peers to determine if the company is trading at a comparatively attractive relative valuation, a practice that differs from absolute valuation techniques, as in enterprise valuation.[140] If the company's P/E is lower than its peer median, an investor is paying less per unit of earnings than the median of its peer group. Investors may be getting a good deal for shares in this case, all else equal, right?

---

[140] A difference between the concepts of relative valuation and absolute valuation is important to define. Relative valuation applies the key metrics of related (other) firms in estimating a firm's value, while absolute valuation applies the unique characteristics of the exact firm one is evaluating in estimating its value.

Well, the problem is that companies are never equal, and even comparisons among companies that are in the same industry or that sell competing or similar products can be misleading. Such companies could have varying competitive advantages that may influence the sustainability of earnings, or require varying levels of reinvested capital to generate the same amount of earnings, or have varying capital structures and degrees of fundamental and financial risk, all considerations that should drive different multiples.

It may also be problematic for investors to apply a company's historical median (or average) P/E ratio to the same company's future earnings stream. Certainly, it's great for investors to have an idea of what "multiple range" a company has traded at in the past, especially for cyclical firms (mainly industrials) that may, from a fundamental standpoint, exhibit similar (but not identical) patterns with respect to both earnings and their P/E ratio through the course of each economy cycle: think Boeing and the commercial aerospace cycle; Ford and consumer demand for auto sales; or United Continental with respect to premium air travel demand.[141]

However, for less-cyclical firms (and even for cyclicals where structural industry dynamics have altered over time), investors may be wrongly assuming that the forward outlook of the past (which determined the historical multiple) will be the same as the forward outlook of the present (which determines the current multiple). This, unfortunately, will almost never be true. One wouldn't, for example, apply the same multiple to Apple's earnings in both 2002 and 2019, or if one did, it would obviously be for different reasons or underlying considerations. This again, points to the pitfalls of using backward-looking ambiguous ratio analysis in trying to explain returns.

Even comparing a company's P/E to the average market P/E is imprecise. A company is simply different from the aggregate market that includes companies from various sectors, so how can this comparison of one company's P/E to the market's P/E be significantly relevant, even if such a comparison provides some context of how the company may be trading relative to other stocks? The application of the P/E or relative value, by comparing one company's multiple to another, often becomes the key source of either systematic undervaluation or

---

[141] The P/E and other relative valuation measures can be used as a way to "triangulate" on a better fair value estimate within the enterprise valuation process, but used by themselves, the risk of using them inappropriately increases.

overvaluation tendencies, or when companies or even sectors can become mispriced in the event of the absence of absolute valuation, as in the enterprise valuation framework. Equities that are priced mainly on dividend yields are subject to systematic mispricings, too, as the dividend, itself, is a symptom, not a driver behind intrinsic value.

But how might systematic overpricings occur with respect to the P/E ratio, for example? Let's say, hypothetically, an analyst publishes a price target for home improvement retailer Home Depot based on peer Lowes' P/E ratio of 20 times. Home Depot jumps higher on the news and then overshoots to trade at a P/E of 25 times. Another analyst then publishes a price target for Lowes based on Home Depot's new P/E of 25 times. The market gets excited, and Lowes then surges to 30 times on the news. Then, another analyst sets another price target for Home Depot based on Lowes' P/E of 30 times, and so on and so forth. Meanwhile, both Home Depot's and Lowes' prices become wholly detached from an *absolute* estimate of their respective intrinsic values, as is derived in enterprise valuation. Though this is a very simplistic example, relative valuation approaches suffer tremendously from systematic overpricing risk that forms in such a manner.[142]

Introduction to Behavioral Valuation

Using enterprise valuation as a lens to interpret share-price movements and as a way to estimate intrinsic value are applications of the framework, but enterprise valuation has behavioral considerations, too, as many finance professionals use enterprise valuation in their work to make critical buying and selling decisions (nearly 79% use a discounted present value approach in equity valuation, according to a 2015 survey by the CFA Institute). The framework benefits from the absolute valuation anchor of public-to-private arbitrage, so it should not be considered a pure behavioral finance tool. This is unlike relative valuation processes, a subset of what I define as behavioral valuation, which can be viewed as the tendency for value investors to buy and sell stocks based on

---

[142] Systematic mispricings can happen when "yield-based" valuation approaches are pursued, too. In comparing equities based on their relative dividend yields, for example, the prices of companies with varying risk profiles and growth rates can drift away from an absolute estimate of their intrinsic value, sometimes materially.

valuation techniques that they believe are most often used by other value investors.[143]

The application of the P/E ratio might be one example of behavioral valuation. On the surface, adding the P/E ratio or a relative-valuation assessment to an investment methodology that already includes an enterprise valuation process may seem to make little sense, or at the very least seems redundant. Why, you may then ask, would a discerning investor use a P/E ratio at all in its process if the measure is so imperfect and can cause widespread problems, especially if its shortcomings may be well known?

Well, there is something more psychological at play, and the answer rests on the core of what drives stock prices: buying and selling activity by the largest investors.[144] Some institutional money-managers--those that have significant influence on stock prices--may pay more attention to a company's P/E ratio, or the price-earning-to-growth (PEG) ratio, in making buying or selling decisions. For example, according to the same survey by the CFA Institute, the most widely-used valuation multiple is the P/E ratio, used by more than 88% of respondents.

Though I view buying and selling based on the P/E ratio as "noise" within the pure enterprise valuation pricing framework, in classic Keynes' beauty contest fashion, if such measures are important to the buying and selling decisions of a great number of investors, they should also be important to one's investment decision-making process. Quite simply, many investors use the P/E ratio to make decisions, for better or worse, and as a result, there exists what can be described as self-fulfilling market forces (buying and selling) that make the P/E ratio a relevant "error" consideration to use in conjunction with the enterprise valuation process in a broader investment framework (more on this later).

In other words, if a portfolio manager likes a stock because its P/E ratio is trading at the lower end of its historical P/E valuation range or is trading at a discount

---

[143] In the text *Misbehaving*, Nobel laureate Richard Thaler posits that most money managers, whether value or growth, are just trying to purchase equities that will go up in value, meaning that they are trying to buy stocks that other investors will later decide should be worth more. The concept is connected to behavioral valuation, which extends to the analytical methods of money managers, themselves.

[144] It may seem contradictory to say that prices are driven by the causal nature of enterprise valuation, while saying that the most widely-used valuation metric in making decisions is the P/E ratio. However, its informative to think of enterprise value as the core pricing framework (the end game for prices) and the buying and selling based on the P/E ratio as pricing "noise."

to its peers' average P/E, the portfolio manager may buy it, and this buying pressure may cause the stock to rise, therefore making the P/E in this form a relevant "error" consideration for investors. This idea hits at the heart of behavioral valuation--developing an understanding of the market forces (value investment philosophies and value processes) that influence the buying and selling behavior that drive stock prices and returns. For this reason alone, a relative value assessment may be included in an investment methodology, as in the forward P/E and PEG (price-earnings-to-growth) ratios, more specifically, as in the Valuentum process (see Chapter 10).

The Theory of Universal Valuation

It is important to draw a distinction between a price-observed P/E ratio (as in observing the price per share and the accounting earnings per share of a company), and a value-derived P/E ratio, as that which is derived within the enterprise valuation framework. The difference basically comes down to saying that a company is trading at 20 times earnings, as in the case of a price-observed P/E ratio, and saying a company *should be* trading at 20 times earnings, as in the case of a value-derived P/E ratio calculated on the basis of its balance sheet and future expected free cash flows within the enterprise valuation context. A stock trading at 20 times may be cheap or expensive in the first case, but a stock trading at 20 times would be considered fairly valued in the second. The former represents the multiple that traders are currently paying for the company's earnings on the market, while the latter represents the multiple an investor might consider paying for a company's earnings to get a fair deal on the stock.

The "correct" P/E cannot be observed in the market, but rather it can only be derived, or rather estimated, through the process of enterprise valuation. The analyst arrives at an estimate of the company's intrinsic equity value as the outcome of the enterprise valuation process. In dividing that intrinsic value by diluted shares outstanding, the analyst then arrives at his estimate of the company's equity value per share. Taking this equity value per share and dividing it by next fiscal year's earnings of the company generates the value-derived forward P/E ratio (the value-derived trailing P/E can also be calculated using last year's historical earnings per share). The enterprise valuation process captures the unique intricacies of the exact company one is modeling at the exact time one is modeling it (and taking into consideration all future factors at the time), so it not as exposed to the potential for systematic "misvaluation" tendencies common in relative valuation practices.

The enterprise valuation explains why companies on the marketplace *should have* different P/E ratios, too. Have you ever wondered why capital-light companies (software, advertising companies) garner higher earnings multiples than capital-intensive companies (auto manufacturers)? Well, capital-intensive companies must reinvest a significant amount of earnings back into their businesses, thereby reducing future enterprise free cash flows, and by extension, the P/E multiple that investors are willing to pay for that earnings stream. Not all earnings streams are created equal, even given equivalent future expected growth trajectories in them. Investors should generally prefer the earnings stream that requires the least amount of re-invested capital, but it is not that simple either (as risk plays a role).

The enterprise valuation process uncovers situations where the health of a company's balance sheet impacts what might be considered a fair P/E multiple to pay for a company's earnings stream. All else equal, companies with billions in net cash should garner higher P/E multiples than companies with billions in net debt. The net balance sheet position is captured in enterprise valuation, but it is not apparent in any P/E multiple assessment that only considers a company's observed stock price and accounting earnings per share. A company's P/E could be elevated for only the reason it has a large net cash position, and a company's P/E could be low just because it has a huge net debt position. In neither case can the P/E reveal whether either company is fairly-valued, undervalued, or overvalued.

Without the application of enterprise valuation, placing a P/E multiple on a company's earnings to arrive at a target price may be mostly arbitrary. Even if that multiple is based on historical ranges (medians or averages) or is comparable to that of industry peers/rivals or the market as a whole, investors may fall short in capturing the uniqueness of a company's future enterprise free cash flow stream and balance sheet. The enterprise valuation process considers all the qualitative factors of a company, from a competitive assessment to the company's efficiency initiatives and beyond. In using an enterprise valuation process, investors think about the key valuation drivers of a company long into the future, as opposed to only a proxy of value for this year or next, as in earnings or EBITDA, for example.

Figure 10: Decomposing the P/E Ratio into the Enterprise Valuation Construct

[(Sum of Discounted Future Enterprise Free Cash Flows – Total Debt – Preferred Stock + Total Cash) / Shares Outstanding]

Next Fiscal Year's Earnings Per Share

The image above shows how the theoretical underpinnings of the P/E ratio rest in enterprise valuation.

The proof of the connection between the P/E ratio and the enterprise valuation framework, as shown in Figure 10, is paramount to explaining how enterprise valuation can be used as a lens to view market prices and changes. The numerator in the value-derived forward P/E ratio above defines how one calculates the fair value estimate of a company's shares in the context of enterprise valuation, while the denominator uses expected net diluted earnings per share, to arrive at the value-derived P/E ratio. Enterprise valuation "solves" what a company's shares should be trading at. It represents the multiple that should be applied to the company's earnings based on forward-expectations within the model.

Here is where the rubber hits the road: Exchanging the numerator, or the enterprise valuation equation, with price, as in the price-observed P/E ratio, the factors of enterprise valuation, the numerator of the definition above, then become the implicit drivers of a company's stock price. The drivers behind the value of the equity in enterprise valuation can be positively or negatively correlated to a company's intrinsic value, and therefore, its stock price, and the list on the next page may be more comprehensive than what many investors may point to as the main reason for varying P/E ratios between companies, the earnings growth rate.[145]

---

[145] It's possible the popularity of the price-earnings to growth (PEG) ratio may have misconstrued the many different reasons for varying P/E ratios, as the PEG ratio only rightsizes the P/E multiple to a company's annual earnings growth. There are many more factors that drive the P/E ratio than just earnings growth as the list in Figure 11 on the next page shows.

Figure 11: List of How Key Value Drivers Impact Share Prices[146]

Revenue Growth: Impacts Enterprise Free Cash Flows (Mostly Positive)

Operating Earnings Growth (EBIT): Impacts Enterprise Free Cash Flows (Positive)

Taxes: Impacts After-tax Earnings (EBI) and Cost of Debt (Mostly Negative)

Capital Expenditures: Impacts Future Enterprise Free Cash Flows via Net New Investment (Depends on RONIC)

Return on New Invested Capital (RONIC): Function of EBI and Net New Investment (Positive)

Risk-free Rate, 10-year Treasury: Impacts WACC (Negative)

Discount Rate (WACC): Impacts Present Value of Enterprise Free Cash Flows (Negative)

Total Debt: Impacts Enterprise Value and Discount Rate (Mostly Negative)

Preferred Stock: Impacts Enterprise Value and Discount Rate (Mostly Negative)

Total Cash: Impacts Enterprise Value (Positive)

Shares Outstanding: Changes in Shares Outstanding (Neutral, assuming reinvestments' RONIC equal the company's WACC)

---

[146] This list is not comprehensive, as theoretically, all future assumptions within enterprise valuation impact the value-derived P/E ratio and therefore the stock price.

It may only be regrettable that without the enterprise valuation framework, the P/E ratio that should be applied to a company's earnings stream may never be appropriately calculated by the investor to assess whether they are getting a fair deal. Interestingly, that enterprise valuation is poorly suited for comparative valuations is considered a limitation of the process by some investment professionals. However, it may be downright scary to now know that when investors use comparative valuation techniques, in assigning a P/E multiple to a company's earnings (based on historical trends or industry peers or the market multiple), they are essentially making estimates for all the drivers behind an enterprise valuation model in just one fell swoop (and hastily!).[147]

The takeaways from bridging the P/E ratio to enterprise valuation are more profound than just an exercise in tying two seemingly separate valuation techniques together. The process establishes the framework behind the Theory of Universal Valuation, the theme of this text, which generally states that value cannot exist in separate vacuums depending on which investment strategy one pursues, whether it is a quantitative strategy or whether it is a fundamentally-based, enterprise-value oriented strategy, or other. The enterprise valuation model transcends styles into quantitative factor-based methods and establishes universal value.

The enterprise valuation framework explains, for example, how a low P/E ratio does not necessarily mean a company is undervalued and how a high P/E ratio does not necessarily mean a company is overvalued, typical considerations in quantitative analysis.[148] Only when the value-derived P/E ratio is compared to the price-observed P/E ratio can a determination about value be made. If the value-derived multiple is higher than the price-observed multiple, the stock may be undervalued. The observed P/E ratio, however, could be a high P/E or a low P/E, and an understanding of this only further highlights the ambiguity of traditional quantitative processes. The enterprise valuation model also derives an implied EV/EBITDA metric, an implied B/M ratio, and a number of other

---

[147] Why do we then see the P/E so much in practice? Well, the P/E, itself, is just shorthand for what the enterprise valuation model implies. Multiples are helpful as a means of communicating value quickly, but they may not mean much if they aren't backed up with enterprise valuation.

[148] A tie-in to the efficient markets hypothesis may be relevant here. For example, random walkers may say that, in an efficient market, stocks with lower P/E ratios should be as likely to be undervalued as overvalued as stocks with high P/E ratios. The idea that the P/E ratio is not a deterministic consideration of a value, as revealed in enterprise valuation, makes this true, not that such a condition implies market efficiency.

metrics that would require a similar value-derived versus price-observed comparison to arrive at an informed statement about value.

There was a study shared by the Enterprising Investor, a blog of the CFA Institute, that collected data on four major stock indices: the S&P 500 (US), the FTSE 350 (United Kingdom), the Euro StoXX 300 (Europe), and the Nikkei 225 (Japan). The analysis compared stocks with the lowest P/E ratios against stocks with the highest P/E ratios over a period of 20 years, for both trailing 12-month ratios and forward 12-month ratios, separated into quintiles. In the US, UK and Europe, the researcher found that the lowest quintile of trailing P/Es did comparatively better than their highest trailing P/E counterparts, but that the performance of the lowest quintile of forward P/Es relative to their highest P/E counterparts wasn't as good as the outperformance of the trailing P/Es (and was even reversed in the US).

The researcher concluded "that trailing P/E ratios are far better value indicators than forward P/E ratios," and that this made a lot of sense because "all the studies on the value factor have been conducted with a trailing P/B and trailing P/E ratios, not forward P/E ratios" and that "relying on forward P/E ratios as a value indicator...can sometimes completely destroy the value premium investors seek to harvest." There are a number of issues with such a conclusion. First, the idea of using ambiguous data in hopes of harvesting a backward-looking-derived factor that may reappear again in the future, just because it was present in the past, has some shortcomings.

More pointedly, however, the enterprise valuation construct shows how the absolute level of the P/E ratio is not deterministic of whether a stock is undervalued or overvalued. Such a value determination can only be accomplished with a comparison between the price-observed P/E ratio and the value-derived P/E ratio, regardless of their absolute levels. A company with a low price-observed trailing P/E ratio could be undervalued as much as a company with a low price-observed forward P/E ratio could be overvalued (it all depends on their respective value-derived P/E ratios). The P/E ratio is ambiguous.

So, what might have been another takeaway from this analysis? Well, the conclusion might be better expressed that the absolute level of the P/E ratio, whether trailing or forward, may not be the best measure of value (or future expected returns), as logically, ambiguous data should not be more predictive of prices than causal data, even if future forecasts are inevitably proven wrong (share prices are still driven by expectations of the future, not the future reality, itself).[149]

The research may have only shown that the P/E ratio, whether trailing or forward, has significant shortcomings in the valuation context, as an investor will always be more interested in the long-term expected forward enterprise free-cash-flow stream of a company, regardless of what its earnings were last year. The unusual results of the study may be best explained within the enterprise valuation construct, not necessarily that backward-looking ambiguous data is more informative than forward-looking ambiguous data.

Enterprise valuation is not only central in explaining the peculiarities of some quantitative observations, but it also shows how growth fits into the value equation, and by extension, how categorizing stocks between "growth" and "value," as in a quantitative setting, or in traditional quant factor-based investing may be largely arbitrary, too, if not misleading. For example, a company such as Alphabet, which is growing fast, may be undervalued with a lofty double-digit P/E ratio, while a company with a single-digit P/E ratio such as IBM can be overvalued. As Warren Buffett once put it, growth is a component of value and the "very term value investing is redundant."[150]

Having been published a few years after Keynes' *General Theory*, John Burr Williams' *The Theory of Investment Value*, was among the collection of works in the 1930s, in addition to Graham and Dodd's *Security Analysis*, that challenged "beauty contest" or "musical chairs" thinking. By 1940, the frameworks for enterprise valuation and behavioral economics had already been established, in theory, but

---

[149] The blog post on Enterprising Investor hypothesized that the trailing P/E may be better because analysts tend to be overly-optimistic with their forward estimates, to the tune of 10%, on average. This data may be inconclusive (or over-generalized), however, as the percentage of earnings beats and misses may change drastically through the course of the economic cycle. In the third quarter of 2018, for example, FactSet reported that about 80% of S&P 500 companies reported a positive EPS beat and about 60% reported a positive sales beat. Analysts, at times, could be too conservative with forecasts, too.

[150] In Warren Buffett's 1992 Letter to Berkshire Hathaway Shareholders, he further explains how a low price-to-book, a low price-to-earnings ratio, or a high dividend yield, even if they appear in the same stock, are far from deterministic about whether shares of the company are truly undervalued. He goes on to say that even the opposite characteristics are not inconsistent with a company that may be truly undervalued. These multiples, and others like them, are insufficient.

a short decade later, quantitative researchers would come to the fore with empirical studies of ambiguous and impractical data.

Perhaps their perspective is best illustrated in the views of Treynor, who believed that what was needed in finance was a more objective approach to portfolio selection (which he believed meant statistical, as put forth by Markowitz in the early 1950s), rather than what he described as more subjective, judgmental work of the security analyst (even going so far as to say that the work of a stock analyst was "rough cut and not very quantitative"). Unfortunately, "empirical" doesn't mean what many believe it to mean, and objectivity within statistics only occurs after the subjective parameters of a study have been set (think model or parameter risk in the case of LTCM). But it is precisely those subjective parameters that matter in advancing our understanding of the markets, and it is in those parameters where the insights of any statistical methods can be gleaned.

In an article titled *"The Superinvestors of Graham-and-Doddsville"* published in the Fall of 1984 in the Columbia Business School magazine, Warren Buffett noted that the academic world had backed away from the teaching of value investing during the past three decades (1954-1984).[151] Richard Thaler noted that the popularity of Keynesian thinking had been on the decline in the 1970s, too, and Keynes' writings were no longer "required reading" by graduate students at the time. What were business schools teaching during this time then? Well, the obvious answer is something that they thought had already been proven, the efficient markets hypothesis, and if they then believed individual stock analysis didn't matter, one of the only other tools, if not the only other tool, was quantitative statistical methods. Hence, the explosion of quantitative research we see today.

The Theory of Universal Valuation, however, inextricably ties quantitative statistical methods (based on price observations of ambiguous and impractical data) to enterprise valuation (based on explicit forward expectations of the drivers of enterprise free cash flows), which in part drives buying and selling activity influenced by real-world public-to-private arbitrage. It also shows how enterprise valuation is not just a way to value a stock, but a lens in which to view the causes behind market

---

[151] The article revealed how many an investor that followed the principles of value investing as instructed by Benjamin Graham had tremendous performance track records. Buffett not only explained, without the aid of hindsight bias, the unusual outperformance of individuals that worked at Graham-Newman Corporation from 1954-1956, but also others that used Graham & Dodd investing principles.

prices and returns. The concept of enterprise valuation forms the Theory of Universal Valuation.

Residual Income and Banking Models

The shortcomings of book equity should almost preclude the reasonable application of the measure under most any analytical framework, even within residual income or economic-profit profit models. It's important to be more precise with my words, however, given how enterprise valuation is also theoretically connected to residual income or economic-profit frameworks. The enterprise valuation construct is driven by earnings before interest, after taxes (EBI), or its equivalent, net operating profit, less adjusted taxes (NOPLAT), which can be decomposed into Invested Capital x return on invested capital (ROIC), an exercise that, more generally (with some massaging), ties enterprise valuation to residual income or economic-profit models with the application of the weighted average cost of capital (WACC).[152]

However, Invested Capital isn't book equity, and it, too, can be measured with and without goodwill. Invested Capital and ROIC are therefore interdependent, revealing that EBI (NOPLAT), or cash flow, is often that which actually drives the function to solve for the other two, in most practical applications. For example, analysts are thinking more about expected earnings (e.g. EBI), particularly in the case of capital-light entities, than they are about driving those expected earnings in a valuation framework as a function of both Invested Capital and ROIC, directly, though all three are important.[153]

---

[152] Residual income or economic-profit models assume clean surplus accounting, where the ending book value equals the beginning book value plus earnings minus dividends, which may not be the case in real-world conditions. With some adjustments (e.g. RONIC = ROIC), however, the enterprise value construct theoretically becomes equivalent to the residual income and economic-profit model. Though this may generally not always occur in practice, the equal relationship speaks to the universal nature of enterprise valuation, itself.

[153] In models that forecast RONIC decay during intermediate stages, for example, it is often forecasts for fading EBI growth within the construct that, in conjunction with the theoretical support for a fading RONIC (i.e. declining competitive-advantage period), then solves for the third variable, the investment rate, defined as net new investment divided by EBI (NOPLAT). The investment rate can also be defined as the growth rate in EBI (NOPLAT) divided by RONIC.

Additionally, there are many instances in which Invested Capital for companies is negative, effectively limiting the usefulness of Invested Capital and ROIC as logical modeling drivers of EBI (NOPLAT), and residual income or economic-profit models, more generally. Within a residual income or economic-profit model, one would have to illogically assume a negative ROIC to drive a positive EBI (NOPLAT) in the case of negative Invested Capital, when the clear intention may just be to arrive at expectations for positive economic-value creation, based on expectations for positive EBI or NOPLAT,[154] an issue that does not occur in enterprise valuation. Future forecasted negative EBI (NOPLAT) within enterprise valuation, on the other hand, is informative and represents the expected value dilution in the near term.[155]

The analyst could possibly consider adjusting negative book equity such that it becomes positive in the residual income or economic-profit construct, and several of these adjustments might consider off-balance sheet items (capitalizing operating leases) or in the instances of certain intangible assets (capitalizing R&D for intellectual "know-how" and advertising expense for "brands"). However, to adjust book equity to economically reflect the intrinsic value of a company's brand (if the value of such an intangible is not properly reflected on the books as goodwill), almost any effort would have to consider how that brand impacts future enterprise free cash flow generation,[156] and therein lies the rub. If those future enterprise free cash flows are the best measure of economic value, then a

---

[154] For example, if we were to pursue the residual income or economic-profit framework for McDonald's, our starting point might be last year's book equity, an approximation for Invested Capital, which stood at -$3.27 billion (negative $3.27 billion) at the end of 2017. Where value might imply Invested Capital + [(Invested Capital x (ROIC-WACC) / (WACC-g)], the structure results in a meaningless negative value. Adjustments to book equity to make the measure positive rely heavily on the core construct of future enterprise free cash flows in enterprise valuation, itself, as in the case of adjusting for understated values of intangible assets (e.g. understated brand equity).

[155] This point is worth emphasizing. That future expected enterprise free cash flows are expected to be negative in the near term is an insightful consideration regarding the enterprise value construct. One shouldn't necessary pursue another method of valuation in situations where there is an absence of near-term positive enterprise cash flows. The timing and magnitude of those cash flows, whether positive or negative, matters.

[156] Interbrand releases an annual Best Global Brands Report, and one of the key components of how it estimates brand value rests in "the financial performance of the branded products or services." The importance a brand plays in customer purchase decisions as well as the brand's competitive strengths, as measured by customer loyalty, are two other more-subjective considerations in the methodology.

focus on those future economic free cash flows should be paramount, as in enterprise valuation.

In many ways, Invested Capital could largely be viewed as a placeholder in residual income or economic-profit models to scale up future measures of EBI (NOPLAT) using ROIC as the lever.[157] What matters is not necessarily Invested Capital, itself, as a meaningful component of enterprise value, but rather the return on invested capital and how that translates into EBI (NOPLAT). Because enterprise valuation considers the cash inflows and outflows of the business, it then becomes a much more intuitive valuation tool. It is much easier to evaluate whether future enterprise free cash flows make sense in a valuation context than to evaluate which ROIC to use, with or without goodwill,[158] and what adjustments to book equity may be needed such that it might be meaningful.

All this said, it may be worth explaining why I make the qualifying statement that book equity may only be irrelevant to operating, non-financial entities, not necessarily all companies.[159] The concept of cash flow is hard to conceptualize at banking-related entities, primarily because banks use cash to generate cash. Unlike a general operating, non-financial company where weight can be placed on the company's balance-sheet net cash position and future expected free cash flows, the survival of a banking entity, at pressure points during the economic cycle, rests more on market confidence than on the trajectory of pretax pre-provision earnings or even its capital position, in my view. If stakeholders and

---

[157] This is an important consideration. For capital-light entities, where initial invested capital may be minimal, for example, the value-driving consideration rests almost entirely in thinking about the trajectory of their future enterprise free cash flows, and then backing into what that may imply for ROIC based on Invested Capital.

[158] The general rule of thumb to consider whether a company's ROIC should be evaluated with or without goodwill may focus on expectations regarding the company's acquisition program. If, for example, prior management made a poor acquisition that resulted in considerable goodwill, but new management is not acquisitive, its operations may be better evaluated excluding goodwill on a forward-looking basis.

[159] It has generally been believed that negative book equity is a sign that a company may be financially distressed, but this isn't always the case for operating, non-financial entities (e.g. McDonald's, Boeing). However, because of the regulatory capital requirements of banking entities, they must hold adequate capital on the books, which makes the residual income or equity profit framework for such entities much more reasonable. In the case of banking entities, negative book equity may very well mean insolvency, unlike in the cases of operating, non-financial entities.

counterparties simply lose confidence in a bank's ability to remain a going concern, the bank will inevitably cease to do business.

The Financial Crisis, in some ways, may have reminded Wall Street that there may be no authentic way to value a banking entity. Banks, for one, use cash to lend to businesses and consumers, and it can therefore be argued that the only practical limitation to their business model rests in the limitations of cash available for lending. During the depths of the credit crunch of 2008-2009, the Fed and Treasury acted to partially nationalize[160] the biggest banks, in effect forcing them to accept new cash. This concept of moral hazard and the idea that the government stands behind the largest banks with a "bazooka"[161] of capital is something difficult to reasonably capture in any valuation context, including the free cash flow to equity model,[162] sometimes used to value banking entities.

For a banking-related entity, assessing the movements of cash going into and out of the business could be considered baseless when it comes to intrinsic value estimation, particularly in light of the implied federal government backstop should any large bank encounter trouble. A residual income or economic-profit model for banking-related entities may be inferior conceptually to the application of enterprise valuation for operating, non-financial entities, but it may be the only practical resource for systematic bank valuation, one that circumvents the issues generated by the arbitrary nature of banking cash flows.

In a residual income valuation (or economic-profit) model, a bank's current tangible book equity is generally grossed up or down by the discounted value of its forecasted annual net income less annual capital charges, the difference being economic profit. If a bank is expected to generate economic profits in the future, it should have a P/B ratio above 1. On the other hand, if the bank is expected to

---

[160] During the depths of the Financial Crisis, Treasury Secretary Henry Paulson ordered the top executives of the biggest banks in the country to agree to allow the government to purchase shares to avoid an impending collapse of the global financial system.

[161] In July 2008, Paulson told a Congressional panel, in reference to the magnitude of financing that would be needed to calm the deepening Financial Crisis, "If you've got a squirt gun in your pocket, you will probably have to take it out…If you've got a bazooka, and people know you've got it, you may not have to take it out." Paulson would eventually have to use more than just a "bazooka" to stave off the crisis.

[162] The free cash flow to equity model utilizes the cash available to equity holders in its framework, while the free cash flow to the firm model, or enterprise valuation, utilizes the cash available to all components of the capital structure, before backing into the value corresponding to a company's equity.

destroy value, it should have a P/B below 1. Book equity within a residual income model should act as an anchor for valuation, but I'd argue only for a small percentage of global equities.

The context of the residual income model for banking-related entities may offer some logical support for why there may have been some justification for the B/M value factor in previous quantitative works decades ago, but there are far more non-banking businesses than banking businesses. In today's fast-changing economy, business models have also evolved greatly, even over the past few years, and have become far more capital-light as software-based enterprises and cloud-hosted companies become more prevalent.

Buybacks and Intrinsic Value

Share buybacks are not always a good thing. The general rule of thumb may be that share buybacks reveal that management believes its stock is underpriced and that the executive team thinks there may be no better investment opportunities out there with firm money than its very own company stock, but while this sounds good, it doesn't always mean that share repurchases will benefit stockholders, or even create value in the long run. Management teams seemingly almost always believe their company's stock is undervalued,[163] and internal company projections that may estimate intrinsic value are subject to as much forecasting error and potential bias as any outside assessment, perhaps more.

A recent example of stock buybacks gone wrong happened with RadioShack, which in August 2010 went on a buying spree for its own shares, specifically announcing an accelerated share repurchase program in August 2010. RadioShack ended up filing for bankruptcy a few years later in February 2015, and then again in 2017.[164] The reasons for the company's demise are well-documented as it failed

---

[163] Perhaps the only time in my recollection that an executive team came close to saying its stock may not be attractive was in Netflix's third-quarter 2013 shareholder letter. The firm noted that its shares were being driven by "momentum-investor-fueled euphoria." That October, Netflix was trading under $50 each, on a split-adjusted basis. Little did management know that shares would hit over $400 in mid-2018.

[164] The example of RadioShack is a good one, not just for the pitfalls of buybacks, but also as it relates to the valuation context. First, in modeling, a company must survive into the long term for it to have any value attributed to the long run. Second, the price-to-sales (P/S) ratio is unhelpful in assessing underlying values. RadioShack generated sales all the way to Chapter 11. Many cite

to reconnect with its customer base in the face of increased competition from more innovative and forward-leaning enterprises. It was clear, in hindsight, however, that RadioShack shareholders would have been better off keeping the money that it had spent previously on buybacks. The takeaways of this one example are many: Not all buybacks are a positive sign, not all buybacks imply the company's shares are underpriced, and not all buybacks will generate value for shareholders.

Let's address where investors may get into trouble with traditional buyback analysis. Many market participants may believe that a stock's price will generally be re-capitalized at a certain earnings multiple based on its forward earnings per share, which, all else equal, will be enhanced as share buybacks are implemented.[165] The thinking goes that a higher earnings per share number multiplied by the same P/E multiple as before will equal a higher stock price than before. Unfortunately, this is not how value generation "works," as the simple mathematical framework ignores the concept of return on invested capital and an important source of value of any company: the balance sheet.[166]

Let's introduce another example. As recently as mid-2014, IBM believed it could attain $20 per share in adjusted operating earnings by 2015, a view that was supported in part by an aggressive share buyback program. Warren Buffett's Berkshire Hathaway may have based the ownership of shares at the time, in part that IBM had been a moaty company, but also that he'd own more of the company over time thanks to the buybacks. During the first quarter of 2014 alone, IBM spent a staggering $8.2 billion on share repurchases, but fundamentals were deteriorating. The same quarter revealed a 1% adjusted decline in revenue and a 22% decline in operating (non-GAAP) income, while revenue in its "growth" markets fell 11%. Management had been using buybacks to disguise underlying

---

the P/S ratio for causing the bubble during the dot-com era when analysts were engaging in suspect valuation techniques.

[165] Incidentally, the idea of capitalizing stocks based on an earnings multiple may be in part why investors fall for the "free dividends fallacy," where investors may wrongly believe they are getting something they didn't already have when they are being paid a dividend (see Chapter 8). Earnings are not impacted by dividend payments, and therefore capitalizing stocks based on an earnings multiple won't be impacted by the dividend, itself, hence the confusion.

[166] Oftentimes, we may hear a company's acquisition is accretive or dilutive to earnings per share. What matters, however, is whether a company's acquisition is value-creating or value-destroying, meaning its net impact on intrinsic value. As with buybacks, accretion or dilution with respect to earnings per share should not be a prime consideration in deal making.

operating deterioration, and what's worse, the company was executing the repurchases at value-destroying prices to do so.

Subsequent quarters at IBM were even worse, sometimes including large charges and lower-than-expected tax rates, two conditions that when combined with revenue weakness implied that earnings quality was deteriorating at a fast rate. It didn't take long before management came around to realizing that buybacks weren't going to save the day. In October 2014, after yet another abysmal fundamental quarter, the company pulled its operating earnings-per-share target of $20 by 2015. Poor earnings quality and arguably too much of a focus on earnings-per-share growth via buybacks likely led management to take its eye of the ball where it matters, economic value creation. Just a few years later, Warren Buffett would sell all his IBM shares.

Focusing too much on earnings per share can get even the most sophisticated investors in trouble. The enterprise valuation framework helps market participants determine whether share buybacks are value-creating (they add to the intrinsic value estimate of a company) or if they are value-destructive (they detract from the intrinsic value estimate of a company). It may seem that talking about the balance sheet with respect to buybacks, which seemingly only serve to enhance the earnings per share on the income statement, is a bit off topic, but the balance sheet is a source of company value, too, and the balance sheet is where share buybacks are financed, either from cash generated from internally-generated free cash flows or from newly-issued debt.

In most cases where companies have a simple capital structure, an intrinsic value estimate of any operating, non-financial equity is generally calculated as follows: the sum of the discounted future expected enterprise free cash flows to the firm (enterprise cash flow) are added to the company's current balance-sheet net cash position (or net debt is subtracted), and that sum (or difference) is divided by current shares outstanding. Share buybacks influence the enterprise value equation as follows: shares are reduced by the number of shares repurchased, and cash on the balance sheet is reduced by the aggregate cost of the share repurchase program (price paid per share multiplied by number of shares outstanding), which may influence the capital structure and the estimate of a company's WACC.

The net impact is either value-creating to the fair value estimate output (it increases it) or value-destroying to the fair value estimate output (it decreases it). It all depends on which change is more powerful. Either the impact of the reduction of the number of shares has a smaller positive impact on the fair value estimate than the negative impact of a reduction in cash on the balance sheet and changes in the WACC, or the impact of the reduction of the number of shares has a greater positive impact on the fair value estimate than negative impact of a reduction in cash on the balance sheet and changes in the WACC. Generally speaking, if share buybacks are completed at a price level that is below an estimate of a company's intrinsic value, the activity can be considered value-creating. If share buybacks are completed at a price level that is above an estimate of a company's fair value, they can be considered value-destroying.

These rules of thumb are very intuitive. Management, just like you and me, should seek to buy stock below its estimate of fair value, not to manage earnings-per-share targets.[167] On a go forward basis, the analyst may generally assume that future share buybacks to be completed at an unknown price in the future are generally fair-value neutral, which may be a reasonable expectation, until the buybacks are completed.[168] After all, if the analyst knew the price at which future buybacks would be purchased on the open market, then that would imply the analyst would be able to predict future prices with precision, rendering most financial analysis and the goal of enterprise valuation mostly irrelevant.

If the examples of RadioShack and IBM aren't enough, the cautionary tale of thinking that buybacks are always a good thing couldn't be more apparent than in the fallout of General Electric during 2018. The industrial conglomerate spent years shedding its financial assets following the Great Recession, perhaps a prudent move, but instead of reinvesting that capital prudently in other free-cash-flow generating enterprises, GE announced April 2015 a share repurchase

---

[167] A 2013 article by McKinsey noted that missing the consensus earnings estimate by a penny or so "just doesn't matter." The research firm studied a subset of Fortune 500 companies during 2010, and the impact five days after an earnings miss of 1% or so was practically negligible.

[168] This line of thinking can be extended to expected share issuances. Within the enterprise valuation framework, it might seem at times that it is required to forecast the number of shares (and the price at which a company will be able to raise equity) to offset enterprise free cash shortfalls in the near term, as in the case of a fast-growing upstart that is burning through cash, for example. The right move, however, is not to, as those negative expected enterprise free cash flows implicitly reflect the dilution that has yet to come. Other methods to capture the dilution effect may result in circular thinking, as in the words of Stern School of Business' Aswath Damodaran, the analyst "will need to forecast a price per share in future years to get an estimate of value per share today." Part of this circular thinking contributed to the bubble prices in Kinder Morgan and most MLPs during 2015, as analysts were not considering the full dilution of deeply negative near-term enterprise free cash flows. Instead, analysts were implicitly offsetting them via the assumption of external capital.

program to the tune of $50 billion, money that turned out was ill-advised to spend. By the end of 2017, it had bought back $29.1 billion worth of its own stock at prices, on average, that turned out to be more than double those where shares settled through 2018. By that time, however, GE had been forced to cut its dividend (twice in roughly a year, and three times since the Great Recession), had announced that it was under an SEC probe with respect to its accounting and could also face action from the Justice Department over subprime mortgages from years prior, and that it may need to raise additional capital, now at depressed prices.

The story with General Electric and its runaway and ill-timed buyback program is an important case study in value destruction, and it could happen to any company *and to any market economy*, in aggregate, even in situations where investors feel a company or market economy is even undervalued (Warren Buffett must have thought IBM was undervalued, for example). Though many tend to group buybacks and dividends together as cash collectively "returned" to shareholders, buybacks are quite different from dividends. With buybacks, cash is not going to the shareholders, even if earnings-per-share measures may be bolstered and existing shareholders own a greater percentage of the business as a result.

As with companies, buybacks act to lever up a market economy (think higher debt-to-equity ratios) and only make sense if repurchases can be had at bargain prices (not at any price). Given that the market isn't greatly inefficient most of the time, most buybacks can then be viewed as essentially value neutral within enterprise valuation.[169] The action of cash being removed from balance sheets, however, still happens (and option value[170] is reduced). Because buybacks amplify a market economy's leverage to both good and bad things, they can create unusual risks, particularly if a fundamental shock to a market economy (e.g. rising interest rates, reversion to less-favorable corporate tax policies) that lowers stock values occurs after a large buyback spending spree.

---

[169] The concept of value-neutrality with respect to buybacks is important to discuss. Because the future is inherently unpredictable and true intrinsic value can only be estimated, buybacks may only technically be value-creating or value-destroying when completed at prices outside a reasonable fair value estimate range (not an estimate of fair value, itself). If buybacks are completed within a reasonable fair value estimate range, which can sometimes be rather large depending on the stock, most buybacks should be considered value-neutral.

[170] The reference to option value in this sense can best be summed up as financial flexibility to take advantage of strategic or other opportunistic situations in the future.

Where the net cash resting on balance sheets prior to share buybacks would retain its value under any economic condition per enterprise valuation, a reset lower in stock values caused by higher-than-expected interest rates or a reversion to less-favorable tax policy, as examples, would effectively mute any perceived benefit from buybacks. Within enterprise valuation, net cash is a source of undeniable wealth of a market economy regardless of changes in future expectations. Once that cash is put to work in buybacks, however, the market economy becomes further leveraged, and should the value of the market economy be reset lower as a result of a change in future expectations (monetary, political or otherwise), those buybacks only compound wealth destruction. An extreme example might be to think about the irrelevance of buybacks on companies that eventually file for bankruptcy (e.g. RadioShack).

According to S&P Dow Jones Indices, S&P 500 stock buybacks alone totaled $519.4 billion in 2017, $536.4 billion in 2016, and $572.2 billion in 2015. In 2018, announced buybacks hit $1.1 trillion. Given all the global wealth that has been accumulated through the 21st century, it may seem hard to believe that another Great Depression is even possible. However, in the event of a structural shock to the marketplace where aggregate enterprise values for companies are fundamentally reset lower, the vast amount of cash spent on buybacks would only make matters worse. The money that had been spent on buybacks could have been distributed to shareholders in the form of a dividend or even held on the books as a sanctuary of value within the enterprise during hardship. Buybacks, unlike dividends, can result in wealth destruction in a market economy, much like they can with companies. This is an important downside scenario that is often overlooked.

6

The Greatest Contradiction of All?

The biggest commonality of stock market bubbles. Some ridiculous valuations. The two separate components of a non-falsifiable hypothesis. Is the market getting its own expectations correct? Getting to know the joint hypothesis problem. Introducing the next best alternative: The Price-to-Estimated-Fair Value Test. Thoughts on the CAPE ratio. If all information is supposedly factored into prices, as in efficient markets theory (and arguably the most critical information in setting prices is forward looking in nature), how can backward-looking factors based on realized ambiguous data be considered logical explanatory drivers behind stock returns? Another perspective on market arithmetic, and an overreliance on mutual fund data. How index investing drives market inefficiencies.

Stock market bubbles have several things in common.

The environment conducive to inflating a stock market bubble is usually one that's filled with excitement or euphoria about what the future may bring, for one. But before we cover other commonalities, what are bubbles? Well, bubbles can generally be defined as a situation when prices detach materially from underlying valuations, but what does this mean exactly? How does one measure value to determine if prices get out of whack? The efficient markets hypothesis may just wave its hands at such things, explaining stock price bubbles as some function of future expectations, any expectations. It doesn't matter how unrealistic prices may be, random walkers[171] believe that investors are incorporating information and

---

[171] "Random walkers" is a term giving to proponents of the efficient markets hypothesis.

fundamental expectations correctly, and such information is being appropriately factored into the stock price (give or take some random unrecognizable errors).

Some bubbles may be created by more willful means than others, with the deliberate intent to separate price from valuation. The stock market in the 1920s, for example, had been openly manipulated, and pools of wealthy investors often inflated the prices of stocks by artificially bidding them higher before offloading them at a profit to mom-and-pop investors that were out to make a quick buck themselves. The rather strange thing is that they knew the game was rigged, but they didn't care (as long as they were making money). During the dot-com bubble of the late 1990s, some analysts would seemingly compete against each other to make the highest target price predictions for stocks, rather than conducting objective analysis. It had been more important at the time to win investment-banking business, so analysts produced rosy reports often at odds with their own personal opinions.

Some bubbles, however, may have less to do with investor euphoria and open market manipulation and more to do with investors not applying a valuation context for their stock investments at all. During the "Roaring '20s," for example, market participants were certainly euphoric about the future, but many were following Ms. Adams' astrological advice, which had no bearing whatsoever on the concept of value at all, much less on that of enterprise valuation. John Burr Williams' *Theory of Investment Value* wouldn't be published until years later. In such a case, the stock price bubble that occurred leading to the Crash of 1929 could also be explained in some ways by investors ignoring some reasonable, or really any valuation context in their purchasing decisions.

But explaining bubbles is more than just explaining how market participants were buying and selling irrespective of some valuation context. Which valuation context? In 1998, for example, Morgan Stanley Dean Witter started assessing the values of some dot-com darlings based on eyeballs, or rather page views, something that was largely unconnected to any sort of free cash flow metric, or really any value metric at all. The research firm would say at the time about a report on Yahoo, "forty million unique sets of eyeballs and growing in time should be worth nicely more than Yahoo's current market value of $10 billion."

In this case, tying valuation to some arbitrary metric as eyeballs didn't hold much substance, and in retrospect appears rather strange altogether.[172]

During the housing bubble in the late 2000s, where everybody wanted to get rich by flipping houses, rising prices were perhaps being driven by systematic means (as loose lending facilitated almost infinite capital to those willing to take extreme risks). For example, if one house in the neighborhood sold for $500,000, another house might be listed at $525,000, and once that house was sold, the next might be listed at $550,000, and so on and so forth, with comparable analysis of prices being the primary driver behind the price appreciation.[173] In this case, comps became disconnected between any sort of logical value metric, whether based on a rent-equivalent analysis or other.[174] In other words, relative valuation or comparing similar instruments amongst themselves, with disregard to their absolute value, was in part responsible for the housing bubble in the late 2000s.

During 2015, most investors were valuing midstream energy equities based on metrics such as distributable cash flow, which ignores a key cash outflow in the enterprise valuation context (growth capital spending), or their financially-engineered distributions in dividend growth valuation models. A focus on distributable cash flow and the dividend led management teams to spend wildly on capital projects in order to keep those metrics moving in the right direction, appeasing the analyst (and income) community. But where the true costs of capital spending in valuation are largely ignored in the metrics of distributable

---

[172] The valuation methods that inflated the dot-com bubble are a big reason why I am generally skeptical of user or subscriber-based valuation methods, as in those perhaps popularly used to justify the valuation of a company such as Uber, for example. In a June 2017 post, Stern School of Business' Aswath Damodaran showed in part that disaggregated valuations as in user or subscriber-based methods could result in more subjectivity and assumptions than the enterprise valuation construct, itself. This line of thinking is similar to how investors that apply the P/E to a company's earnings may not know that, in doing so, they are making as many assumptions as they would within an enterprise model, but without scrutinizing such implicit assumptions to see if they make sense. Quickly applying a P/E ratio to earnings may be simpler, but it may just be wrong, too.

[173] Anecdotally, in search of a condo in Chicago during 2004, years before the housing bubble burst, the justification given to me by a seller was that the asking price "was only 5% over what he bought it for a few months ago." Though not likely the case in this instance, real estate transaction costs may be a contributing factor to systematic housing price advances, as each seller may embed commissions in the listing price just to break even.

[174] There are a few basic measures to assess housing values, including a house P/E ratio [(house price / (rent less expenses)] and the house price-rent ratio [(house price / monthly rent x 12)]. The capitalization (cap) rate may be most popular, however, and it is calculated by dividing a property's annual net operating income by the cost of property.

cash flow and a dividend supported by external financing measures, capital spending is captured in its entirety within the enterprise valuation framework (see Chapter 5).

Eventually, the Crash of 1929 happened. The dot-com bubble burst in the early 2000s. Housing prices flopped during the Financial Crisis, and the collapse in prices of midstream energy stocks happened during late 2015. What did all these bubbles have in common? It wasn't necessarily a detachment in prices from a general definition of fundamentals or valuation, as in relative valuation analysis, but rather a more pointed one. These bubbles happened because prices detached significantly from the reasonable application of enterprise valuation, despite full information dissemination. Even if markets are fully aware of all information, participants can still misuse that information, as in applying inadequate or ambiguous valuation frameworks, which can drive bubbles and therefore market inefficiencies.

Identifying bubbles continues to be an area of study captivating researchers, in light of the view that a systematic identification of such bubbles *in real-time* would provide even more evidence against the efficient markets hypothesis. There seems to be some evidence that investors can recognize bubbles when they are happening, but it turns out most may not care. A 2006 study, for example, surveying investors that bought technology stocks during the dot-com bubble in the 1999-2000 period suggested they did so even though they felt shares were overvalued (they just expected the price to continue to go higher). Another poll from Gallup in February 2000 suggested that nearly half of investors at the time thought the market was overvalued. Investors have some sense of when conditions can get overheated after all, but simply have no problem being greater fools,[175] it seems.

---

[175] "Puts forth the view that any price, as unrealistic as it might be, is warranted if one buyer believes that another buyer will pay an even higher price for the same item. This line of thinking drives stock market and commodity market booms and manias. Busts and paranoias jump in when the bubble pops." – Black's Law Dictionary

What Matters in Testing for Efficiency?

Efficient markets theory is a hypothesis that generally states "security prices at any point in time 'fully reflect' all available information," implying that any price is as good as the next and that prices generally reflect intrinsic value, give or take some unrecognizable random error. Infospace at $1,305 in March 2000, at the top of the dot-com bubble?[176] Reasonable. Netscape at 70 times revenue?[177] Okay. Lehman Brothers near the peak in 2007? Priced right. Yahoo at 1,400+ times earnings.[178] You get the point. The theory further supposes that it is impossible to beat the market on a risk-adjusted basis and that stock selection and market timing are generally fruitless endeavors. The hypothesis, in many respects, distills into two separate components: are stocks priced correctly, and if they aren't, why can't active fund managers consistently outperform the S&P 500? However, whether stocks are priced correctly is a distinctly different concept than whether a small subset of the corporate equity market such as active fund managers can outperform a benchmark consisting of the 500 largest US publicly-traded companies by market capitalization.

Regarding the first component, it would seem that the nature of outperforming public-to-private arbitrageurs (private equity returns, Berkshire Hathaway, etc.) would imply that stock prices aren't always priced correctly relative to their true intrinsic values. The misapplication of information within valuation models, or the use of inadequate valuation methods (e.g. the use of the dividend discount model to value Kinder Morgan and the MLP sector in 2015), would imply that stock prices may not even be priced correctly relative to the market's *own* expectations at times, even under the assumption that markets have all available information. This observation is key and where testing for market inefficiencies should rest, as it's not whether prices always "fully reflect" available information as much as it is whether the market is correctly using the information to set prices. Regarding the second component, the attention given to underperforming active fund managers, or perhaps the concept of the Arithmetic of Active Management, as written by Nobel laureate William Sharpe, makes assessing active fund

---

[176] Infospace's shares would trade under $3 by June 2002. At its peak, the company would command a market capitalization greater than $30 billion, more than Boeing's at the time.
[177] In 1995, Netscape would go public and see its market capitalization rise to $6 billion on a yearly revenue base of roughly $85 million.
[178] Yahoo's stock price stood at about $225 per share in January 1999, implying a P/E ratio of 1,406.

performance, one of the biggest sources of perceived support for efficient markets theory, highly inadequate.

In a world where only three types of stocks can exist--those that are fairly-valued, undervalued and overvalued, on the basis of a comparison between price and estimated fair value--the distribution of fairly-valued, undervalued, overvalued stocks on the global marketplace is likely to be undefined at any time, as both price and estimated fair value are non-static variables, both moving in successive time periods. Models that test for market efficiency or inefficiency must consider this notion. Fama's efficient markets hypothesis presupposes that the distribution of price returns of fairly-valued, undervalued, and overvalued stocks may be independent, identically distributed in successive forward one-time periods, but this may not take into account the core component of investing. That is, it may take each stock uniquely more than one period--not successive days or weeks or months, but rather sometimes years--to be categorically reclassified as a result of both price and fair-value-estimate movements (i.e. an undervalued stock's price advances to become fairly valued). That price returns may be independent, identically distributed in successive one-time periods across undefined sets of fairly-valued, undervalued, or overvalued stocks may not, or rather should not, translate into the view markets are efficient, or that stocks are priced correctly.

It seems only reasonable to assume that the time for a stock to theoretically move from undervalued to fairly-valued or from fairly-valued to overvalued, as examples, is and will always be undefined for each individual stock. In other words, to the viewer of stock price movements alone, shouldn't the observer only see randomness, whether those prices are truly random or not?[179] For example, that it took two years instead of two months for price-to-estimated-fair value convergence to occur in a stock should not make the original mispricing of the stock, or market inefficiency less true, even if successive price movements of the

---

[179] This is an important point. Many give credit to John Burr Williams' *Theory of Investment Value*, published in 1938, for shifting studies from the analysis of the time series of stock prices (i.e. forecasting stock prices) to an evaluation of the future fundamentals of businesses. The proliferation of quantitative finance more recently, however, suggests, in part, a reversion to pre-Williams financial theory. In the 1999 book, *The Psychology of Investing*, in Chapter 11, Steven Halpern refers to Warren Buffett as having said that investment intelligence has gone backward during the past four decades. It seems that, while the statistical methods and data used to analyze stock prices have advanced significantly since the Great Depression, the logic behind most quantitative theory may not have followed.

undervalued stock appear to be random to the observer during the convergence period.

Before talking about an efficient markets test, let's address a few related considerations. Random walkers may point to an inconsistency in a view where value investors somehow need the market to be inefficient, as in identifying a mispricing, and efficient, as in price-to-estimated-fair value convergence (or when prices equal fair value). However, this isn't necessarily a required condition to explain the markets, or value investing, in general, as stocks might move from inefficiency to inefficiency, too (e.g. undervalued to overvalued). Stock price movements based on new "news" should not be extended, in theory, to assume stocks are appropriately priced either. A mispriced equity can move on new "news" and reflect a further mispricing as much as an equity that may be more fairly priced move to better "accurately" reflect its "true" intrinsic value.

The idea of efficient markets, as in measuring whether stocks are priced correctly, could generally be evaluated on the difference between price versus *estimated* fair value (not true value), namely a test that measures the difference in expectations, a test that would capture modeling errors, and a test that would identify the conditions of bubble prices driven by inadequate valuation techniques. The proper test therefore comes down to measuring whether the market is pricing in its *own* expectations correctly, not whether those expectations actually come to fruition, per se, as in the case of true intrinsic value. True intrinsic value, because it is based on realized future expectations, of which have not been realized yet, might be best left out of the conversation.

The proper test may only consider whether stock prices accurately reflect what the market *should* think is a company's correct intrinsic value, and because of inadequate valuation techniques, a disconnect between what the market or analysts *believe* to be intrinsic value and what they *should believe* to be intrinsic value can exist, a market inefficiency. One prominent example where the test might flag an inefficiency may have occurred in 2015 when financially-engineered dividends were being applied within the dividend discount model, as in the case of Kinder Morgan and most MLPs.

But who gets to decide which valuation approach represents the correct model by which all prices are to be assessed against? In some ways, this is the primary reason why the efficient markets hypothesis has stuck around so long in financial literature. It suffers from the joint hypothesis problem. To test for market efficiency, an equilibrium asset pricing model[180] is needed, but there's no way to confirm that the equilibrium asset pricing model, itself, is accurate. Quite simply, the efficient markets hypothesis can't be disproven, or falsified. Some say a hypothesis must at least be testable (falsifiable), or else it cannot be a hypothesis or theory to begin with.[181]

Is this philosophical view enough to retire the efficient markets hypothesis for good? As the ranks of behavioral economists swell in the coming decades, it is possible. Until then, the next best thing may be the application of systematic enterprise valuation in a test of market efficiency. The enterprise valuation framework is the most robust method to capture future expectations, and whether those expectations make sense through explicit forecasting. During most observed bubbles, arguably, prices didn't just detach from fundamentals or some value metric in general, but more specifically, prices detached from *enterprise valuation methods*. The test may measure whether the price at time t eventually at some point in the future (time Φ) converges to estimated fair value at time t:

Figure 12: The Price-to-Estimated-Fair-Value Test

$$Fair\ Value\ Estimate = \lim_{t \to \phi} Price\ (t)$$

This figure explains that it is not price movement itself over successive time periods that may matter in evaluating efficient markets or inefficient markets but rather it is whether over an undefined time period for each company that price-to-fair-value convergence eventually occurs more often than not. The limit of function "Price" of t (time) as t approaches Φ is expected to be the fair value estimate. This represents a singular representation of price-to-estimated-fair value convergence, as the fair value estimate is also dynamic over time.

The Price-to-Estimated-Fair-Value test determines whether there may exist an elevated percentage of instances of price-to-*estimated*-fair value convergence on the market over various time periods, including multiple instances of price-to-

---

[180] The CAPM or Fama-French's three- or five-factor models can be considered equilibrium models. In the Price-to-Estimated-Fair-Value test, the enterprise valuation framework is used as the equilibrium model.

[181] Karl Popper, one of the greatest philosophers of the 1900s, held that the main criterion for separating science from non-science was the idea of falsifiability. Popper would say that theories that are not falsifiable are unscientific and that an unfalsifiable theory that is believed to be scientific is pseudoscience.

estimated-fair value convergence even with the same stocks over time (as fair value estimates change over time, too), implying inefficiency. The test would identify the instances where there may have been a mispricing, and whether such an inefficiency was "corrected" by the market over longer periods of time. I use the term "correct" to mean that the market comes to more appropriately value its *own* expectations.

It should not necessarily be whether prices reflect a "random walk" or "random walk with drift" in t+1, as in efficient markets theory, but rather whether prices reach an estimated fair value at some point at undefined time Φ. The limit of a company's stock price as t (time) approaches undefined time Φ should be the fair value estimate in more cases than not, in what might be called an inefficient market. Though there have been intriguing studies on the predictive power of *forward-looking* fair value estimates,[182] they are unfortunately quite few in number given the prevalence of target prices on Wall Street. There are even fewer studies that test systematic price-to-*estimated*-fair-value convergence based on enterprise-valuation techniques, with Valuentum's efforts in 2017 one study.[183]

The subjective element of the Price-to-Estimated-Fair-Value test may represent a valuable attribute for testing for efficiency relative to other equilibrium models (as in whether the market is factoring in its *own* expectations correctly), given that the test captures explicit future expectations, or the drivers of prices, similar to how the efficient markets hypothesis considers future expectations, except in its case, they are only implied. Proponents of the efficient markets hypothesis generally may believe that prices theoretically capture future expectations best (or that all available information is being "correctly" factored into the prices), but this must also assume unrealistically a frictionless environment where capital is readily-available to the very best capital allocators to "set" prices and that systematic mispricings caused by inadequate valuation techniques cannot be

---

[182] In a study published in the October/November 2013 edition of *Morningstar Advisor*, the research firm found that the outperformance of undervalued stocks calculated by the enterprise value method during the period January 2003 through March 2013 were statistically significant at the 1% level, even after controlling for key variables such as the book-to-market ratio, size, volatility, and momentum.

[183] The study in this paper revealed a higher rate of price-to-estimated-fair value convergence for both undervalued and overvalued stocks, in aggregate (59%), as defined by the enterprise valuation process, than what otherwise might have been expected under "random walk" or efficient market theory. See Notes to read more about the conclusions of this study.

recognized despite full information dissemination, as in what happened with Kinder Morgan and the MLPs during 2015.

At the very least, the concept of the Price-to-Estimated-Fair-Value test could be considered a better theoretical model in testing for market efficiency than perhaps just embracing the randomness of successive one-period martingale or submartingale[184] views on security prices as justification for the view that prices equal true or even estimated intrinsic value with some random error. The point that the Price-to-Estimated-Fair-Value test measures variant expectations (e.g. errors in factoring in expectations) as reflected in the price, is an important point of emphasis, distinct from a test that measures price versus true intrinsic value, where hindsight bias may be applicable. In short, the test measures where the markets may trip themselves up with their own valuation mistakes, not necessarily whether markets can predict the future with precision.

But the enterprise valuation framework and efficient markets hypothesis aren't completely inconsistent. The idea of a submartingale for security prices does not clash with the value composition of the enterprise free cash flow model, where value estimates, all else equal, advance over time and cash is collected, what may be considered the foundational element in support of long-term index investing (i.e. stock prices have an upward drift). In other words, an inefficient market may behave exactly like the one determined to be efficient, possessing submartingale properties. In studies where a high rate of price-to-estimated-fair value convergence for both undervalued and overvalued stocks may occur, the price behavior in those studies would not necessarily have to be different than the same price behavior supporting random-walk theory.

---

[184] A submartingale is generally defined as a stochastic process, in which the expected value in the next period is greater or equal to the current period's value. The time value of money property within enterprise valuation is consistent with observed submartingale properties of equity prices.

Figure 13: Same Prices – Efficient or Inefficient Market?[185]

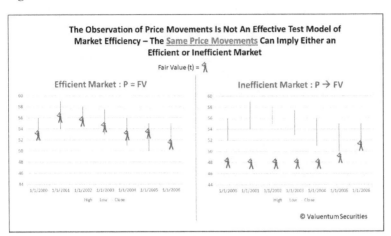

The image above shows how the observed behavior of prices can be the same in an efficient market as in an inefficient one. The lines, prices, reveal identical behavior, but expectations of intrinsic value are changing. In the efficient market, value (baseball batter) is always on the line (price). In an inefficient market, the value eventually converges to the price. However, the price behavior is identical in both markets.

From a practical standpoint, if the enterprise valuation framework does not necessarily contradict the view equity values and prices may have an upward bias over the long run, as in the merits of index investing, why then should the investor even care whether markets are inefficient or efficient? Well, where long-term index investing may fit well into modern portfolio theory and long-term financial planning, in assessing how the stock market has performed in the past and how it may be expected to perform in the future, enterprise valuation not only offers a framework as to *why* stock prices may advance into the future, but it also reveals

---

[185] This is where the conversation regarding the efficient markets hypothesis approaches the non-falsifiable component. Random walkers may say that market efficiency does not necessarily require the market price to be equal to true value at every point in time. The market can have errors if those errors are random, too. Therefore, to satisfy conditions of the hypothesis, not only would there have to be an objective equilibrium model that identifies stocks that are fairly-valued, undervalued and overvalued (a resolution of the joint hypothesis), but that in situations where there are value deviations from the price--or the market's "unbiased" estimate of fair value--these errors would also be unbiased and random (the application of the equilibrium model satisfying the joint hypothesis). Efficient markets theorists, it seems, are very good at defending a non-falsifiable hypothesis. The Price-to-Estimated-Fair Value test pays no mind to the concept of true intrinsic value, but rather whether the market's estimate of true value in the price is different than what the market's estimate of true value *should be*, applying enterprise valuation as the equilibrium model.

how the interaction of the drivers can result in declining fair value outcomes, too, as in the declining fair value of an index, for example, and by extension, declining prices. In this light, the difference may be profound.

For example, there may be research that shows how equity prices have performed relative to changes in interest rates, and that in the past there may have been periods where equity prices advanced while interest rates increased.[186] Though this may be true at certain points in history, it's also informative to view interest rates in the context of the ceteris paribus assumption, or all else equal, with other conditions remaining the same. In such studies, it may be very difficult to back out or adjust for the impact of expectations of improving fundamentals that may be contemporaneous with a rising interest-rate environment,[187] as such expectations can theoretically completely offset the negative impact of a higher discount rate. Within the enterprise valuation framework, however, the analyst can hold everything else constant and adjust the interest rate to evaluate the impact on the estimated value of the equity, or an aggregate market. Under a higher discount rate (higher benchmark interest rate and/or wider credit spread), equity values adjust lower, all else equal.[188]

The idea of presenting the enterprise valuation framework in the context of efficient markets hypothesis, as in the Price-to-Estimated-Fair-Value test, is to help move the discussion in finance away from studying the behavior or movements of prices alone and more to the behavior of price-to-estimated-fair value ratios over longer duration time periods as tests for market and information efficiency. Incidentally, this concept may be somewhat connected to Shiller's cyclically adjusted price-to-earnings ratio, or the CAPE ratio, which measures

---

[186] Investing columnist Josh Brown noted in a May 2015 Fortune article, using data going back to 1976, that S&P 500 stocks tend to do better in the one-year periods leading up to and after rate-hike cycles, and that returns for stocks during rate-hike cycles, while below average, were still positive.

[187] In the "real world," there is no such thing as "all else equal," as changes in one variable often have implications on another, which may impact something else and so on. However, causality is an important consideration. For example, if stock prices have still increased during various periods of rising interest rates, it does not mean that rising interest rates are good for stock values and prices. Josh Brown noted in the study of credit cycles since 1976 that stocks typically do worse than average during the rate-hike cycles, themselves (Brown 2015).

[188] The higher discount rate in this case is typically referred to as the "denominator" effect of rising interest rates on equity values. During periods of rising interest rates, the "denominator" effect has shown to have a greater impact than the "numerator" effect (i.e. expectations of higher profitability and growth).

changes in a long-term P/E ratio, using the current stock price of an index and the average of the *prior* 10 years of earnings of that index. The Shiller P/E has shown reversion-to-the-mean behavior over time, but unlike forward-looking enterprise valuation, the CAPE ratio is backward-looking and uses GAAP earnings, meaning it suffers from the same pitfalls of most quantitative research applications when it comes to having predictive value.

In other words, the CAPE ratio does not account for structural changes in the data that influence the future expected enterprise free cash flow streams or underlying value composition of equities and therefore their prices. In the event of corporate tax cuts, one might expect the CAPE ratio, which is primarily based on the average of the last 10 years of earnings, which did not benefit from corporate tax cuts, to be much higher than in years' past, as investors look to better earnings in the future as a result of a lower tax burden in setting prices. Further, all else equal, one might expect the CAPE ratio to be impacted by any number of the measures impacting the P/E ratio itself, not the least of which is non-earnings-specific items, including changes in interest rates. The backward-looking nature of the CAPE ratio makes it less predictive under situations when structural changes occur, ones that *should* reset intrinsic values and therefore prices (and the CAPE ratio) to a higher or lower threshold, respectively.

Logical Inconsistencies of Efficient Markets Hypothesis and Factor Investing

Random walkers may say that investors may have been pricing in an impending recession prior to the Crash of 1987, which in turn, may have impacted future fundamental expectations to actually cause the Crash of 1987, resetting values. That the value of the market changed 20% overnight is perfectly plausible to them. Efficient market theorists may also say that prices of tech stocks in the dot-com bubble were reasonable because "most people were saying the Internet was going to revolutionize business, so companies that had a leg up on the Internet were going to be very successful." These two examples point to how the efficient markets hypothesis generally cannot be falsified (as everything can just be explained away as a function of future expectations), questioning whether it as a testable hypothesis altogether.

However, if the support for efficient markets hypothesis, as explained in the case of bubbles, rests primarily on future expectations, it brings up a very damaging consideration as it relates to backward-looking factors based on *realized* ambiguous data. If all information is supposedly factored into such prices, as in efficient markets theory (and arguably the most critical information in setting prices is forward looking in nature), how can backward-looking factors based on realized ambiguous data be considered logical explanatory drivers behind stock returns?[189] They can't, and the very idea that backward-looking factors based on realized ambiguous data aren't necessarily capturing what they are intending, as in the traditional B/M value factor, for example, should only add a greater degree of skepticism. Going wherever the data takes you, as in the case of data mining, can be perilous, as Gabrielle Baum and Gary Smith noted in their paper, *Great Companies: Looking for Success Secrets in All the Wrong Places*:

> Statistical tests assume that a researcher starts with a theory, collects data to test the theory, and reports the results--whether statistically significant or not. However, many people work in the other direction, scrutinizing the data until they find a pattern and then formulating a theory that fits the pattern. Ransacking data for patterns is fun and exciting--like playing Sudoku or solving a murder mystery. Examine the data from every angle; look for something, anything that is interesting; after a pattern is discovered, think about the reasons behind it.

> This pillaging is known as data mining (or data grubbing, data dredging, fishing expedition). The problem with this approach is that even random coin flips from patterns that appear to be meaningful but are, in fact, meaningless. When a fair coin is flipped 10 times, a streak of four heads in a row (or four tails in a row) seems too remarkable to be explained by chance, although streaks this long, or longer, can be expected 47% of the time. One may think something must be unusual about the coin or the

---

[189] It may be worth emphasizing the critical difference between implied expectations as observed in prices in quant applications and explicit expectations as determined within enterprise valuation. For example, an observer of a low B/M ratio cannot make a determination about what is implied with respect to future expectations by just looking at that measure, by itself. Therefore, the B/M ratio should not be considered a predictive variable, given other potentially confounding variables that drive its ambiguousness. See Jiang (2017) about how low B/M ratios can be a function of "high growth and moderate ROIC, low growth and high ROIC, or high growth and high ROIC," for example. The enterprise valuation framework, on the other hand, explicitly captures these future expectations.

person flipping the coin and thus underestimate the importance of luck. This is instead another version of the Texas sharpshooter fallacy, in which a person with no talent for shooting fires randomly at the side of a barn and afterward, paints a bullseye around the cluster of bullet holes.

Even randomly generated data typically contain clusters and, should an explanation for a particular cluster be sought, it will inevitably be found. In a cancer study, for example, one might discover that several cancer victims happened to live near power lines, a Little League field, or a water tower--which proves nothing at all. Data mining demonstrates little more than a researcher's endurance. Data without theory is treacherous, and one should be deeply skeptical of any supposed results gathered through data mining.

Stock prices are a function of future expected data, an important building block of finance, consistent with the efficient markets hypothesis and enterprise valuation, but with far-reaching ramifications on backward-looking factor-based research, of which has been growing in popularity in the field of finance for the past couple decades. This is not to say realized fundamental data (e.g. net cash within enterprise valuation) or realized pricing data (e.g. a "technical pattern") that may influence future buyer behavior cannot be an important factor of future stock price returns, but realized fundamental or pricing data, by itself, if not logically connected to future buying or selling decisions, cannot reasonably be considered a logical explanatory factor of stock returns.

It's the market's expectations of future data, *realized or not* (e.g. in the case of a bubble, overly optimistic future data that is not realized), that's important when it comes to explaining stock returns. Future expected data that is realized or not also logically captures the human behaviors of greed and fear. That the general approach of most factor-based analysis, however, is based on backward-looking ambiguous and sometimes impractical data (e.g. t-1, B/M ratio from last year), but also based on *realized* data (which may or may not be tied to prices, as prices are driven by expected data, realized or not) are huge theoretical shortcomings and ones that are even inconsistent with the efficient markets hypothesis.

In certain cases, the term "empirical," as in the application of backward-looking ambiguous analysis, becomes equivalent to "wrong." Either the efficient markets hypothesis doesn't hold, or most backward-looking factors may not hold, but it may be most logical to assume that both may not hold. Market anomalies[190] derived through backward-looking processes based on ambiguous multiple analysis or impractical data generally should not be expected to continue.

As the theoretical underpinnings of finance evolve, particularly as behavioral thinking is increasingly embraced, I would not be surprised to bear witness to a Copernican shift from backward-looking approaches to forward-looking approaches. Quantitative methods can just as easily be applied to forward-looking expectations as they can with backward-looking ambiguous or impractical data, and it is within the subset of forward-looking information where price behavior can be explained. Even random walkers should agree. Such a Copernican shift may be decades away, however, if the time it took for many in the financial community to embrace behavioral thinking is any indication.

Nonetheless, I believe the shift will happen.

Rewriting the Arithmetic of Active Management to the Investor Level

It was 1973, and a Princeton economist by the name of Burton Malkiel had just published *A Random Walk Down Wall Street*, a book that would turn into one of the most influential studies in support of the efficient markets hypothesis. Malkiel's book would suggest that asset prices typically exhibit signs of a random walk, and as a result, an investor could not consistently outperform market averages in part due to powerful reversion-to-the-mean tendencies: "…the market prices stocks so efficiently that a blindfolded chimpanzee throwing darts at the *Wall Street Journal* can select a portfolio that performs as well as those managed by the experts." Others have subsequently hypothesized that monkeys might even do better than the experts.

A few years following the original publishing of Malkiel's work, the book's popularity would add support for the launch of the first "passive" index fund, and the ideas within it would serve as the foundation for indexers far and wide

---

[190] The underpinning of most traditional quant factors that are derived by backward-looking ambiguous or impractical data rests on the idea that an anomaly will continue in the future. There may be no basis for such a view.

for decades. According to the Investment Company Institute, as of the end of 2017, hundreds of index mutual funds manage a collective sum of $6.7 trillion. Index mutual funds' share of total net assets[191] has swelled to 18% at the end of 2017 from just 9% in 2007. The percentage of assets passively managed (both funds and ETFs) has advanced to 35% of total net assets from just 15% prior to the Financial Crisis. Much of popular finance has generally operated under the following assumptions of the arithmetic of active management, with variations of such arithmetic being reproduced during the past several decades in many forms and formats.

Figure 14. Sharpe's Arithmetic and Bogle's Syllogism

> If "active" and "passive" management styles are defined in sensible ways, it must be the case that
>
> (1) before costs, the return on the average actively managed dollar will equal the return on the average passively managed dollar and
>
> (2) after costs, the return on the average actively managed dollar will be less than the return on the average passively managed dollar. (Sharpe 1991)

> 1. All investors own the entire stock market, so both active investors (as a group) and passive investors—holding all stocks at all times—must match the gross return of the stock market.
>
> 2. The management fees and transaction costs incurred by active investors in the aggregate are substantially higher than those incurred by passive investors.
>
> 3. Therefore, because active and passive investments together must, by definition, earn equal gross returns, passive investors must earn the higher net return. QED. (Bogle 1999)

---

[191] According to the Investment Company Institute, total stock market capitalization for passive and active mutual funds and ETFs was 29% of the U.S. stock market in 2017. The balance is held by hedge funds, pension funds, life insurance companies and individuals. This percentage is slightly different than Goldman Sachs data discussed later (30%), but both reveal how small mutual fund/ETF holdings are to the stock holdings of individuals and other institutions.

It's perhaps not obvious, but also consistent with such syllogisms that some investors can and do outperform a market benchmark (index), and some consistently so. The syllogisms above, which don't quite describe the market from the perspective of the investor, assess outcomes in terms of "average dollars" and in "aggregate returns," respectively, and not on the number of investors (percentage of active investors, or average returns of those investors), arguably what matters most. For illustrative purposes, and to show the hazards that may materialize from oversimplified generalizations of the stock market, a hypothetical example shows how 80% of active funds (and an even larger percentage of active investors) can exceed a market return after fees and transaction costs in a given year.

Figure 15: Extreme Proof -- Active Management at the Investor Level[192]

Fund Type	Number of Investors in Fund	1-Jan	31-Dec - prior to the deduction of fees	Total Gain - prior to the deduction of fees	Fees	Total Gain after Fees	Active Gross Return	Active Net Return	% of Active Investors Earning Active Net Return
Active Fund 1	100	1,000.0	1,212.0	212.0	12.1	199.9	21.2%	20.0%	12.2%
Active Fund 2	100	1,000.0	1,212.0	212.0	12.1	199.9	21.2%	20.0%	12.2%
Active Fund 3	100	1,000.0	1,212.0	212.0	12.1	199.9	21.2%	20.0%	12.2%
Active Fund 4	100	1,000.0	1,212.0	212.0	12.1	199.9	21.2%	20.0%	12.2%
Active Fund 5	100	1,000.0	1,212.0	212.0	12.1	199.9	21.2%	20.0%	12.2%
Active Fund 6	100	1,000.0	1,212.0	212.0	12.1	199.9	21.2%	20.0%	12.2%
Active Fund 7	100	1,000.0	1,212.0	212.0	12.1	199.9	21.2%	20.0%	12.2%
Active Fund 8	100	1,000.0	1,111.0	111.0	11.1	99.9	11.1%	10.0%	12.2%
Active Fund 9	10	100,000.0	98,000.0	-2,000.0	980.0	-2,980.0	-2.0%	-3.0%	1.2%
Active Fund 10	10	100,000.0	95,000.0	-5,000.0	950.0	-5,950.0	-5.0%	-6.0%	1.2%
Total Active Investors (aggregate)	820	208,000.0	202,595.0	-5,405.0	2,026.0	-7,431.0	-2.6%	-3.6%	100.0%
Total Active Investors (average)		Weighted average return of all active individual investors (18.2%) ⟶						18.2%	100.0%
		Aggregate net percentage return is greater for passive (-2.6%) than active (-3.6%)							

Fund Type	Number of Investors in Fund	1-Jan	31-Dec	Total Gain	Fees	Total Gain after Fees	Passive Gross Return	Passive Net Return	% of Passive Investors Earning Passive Net Return
Index Fund (aggregate)	300	50,000.0	48,700.7	-1,299.3	1.0	-1,300.3	-2.6%	-2.6%	100.0%
Total Passive Investors (aggregate)	300	Aggregate gross percentage return is equal for both active and passive (-2.6%)						-2.6%	100.0%
Total Passive Investors (average)		Average active investor's return (18.2%) is greater than the average passive investor's return (-2.6%)						-2.6%	100.0%

By illustrating how both the majority of active funds and the majority of investors can outperform a broad market index, this figure shows how the arithmetic of Sharpe (1991) and the syllogism of Bogle (1999) may not be perfect representations of the stock market on the investor level.

In the rather extreme proof in Figure 15, there are 10 actively-managed funds (Active Fund 1, Active Fund 2, and so on) and one index fund (Index Fund). The stock market, as measured by the gross return of the 'Index Fund' fell approximately 2.6%, matching the aggregate gross decline of all actively-managed funds (-2.6%). Assumed in such an example is that active funds, in aggregate, performed worse than the 'Index Fund,' consistent with such syllogisms, as a

---

[192] This extreme proof assumes that mutual funds represent the entire corporate equity market. I have expanded this analysis to the entire corporate equity market later in this text.

result of the deduction of fees and expenses. Such a comparison, however, matters little to the investors of either Active Fund 1, or Active Fund 2, or Active Fund 3 and so on through Active Fund 8, all of which outperformed the return of the Index Fund. The biggest active funds in this hypothetical example, Fund 9 and Fund 10, vastly underperformed the market's return.[193]

In the hypothetical illustration, 80% of active funds outperformed the return of the 'Index Fund' after fees and expenses, and active funds generated an *average return*, equal weighting the return of each active investor (not fund), of 18.2% (including the poor performance by investors in Active Fund 9 and Active Fund 10), even as the aggregate net return of active funds was -3.6%, below that of the aggregate net return of -2.6% for the 'Index Fund,' again due to the deduction of fees and expenses. As the number of investors that held Active Funds 1-8 significantly exceeded the number of investors that held Active Funds 9-10, as shown in the example, a far greater percentage (number) of active investors outperformed the 'Index Fund' after fees and expenses than even the percentage of active funds that did.

In light of this extreme proof, one might suggest that a more logical (and fairer[194]) pie theory of the stock market might consider average investor returns and read from the perspective of the investor, as follows.

Figure 16: Nelson's Syllogism of the Stock Market

1. All investors own the stock market.

2. The aggregate returns of all investors after all fees and expenses do not equal the average returns of all investors after all fees and expenses (as shown in Figure 15).

3. In any given year, the probability that the average return of all investors after all fees and expenses will be more or less than the aggregate return

---

[193] Though I have labeled this proof "extreme" for illustrative purposes (underperforming Funds 9 and 10 are abnormally large), there is some evidence that "asset bloat" or when stock funds, in particular, become too large, their ability to react quickly to market events or capitalize on new or smaller ideas becomes diminished. When it comes to equity funds, there is a disadvantage to asset size, something magnified in this "extreme" proof.

[194] The goal in presenting Nelson's Syllogism of the Stock Market is to provide a fair and unbiased representation of the stock market to investors.

is not defined. Each passing year has a unique outcome, independent of the past.

4. The percentage of investors outperforming the index after all fees and expenses can be greater or less than the percentage of investors underperforming the index after all fees and expenses in any given year, every year.

It is not immediately clear why Sharpe's arithmetic and Bogle's syllogism view the market in terms of "average dollars" and in "aggregate returns," respectively, and not on the investor level, which arguably is what matters most to the investor. In the work of Sharpe, the possibility of active outperformance is mentioned, but the work does not extend the view that those that may "manage a minority share of the actively managed dollars" can also possibly comprise a majority share of investors. In *Common Sense on Mutual Funds*, Bogle reveals that during the years 1963-1998, the S&P 500 Index outperformed the majority share of mutual funds in 8 more instances than it was outperformed by the majority share of mutual funds over the 36-year period. If only four years out of 36 had gone the other way, the distribution between active and passive outperformance would be even. Bogle notes there were also three major periods in which the S&P 500 Index lagged the average return of a mutual fund during the time period studied, 1965-1968, 1977-1980, and 1991-1993.

It may be clear that the case for indexing could be compelling at certain points during the economic cycle, but it is not an absolute certainty, or a "self-evident certainty," as in Bogle's words. Indexing's popularity recently may instead be a function of misunderstood randomness or the drivers behind the gambler's fallacy, perhaps exacerbated by the presence of recency bias, as the majority of large-cap, mid-cap, and small-cap managers have more recently trailed their respective benchmarks, after fees. With the gambler's fallacy, an investor may believe that indexing may continue to outperform because it has in the past (hot streak), or an investor may believe that active funds may now be due to outperform (self-correcting). The reality is that the distributions of future performance may be completely independent from the past. Every new year is different, just like every flip of a fair coin. Recency bias occurs when investors place too much weight on what has happened in the near past and forget about what may have occurred even further back, or during 1965-1993 as it relates to index funds, for example.

The streaks of outperformance and underperformance for both the majority of active funds and the S&P 500 Index, respectively, brings up an interesting consideration. Said plainly, if a 15-year consecutive streak of beating the market's return, as in Bill Miller's Legg Mason Value Trust,[195] for example, can be considered luck in some circles, shouldn't such a view also apply to the streak of how indexes and/or "benchmarks" have beaten the returns of 90%+ of funds over the 15-year period ending 2017? The logic seems consistent. Michael Mauboussin is credited for saying, "if you can't lose on purpose, then you can't win on purpose either." If indexers and "bench-markers" cannot lose on purpose, then what can we make of the recent outperformance streak of indexing relative to active management? Luck or skill?[196]

The statistical dynamic illustrated in Figure 15, where both the majority of funds and the majority of investors can outperform the return of a broad market index, may seem unrealistic, but it can be theorized from the data found in Bogle's text *Common Sense on Mutual Funds*, where both mutual funds and index funds outperformed each other for extended and different periods of time (and perhaps the number of investors, too). In some ways, this statistical dynamic may be more common than some believe. In the zero-sum game of professional baseball, for example, where either one team wins or one team loses a game (as in the zero-sum game of stock-market outperformance), there are recurring annual instances where there are fewer teams with losing records (those with more losses than wins) than winning or average records (those with more wins than losses or those with an equal number of wins and losses). In the 15-year period ending 2014, the outcome happened in 2012, 2010, 2009, 2008, 2007, 2005, 2004, 2003, 2001, and 2000, or two thirds of the time. In 2003, 18 teams had a winning record and only 12 a losing one.

---

[195] Famed money-manager Bill Miller, formerly of Legg Mason, developed a remarkable streak of exceeding the S&P 500 Index return for 15 consecutive years starting in 1991, in part by investing in growth-oriented stocks that seemingly had a value-tilt, with such stocks forming a large portion of his value fund, the Legg Mason Value Trust. During part of his streak, for example, some large holdings in the Legg Mason Value Trust, namely companies with high P/E ratios such as Amazon, eBay, and Google, may have had more characteristics of growth at the time than value, but arguably such stocks had both characteristics if their subsequent fundamental and equity price performance is any indication. High P/E stocks can be undervalued.

[196] Fees do play an important role when it comes to long-run mutual fund returns (fees compound over multiple time periods). Nonetheless, index investors could still be on nothing more than a lucky streak, something tied more to randomness (i.e. gambler's fallacy) and exacerbated by recency bias.

Figure 17: The Skill Ratio

Skill Ratio = Avg. Rolling 5-year Excess Return / Avg. Rolling 5-year Excess Return Standard Deviation

This figure shows how the Skill ratio is calculated in assessing active fund manager performance. A manager is considered to have skill if this ratio is above 1.

A new metric called the Skill Ratio, as presented by the CFA Institute, may help further conceptualize this point. The Skill Ratio can be calculated "by dividing the average excess rolling returns by the standard deviation of excess rolling returns," where a skilled manager would have a ratio greater than 1. The implications with respect to indexing are clear. Because index investors are merely tracking the benchmark, definitionally, they cannot generate a positive excess return. Therefore, the Skill Ratio for index investing is nil, and the returns emanating from the strategy of index investing are luck, by definition. The enterprise valuation framework offers the context for why index investors may expect rising equity values and prices over time, but merely expecting this to happen just because it has happened in the past is a framework built entirely on chance.

Much of the financial industry has applauded the proliferation of low-cost index investing, and for good reason. When it comes to long-term returns, fees matter. However, the pure luck, or rather speculative, component of indexing is not changed just because these instruments are cheap to hold, and the luck-versus-skill discussion may have implications on the level of fees the advising community may be able to charge their clients in time to hold such passive products.[197] Index funds should be applauded for making it easier for investors to get into the stock market (i.e. to capture rising equity values and prices via the enterprise valuation framework), but making it easier to get into the stock market doesn't mean that

---

[197] It may be puzzling to some that there is considerable information dissemination regarding the importance of fees when it comes to their impact on mutual fund returns, but such information is not readily available when it comes to the impact advisor fees may have on long-run client portfolio returns. Over a 20-year look-back period ending June 1, 2017, for example, it can be hypothesized that fees on passive index products held in advisor accounts that charge 1% on assets under management per annum may have resulted in as much as 17 percentage points of cumulative underperformance relative to the index itself during the 20-year period, excluding the reinvestment of dividends, which may have only widened the underperformance gap. Such cumulative underperformance amounts to approximately 66% of the initial value on August 1, 1997, in the hypothetical example.

there is skill involved with holding such assets, or that advisors should receive outsize compensation just for holding such assets.

In many ways, the practice of index investing is a lot more like speculating than investing.[198] Indexers may be betting on a stock market advance over the long haul, irrespective of current intrinsic-value estimates or risks involved that could impair their capital permanently. Indexers are essentially buying everything at any price and holding it no matter what. That can be very risky at expensive valuations. If one is buying index funds or theme-based ETFs merely on hopes that their prices will be higher in the future with no justification or thesis, one is speculating or playing the "greater fool" game. In any case, however, a new age is upon the financial industry, with Fidelity introducing zero expense-ratio index mutual funds.

Speculating on the stock market via indexing is now free, but free can be so very expensive, if you know what I mean.

Bad Math? Finance Does Not Have the Complete Picture

Efficient markets theorists may further argue that, if prices aren't correct on the marketplace, or at least very close to being correct, why can't active fund managers outperform the S&P 500 Index. It's a good question. However, it is vitally important to separate the idea of whether stock prices are priced "correctly" based on future expectations, as in the Price-to-Estimated-Fair-Value test, from the idea of whether investors can outperform their respective benchmarks. These are two different components and have likely only been wrongly intertwined during past decades as research supporting the efficient markets hypothesis has proliferated.

For example, there seems to be an overreliance on mutual fund data in showing active fund manager underperformance to try to *prove* that markets are efficient

---

[198] At a very high level, index investing seems to replace due diligence with diversification. In diversifying away most firm-specific "risk," however, the proliferation of indexing and thematic ETFs may actually increase systematic risk, which could cause overall (total) portfolio risk to increase. Increased stock return correlations speak to this dynamic. See Sullivan (2012).

(something that cannot be done). We have the following excerpt from an abstract, connecting the two separate components: "In recent years financial economists have increasingly questioned the efficient market hypothesis. But surely if market prices were often irrational and if market returns were as predictable as some critics have claimed, then professionally managed investment funds should easily be able to outdistance a passive index fund (Malkiel 2005)."

However, what may not be more broadly known is that mutual fund data is but one part of the entire corporate equity market. According to data from Goldman Sachs, "households directly own 36% of the $46 trillion U.S. equity market.[199]" This may not seem like a lot, but according to the same data set, mutual funds account for just 24% of stock ownership, while ETFs account for just 6%. If you include household ownership of mutual funds and ETFs, the percentage of retail share ownership (mom and pop investors) is indirectly more than half of the market, but it is the share of households, excluding their ownership of mutual funds and ETFs, relative to that of mutual funds that matters to this analysis.

Retail investors may own small parts of the market individually, but in aggregate, their share, excluding their ownership of funds and ETFs, is 50% larger than the share attributed to mutual funds. Can conclusions be drawn about active stock selection or the efficient markets hypothesis on mutual-fund data alone? We suspect no, and the idea of underperformance, gross of fees, by active fund management,[200] a subset of mutual fund data, may actually imply outperformance in other areas, possibly including households, under the broader assumption that underperformance is generally offset by outperformance elsewhere, all else equal, as in Sharpe's Arithmetic of Active Management.[201]

---

[199] This data is important in separating the various verticals within active stock selection in the vast corporate equity market. Active funds are one subset, but active individual stock selection is another, larger subset. Some investors may only evaluate the performance of active management based on active fund returns, but this is an incomplete assessment.

[200] This is worth some clarification. The performance of active fund management, gross of fees, can vary. A study by Morningstar over the trailing 20-year period ending September 2018 has shown that "the average dollar invested in U.S. stock funds outperformed its blended index and 80% of other funds before fees." This gross performance might imply that other sectors such as households may have underperformed the market index over this time period. More importantly, however, the data points to potential active stock-selection outperformance for the skilled do-it-yourself investor that can avoid active fund fees altogether.

[201] I draw on Sharpe's observation that before costs "the return on the average actively managed dollar must equal the market return," and that "the market return must equal a weighted average of the returns on the passive and active segments of the market." Therefore, if active mutual

But it is more than that. Variations of the arithmetic can be expanded to the broader corporate equity market, too. For example, theoretically, the number of individual stock investors that comprise 36% share of the market and those investors in mutual funds with 24% share is undefined, each and every year, and each individual's outperformance or underperformance, after fees and expenses, is also undefined. Many investors today may own stocks, funds, ETFs and a variety of other assets, so the idea is not necessarily to explain, in theory, how the majority of investors may be performing, but rather that the application of mutual fund data alone in support of efficient markets hypothesis, as in showing data only for active fund managers, may not provide the complete picture.

What are the key takeaways? One, research on mutual funds alone, while accounting for a large percentage of assets, may still be too small of a sample to test the efficient markets hypothesis within the entire corporate equity market. Two, the traditional definition of the Arithmetic of Active Management suggests that underperforming active fund managers, gross of fees, may only imply outperformance elsewhere in the corporate equity market, perhaps with individual stock investors.[202] Three, because the number of investors holding each mutual fund is undefined, the distribution of individual investor fund returns is also undefined, regardless of fees and expenses. Finally, because each individual investor's mix of stocks, funds, ETFs and other assets is undefined, the distribution of their total returns is also undefined, regardless of fees and expenses.

The Arithmetic of Active Management, as presented by Sharpe, says that "after costs, the return of the average actively managed dollar will be less than the return of the average passively managed dollar." What is shown in this text is that, while the average actively managed dollar may underperform the average passively-managed dollar, at the same time, the number of investors that outperform the index may be far greater than the number of investors that underperform the

---

funds underperform as a group, gross of fees, another segment of the corporate equity market must be outperforming to arrive at the market return, gross of fees. Since it can be presumed that the household segment, the largest segment of corporate equity market, may be free of mutual fund or ETF fees and is highly fragmented, the majority of active investors could still outperform, even when the majority of active mutual funds underperform.

[202] Hypothetically speaking, it seems possible that 100% of active mutual funds can underperform a market benchmark, gross of fees, a condition, however, that would only imply outperformance in other areas of the corporate equity market, not that index investors are outperforming the majority of active stock investors.

index, and the average active investor return, equal weighting the return of each active investor, can be greater than that of the index return. Do investors care about the return of the average actively managed dollar, or do they care about their own returns?

Indexing Moves Markets and Drives Inefficiencies

There continues to be debate within the investment community about indexing's impact on the stock market. It would seem to the reasonable observer that, because all buying and selling activity impacts stock prices, that indexing, too, would have an impact on stock prices.[203] By extension, because most indexers aren't paying attention to valuations with respect to their buying and selling behavior (and are only looking to fill an index weight at any price) that they could themselves cause severe mispricings and inefficiencies. One only has to look at the title of a recent *Economist* article, however, to assess the contradicting, and perhaps more broadly-held, opinion by the marketplace: "The growth of index investing has not made markets less efficient."[204]

Let's first examine an example that may shed some light on the debate. On February 14, 2018, FTSE Russell announced that it would add Longfin Corp to the Russell 2000 and 3000 indices. The news caused Blackrock and other index trackers to buy nearly half of the freely available float in Longfin, "pushing the shares up from their February low of $32 to above $71," according to the *Financial Times*. Once FTSE Russell noted they made a mistake, and that Longfin did not meet the 5% free float requirement to be included in the Russell indices, the stock was removed from the indices after the close March 28, 2018, meaning Blackrock and other index tracking funds, including Vanguard and Charles Schwab, also had to sell their shares at a loss.

---

[203] This is worth emphasizing. Many may believe that indexers are merely passive participants that have no influence whatsoever on prices. This is simply not true.

[204] Incidentally, this may be one of the most loaded article titles I have ever read. It not only assumes the markets are efficient, but it also assumes that index investing has not made the markets less efficient.

Figure 18: Index Fund Impact on Share Prices

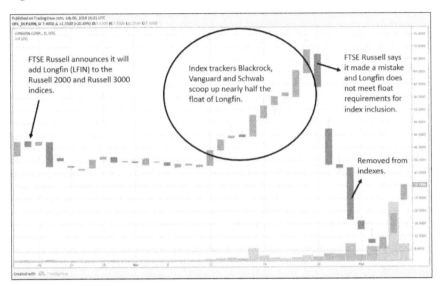

The figure shows how pricing action does not discriminate between the active or index buyer. Indexing drives prices, and indexing activity, itself, can create market inefficiencies, as shown in the Longfin Corp example.

The mistake wasn't necessarily material to index fund returns, but the example is important because it shows directly how indexing, itself, moves markets and may cause mispricings or inefficiencies. The takeaway may be more along the lines of the following: If we can see the impact plainly in this example, what aren't we seeing with respect to the impact indexing is having on other companies? One may even theorize that, given this example, the degree of market inefficiencies caused by indexing can be presented as a function of the company's weight in the index, and how many shares are required to be owned by index trackers versus the company's outstanding float. Should the weight of the company in an index cause a large percentage of the float to be purchased by index trackers, there may be greater potential for index-driven inefficiencies over an undefined time period.

Figure 19: Framework for Estimating Index-Driven Inefficiencies[205]

$$Index - driven\ inefficiencies = \frac{shares\ purchased\ by\ index\ trackers\ to\ achieve\ index\ weight}{shares\ in\ outstanding\ float}$$

The image shows that the price inefficiencies caused by indexing are, in part, a function of the shares purchased by index trackers to achieve their respective index weightings and the shares in the outstanding float, where there may exist a positive correlation between index-driven inefficiency and the ratio over an undefined time period.

A 2010 study by Jeffrey Wurgler of the Stern School of Business noted, in particular, that the popularity of index investing has "created underappreciated side effects," stemming "from the finite ability of stock markets to absorb index-shaped demands for stocks." Wurgler observed that stocks added to the S&P 500 between 1990 and 2005 increased almost 9% around the event, while stocks removed from the index "tumbled by even more." He defined this phenomenon as "detachment," or when index members slowly drift away from the rest of the market over time. Another study in 2012, *How Index Trading Increases Market Vulnerability*, written by Rodney Sullivan and James Xiong and published in the *Financial Analysts Journal*, evaluated the connection between higher return correlation among stocks and a declining dispersion in trading volume changes (higher trading commonality among stocks). They found the behavior consistent with the view that the rise of index investing and thematic ETF trading may lead to higher systematic (common trading) equity market risk. This isn't good for active or passive investors.

All told, since the dawn of the new century, value-conscious investing, or investors that buy and sell on firm-specific intrinsic value calculations, has been slowing as index and quantitative investing have become a greater part of trading activity. The example of Longfin shows how index investors (and those anticipating changes in index fund composition) drive share prices, and more pointedly, how indexing can create market inefficiencies, significantly in some cases and less materially in others. The example also reveals how price-agnostic trading could lead to huge losses, as Longfin would eventually become a penny stock, trading under a $1 per share by the end 2018. Several studies indicate that stock prices are being driven in part by their index membership and, by extension, the trajectory of other stocks in the index. What might a stock market look like if

---

[205] The framework is loosely connected to the violation of the law of one price in the Palm-3Com example, where a small float caused a dislocation (and a limit to arbitrage), albeit temporarily.

most trading becomes index or quantitative-related, driven by price-agnostic decisions that are largely dislocated from fundamental enterprise valuations? Could most stocks, even large caps, and maybe even an index fund such as that tracking the S&P 500 trade in such a volatile manner as that of Longfin?

Probably not to such a degree, and probably not all the time, but only time will tell.

III.

PRACTICAL APPLICATION

7

The Latest Bubble to Pop

"Bogle's folly" and the resistance to change. A 10-point thesis on Kinder Morgan. Some quality financial analysis. The market reacts quickly to correct structural mispricings. The role that falling energy resource prices played. Distribution cuts and MLP business-model rollups. Traditional free cash flow analysis and assessing capital-market dependence risk. A plea to retire a controversial non-GAAP measure. Thinking about maintenance versus growth capital spending. How to tie price-to-distributable cash flow to enterprise valuation. A unique way to look at financial leverage.

"Kris, I think we should remove it."

I walked over to his desk. I had just picked up a piece of paper off the printer, and now had a print out of the company's balance sheet in hand. Valuentum included a simulated dividend growth portfolio in its monthly Dividend Growth Newsletter.[206] Our company was only a few years old in 2015, and Kris had joined the firm full time that year. Located in DeKalb, Illinois, a couple miles from Northern Illinois University, the office interior was painted blue, and it had everything we needed, even a bagel shop in the same building.

"I'm not comfortable with its free cash flow and balance sheet anymore," I added, placing the piece of paper on his desk. Prior to this point, I had been giving the company the benefit of the doubt that distributable cash flow was tied to the

---

[206] The Best Ideas Newsletter portfolio, Dividend Growth Newsletter portfolio, and High Yield Dividend Newsletter portfolios are not real money portfolios. Any performance, including that in the Exclusive publication, is hypothetical and does not represent actual trading. Past performance is not a guarantee of future results, and actual results may differ from simulated performance being presented in this book. Valuentum is an investment research publishing company.

operating dynamics of the company. "Significantly negative free cash flow, net debt through the roof, and yet a huge and growing dividend payment?" Something just wasn't adding up, and Kris agreed. In the next few days, I wrote up "Why We're Dumping Kinder Morgan Right Now," and the piece would get far more attention than I could have ever imagined.

The More Things Change...

Vanguard's Jack Bogle is one of the more inspirational people in finance. His story about what he had to overcome to explain to the investment community the benefits of index funds is a great one. When Bogle launched the first index fund decades ago, it could probably be described as nothing short of a failure, at least in today's terms. Index funds, at the time, were called un-American, brokers and even former Fidelity Chairman Edward C. Johnson III argued that nobody would want just "average returns," and Vanguard in its early days didn't even have enough money to invest in all the stocks of the S&P 500 Index in their exact proportions. The initial index fund on the S&P 500 Index held just 280 stocks.

But that didn't stop Jack Bogle. "Bogle's folly" (i.e. the index fund) is now arguably among the most successful product idea launches in the history of the markets, with indexed assets accounting for a growing percentage of all mutual fund assets today. Those that had been in the finance industry for 30 or 40 years or longer in the 1970s simply couldn't believe that such a product like an index fund would be successful. This resistance to new ideas has seemingly been a staple to incumbents that have grown comfortable with the status quo, as for many years the lack of change may have made them wealthy. In corporate finance, the challenge for others to embrace new ideas, or ways of looking at things, seems to be no different.

In mid-2015, when we presented the opinion that Kinder Morgan and midstream energy equities, most of which used the MLP business model, should be valued the same way as any other company, the opposition to this very basic idea was tremendous. But why should pipeline companies be valued differently? All companies generate operating cash flow and all companies have growth and maintenance capital spending, and capital raised in the marketplace is still shareholder capital regardless of the business model attached to it. Most of the midstream MLPs in mid-2015, however, were being systematically assessed on a price-to-distributable cash flow (P/DCF) basis,[207] which ignored a key cash outflow (growth capital spending), or valued on a dividend discount model with an artificially-elevated payout.

The marketplace, in applying distributable cash flow or distribution analysis, was ignoring the concept that growth capital associated with driving future distributable cash flow is also shareholder capital, a condition that only exacerbated a disconnect between what the market *believed* shares, or units (investors in MLPs buy units of the partnership), were worth and what they *should have believed* shares, or units, were worth, a mispricing or market inefficiency, by definition (i.e. the Price-to-Estimated-Fair Value test). Because their distributions were not reasonably tied to the operating cash flow movements in and out of the enterprise, net of all capital spending, using a dividend discount model made very little sense in valuing the business. In the market's valuation context, Kinder Morgan and most MLPs were getting a free pass on growth capital from new equity and debt issuance, artificially bolstering their distributions, and only through an enterprise valuation model could such a dynamic be revealed (all capital spending is considered in enterprise valuation, see Chapter 5).

In all, there were 10 reasons[208] why we expected Kinder Morgan's shares to collapse in our June 2015 thesis. We said in point 1: "valuation adjustments consistent with MLP evaluation no longer apply. We don't think the market is anywhere close to fully making this valuation adjustment," pointing to the enterprise valuation paradigm shift. In point 2: "Kinder Morgan's dividend growth endeavors will disappoint. Kinder Morgan's free…cash flow, as measured by cash flow from operations less capital expenditures, was $850 million, $753 million, and $786 million in 2014, 2013, and 2012, respectively. Cash dividends paid, and this excludes distributions to non-controlling interests, were $1.76 billion, $1.62 billion and $1.18 billion for those same years, respectively. Kinder Morgan cannot cover its dividend with free cash flow generation…We would not be surprised to see Kinder Morgan raise equity in the next 12 months." Point 3 was no less subtle: "Debt, net of cash was $42.8 billion in the first quarter of 2015, up from $40.6 billion in the first quarter of 2014. The company's debt-to-EBITDA ratio stood at 5.8 times, up from 5.5 times in the last year's quarter.

---

[207] Distributable cash flow is not to be confused with discounted cash flow, as in enterprise valuation, though both go by the acronym DCF.

[208] See Notes for list of the "10 Reasons."

This is junk territory, in our view, but the company is rated investment-grade by the credit rating agencies."

In point 4, the P/E ratio was used to help explain the valuation disconnect. The P/E ratio has significant shortcomings, but generally speaking, elevated P/Es in the context of huge net debt positions make very little sense, in almost all cases: "In the first quarter of 2015, Kinder Morgan generated $0.22 in earnings per share, and consensus forecasts put fiscal year 2015 earnings close to $0.90 per share at the high end (and close to $1 in fiscal 2016). Kinder Morgan is trading at ~$40 per share. That's 40 times earnings for a company whose revenue and operating income fell during the first quarter of 2015 on a year-over-year basis. The company's market valuation makes little sense." Point 5 explained how we understood our perspective would be viewed with skepticism and disbelief, given how many currently view the financials of midstream equities: "Kinder Morgan's shareholders...may be extremely skeptical and not believe the numbers we've put forth in this report...something isn't quite right when entities go up on news that they're creating an MLP and up on news that they're re-consolidating their MLP structure or dissolving an MLP. If one is good, the other can't also be good. Kinder Morgan significantly overpaid for its very own assets."

Our counter to Credit Suisse's rebuttal included five more reasons why we thought Kinder Morgan's shares would collapse, and that note is reproduced below:

Figure 20: 5 More Reasons Why We Think Kinder Morgan's Shares Will Collapse

June 19, 2015

The credit rating agencies have a lot to think about. Kinder Morgan's investment-grade credit rating is in part supported by the firm's ability to access the equity markets to sell its own stock. But its share price is artificially propped up by the incorrect application of dividend discount models that are using financially engineered dividends, which themselves are in part supported by the debt raised from an investment-grade credit rating, which is then used to keep raising debt and growing the dividend -- and so on.

Kinder Morgan is now a corporation (not an MLP), and tax implications aside, that means it should be valued like any other corporate: on the internally generated (organic) future free cash flows it generates for its shareholders discounted back to today. The following analysis on KMI is separate and distinct from previously publicized analyses from Barron's and Hedgeye on Kinder Morgan Energy Partners, formerly trading under the ticker symbol KMP.

In business analysis, the most prevalent form of discounted cash-flow valuation analysis is the application of an enterprise free cash flow model, the framework we use at Valuentum to value all companies in our coverage universe. In all cases for non-financial operating companies, we calculate the present value of future free cash flows to the firm (FCFF) and then deduct the book value of a company's debt, net of cash, from that sum to arrive at a firm's equity value. We then divide equity value by weighted average diluted shares outstanding to calculate an intrinsic value estimate of a company's shares.

In this widely accepted process in both the academic and professional worlds, dividends are a symptom, an output, of the enterprise free cash flows that a company generates for all of its stakeholders -- debt, equity and preferred, where applicable. Dividends are not a driver behind the valuation equation of a business for one very important reason: a company can artificially and unsustainably prop up a dividend via external financing activities, as in the case of raising debt or issuing equity, to achieve a payout that is completely detached from what its internal operations can feasibly support. An enterprise free cash flow model values the operating assets of a business, not a company's ability to engage in financial engineering to create a valuation construct around its dividend that is unrelated to its ongoing, underlying operational performance.

It is clear that Kinder Morgan cannot internally support its dividend, let alone increase it year after year. This is not a question, but a matter of reality at the company. The boards of most every corporation like Kinder Morgan, not MLPs, set their respective dividend policies on the basis of either a payout ratio of earnings and/or a target of free cash flow, as measured by cash flow from operations less capital expenditures. This makes sense because free cash flow is what's left over to allocate to dividends, buybacks and/or acquisitions. In Kinder Morgan's case, the company's internally generated free cash flow was $850 million, $753 million, and $786 million in 2014, 2013, and 2012, respectively.

Is Kinder Morgan's organic free cash flow stable? Yes. Is Kinder Morgan's organic free cash flow consistently positive? Yes. Does Kinder Morgan have a great business model? Yes. But to the point: Is Kinder Morgan's organic free cash flow insufficient? Absolutely, 100% yes. Based on the 2.159 billion weighted average shares outstanding at the end of the first quarter of 2015 and the company's current $1.92 per share annualized dividend, Kinder Morgan will pay over $4.1 billion to shareholders in dividends this year alone. That's more than 5 times what the company generated in internal free cash flow in each of the past three years from its own operations.

In being presented with such data, most management teams would come away with the view that perhaps they should ratchet back dividend "spending" and de-risk their cash-flow profile, but Kinder Morgan is instead plowing ahead with dividend increases! Management says it's on track to meet its full-year dividend target of $2 per share, up from today's levels, and even expects strong year-over-year growth for years after that. Kinder Morgan seems to not care about its earnings, free cash flow, or leverage in setting dividend policy, unlike most every other operating company. And with "unlimited" access to capital whenever it wants it, or so it seems at the moment, and with arguably brazen confidence, management believes it can do just about anything it wants with its dividend growth plans, regardless of its actual consolidated financial statements.

But how long before the chickens come home to roost? Before proceeding, we think it makes sense to address the "maintenance and growth capital" question. To many, this is old news. To us and to shareholders, both matter. Both maintenance and growth capital spending are shareholder money that is used to support future cash flow from operations. In this regard, Kinder Morgan is no different than any other corporate: every company uses large amounts of capital each year to grow its cash-generating capabilities not just to replace their cash-generating capabilities. Every single company.

But we have to put to numbers this dynamic for each and every one of them. We cannot ignore growth capital for Kinder Morgan in its valuation equation. Not only is growth capital spending a cash outlay in the calculation of economic value estimation, a vital component of the investment merits of Kinder Morgan at an appropriate price, but the timing of such outlays are absolutely critical in estimating intrinsic value. A dollar spent today is worth significantly more than a dollar earned 20 years from now. The time value of money matters.

As is traditionally the case with corporates, the most a company can organically pay to shareholders as dividends each year is a function of its long-term free cash flow generation, not its long-term operating cash flow generation. The distinction between these two cash-flow measures is extremely important. For example, in looking through the lens of a dividend discount model within the context of business valuation, only organically supported dividend payments should be used in the valuation process. A range of $750-$850 million of dividends each year, or an approximate of the amount of annual free cash flow generated during the previous three years, is a much more reasonable dividend input to ascribe to Kinder Morgan than its current pace of annual dividends of ~$4.1 billion. The difference between the ~$4.1 billion and the $750-$850 million range is textbook financial engineering, completely unrelated to the value of Kinder Morgan, itself.

If, for example, a brokerage house has a price target of ~$50 per share on shares and uses a dividend discount model to support the valuation, approximately 20% of the value, give or take, behind that price target ($850 million/$4.1 billion) corresponds to Kinder Morgan's organic business, while the balance of the value behind the price target is supported via external financing activities. The dividend discount model should not be used to value businesses where earnings and free cash flow are completely and undeniably disconnected to the dividend payment. Kinder Morgan, a corporation (not an MLP), is expected to earn ~$0.90 per share this year and ~$1 per share next year, while paying ~$2 per share in annual dividends going forward. A large portion of Kinder Morgan's equity value defended by a dividend discount model is fictitious.

We can understand why supporting and growing the dividend at all costs is everything to management when Wall Street is using dividend discount models to value its company. That doesn't change the fact, however, that applying a dividend discount model on financially engineered dividend payments is a mirage--which brings us to the next tangible point. One of the dual and perhaps lesser-known benefits of the dividend discount model is that it seconds as a calculation of the present value of future cash dividend obligations. For example, the higher the "perceived" equity value that is supported by the dividend discount model, the more the present value of cash obligations the company has to shareholders, and by extension, the lower implicit credit quality of the organization, assuming a company continues to pay and increase its dividend irrespective of what the credit rating agencies say.

In any case, what matters most is not the absolute level of the debt on Kinder Morgan's books, which is striking by itself, but whether Kinder Morgan can service all of its debt-like, cash obligations with its own organically generated EBITDA, which pays no mind to capital spending in any form. Kinder Morgan currently has $42.8 billion in debt, net of cash, on the balance sheet, and implicitly, on the basis of the price targets of some brokerage houses that employ a dividend discount model, it has another ~$100 billion in "mandatory" obligations to shareholders in the form of dividends (though if you ask a shareholder, the dividend payment is as contractual as it gets).

We think that, as the credit rating agencies evaluate the firm's die-hard commitment to shareholders and its unwavering backing of an explosive future dividend growth plan, the implied leverage of cash, debt-like commitments at Kinder Morgan should approach $140 billion. The company's reported debt-to-EBITDA is 5.8 times, already a consideration for junk-rated credit status, but its implied debt-to-EBITDA is closer to 19 times ($140 billion/$7.35 billion) after factoring in all cash, debt-like commitments! The company is buried under cash, debt-like obligations.

No matter how much one likes Kinder Morgan's reliable, toll-road-like business model, $140 billion in present-value, cash debt-like commitments is a lot to service with only $7.35 billion in annual adjusted EBITDA, a measure that ignores all forms of capital spending, as most would prefer to look at its business model. If we use the high-water-mark of free cash flow that Kinder Morgan generated during the past three years, it would take 50 years to pay off its tangible debt load on the books today, and that's if it doesn't pay one penny of free cash flow to shareholders as a dividend.

Bond holders should take note of the existing tangible leverage on the books and Kinder Morgan's commitment to paying out more than 5 times its internally generated free cash flow as dividends to shareholders, as it has done the past three years, coupled with management's commitment to keep growing its cash dividend obligations to shareholders in coming years. Kinder Morgan's track record may matter, but if it can't cover all of its cash, debt-like obligations, it can't. At the end of the first quarter of 2015, Kinder Morgan had just $259 million of cash on its books.

At an implied leverage of 19 times all cash, debt-like commitments, the credit rating agencies have a lot to think about. Kinder Morgan's investment-grade credit rating is in part supported by the firm's ability to access the equity markets to sell its own stock. But its share price is artificially propped up by the incorrect application of dividend discount models that are using financially engineered dividends, which themselves are in part supported by the debt raised from an investment-grade credit rating, which is then used to keep raising debt and growing the dividend - and so on.

We don't care what you call it -- "a debt-infused stock bubble" or some other name -- but the situation isn't sustainable in its current form. The "circular flow of unsubstantiated support" will last as long as the credit rating agencies and sell-side analyst community allow it to, and from implied levels of leverage to understanding the pitfalls of dividend discount models, the story will take some time to evolve and for others to figure out. But does Kinder Morgan have a way out?

The first option for consideration would be for the board to scrap its dividend growth plans to reduce its level of implied leverage. But this may not matter. In cutting the dividend, the board would just reduce its firm value in the context of wrongly applied dividend discount models, and this would then further reduce its attractiveness as a credit because the price in which it can raise equity to support its capital position would then be substantially reduced. In this event, the credit rating would likely face pressure anyway -- thereby starting the spiral lower. The above scenario also helps to reiterate the fragility and irrelevancy of the dividend discount modeling framework in Kinder Morgan's case. In the above scenario, there would be no actual change to Kinder Morgan's business operations at all, but the firm's equity value, as measured by the dividend discount model, would plummet.

The second option for consideration would be for Kinder Morgan to start paying down its abnormally high levels of leverage with excess free cash flow, but then the company wouldn't have any organically derived free cash flow to allocate as dividends to shareholders at all. In this light, the financial engineering would become even more obvious, and the move in turn, would then force a decision on the company to cut its own dividend, which would then yet again hurt its "perceived" value in the eyes of those using a dividend discount model, thereby starting the spiral lower anyway.

From our perspective, management's best option may be to raise as much equity capital as it can while the times are good. The company knows how important its equity price is to the "circular flow of unsubstantiated support" better than anyone, and from our perspective, that's the predominant reason why insiders are buying back stock at present levels. From our vantage point, we don't view the highly-publicized insider purchases as a sign of confidence at all,[209] but recognition that the company's shares are incredibly vulnerable.

A fresh, unbiased voice is saying: "Your stock is trading at ~100 times the trailing 3-year average of free cash flow, ~40+ times forward earnings, the company has implied leverage of 19 times after considering all of your cash, debt-like commitments, and it has negligible cash on the

---

[209] In some cases, the signaling aspect of the dividend, share buybacks, or insider purchases is not something in which I put much value. It's somewhat psychological. For example, management knows that investors view the dividend as a sign of strength, but because management knows investors will interpret a dividend raise as strength, dividend increases, themselves, generally lose their signaling value. The same could be said about share buybacks or insider purchases. Because management knows the market will view them positively, they can't generally be viewed as having any informational or signaling value, per se.

books. Yet 'everybody' loves both your equity and your debt?" Clearly, something is wrong.

The credit rating agencies can keep giving Kinder Morgan investment-grade marks and the brokerage houses can keep valuing the company on financially engineered dividends. But we're certainly not sticking around! Frankly, we're sleeping better at night knowing the company is no longer in the Dividend Growth portfolio. The low end of our enterprise free cash flow derived fair value estimate is $29 per share.

Shortly thereafter, we would reduce our intrinsic value estimate of Kinder Morgan to a point estimate of $29 (the low end of the fair value estimate range had been $29 previously, as in the note above), with the company registering a 1 on the Valuentum Buying Index, one of the worst ratings (as shown in Figure 22). Shares of Kinder Morgan would eventually converge to our $20 fair value estimate, and almost everything happened that we said would happen, including the dividend cut in December 2015, almost as if our prediction in June 2015 acted as some sort of script the markets were following. Other midstream equities reacted similarly, converging to valuations that captured the cash outflow of growth capital spending.

Figure 21: Market "Corrects" Structural Mispricing in Kinder Morgan

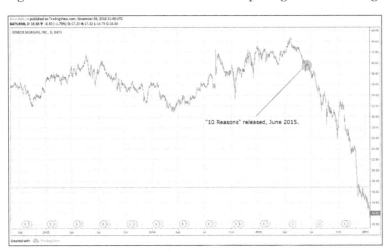

Kinder Morgan's shares peaked in April 2015 and collapsed to the low teens by January 2016. Image: TradingView.

Figure 22: Valuentum's Rating History of Kinder Morgan

KMI Rating History	Price	Fair Value	VBI
25-May-18	$15.89	$20.00	6
26-Jan-18	$18.77	$20.00	6
22-Sep-17	$19.27	$20.00	3
21-Jul-17	$20.69	$20.00	6
9-Jun-17	$19.08	$20.00	3
24-Feb-17	$21.24	$20.00	3
29-Aug-16	$21.92	$20.00	6
5-Aug-16	$20.36	$21.00	6
8-Apr-16	$17.94	$21.00	6
22-Jan-16	$15.34	$20.00	5
7-Dec-15	$15.72	$20.00	5
29-Oct-15	$27.20	$26.00	5
14-Aug-15	$33.96	$29.00	3
19-Jun-15	$39.54	$29.00	1

The image shows the rating history of Kinder Morgan. The company registered the worst rating on the Valuentum Buying Index (VBI) in June 2015, only a few months before shares collapsed to the mid-teens.

In March 2017, I was invited to give a speech to my fellow CFA charterholders at the CFA Society of Houston about my analytical experiences with respect to Kinder Morgan and other midstream equities, *"Trust the Numbers, Not Just Management: How Simple Financial Statement Analysis Could Save You Big."* In the presentation, I walked through a variety of instances where operating earnings and leverage metrics seemed too optimistic. I explained what true free-cash-flow coverage meant, but perhaps most interestingly, I put together a slide that compared Kinder Morgan's credit rating metrics to those across the rating spectrum, using *Moody's Financial Metrics* as a resource. For example, what level of EBITA/interest expense ratio is typical of a Ba-rated equity or what level of FFO/Debt would suggest a B-rated entity? Kinder Morgan's metrics would imply a junk rating for almost every key ratio in the book. Viewing individual metrics, by themselves, won't necessarily capture the company's entire credit perspective, but when the vast majority of them point in one direction, it can be a red flag.

But how can we possibly know whether it wasn't just falling energy resource prices that drove the collapse in Kinder Morgan's and MLP's shares, and that our call wasn't just completely lucky because of them? How can we know that we recognized a market inefficiency? Well, falling energy prices certainly played a role,[210] the threat of impending rate hikes had an impact,[211] and there had to be some degree of luck, of course, but the answer is mostly twofold.

First, other industry observers and most executive teams in the midstream energy space have long-maintained that part of the attractiveness of pipeline companies is that they are largely immune to changing energy resource prices thanks in part to their volume-based contracts. Though we believe the health of a midstream energy entity is inextricably tied to the health of its customer base, which *is* impacted by energy resource pricing, particularly during tough economic times, the view that midstream equities were more volume-based players was widely held at the time.

Second, and more telling, energy resource prices bounced back significantly in the years that followed the collapse, but the equity prices of Kinder Morgan and most other midstream MLPs did not. Swooning energy resource prices seemed to only act as the catalyst for the markets to systematically reevaluate the lens by which to value shares (from the basis of distributable cash flow and the dividend discount model to a "fairer" valuation with respect to the enterprise valuation context).

---

[210] In 2015, it was estimated that $1 per-barrel change in the price of oil would have a $10 million impact on Kinder Morgan's distributable cash flow, while a $0.10/MMBTU change in the price of natural gas would have a $3 million impact on the measure.

[211] Approximately $11 billion of the $40+ billion of consolidated debt Kinder Morgan held on its books in 2015 was subject to variable interest rates.

Figure 23: Energy Prices Bounced Back But Not Kinder Morgan's Stock

Falling energy resource pricing (USO) served only to expose the share mispricing in 2015. As energy prices have recovered (top) in the years since, Kinder Morgan's equity did not. Image: TradingView.

Figure 24: Midstream MLPs Did Not Recover Despite Higher Energy Prices

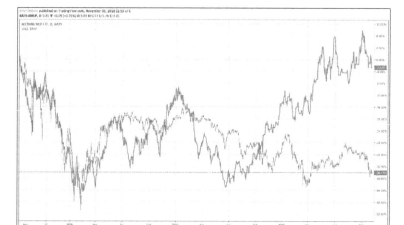

As with Kinder Morgan, falling energy resource pricing (USO) served only to expose the share mispricing in 2015. As energy prices have recovered (top) in the years since, midstream MLPs did not. Image: TradingView.

Since Valuentum shared its work with Barron's on Kinder Morgan and MLPs in mid-2015, dozens of MLPs have cut their distributions and many of them have rolled up or simplified their business operations, with operators shunning the MLP business model preferring C-Corps instead. Most midstream equities are now being more reasonably valued on an enterprise valuation basis. According to work from Global X Funds, now roughly 40% of the energy infrastructure market capitalization consists of C-Corps, up considerably from practically nothing prior to Kinder Morgan's roll up in 2014. Though one can never rule out a reinflation of the prior bubble based on human behavior, pricing advances, even those that may return such equities to their prior levels and beyond, will likely be more fundamental-driven in nature, augmented in part by the time value of money.

Capital-Market Dependency Risk

It's important to differentiate the concept of enterprise valuation and capital-market dependence. The former refers to the view that Kinder Morgan and most midstream MLPs were systematically overvalued in mid-2015, or that their prices were trading above what we thought the market *should view* as a fair representation of intrinsic value (driven in part by investors' thirst for dividends and a lax lending environment of ultra-low interest rates). On the other hand, the idea of capital-market dependence, or a condition where operating cash flow does not consistently cover all capital spending and all distributions or dividends, the latter suggesting that companies will continue to require new external capital from the debt or equity markets. But why is this difference important?

Well, assessing the inherent risk of a dividend payment, in part, rests on traditional free cash flow analysis, which while connected remains distinct from the enterprise valuation construct, which applies enterprise free cash flow. Where enterprise free cash flow analysis mostly focuses on generating a fair value estimate for shares, capital-market dependence analysis, on the other hand, focuses on evaluating how dependent a company is on external capital to keep funding its business model, or a distribution/dividend. One can evaluate capital-market dependence risk by assessing whether operating cash flow covers both capital spending (both growth and maintenance) and distributions/dividends paid, all items that can be found on the cash flow statement.

Figure 25: High Capital Market Dependence Risk

Cash flow from Operations < Sum of Capital Expenditures (both growth and maintenance) and Cash Distributions (Dividends)

Under situations where operating cash flow does not consistently cover *all* capital spending *and* dividends/distributions paid, the dividend or distribution might be considered artificial or financially-engineered, as it is literally supported by the *financing* section of the cash flow statement. Generally speaking, the lower explicit cost form of equity capital[212] is generated from internal funds (operating cash flow), and such funds are theoretically allocated to the highest-return projects (growth capital spending) first, prior to new-equity issuance, which is comparatively higher cost. Once internally-generated operating cash flow is exhausted from all capital spending, including growth-related endeavors, external equity capital issuance, which is higher explicit cost funding, should then be viewed theoretically as the capital in support of a capital-dependent distribution, a payout that is greater than internally-generated free cash flow (cash flow from operations less all capital spending).[213]

When it came to Kinder Morgan and most MLPs in mid-2015, they were considerably capital-market dependent at a time when the energy complex was starting to feel the pain from falling energy resource prices. The lessons from the Financial Crisis with respect to the banks were clear. Not only were their dividends and distributions at risk, but stocks that were capital-market dependent during the Financial Crisis were punished as the probability of an adverse outcome was eventually factored into their share price. With energy resource

---

[212] A distinction is made between "explicit" and "opportunity" costs. Even internally-generated operating cash flow, when reinvested, has opportunity cost, as expressed more theoretically as the cost of equity. In a less-theoretical sense, absent negative interest-bearing corporate debt, internally-generated operating cash flow may practically be the lowest-cost source of funding, even lower than new debt financing, given the lack of explicit costs.

[213] Due to issuance costs, internally-generated funds will always be lower cost than raising new equity. For example, in a project financed 50% with new debt and 50% with new equity, the use of internally generated funds for the equity portion of the project would be less than the cost of raising new common equity. This might assume shares of the equity are trading at fair value. In the event shares of the company are overvalued, raising equity may make sense as it could represent a value-creating endeavor, itself. Firms that pursue all-debt financing may indirectly raise their overall weighted average cost of capital, in the event bankruptcy risk becomes elevated. In other words, what may appear to be lower-cost debt financing may indirectly increase the overall WACC under certain situations, providing further support for the use of internally-generated funds as perhaps the lowest-cost consideration from a practical standpoint.

prices falling, putting into question the health of independents, which were customers of most midstream MLPs, the writing was on the wall for a big fallout that eventually happened.

But how did we get ahead of this? Why Valuentum?

For starters, the systematic application of the enterprise valuation construct across our coverage universe helped, meaning it's likely we had a better chance of identifying market outliers across industries and sectors than other research firms whose business models have analysts focusing purely on one industry or one sector. To us, it was clear that an imbalance was present when comparing the modeling framework for Apple or Boeing to Kinder Morgan or Energy Transfer Partners.[214] The MLP model, from where we stood, had primarily been used as a financing mechanism that could raise equity for the corporate umbrella at a price that was more reflective of its distribution yield, not on enterprise valuation (or intrinsic value). Prior to the collapse, MLPs could rather easily float equity, attracting new investors with a lofty distribution that wasn't necessarily reflective of the economic substance of the business. This translated into equity unit prices for MLPs of bubble proportions that eventually popped as the energy resource markets began to swoon in late 2015 and early 2016 as credit conditions deteriorated.

The Plea to Retire Distributable Cash Flow

Where in quantitative research, there is a zoo of factors. In corporate finance, there is a zoo of measures of cash flow. Cash flow is more broadly accepted as cash flow generated from operations, or operating cash flow. Enterprise free cash flow, unlevered free cash flow, or free cash flow to the firm are all one and the same, representing the cash flow generated to value equities in the enterprise value framework (see Chapter 5). Free cash flow to equity is that estimated to accrue to equity investors, typically used to value banking entities. Cash flow from

---

[214] Looking at the cash flow statements and balance sheets of Apple and Energy Transfer Partners side-by-side is an insightful analytical exercise. On one hand, there is a company with substantial net cash and tremendous free-cash-flow coverage of the dividend. On the other hand, there is a company with substantial net debt and significantly negative free cash flow, despite paying a lofty distribution.

investing and cash flow from financing are two other measures found on the GAAP cash flow statement.

It is important to draw a distinction between the midstream industry's definition of distributable cash flow and traditional free cash flow, the latter generally defined as cash flow from operations less all capital spending, and to use the SEC's guidelines for free cash flow as the basis for why the measure distributable cash flow, itself, should be retired. For illustrative purposes, there are myriad examples of companies that use free cash flow in non-GAAP reporting, as measured by cash from operations less all capital spending, including Facebook and even research provider Morningstar.

Traditional Free Cash Flow =

Cash flow from operations less *all* capital spending (additions to purchase of property, plant and equipment)[215]

There are variants of free cash flow representation, too, and while we generally do not like situations where companies deviate from cash flow from operations less all capital spending as the measure of free cash flow in disclosures, the concept of cash flow from operations less all capital spending remains the key relationship in assessing traditional free cash flow. For example, Exxon Mobil includes 'Proceeds associated with Asset Sales' in the calculation of free cash flow, something that we'd prefer not to be in there, though we do give the company credit for transparency (it provides a clear breakdown of how it defines free cash flow). We may have our preferences, but the construct is the same in assessing operating cash flow less *all* capital spending in arriving at free cash flow.

In the SEC's guidelines for free cash flow, updated April 2018, it reads in response to a question that defines free cash flow as cash flow from operations… less capital expenditures: "Companies should also avoid inappropriate or potentially misleading inferences about its usefulness. For example, 'free cash flow' should not be used in a manner that inappropriately implies that the measure represents the residual cash flow available for discretionary expenditures, since many companies have mandatory debt service requirements or other non-discretionary expenditures that are not deducted from the measure." The guidelines make a lot

---

[215] This definition of free cash flow is widely-accepted in the financial community. However, for an authoritative source of the definition, please see Corporate Finance Institute, "The Ultimate Cash Flow Guide (EBITDA, CF, FCF, FCFE, FCFF).

of sense (every financial metric has some shortcomings). However, when we think about the SEC's guidelines for traditional free cash flow, a punitive metric that deducts for all capital spending, it becomes questionable whether distributable cash flow, because it does not deduct for growth capital spending, is a helpful measure for investors at all.

Figure 26: Midstream Example of "Distributable Cash Flow"[216]

	Net Income
+	Depreciation and Amortization
+	Other Non-Cash Items
--	Distributions to Preferred Units
--	Maintenance Capital Expenditures[217]

| | "Distributable Cash Flow" |
| = | |

That midstream equities have designated the term distributable cash flow to mean one thing should not make it so.[218] Hypothetically, why couldn't an operating company call revenue some form of extreme measure of distributable cash flow? Where, for example, the midstream energy industry's measure of distributable cash flow backs out growth capital spending, an operating company could consider revenue an estimate of "distributable cash flow," if one backs out all costs. In both cases, any cash shortfalls caused by a distribution payment tied to "distributable cash flow" could be made up by floating new debt or equity to keep paying an outsize distribution/dividend.

Distributable cash flow is an imbalanced metric that gives credit for growth in net income but does not deduct for the growth capital spending that was

---

[216] In its third-quarter 2018 press release, for example, Energy Transfer Partners defined distributable cash flow as "net income, adjusted for certain non-cash items, less distributions to preferred unitholders and maintenance capital expenditures."

[217] Note how the traditional definition of "distributable cash flow" only includes a deduction for maintenance capital spending, not growth capital spending. The enterprise valuation framework, however, does not differentiate between growth and maintenance capital spending, as it deducts for all capital spending in the year in which it happens. The value generated by the growth capital spending is captured in the incremental improvement in future EBI (NOPLAT).

[218] The term "distributable cash flow" implies the measure represents cash available for distributions. However, distribution coverage ratios vary quarter-to-quarter and are not fixed at 1, dozens of midstream equities have opted to cut their distributions during the past several years, and many have chosen to pursue business-model simplification initiatives, rolling up subsidiaries and adjusting their payouts along the way. The term could be considered a misnomer.

necessary to drive the net income expansion. If traditional free cash flow, which deducts for growth capital spending, should not be viewed as a measure representing "the residual cash flow available for discretionary expenditures," per the SEC guidelines, including dividend policy (which is discretionary), some may reason that distributable cash flow should probably not be allowed at all. At the very least, it seems to make sense that there should be at least some reconciliation between distributable cash flow and free cash flow within midstream energy press releases to help the individual investor better understand the substantial differences between these two metrics.

We hope we may eventually see a systematic measure of free cash flow as a mandatory release for all companies--hopefully one as simple and straightforward as cash flow from operations less all gross capital spending (companies sometimes like to use net capital spending). The transparency and consistency that this one move would make across the financial markets would be phenomenal, and the move may encourage market participants to migrate away from near-term thinking and quarterly earnings-per-share beats and misses to evaluate a core value driver of the company, free cash flow.

Maintenance and Growth Capital Expenditures

Some analysts may subjectively separate capital spending into the categories of maintenance and growth capital outlays. The key, however, is achieving balance within the modeling framework.[219] If one isn't assuming any EBI (NOPLAT) growth from growth capital spending, for example, then one shouldn't assume any growth capital spending. On the other hand, if one is assuming EBI (NOPLAT) growth from growth capital spending, then one should assume growth capital spending. The timing of enterprise free cash flows (including negative ones) matter, so modeling inclusive of all capital spending

---

[219] Aswath Damodaran, in his text *Investment Valuation*, notes the generally lumpy nature of capital expenditures, and that in estimating them going forward, seeking normalization may make the most sense. Though explicit forecasts of capital expenditures are always best to use in the near term, in my view, seeking a normalizing of key value-drivers immediately prior to latter stages of the enterprise valuation model will be important in the context of balance.

makes the most theoretical sense.[220] Most every company has some degree of maintenance and growth capital spending, and even some capital-light technology companies could have lower total capital-spending profiles than just the maintenance requirements of many midstream pipeline entities.

Xilinx is a good example of this. The company makes programmable logic devices (PLDs), including programable System on Chips (SoCs) and three-dimensional integrated circuits (3D ICs), and its intellectual property is a key component of its value proposition. During the three fiscal years ending 2018, Xilinx's operating cash flow averaged over $830 million, while its entire cash bill for capital spending, including growth and maintenance, averaged just over $50 million, meaning all capital spending represented, on average, approximately 6% of operating cash flow. By comparison, for the three years ending 2017, midstream equity Energy Transfer Partners' operating cash flow averaged approximately $3.5 billion, while just its maintenance capital spending, on an accrual basis, averaged more than $425 million, approximately 12% of operating cash flow, nearly double that of Xilinx's on a common-size percentage basis.

As in the example of Xilinx, many capital-light operations, almost by definition, do not have tremendous growth capital spending, as fixed cost investment may not be a core driver behind their future EBI (NOPLAT) stream. On the other hand, many midstream entities do. During the three fiscal years ending 2018, Xilinx generated substantial free cash flow, averaging roughly $780 million per year. Energy Transfer Partners' free cash flow was significantly negative during the three years ending in 2017, however. The midstream equity's total capital spending of $8.3 billion, $7.6 billion, and $9.1 billion during 2017, 2016, and 2015, respectively, completely overwhelmed the company's operating cash flow generation in each of those years. Though the maintenance-versus-growth capital spending ratio varies across sectors of the economy and for different types of companies, how maintenance and growth capital spending is treated in the enterprise valuation framework should not change with the company.

Midstream energy MLPs, for example, are like any other company, even if the magnitude and duration behind the composition of their value drivers are

---

[220] Though the timing of cash inflows and outflows matter within the near-term explicit forecast horizon, it is important for the analyst to estimate a pure measure of the company's RONIC such that appropriate measures of net new investment can be assumed during latter stages of the model in arriving at corresponding enterprise free cash flow.

different. Said plainly, many pipeline companies may have relatively low maintenance capital spending, all else equal, but so do many software companies and other asset light entities, too. The midstream space seems to encourage analytical thinking on a project-by-project basis, which is reasonable with respect to net present value (NPV) considerations, but all projects inevitably roll up into a cumulative forward trajectory of enterprise free cash flows for each and every entity and form the basis of an enterprise value estimate for each and every entity. Within the construct of enterprise valuation, the timing and magnitude of all capital expenditures must be considered.

Valuing MLPs

There are a number of ways to account for business performance across various business structures, whether an entity is a corporate, real estate investment trust (REIT), or MLP, but cash flow will always be cash flow. In finance (and in valuation), a business cannot be worth more or less than the present value of its future enterprise free cash flows, adjusted for its net balance sheet (a net debt or a net cash position), as well as any other "hidden" factors (e.g. an overfunded pension)--no matter if the entity is structured as a corporate, a REIT or MLP.

The prices of these entities may become disconnected from their true intrinsic values, or even estimates of what the market should believe is their true intrinsic value, if for example, "yield-based pricing" (systematic valuation on distributable cash flow) is pursued in an ultra-low interest rate environment (as in what happened with midstream MLPs in 2015). However, value will always be value, distinct from price. A dollar of enterprise free cash flow generated by a retailer is a dollar generated by a software company is a dollar generated by a midstream entity. The present value of dollars coming in versus dollars going out forms the basis of any robust valuation context.

For those focused on value-contributions of each individual project of a pipeline operator as only being incremental (using arbitrary and impractical book equity as a base in economic-profit models), what may be helpful is to consider an MLP as one big project, one big NPV calculation, and therefore, one enterprise free cash flow model, where the timing of enterprise cash flows matters and net debt is considered. In the image on the next page, the link between the industry-specific metric distributable cash flow and the basic construct of an enterprise free cash flow model is established.

Figure 27: Formula That Ties Enterprise Value to Distributable Cash Flow

Master Limited Partnership Valuation

It has become common practice to value master limited partnerships on a Price to Distributable Cash Flow (DCF) basis. However, such a valuation technique, if not supported by an enterprise free cash flow process (1), is susceptible to systematic overvaluation when comparable company analysis is applied.

The following formula links enterprise free cash flow valuation to the P/DCF multiple, showing how the latter is a function of the former, much like enterprise free cash flow valuation *derives* the P/E multiple. The numerator is the standard function used in corporate valuation, while the denominator is an MLP's forward distributable cash flow.

Note how the timing of large capital expenditures (negative) and outsize net debt positions (negative) impact the intrinsic worth of capital-intensive and debt-heavy MLPs.

Forward Price / Distributable Cash Flow (P/DCF) Ratio Derived

$$\frac{\left[\sum_{t=0}^{\infty} \frac{A(t)}{(1+d)^t} - B(0) - C(0) + D(0)\right] \Big/ E(0)}{F(1)}$$

where A (t) is an Enterprise Free Cash Flow (1) at year t,

    B (0) is a Total Debt at time 0,

    C (0) is a Preferred Stock at time 0,

    D (0) is a Total Cash at time 0,

    E (0) is Weighted Average Diluted Shares Outstanding at time 0,

    F is Distributable Cash Flow per Share, and

    d is Weighted Average Cost of Capital (WACC).

(1) Enterprise free cash flow, or free cash flow to the firm (FCFF), is calculated as earnings before interest after taxes less net new investment (total capital spending less total depreciation) +/- working capital changes.

Similar to how enterprise valuation is tied to the P/E ratio, the numerator of the ratio in the image above represents a construct of the enterprise valuation model, which takes the present value of a company's enterprise free cash flow and net balance sheet impact and divides that by units outstanding. The denominator is the industry-specific term distributable cash flow estimated for next year. The formula derives the value that should be placed on the business via the enterprise valuation construct, and then this value estimate helps to inform the multiple of forward expected distributable cash flow that may be reasonably applied to units on the market to determine a fair price. As with the P/E ratio, the value-derived distributable cash flow multiple differs from the price-observed multiple, which is taken by dividing a unit's share price observed on the marketplace by its future distributable cash flow.

Introducing Dividend-Adjusted Leverage

Financial leverage is a very subjective consideration and can be measured in a variety of different ways depending on its relevance to a stakeholder, whether it be an equity holder or debt holder. Some measures of leverage include assets-to-equity as in the third product of the DuPont equation,[221] for example, or total debt-to-EBITDA, or net debt-to-EBTIDA, or total debt-to-equity, among many others. Most leverage metrics, however, tend to focus more on assessing credit quality, as in evaluating the ability of a company to repay its debtholders, or in measuring and ranking the probability of default.

The credit rating agencies employ a wide variety of adjusted financial metrics that have myriad subjective judgments embedded within them. Moody's, for example, uses debt-to-equity and debt-to-book-capitalization, as well as a unique measure called retained cash flow to net debt (RCF/net debt). The definitions for many credit metrics can be relatively complex, in some cases. According to Moody's, RCF/net debt decomposes into the following: (FFO – preferred dividends-common dividends – minority dividends) / (short-term debt + long-term debt, gross – cash and cash equivalents).

The ratio RCF/net debt is a rare credit metric, in our view, that may be applicable to that of the dividend growth or income investor. Where a bond holder may implicitly assume that dividends can be reduced in order to shore up cash flow to

---

[221] The DuPont equation is a measure that breaks return on equity (ROE) into three components: (Net Income/Sales) x (Sales/Assets) x (Assets/Equity).

service debt repayment, from the perspective of the equity investor (one that is counting on that dividend for income), the view is quite different. In the eyes of many committed dividend growth or income investors, the dividend payment is often viewed, in great substance, as the equivalent of a debt-like cash commitment. RCF/net debt provides some context in how much cash flow is left over after paying dividends or distributions to service the debt, but it may not be a pure measure of dividend-adjusted leverage, as in the traditional sense (where EBITDA may be in the denominator, for example, as in net debt-to-adjusted EBITDA).

In any case, one strong quality of the RCF/net debt ratio is that it does not assume that dividends are not going to be paid, as in the case of other traditional credit metrics that effectively ignore the dividend or distribution as an important cash outflow (and an implicit reduction to credit quality). The RCF/net debt ratio assumes that the dividend is a debt-like cash commitment reducing funds from operations, something we believe is very relevant to the dividend growth or income-oriented shareholder that is depending heavily on that dividend or distribution payment. What RCF/net debt also considers is that the same money distributed to shareholders or unitholders is not also "used twice" as the same money that can be used to service the debt (double counting). In my view, it should be generally assumed that such capital can only be used once; if it's expected to be paid out as a dividend or distribution, it generally should not be assumed that it is also capital that can be used for debt repayment.

The idea of a new measure of leverage for dividend growth and income-oriented shareholders/unitholders that considers dividend/distribution obligations originated in the June 2015 analysis of Kinder Morgan when we explained how a dividend-growth or income-oriented investor that, if they are truly counting on the dividend/distribution to be paid in the future for their income stream, they should evaluate the company's financial leverage in the context of both its net debt and the present value of those dividends/distributions to shareholders/unitholders. Once the capital corresponding to dividend payments is released to shareholders/unitholders, that same capital shouldn't also be considered as a means to repay debt as well.

A dividend-adjusted measure of leverage, or financial leverage as it should be viewed in the eyes of the dividend-growth and income-oriented investor, can be considered as follows:

Figure 28: Dividend-Adjusted Leverage Ratio

$$Dividend-adjusted\ Leverage = \frac{LFY\ Net\ Debt + \dfrac{LFY\ Cash\ Dividends\ Paid\ (1+growth\ rate)}{Discount\ Rate}}{LFY\ EBITDA}$$

This measure calculates dividend-adjusted leverage, which considers both the company's debt and the present value of its future expected cash dividend obligations, which, in the eyes of committed dividend-growth or income-oriented shareholders, may be implicitly assumed to be debt-like commitments in substance. The ratio ignores the growth rate in the perpetuity calculation such that it is less sensitive to subjective dividend growth estimation.

The concept of financial leverage should be viewed differently as it relates to the perspective of either the debt holder or the dividend-growth and income-oriented equity holder. In the case of Kinder Morgan in 2015, many holders of its stock were committed dividend growth investors, and they were counting on the company's dividend no matter what. This assumption should be an important part of leverage analysis for the dividend growth and income investor. Looking at financial leverage from the perspective of that of a bond holder, or as one that assumes the company can cut its dividend to repay debt, may not be an accurate representation of actual cash, debt-like obligations in the eyes of dividend-growth or income-oriented shareholders, which are counting on the dividend to be paid through thick and thin.

Where RCF/net debt effectively reduces the numerator by dividends paid to explain just how much cash is left over to service the debt, an implied measure of leverage that views dividends as cash, debt-like commitments may be of equal usefulness. It makes little sense from the perspective of a dividend-growth or income-oriented shareholder to evaluate a company's financial leverage as if one is never going to get paid a dividend or distribution. Financial leverage from the perspective of the dividend-growth or income-oriented shareholder might consider all net debt and the present value of all future expected dividend obligations. Much like rent can be capitalized to arrive at a present value of debt equivalent (as if a retailer were to finance a building instead of paying rent), dividends can be capitalized in much of the same way through either the construct of a dividend discount model or through a modified growing perpetuity function with a reasonable discount rate.

8

The Dividend Misunderstanding

Monopoly. The role of the market specialist. The dividend as a possible symptom of value, not a driver of it. Dividend irrelevance and enterprise valuation. A Yogi-ism. An ex-post construct of enterprise present value? Ask why a lot, and then some more. Why have stocks that continue to pay and grow their dividends do well? Thinking about total return the right way. The "free dividends fallacy." Overheated consumer staples stocks. Price versus value is paramount. The Dividend Cushion ratio demystified. A warning on the implications of share price declines on high-yield stocks.

D ividends have always been important to many investors.

But not one time in my recollection during my buyside experience or as an independent stock analyst did I ever get the sense of just *how* important the dividend had become to investors. My time at Driehaus and Morningstar had been focused on different areas of analysis, and for someone laser-focused on enterprise valuation, the dividend just wasn't a consideration in the value context. However, labels such as "Dividend Aristocrats," a listing of S&P 500 Index constituents that had increased their dividends for the more than 20 years, would soon become part of my vocabulary.

During the 2000s, but prior to the Financial Crisis, the Fed had not yet aggressively pursued zero-interest-rate policy, so perhaps the environment hadn't yet been set up for income and dividend growth investing to flourish. Looking back to the late 1990s and early 2000s, certificates of deposits (CDs) could be had at a yield of 6% or even higher at the local community bank, so perhaps dividend yields just weren't as important a part of the decision-making landscape for equity investors then. High yields could be found elsewhere in risk-free, government-backed instruments.

It might also be reasoned at the time that, if the lofty yields on CDs weren't sufficient, the fixed-income markets might then be more appropriate. Income investors that didn't want to worry about market price fluctuations of comparatively lower-yielding dividend-paying stocks, for example, would only have to hold the bond to maturity and collect the coupons along the way to get their money back and then some, provided an event of default that harmed bondholders did not occur. If seeking income but not taking risks of share-price volatility in the marketplace was one's cup a tea, income or dividend growth stocks may not have been the best fit in the late 1990s and early 2000s, despite the long-term prospects of dividend growth. Yields were already elevated.

We learn a lot from the culture we live in, the education system we promote, and the games we play. Who hasn't played Monopoly, the age-old game that Hasbro scooped up from Parker Brothers, first distributed in 1935? For more than 80 years now, men and women of all ages have been collecting $50 from the "bank" after pulling one of the more-fortuitous Chance cards. Ingrained in society has become the belief that a dividend is incremental, that something is given to shareholders that otherwise was not there. After all, the Monopoly player now has $50, when prior to pulling the Chance card he or she didn't. But unlike the make-believe Monopoly game, a stock's dividend is nothing like this.

The enterprise valuation framework makes it clear that the dividend is but a symptom of value, not a causal driver behind a company's value, and market observers know that on the stock exchange, the share price of a dividend-paying company is marked downward by the market specialist in the amount of the dividend on the ex-dividend date. A dividend then becomes, in theory, capital appreciation that otherwise would have occurred had the company not paid a dividend at all. The value of a dividend-paying company, instead, rests in the actions the dividend-paying company takes to replenish that income stream such that it is sustainable long into the future.

Figure 29: The Market Specialist Marks Down the Price by the Amount of the Dividend

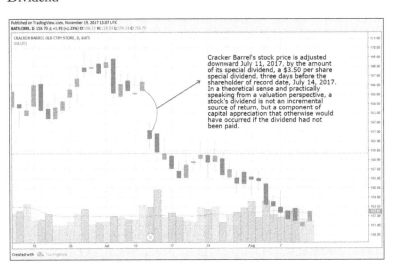

This figure illustrates how the dividend is a component of capital appreciation that otherwise would have been achieved had the dividend not been paid. Such a situation applies to both regular and special dividends.

A company is worth more because its operations generate more free cash flow, not just because it may or may not pay an increasing dividend. In an extreme case, receiving a dividend payment can be largely described as getting paid with your own money because that dividend you just received had already been reflected in the price of the stock you already owned prior to the dividend payment (as with all assets of the business, shareholders already have a claim on the cash dividend they receive, even before its paid).

That said, many investors may prefer the dividend for cash-flow reasons (and tax implications can impact how investors would like to receive their returns), but in many respects, perhaps the primary utility of the dividend payment, whether a monthly or quarterly one or other, is the structure and timing of the income payment to the investor. The idea that paying a dividend keeps excess capital out of the hands of management, which may be tempted to pursue what could end up being value-destroying endeavors (if it sees its cash coffers swell), may be another reason to like dividends. One might think of this reason as perhaps similar in thinking to how companies load up on debt to provide a layer of discipline on operations such that debt servicing costs can be met.

But could the significance of the dividend be overstated? Shouldn't the focus be primarily on the company's intrinsic value generation, not on what could largely be considered a discretionary dividend policy? Is Berkshire Hathaway any less attractive of an investment idea because it hasn't paid a dividend in 50+ years? Are there other ways for financial advisors to structure income payments to meet their clients' requests without stretching needlessly for "getting paid with their own money (i.e. the dividend)," especially if it leads to overpaying for stock? In this sense, is the tail (the ease of income policy with dividend payments) wagging the dog (the decisions in setting prudent investment policies for retirees)?

Management teams should do a better job explaining what a cash dividend is and what it is not. This might save many executive teams from encountering a lot of trouble in trying to pay out more than the business can handle.

How Dividends Impact Enterprise Valuation

Let's imagine for a minute that you gave $1,000 to your co-worker for a piece of paper, and the co-worker said that in exchange he or she would pay you a $1 per year and increase the payment 5% each year until the $1,000 ran out (was completely transferred back to you). At any time during the arrangement, you could give the paper back, and your co-worker would return the remaining money left (less cumulative dividends already paid) to you in full. Let's ask two questions. Absent the time value of money (i.e. the discount mechanism that links the value of cash flows generated tomorrow to today), what is the value of this hypothetical relationship to you? And when he or she pays you more and more each year, should you grow more and more excited about the payment?

The answer to the first question is that the relationship to you isn't worth anything. You could have your $1,000 back right now by returning the paper, or your co-worker would eventually over time provide you with an annual income stream until you finally receive $1,000 in its entirety in the future. Absent the time value of money, these two scenarios are equal. Raising the payout to you each and every year (as in dividend growth), and paying you back with your own money, shouldn't make you more or less excited in this example (it is not value creating). The only value of such a relationship would occur if your co-worker grows the

$1,000 you gave him for your benefit. If instead, the co-worker would replace all payments that are given to you with his or her own personal earnings such that at any time he or she would have $1,000 to give to you in exchange for the paper (even though he or she keeps paying you a growing dividend).

Now that would be fantastic deal! The value of this relationship to you, instead of being net-neutral ($0) in the scenario where the co-worker did not replace the dividends paid to you, would be a growing perpetuity function: [$1 x (1.05)]/(0.10 - 0.05) = $21.[222] Essentially, the co-worker is creating $21 in value for you because he or she is generating earnings for you (replacing the dividends paid to you). The value of a relationship where one party pays an income stream to another is not in the income stream itself, but in the actions one party takes to replenish that income stream such that it can continue to be paid in the future. Perhaps in more relevant terms, the value of a dividend-paying firm is not in the income itself, but in the actions the dividend-paying firm takes to replenish that income stream such that it is sustainable. Generally speaking, a company can increase its intrinsic value if it drives better-than-expected enterprise free cash flows (relative to future forecasts), which would increase the value estimate by bolstering total firm (enterprise) value.[223] The analytical focus therefore should be on the operations of the business that generates enterprise free cash flows to replace cash dividends paid, not necessarily on the dividend itself.

When a company pays a dividend, the intrinsic value of the company is adjusted lower by the amount that the company pays to shareholders in cash. Similarly, within enterprise valuation, a cash dividend payment reduces the intrinsic value of a company, much like paying yourself a personal dividend in the form of a vacation for yourself reduces your net worth (you may get great utility from vacationing, but it reduces your net worth). Enterprise valuation is largely consistent with Modigliani and Miller's dividend irrelevance theorem, which states that in a perfect capital world with no taxes, a company's dividend policy should be irrelevant to valuation.[224] Modigliani's and Miller's dividend irrelevance theorem can probably be best summed up in a famous passage in the Abilene Reporter from 1971:

---

[222] This example assumes a hypothetical 10% discount rate.
[223] A company can increase its intrinsic value by reducing fundamental risk as well.
[224] Of course, we do not live in a world where there are no taxes, so dividend policies do matter, especially when it comes to the after-tax returns investors actually receive.

Seems Mantle, Berra and Whitey Ford went looking for a bite to eat after a night game in Baltimore (I think) and stopped in at a pizza parlor. They each ordered a large one, and when the waitress asked Yogi (Berra) whether he wanted his sliced in eight pieces or four, he shot back, "Four. I don't think I can eat eight.[225]

Obviously, this is one of the more famous "Yogi-isms," but the analogy is a good one. Whether total returns are distributed via capital appreciation or dividends, tax considerations aside, it generally shouldn't matter to the investor. Even more apparent, however, is that given the various dividend policies and payout ratios across companies, the relevance of the dividend discount model becomes highly questionable. The bird in the hand hypothesis, which suggests that companies that pay higher current dividends today should have higher stock values and stock prices, is also suspect. Entities that don't pay dividends can still have value. In some ways, the dividend discount model should have been dead for a while, and its application today might just be confusing analysts about how value is generated for shareholders.

That said, many, including Nobel laureate Robert Shiller, at least in some of his earlier works and in his book *Irrational Exuberance*, explain that the value of an equity is tied to its future dividend payments. Shiller developed the concept of dividend present value, which "subsequent to any given year is the (as yet unknown) true fundamental value of the stock market in that year." By tying value to a future realized stream of dividends, he was able to show that stock prices are far too volatile to be accurate predictors of intrinsic value. Though the work was fascinating, theoretically, there should only be a very loose relationship between dividend present value and the share price anyway, if at all, for most companies (as, in most cases, the dividend is paid from only a portion of the enterprise cash flow stream). It may be more definitive to extend Shiller's concept of dividend present value to enterprise cash flows, but one may hypothesize that "enterprise present value," or using realized enterprise cash flows in the same ex-post construct as the dividend present value, may result in a similar conclusion as Shiller's: stock prices are too volatile to accurately reflect intrinsic values.

---

[225] Incidentally, this is how investors should think about stock splits. The size of the pie (business value) available to shareholders has not changed. It is now just broken into more pieces (shares).

The Importance of "Why"

History has revealed that some of the best performing stocks during the previous decades have been those that paid ever-increasing cash to shareholders in the form of dividends. In a recent study by Ned Davis, for example, S&P 500 stocks that initiated dividends or grew them over time registered roughly a 10% annualized return since January 31, 1972 (through December 31, 2017), while stocks that did not pay out dividends or cut them performed poorly over the same time period (the group of Dividend Cutters & Eliminators declined during the period). Not only did these strong dividend payers turn out to be great investments, but investors that reinvested dividends received a greater percentage ownership of these companies in time. Dividend growth investing not only capitalizes on reinvested dividends into the accumulation of more shares of stock, but also on the increased per-share dividend on the greater number of shares held, both dynamics further augmented over time if such a stock appreciates considerably.

But paying a dividend, in itself, is not a value-creating move by a company. Dividend growth investors know that Apple hasn't been one of the best performing stocks in history just because it started paying a dividend a number of years ago (it even cut its dividend in 1995), and income investors know Berkshire Hathaway has value even though it hasn't paid a dividend in 50+ years. Letting backward-looking studies, alone, guide an investment process could simply lead investors astray. In this case, drawing empirical deductions from historical data without having a theory for why something is happening could cause investors to rush out and buy companies that have paid a growing dividend in the past, almost at any share price and irrespective of other considerations. It's far more important to understand the "why" behind the evidence in any study as the data observed may not be causal to the outcome.

Toyota is perhaps most admired for the Toyota Production System, pioneered by former executive of the auto giant Taiichi Ohno in the 1950s. Ohno viewed any problem as an opportunity in disguise and encouraged root-cause thinking on the production floor. Toyota would later come to enjoy a reputation for the quality of both its products and processes for decades. Ohno emphasized that uncovering the root cause of any issue is the key to finding a sustainable solution. He believed that data was important to understand the manufacturing process, but he placed the "greatest emphasis on facts," or what is driving the data.

Ohno would advise his staff on the production floor whenever a problem arose, "Ask 'why' five times about every matter." Only through persistent enquiry could the root cause of why something is happening be established. Ohno would use an example of a welding robot breaking down on the factory floor to illustrate his "five why's" method, but this method has other applications and it can even take more than five "why's" to get to the root cause. The answer to each series of "why's" may be different depending on the investor's viewpoint, but let's apply the exercise to help explain why perhaps the performance of dividend-paying and dividend-growing stocks may have been so good.

1. Why have stocks that have paid and grown their dividends over time generated significant total returns for investors in the past?

> Many investors would say that the reinvestment of dividends and the power of compounding have accounted for more than 80% of the total return, and therefore these are two of the primary reasons why.

2. Why are companies able to continue to pay and grow their dividend so investors can reinvest the dividend, and why is compounding important to the total return equation?

> For an investor to continuously reinvest a growing dividend, a company must be able to generate enough free cash flow to keep paying and raising the dividend over time. Compounding only works if the company's business value, and by extension, its market capitalization also advances over time.

3. Why are some companies able to generate strong and growing free cash flows while others cannot, and why do the value of some businesses increase over time while others don't?

> Some businesses have competitive advantages, great products, and pursue continuous innovation such that their operations generate strong and growing free cash flows for long periods of time. Investors building in changes in expectations for future free cash flow generation by the company impacts the estimated value of the company over time, and therefore its subsequent market capitalization, all else equal. Higher expected future free cash flows generally translate into higher values and market capitalization, all else equal.

4. Why do some companies have strong competitive advantages, great products, and pursue continuous innovation while others do not, and why are some

companies able to continuously grow free cash flows over time and the market's expectations in them while others cannot?

These two questions are somewhat connected and may converge upon one answer, and while luck may be part of it, particularly with respect to the market's expectations of future free cash flows, the structure of the industry in which a company operates has a lot to do with whether a company can carve out competitive advantages and a profitable niche, and by extension, whether a company can generate substantial free cash flows to support a growing dividend payment.

5. Why might that be?

How a company interacts with customers and suppliers, the intensity of existing competition and the threat of new entrants and substitute products are a few considerations that, here it is: separate winning businesses from losing businesses. The airline business, for example, has notoriously been a bad one, and that simply wouldn't have changed based on dividend policies, and whether investors reinvested those dividends (many an airline has gone belly up!). On the other hand, companies such as Alphabet or Facebook, which operate near-monopolies, have generated substantial total returns since going public, despite not ever paying a dividend to shareholders. Keynesian beauty contest analogies aside, total return, in part, comes down to whether the company, itself, is a winning or losing business, no matter if it pays a dividend or not.

The S&P High Yield Dividend Aristocrats Index comprises stocks that "have consistently increased their dividend for at least 20 consecutive years." As of October 2018, there were only approximately 110 holdings out of the roughly 1,500 possible stocks in the S&P 1500 Composite Index that met the criteria (or approximately 7% of the total). Without a doubt, it is no small feat for a company to increase its dividend each year for 20 consecutive years (and these companies should be proud of this accomplishment), but the dividend should not be viewed as causal to a business' success, but rather, the dividend should merely be viewed a symptom of a business' success. This distinction is important but frequently overlooked by dividend growth and income investors focusing primarily on the dividend payment, itself.

Strong dividend-paying companies have more than likely done a better job generating economic value and strong free cash flows over time. This has allowed them to pay out increasing dividends to shareholders, but more critically, it has provided the support for the market to re-value their businesses ever higher, facilitating a higher market capitalization and compounding returns on reinvested dividends. It's not that these companies paid a growing dividend, itself, that has led to their success, but rather that their operations and free cash flows have improved considerably in time, resetting their valuations higher. Reinvesting dividends in a company that eventually files for bankruptcy is never a good strategy, while outperforming dividend-paying stocks would still have been winning stocks had they never paid a dividend at all.

Theoretically, one might hypothesize their total returns would still be the same, too, whether they paid a dividend or not. For example, you may be familiar with studies that show the S&P 500 total return with reinvested dividends versus the S&P 500 price-only return with no dividends. From December 1960 through December 2017, the growth of $10,000 in the S&P 500 with reinvested dividends was nearly $2.6 million. By comparison, the growth of the S&P 500 over this time period, its price only, amounted to about $0.46 million. The difference is astounding. However, what is left out of the price-only return is the theoretical return that otherwise would have been price had the company not paid the dividend in the first place (investors now would have this money in their pockets). Not only this, but had investors used the money in their pockets to invest in non-dividend-paying companies that may have been tremendously undervalued (and these companies subsequently performed relatively better), it is possible that the total return could have been even greater than the S&P 500 return with dividends reinvested!

My opinion is not that the dividend is not important (it is to many investors), or that dividend reinvestment strategies may not lead to great returns (they have in the past), but rather that stock selection (and a focus on enterprise valuation) will always matter, even in the context of an income-oriented or dividend growth strategy that may not emphasize it, or at least not emphasize it enough. A focus on the dividend alone won't lead you to riches. There's much more to it than that.

Understanding Total Return

That investors are interested in dividend payments is quite understandable. Each month or each quarter, there is a tangible dividend check in the mail (think of that Chance card in the board game Monopoly; it "feels" incremental when you receive Monopoly money you didn't have before), and this concept is quite appealing in a stock market that may seem rigged to the casual observer. The benefits emanating from reinvesting dividends over time in an appreciating equity can be quite profound, and dividend growth strategies where yield on cost can increase materially in time are attractive.[226]

Studies that show the outperforming nature of dividend payers and growers may only add conviction to the dividend investor's psyche, and a breakdown of long-term stock returns that show how the percentage of total return attributable to dividends can be considerable helps to create a sense that the dividend is somehow incremental to capital appreciation when it is a part of it. One of the more popular total-return breakdowns, for example, comes from *Common Sense on Mutual Funds*, written by John C. Bogle:[227]

> These variables determine stock market returns over the long term:
>
> 1) The dividend yield at the time of initial investment.
>
> 2) The subsequent rate of growth in earnings.
>
> 3) The change in the price-earnings ratio during the period of investment.
>
> The total of these three components explains nearly all of the stock market's returns over extended holding periods. By analyzing the contribution to total return of the three factors, reasoned consideration of future returns can take place. The initial dividend yield is a known quantity. The rate of earnings growth has usually been relatively predictable within fairly narrow parameters. And the change in the price-earnings ratio has proven highly speculative. Total return is simply the sum of these three factors. For example, an initial dividend yield of, say, 3 percent plus a forecasted earnings growth of 7 percent annually over the next 10 years would bring the return to 10 percent. A change in the

---

[226] The concept of yield on original cost is attractive to long-term dividend growth investors. Realty Income is an excellent example. Investors who purchased $800 worth of shares of the REIT on October 18, 1994, would have received annual income of $90 on their original investment of $800 at the time for a yield of 11.3%. By 2018, thanks to successive dividend increases, that annual income would grow to $265, implying a yield on original cost of 33%.
[227] For what could be considered additional criticism of the total-return framework explained by Jack Bogle, please see McKinsey *Valuation* (2010), page 50-51.

price-earnings ratio—from, say, 15 times at the beginning of the period to a forecasted 18 times at the end—would add 2 percentage points to that total, bringing the return on stocks to 12 percent. – *John C. Bogle, Common Sense on Mutual Funds*

One might think that, given this breakdown of expected long-term returns, if one were to hypothetically assume that, if all companies were to stop paying dividends, the total expected total return should fall to 9%, a reduction by the amount of the dividend yield (3%). However, total return expectations shouldn't necessarily change in this case, provided there is not a major disruption in the marketplace as a result of companies doing away with their payouts. Whether the dividend yield is 1% or 3% or 8%, the total expected return in Bogle's example should still be 12% with the balance relative to the dividend yield coming from capital appreciation under any distribution of outcomes. Though presented as such, the dividend is not incremental or a driver of total return, but rather capital appreciation that otherwise would have accrued to the shareholder had the dividend not been paid.

Part of the confusion regarding the dividend may arise almost entirely from broad generalizations about expectations of long-term returns that break total return into a dividend and capital-appreciation component. Also contributing to the misunderstanding is an investor's use of the P/E ratio, where in applying a multiple to earnings, it makes the dividend, itself, look like it's incremental, as the stock price is capitalized based on earnings, irrespective of changes on the balance sheet. What's more, in the dividend discount model, when the dividend is applied as the driver behind an estimate of intrinsic value, an understanding of what *actually* drives a company's value, and therefore, its total return almost entirely becomes lost. In a paper, *The Dividend Disconnect*, Samuel Hartzmark and David H. Solomon define the situation of many investors viewing the dividend as separate from the price appreciation of the stock as the "free-dividends fallacy." The duo even found that when investors tend to choose stocks just for their dividends, it could cost them as much as 2%-4% less per year than what otherwise might have been expected.

Let's use a couple examples to explain this "free dividends fallacy" a bit more. 3M, for example, has a long track record of annual dividend increases, but had the company never paid a dividend in its corporate life, its market capitalization would be significantly higher today, all else equal. The cash on 3M's balance sheet, for one, would be much larger than it is today, and because net cash is a source of intrinsic value, its market capitalization should theoretically be much bigger today, too, even if such cash had not been used in the past to drive even more value. On the other hand, had Berkshire Hathaway been paying shareholders a consistent dividend during its corporate history, its market capitalization today would be much lower, all else equal. The net cash on its books would be lower than it is today, and the cash that it reinvested into other businesses would not have compounded in time.

In a more practical, less theoretical sense, why might some dividend stocks be doing well? Keynesian beauty contest theorists may say that the advent of dividend growth equities as a substitute for low-yielding debt instruments in ultra-low interest rate environments (as that in the years following the Financial Crisis) has driven more buying from income-oriented investors, and this has in turn, has attracted more and more investors, driving up shares of dividend paying stocks. In August 2016, I made a reference to consumer staples equities being like the stocks of the "Roaring '20s:"

> ...at arguably no time in the history of the stock market have investors been willing to pay so much for each unit of earnings to capture a dividend yield of just a few percentage points...In many ways, the strongest business models have become some of the most risky stocks, to no fault of their own...The makings of a dividend-growth bubble are well underway on some of the strongest business models in the market and have been for some time. It sounds so backward, but it's true--you know as well as I do that a good company a good stock does not always make. But at what earnings multiple do market participants finally say that it has become too expensive to stretch for that 2-3% dividend yield? Today, the consumer staples sector stands at a forward P/E ratio of 21 times, well above its 5-year and 10-year averages and significantly above the market multiple... it's the "Roaring '20s" in the US, and investors can't get enough of dividend-paying companies!

Everyone seemed to be interested in consumer staples stocks at the time, in part due to their strong, recession-resistant business models, but probably more truthfully because of their steady track records of consecutive annual dividend growth (and if not, perhaps because others were interested in their steady track records of consecutive annual dividend growth).[228] Something wasn't quite right with how the market was pricing their shares, however. These stocks were fetching 20+ earnings multiples, while revenue growth was practically nil, and many had considerable net debt positions. For example, Kimberly-Clark reported a net sales decline of 1.2% in its second-quarter 2016 report, but the stock still traded at 21 times adjusted 2016 earnings. Coca-Cola experienced a net revenue decline of 5% during its second-quarter 2016, but the beverage giant still fetched a 23 times 2016 earnings multiple at the time. Colgate-Palmolive's sales fell more than 5% during the second quarter of 2016, but the company would still garner a high-20s multiple on 2016 bottom-line numbers.

Did these companies have huge net cash positions that may help justify an unusually-large value-derived earnings multiple within the enterprise valuation framework? *Not even close.* Kimberly-Clark's total debt was $7.7 billion versus a cash balance of $0.7 billion at the end of the second quarter of 2016, meaning it had a huge net debt position. Coca-Cola's total debt load, including loans and notes payable, was north of $48 billion relative to a total cash balance of $21.4 billion at the end of the second quarter of 2016, again another huge net debt position. Colgate-Palmolive's total debt load stood at $6.6 billion against a total cash balance of $1.1 billion at the end of the second quarter of 2016, revealing that, it, too had a large net debt position. The enterprise valuation framework will tell you that it is highly unlikely for shrinking companies with huge net debt positions to garner value-derived earnings multiples north of 20 times, across the board.

What was going on? Why were investors paying up for these companies? Well, most were scooping them up for their dividends, of course, sometimes irrespective of their valuations, and mainly because they fit neatly within the dividend growth framework.[229] After all, they have widely-recognized brand

---

[228] This line of thinking is connected to what is commonly called the clientele effect, where a set of investors are attracted to certain securities (e.g. consumer staples) because the companies pursue certain policies (a growing dividend, for example). The clientele effect can impact the pricing of a security significantly, both up or down.

[229] A few months prior to our "Roaring '20s" reference, in June 2016, we felt the dividend growth "track record" craze might play out a lot like that of the "Nifty Fifty" craze of the late 1960s and 1970s. The 'Nifty Fifty' was a group of "buy-and-hold" large cap stocks that were largely credited with driving the market to new heights during the early 1970s, with their average P/E ratio of 37 in 1972. Many called these stocks with stable earnings one-decision stocks--they were to be bought and held forever. Most of the 'Nifty Fifty' underperformed during the bear market of the late 1970s, early 1980s, after their run higher, but they had their time in the limelight.

names and long, dependable dividend growth track records, and some with tremendous competitive advantages. Many investors, however, weren't paying attention to the price they were paying for shares, and to an even larger degree, they weren't considering how net debt fits within the enterprise valuation framework, creating a wide dislocation between price and estimated intrinsic value. Something other than enterprise valuation was driving their stock prices, and that meant market inefficiency, perhaps best defined in this text as the market not pricing its *own* expectations correctly (not necessarily a difference between price and true intrinsic value). The consumer staples sector would end up underperforming considerably from August 2016 through October 2018.

Figure 30: The Significant Underperformance of Consumer Staples Stocks

The price performance of an ETF tracking the S&P 500 (SPY), top, relative to the price performance of an ETF tracking the consumer staples sector (XLP), bottom from August 2016 through the end of October 2018. Image: TradingView.

The popularity of dividends tends to go in and out of favor over market cycles. During the 1990s, dividends had been de-emphasized as the world ushered in an age of irrational exuberance[230], and many were chasing the next dot-com darling. Returns during the 2000s, however, were atrocious as a result of the Internet bubble bust followed by the Financial Crisis, and dividend investing came back

---

[230] Former Federal Reserve chairman Alan Greenspan coined the term, "irrational exuberance," at a December 5, 1996 speech at the American Enterprise Institute. It would later become the title of Nobel laureate Robert Shiller's book, released a few years later.

into vogue, its popularity largely continuing through today, buttressed by ultra-low interest rates. However, the dividend will always be a source of capital appreciation that otherwise would have accrued to the shareholder, had the company not paid a dividend, and buying stocks solely based on their dividends opens the door to serious overpayment risk.

Never forget: Enterprise valuation is independent with respect to a company's dividend policy, and intrinsic value is reduced by the amount of the dividend payment, much like the specialist marks down a stock price by the amount of the dividend on the exchange. Such dynamics get misconstrued, however, as market participants may only focus on a re-capitalization of earnings per share in valuation (e.g. the P/E ratio), and as the stock price experiences considerable volatility the day it trades ex-dividend.

Time Often Does Not Determine the Time Horizon

Each investor has different goals and risk tolerances, but it may be important for investors to understand that, tax-considerations aside, a dollar is a dollar, whether it comes from income or from capital appreciation. Investors that try to "force" their returns to be generated strictly via income over the long haul are, in some ways, trying to tell the market what to do, which could end badly. If the market hands you lemons, make lemonade. Said another way, if an income idea jumps 30% in a few months, handing you the equivalent of perhaps 5-10 years' worth of income in the form of capital appreciation, why not consider taking it, even if you may have been planning to hold the stock for longer than 5 years? Surely, one can't be disappointed by taking profits?

Some investors could be. Why? Because achieving the goal didn't take years, and the return didn't come in the form of a dividend payment. It seems these investors want to tell the market what to do, and this seems so silly to me. If you may be disappointed because income ideas are providing you with significant income through alternative means such as in the form of capital appreciation, strive to be flexible and open your mind on ways you might be able to convert that capital appreciation to income to achieve goals. To paraphrase Buffett, if you want a dividend, you can sell some stock and make it.[231] An investor can never control the distribution of returns they receive from the market, but only seek to achieve their investment goals from the market. If the market hands you a winning ticket, it's okay to cash it in.

In some respects, the market is often going to tell you when profit taking might be prudent. If a stock is purchased at $10 and doubles to estimated fair value in a matter of weeks, an investor may be interested in unloading it for a profit at that time...in a matter of a few weeks...as upside from that point may be rather limited. On the other hand, if a stock is purchased at $10 and it takes 10 years for it to double to estimated intrinsic value, the holding period for an investor might be 10 years, if he or she would like to sell at an estimate of intrinsic worth. The price-to-estimated-fair value equation matters much more in determining the time horizon than the passing of time, per se. Investors wouldn't hold a significantly overpriced stock just for the sake of holding it because they made money too quickly, would they?

A Financial Construct for Assessing the Capacity for Dividend Growth

The construct that alerted us to the concerns with respect to Kinder Morgan and most midstream MLPs in mid-2015 form the backbone of what is the Dividend Cushion ratio. Since the development of the Dividend Cushion ratio, it has forewarned of the dividend cuts of approximately 50 companies, meaning members to Valuentum's website were well-aware of the significant risk to stocks' dividends before they cut or suspended them.

Some high-profile dividend cuts that the Dividend Cushion ratio has warned about in advance were StoneMor, Mattel, Exelon, BHP Billiton, ConocoPhillips, General Electric, Seadrill, and JC Penney, among dozens of others. We estimate that the ratio's efficacy in predicting dividend cuts is just less than 90%. The measure should be viewed as just one factor to use in assessing the overall health of a company's dividend, as business model and secular demand trends are very

---

[231] In his 2012 Letter to Berkshire Hathaway shareholders, using a variety of assumptions, Warren Buffett explained how not paying a dividend, but rather investors making the dividend by selling Berkshire shares themselves (a "sell-off" scenario), could end up being a better deal for investors.

important qualitative considerations, too, as is information retrieved from market prices (e.g. an outsize yield could itself be foretelling of a cut).

The Dividend Cushion ratio highlight risks, but the calculated 'cushion' behind the ratio also reveals how much financial capacity a company may have to continue growing its dividend in the future, above and beyond existing analyst forecasts. The foundation of the measure rests on assessing future free cash flows relative to future cash dividend payments in the context of a company's balance sheet.

Figure 31: Construct of the Dividend Cushion Ratio

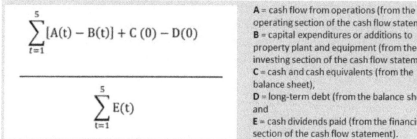

$$\frac{\sum_{t=1}^{5} [A(t) - B(t)] + C(0) - D(0)}{\sum_{t=1}^{5} E(t)}$$

A = cash flow from operations (from the operating section of the cash flow statement), B = capital expenditures or additions to property plant and equipment (from the investing section of the cash flow statement), C = cash and cash equivalents (from the balance sheet), D = long-term debt (from the balance sheet), and E = cash dividends paid (from the financing section of the cash flow statement).

The Dividend Cushion ratio is only one factor used in assessing the overall health of a company's dividend. Business model and secular demand trends are very important qualitative considerations, too, as is information retrieved from market prices (e.g. an outsize yield could be foretelling of a cut in itself).

But why is the Dividend Cushion ratio primarily forward looking? Well, a historical dividend track record only says so much about the dividend, and mostly with respect to management's willingness to keep paying a growing dividend, or a dividend at all, not that the company has the financial wherewithal to keep the payout healthy.

Many companies can fall from grace, even those that had been a part of the coveted S&P 500 Dividend Aristocrats list. In 2009, nine companies, including Anheuser-Busch, Bank of America, Comerica, Fifth Third Bank, Keycorp, Progressive Corp, Regions Financial, Synovus Financial, and Wm. Wrigley, were removed from the list as a result of the Financial Crisis. In 2010, ten more companies failed to stay on the list. Avery Dennison, BB&T, Gannett, General Electric, Johnson Controls, Legg Mason, M&T Bank, Pfizer, State Street Bank, and US Bancorp disappointed. In 2012, CenturyLink was removed, and in 2013, Pitney Bowes was dropped as a result of its own dividend cut.

It is difficult to become a Dividend Aristocrat, and during tough economic times, it may be even more difficult to hold onto that distinction. In any case, what a company has done in the past with respect to its dividend says very little about what it has the capacity to do in the future. Forward-looking analysis is key and measuring the financial capacity of a dividend payer to keep raising its dividend over time is where the Dividend Cushion ratio comes into play.

Figure 32: Example Dividend Cushion Cash Flow Bridge

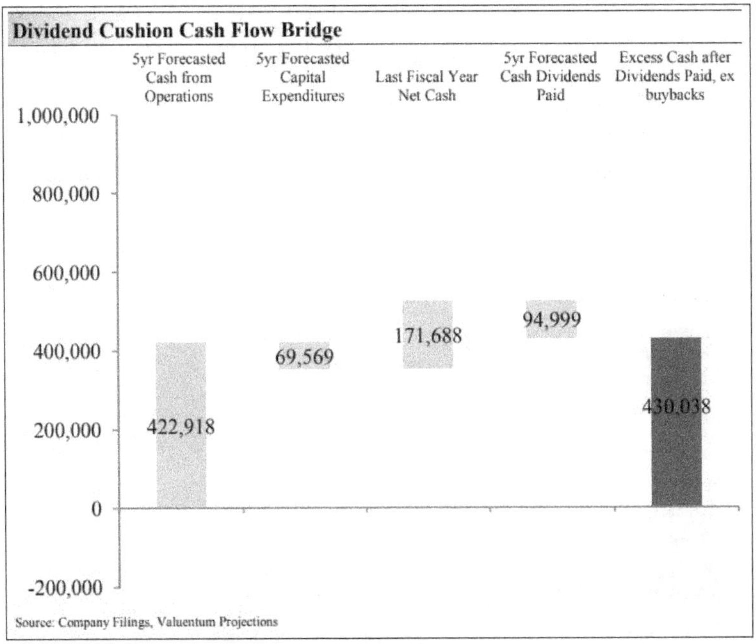

This figure shows the various drivers behind the Dividend Cushion ratio. Source: Valuentum's 16-page equity report of Apple, September 2018.

The image illustrates the components of Apple's Dividend Cushion ratio, revealing the sum of the company's five-year cumulative free cash flow generation, as measured by cash flow from operations less all capital spending, plus its net cash (or less its net debt position) on the balance sheet, as of the last fiscal year, is greater than the sum of the next five years of expected cash dividends paid. The Dividend Cushion ratio is forward-looking and captures the trajectory of the company's free cash flow generation and dividend growth, and it reveals whether there may be a cash surplus or a cash shortfall at the end of the five-year period, taking into consideration the leverage on the balance sheet, a key source of risk.[232]

On a fundamental basis, companies that have a strong net cash position on the balance sheet and are generating a significant amount of free cash flow are better positioned to pay and grow their dividend over time. Companies that are buried under a mountain of debt and do not sufficiently cover their dividend with free cash flow are more at risk of a dividend cut or a suspension of growth, all else equal. Generally speaking, in Figure 32, on the prior page, the greater the 'bar' furthest to the right is positive, the more durable a company's dividend, and the greater the 'bar' furthest to the right is negative, the less durable the dividend.

Figure 33. Example Dividend Cushion Calculation

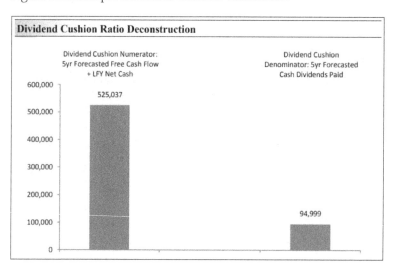

This figure shows the numerator and denominator of the Dividend Cushion ratio. Source: Apple's 16-page equity report, September 2018.

---

[232] The construct of the Dividend Cushion ratio doesn't necessarily imply that all debt will be paid back within the five-year forecast horizon, as much as it uses the debt to capture the financial risk of the dividend payment emanating from the balance sheet. Think of the Dividend Cushion ratio as one might think of a credit rating for a corporate. The Dividend Cushion ranks the financial risk of the dividend, while a credit rating ranks companies by probability of default.

To arrive at the Dividend Cushion ratio for Apple, in Figure 33 on the prior page, we divide the numerator ($525 billion) by the denominator ($95 billion). The numerator represents the sum of the company's net cash position and its cumulative 5-year expected free cash flows, as measured by cash flow from operations less all capital spending. The denominator represents the sum of the company's cumulative five-year expected cash dividends paid. Apple's Dividend Cushion ratio of 5.5 implies considerable dividend strength on a go-forward basis, as in most cases, the higher the ratio above 1, the better.

The Dividend Cushion ratio often exposes the capital-market dependence of most MLPs and some REITs, and the ratio's generation led to the creation of one other variant, the adjusted Dividend Cushion ratio, that considers the conditions of the credit markets at any given time. For example, many MLPs and REITs may not generate sufficient traditional free cash flow to keep paying out an ever-increasing distribution or dividend, meaning these particular entities tend to be very dependent on access to new capital.

As a result, their distributions or dividends are more dependent on the health of external capital market conditions than perhaps on anything else, including underlying fundamentals. The adjusted Dividend Cushion ratio augments the numerator of ratio, bolstered by the assumption of new external capital, creating a positive adjustment during times of good credit. The analyst may revert to the standard Dividend Cushion ratio for these business models during times of tight credit, however, when a dividend cut may grow more likely as external financing support wanes.

Price Declines Are Fundamental for High Yield Stocks

Investing for capital appreciation and investing for yield are two separate things, analytically independent of each other, but sometimes misunderstood by the marketplace. What a company pays out today as a dividend or distribution relative to its share price today has little, if anything, to do with the drivers of its long-term intrinsic value calculation, which is based on balance sheet health and future forecasts of enterprise free cash flows, from which dividends are paid. Where investors that are focused on dividend growth may seek companies that have elevated Dividend Cushion ratios, those that venture into high-yield equities may find most high-yield considerations with Dividend Cushion ratios below 1 or even well below 0, meaning they are significantly capital-market dependent.

In other words, most entities in the high-yield equity arena are already maxing out their payouts and don't have much to guard against exogenous events or cash-flow shortfalls at all. This is what makes them inherently riskier as income vehicles, and in some respects, high-yield stock investing can be viewed as synonymous with high-risk stock investing. Dividend cuts are not only possible but may even be probable. In the event a high-yield equity comes under suspicion of a dividend cut, its price may experience a considerable decline in advance of the dividend cut, given the income-oriented composition of its investor base, resulting in not only capital impairment but also reduced income if the dividend cut eventually happens. The likelihood of prices becoming disconnected from intrinsic values may also be more probable with high-yield stocks, given a greater focus by the marketplace on chasing yield than on calculating an informed intrinsic value estimate.

Broadly speaking, the market price of a stock offers clues that there may be something else impacting the thesis on the company more heavily than an investor's original expectations. For example, if the analyst thinks a stock's shares are worth $50 each, but the stock is trading at $10 on its way to $5, there's probably something not quite lining up (rather than the market being that far off). Price movements could indicate situations when an analyst may be too aggressive, or even too conservative, with forecasts and the corresponding fair value estimate of a company. Some may call this "the information contained in prices." The market can be wrong at times, but sometimes the market price can also offer clues to help assess risks that may not have been extensively presented within the GAAP fundamentals.

There's a very important reason why evaluating market price activity may even be more critical within the high yield equity space. An often-overlooked component of high-yield equity analysis is that the market price, itself, is a key component of the fundamental dividend and distribution thesis of the company given the capital-market dependency of many constituents. For example, during the Financial Crisis of the late 2000s, information in the share-price activity of banking stocks suggested something was very wrong despite items in their financial statements that may have suggested their share-price moves may have been unwarranted. Equity price declines during the Financial Crisis depleted a bank's ability to raise equity, creating an avalanche effect and self-perpetuating weakness, at the very time that access to the capital markets was needed.

Similarly, the decline in the share prices of high-yield equities directly impacts their ability to raise funds, and as a result, impacts their credit strength, and therefore the strength of their dividend or distribution, revealing a similar potential risk as that of banking equities under stress needing to shore up their own capital positions. There is an increased likelihood of a price-avalanche effect in the high-yield space (REITs, MLPs and the like) than in other arenas, per se. This view runs counter to that of many lower-yielding, net-cash-rich corporates that can cover cash dividends paid with free cash flow, meaning that these strong companies do not need continued access to the capital markets.

For high-yield equity considerations, however, capital-market dependence risk remains very real for them given the relationship of their dividends to free-cash-flow generation, and as a result, their share prices are contributing factors to overall financial and dividend health. The need for continued access to the capital markets for many in the high-yield space is why, with respect to high yield ideas, it may be worth paying the most attention to credit quality, as offered by the rating agencies, and share-price movements (as equity is a key source of funding). The health of the payout of a high-yield entity's dividend or distribution may, in some cases, be beyond its control, given the need for ongoing debt or equity capital assistance.

All things considered, however, the focus on the dividend more recently by investors has been a net positive development, but it could also be a concerning one. On one hand, investors that are interested in dividend-growth investing are allocating capital to strong, stable, dividend-paying companies such as Microsoft,[233] for example, and this is great. Doing so prevents many an investor from getting involved in speculative, high-risk companies, which in many cases is the last thing a retiree should be interested in doing. But on the other hand, dividend-paying companies have, in other cases, been transforming into speculative investments, themselves. Many MLPs and REITs, for example, remain overly-dependent on the healthy functioning of capital markets,

---

[233] Microsoft is an idea that we've frequently highlighted as one of the strongest dividend payers on the market. As of November 2018, the company's Dividend Cushion ratio was a very healthy 3.6.

necessitating credit health for survival, and many investors are stretching for 8%+ yielding entities, whose payouts may not survive for long.

This is not a good thing at all.

9

Economic Moats and Economic Castles

Some medieval nomenclature. How to think about the concept of economic value. Pitfalls of some common return metrics. Negative invested capital, and why it could signal a fantastic business. Good companies, but bad stocks. The Oracle of Omaha. The competitive-advantage period. Thinking about mispriced moats, not moats themselves. Magnitude and duration of economic profit. Not a wooden palisade, but a royal castle. Airlines and garbage: which is the better oligopoly? The wider the moat, the lower the stock return?

"**M**oat" wasn't part of my vernacular until 2006.

That's when I first walked through the doors at Morningstar. The company's equity department truly "lived" competitive-advantage analysis, and there, I met some of the smartest people that I will ever come to know. Having worked a couple years on the buyside, I was just getting my bearings in independent research at Morningstar during the years prior to the Financial Crisis. I would soon have 30+ companies under full coverage, however, from airlines to environmental services companies to engineering & construction firms and beyond. By the time I had left the company in 2011, I believe I had written more articles than perhaps any other person employed at the firm through that date. I'm proud of the time I spent there.

One of the most valuable experiences was having the opportunity to cover one of the worst industries out there, the airlines, while covering one of the best industries out there, the garbage haulers (more on this later). It was truly a dichotomy that perhaps few other analysts get to experience, but I think every analyst should. It seemed one week I'd be writing about a failed airline, and then the next I'd be writing about the strong fundamental backdrop and increasing value of airspace emanating from a garbage hauler's disposal capacity. It was great. These industries represented two textbook case studies on both sides of the spectrum of Michael Porter's 5 forces, and I couldn't think of a better experience to soak up as much as there was to know about competitive-advantage analysis.

Though Warren Buffett coined the term "moat" in 1999, Morningstar deserves a tremendous amount of credit for making the term "economic moat" go mainstream. The research firm has written several books about economic moats, and I'd be remiss if I didn't give them a shout out. Pat Dorsey's *"The Five Rules for Successful Stock Investing"* and *"The Little Book That Builds Wealth"* are two fine pieces of literature on the topic, and more recently the Morningstar team wrote *"Why Moats Matter,"* which dives deep into what the firm believes are the five sources of an economic moat: intangibles, cost advantage, switching costs, network effect, and efficient scale.

Because competitive-advantage analysis, or economic-moat analysis, has become so engrained in my thoughts after years of training new analysts at Morningstar as Director of Global Equity and Credit Research (Training and Methodology), I can't possibly begin to tell you how much it influences the way I think about individual equities. Thinking about the competitive advantages of a company is about as natural as breathing for me. It just happens, and I think for any investor, a solid fundamental framework in economic moat analysis is simply par for the course. Investors can go wrong in a great many ways, but there's only upside to learning the in's and out's about what separates the best companies from the worst ones, often separated by those with product or service pricing power and those without.[234]

---

[234] There's nothing that quite drives returns like product or service pricing strength. The stronger the competitive advantage, the stronger the pricing power in most cases, and the easier it is for the company to drive higher RONIC.

ROIC versus RONIC

The measure of a company's ability to generate value for shareholders is not expressed in accounting earnings per share, or really anything found only on the income statement. What makes a good business is not necessarily how much it generates in earnings, but rather the efficiency at which it uses shareholder capital to generate those earnings and resulting free cash flow. For example, a business that spends $100 million to generate incremental earnings of $1 million may experience earnings-per-share expansion, but its economic returns on investment are terrible. On the other hand, a company that can generate $1 million in incremental earnings on negligible new investment may be a great business.[235]

But even the widely-used measures return on assets and return on equity, which consider some comparison between the income statement and balance sheet, fall short of telling the whole story. After all, why should the view of the strength of a company's operations be impacted by the amount of cash held on the balance sheet, as in ROA, and why should businesses be viewed to be better than others if they just take on more leverage, as in ROE? They shouldn't. The measure that best evaluates the value-generating capacity of a business is return on invested capital, or ROIC, and more specifically, return on new invested capital, its first derivative RONIC.

ROIC is generally expressed as earnings before interest, after taxes, or EBI (NOPLAT), divided Invested Capital, or the difference between the operating assets of the business--the sum of net PP&E, inventories, accounts receivable, and other current assets--and the operating liabilities of the business such as accounts payable and other current liabilities (including deferred revenue). ROIC gives a pure measure of the return on the net operating assets of the business, and it can be calculated with and without goodwill. RONIC evaluates the return of a business' next incremental dollar invested, and it is generally calculated as the change in earnings before interest, after taxes (EBI or NOPLAT), divided by the change in invested capital, or net new investment.[236] Companies that can drive EBI improvement at a fast rate with little change in invested capital are generating

---

[235] These two examples show that not all growth is good. Companies that can invest new capital at high rates of return should grow fast. However, the same is not true for companies that are destroying capital. They should work on improving returns first.

[236] Net new investment in any given year generally represents the difference in capital expenditures and depreciation +/- changes in non-cash net operating working capital.

significant value for shareholders, provided that the incremental return on invested capital, or RONIC, is in excess of the company's weighted average cost of capital.

Figure 34: The Formula for RONIC

RONIC = Change in EBI, or NOPLAT / Change in Invested Capital, or Net New Investment

In Warren Buffett's 1992 Letter to Berkshire Hathaway shareholders, he talks about what kinds of businesses are the best. Paraphrasing the Oracle of Omaha, if we were to throw out a comparison between price and estimated intrinsic value, the best kind of business is one that can invest incremental capital at elevated rates of return over long and sustained periods of time. The worst kind of business, however, is the opposite, or one that continues to invest heavily in very low-return endeavors. The Oracle of Omaha would add that the first type of business is rather difficult to find, mostly because the companies usually don't need a lot of capital.

The point is worth emphasizing. A company is not generating value for shareholders because its accounting earnings have expanded, or that earnings per share was augmented by buybacks at any price, for example. A company generates value for shareholders when its operations generate incremental returns on invested capital that are greater than its weighted average cost of capital (WACC), meaning that it can access capital at a cost that is less than the returns it will generate once it puts that investment capital into place. A company that generates incremental return on invested capital of 20%, for example, and has a WACC of 9.5% would be considered one that is generating value for shareholders. In this example, the company has a positive RONIC-less-WACC spread.

Part of the analytical benefits of using the framework of ROIC and its first derivative RONIC in assessing business quality is that it captures the capital intensity of a company, in aggregate, and on each new dollar invested, and it brings to the fore some of the most attractive business models that may be self-funded. For example, auto manufacturers such as General Motors and Ford that have a significant amount of fixed assets won't necessarily generate high returns on invested capital, while asset-light companies or licensing or franchising entities may generate significant returns on invested capital. A great example of a company with tremendous returns on invested capital is Domino's, which to many may just be a pizza company, but really is a tremendous capital allocator with profits driven primarily by franchise royalties. Its franchisees take on most of the operating risk and capital investment, not Domino's itself.

ROIC also shows the enviable position of some companies that have negative invested capital. These types of businesses collect cash from customers at such a rate that they are practically self-funded. A good example of this today is the capital-light subscription-based business model, where cash receipts in the form of deferred revenue, an operating liability, can completely overwhelm any operating assets, including land and property, causing negative invested capital. Where negative ROIC driven by negative EBI reveals a company that may be under operational stress, negative ROIC driven by negative invested capital may signal a fantastic business. Such businesses can practically be launched with no capital, and each new dollar of earnings is generated without the need of further investment.

A subscription-based business, itself, Valuentum was launched for less than $5,000.[237]

Good Companies Don't Always Make Good Stocks

Believing good companies will also be good stocks might be a prevalent view among some investors, to the degree that many may focus almost entirely on evaluating a company's long-term fundamentals, not necessarily on whether a company's price is trading at a discount to an informed estimate of its intrinsic value, which captures those long-term fundamentals. Long-term fundamental considerations contribute to the most important component of equity value and stock market capitalization, and it may be the case that it is easier to identify potential mispricings in companies that have more stable, long-term fundamental make-ups, but this doesn't change the supreme investment consideration, which

---

[237] Incidentally, I would never consider the value of Valuentum's assets as a function of this initial investment in book equity. It's much more intuitive to base value on forward-looking enterprise free cash flows.

rests in a comparison between a company's share price and an estimate of its intrinsic value.

During times of euphoria, even the prices of good companies can become detached from what may be considered a reasonable estimate of their intrinsic values. For example, had you bought Microsoft at the peak of the dot-com bubble in December 1999 at a split-adjusted price close to $60 per share (a move of terrible timing in hindsight), absent dividend considerations, it would have taken until October 2016 for investors to recoup their initial investment, almost 17 years later. If anything, however, Microsoft became a stronger company during that 17-year period. Another example is Amazon, which on a split-adjusted basis surpassed $100 per share during the go-go years of the late 1990s. However, it would take almost 10 years for the stock to get back to those split-adjusted levels, despite the company's fundamentals getting ever-stronger.

Where in the cases of Microsoft and Amazon, things eventually worked out for long-term holders, with Microsoft's shares surging to $100+ and Amazon breaching $2,000+ during 2018, this doesn't always have to be the case. Many an investor likely sold Microsoft's shares following the dot-com bust, and many an investor probably didn't stick around to watch Amazon rise to the top. Where both Microsoft and Amazon became only better companies following the late 1990s, investors could have lost a lot of money in their shares along the way, and many that may have avoided losses probably didn't have the nerve to continue holding after breaking even following all those years.

The examples are less about explaining the potential merits of a long-term holding period in staving off losses on companies that survive and then thrive (or the potential benefits of dollar cost averaging on stocks that eventually recover and set new highs), but more to explain the idea that investing rests on identifying whether the characteristics of good companies are mispriced at any particular time, rather than on whether a company has strong fundamentals or not, in an absolute sense. What mattered most to returns is the investors' assessment of price versus estimated intrinsic value at any point in time, as even great companies such as Microsoft or Amazon, if bought at the wrong price, can be horrible investments.

Warren Buffett's Economic Moat

No other saying on the topic of moats may be more widespread than Warren Buffet's: "In business, I look for economic castles protected by unbreachable moats." The teachings of Warren Buffett have become a favorite among individual investors and have been embraced by money-management firms and sell-side firms alike. The phrase 'economic moat'--or sustainable competitive advantage--may have become ubiquitous in the investment world, and the term may have perhaps lost much of its significance and meaning along the way. Most management teams across the globe are now eager to tell you about their business' very own 'economic moat,' while research analysts will talk frequently about the moaty characteristics of a company's division or the moaty characteristics of a firm's enterprise. Flipping on a business channel for a couple hours may have a guest or two that says that their favorite idea has a nice moat.

Certainly, companies can have several sustainable advantages, or moaty characteristics, but the intrinsic value of the company will always be based on the company's future free cash flow stream and its net balance sheet (net cash position), not necessarily on a qualitative opinion of competitive advantages, per se. Stocks are not priced in number of moats, but rather by the size of their future enterprise free cash flow streams, which of course, can be influenced by their "moat," but nonetheless, it is enterprise free cash flow, itself, that drives the value equation. An economic moat assessment will never trump that of an in-depth cash-flow-derived valuation process (price matters immensely). Nevertheless, without an economic castle,[238] or a high-return generating enterprise, a moat to protect the business doesn't much matter. Quite simply, it doesn't make a lot of sense to be happy to have a wide moat full of alligators just to protect a dilapidated wooden palisade. That's why when Buffett talks about the best kinds of businesses, he leads with "leaving the question of price aside." The question of price versus value is paramount.

One of the early pioneers of the economic moat concept is BlueMountain Capital's Michael Mauboussin, and his work may have paved the way for widespread application of the analytical structure across numerous investment frameworks. Mauboussin states that "sustainable value creation is rare" and

---

[238] The term "economic castle" in this text is defined as the magnitude of economic profit. The Economic Castle rating is a registered trademark of Valuentum Securities, Inc.

sustainable competitive advantages are even "more rare" (given that a firm must perform not only better than its cost of capital but also better than its peer group to achieve both). The widely-accepted view within the investment community is that at some point in the future, competitive forces will erode a company's competitive advantages and drive return on new invested capital (RONIC) toward a company's cost of capital (WACC) over time.[239] The framework stipulates that no company can generate outsize economic profits forever, and even the strength of a company's competitive advantages may only tend to delay inevitable RONIC-WACC (economic profit) convergence.

The structure of the industry acts in such a manner where forces tend to exert downward pressure on ultra-high RONICs (e.g. new entrants seek to capitalize on opportunity and drive down prices for market share) and upward pressure on ultra-low RONIC (business failures leave the industry, lessening competition), such that over time, a company's RONIC will converge to its WACC.[240] Michael Porter's 5-forces model is one way to evaluate a company's interaction with participants in its industry vertical, as it relates to forces both horizontal (threat of substitute products, threat of existing rivals, and the threat of new entrants) and vertical (bargaining power of suppliers and bargaining power of customers). The strength of a company's economic moat, or its competitive advantages, is largely influenced by its position with respect to these 5 forces, and theoretically determines expectations for the duration of a company's RONIC-WACC spread.

Cumulative Economic Profit Is What Matters Most

The concept of an economic moat, or sustainable competitive advantages, however, generally focuses purely on the sustainability and the duration of the competitive advantages that a company possesses. The concept generally does

---

[239] A study of ROIC decay analysis completed by McKinsey, bucketing companies based on their ROIC and evaluating returns over the following 15-year period, showed a reversion-to-the-mean pattern. The returns in high ROIC buckets faded over time, while the returns of low ROIC buckets increased over time.

[240] A distinction is made in this text between ROIC and RONIC with respect to the latter's convergence to WACC. As RONIC fades to WACC over time, the company's firmwide ROIC could still be greater than its WACC.

not emphasize the cumulative sum of a company's potential future economic profit creation as a consideration of the quality of the business, but only that at some point in time in the future, a moaty company will continue to have an economic profit spread (i.e. RONIC is greater than its WACC) and a no-moat firm will not. In most cases, it will be the moaty company that has the largest cumulative economic profit stream, but a potential problem might arise if one focuses only on companies that have economic moats, or sustainable and durable competitive advantages, and overlooks those with shorter-duration, high-magnitude economic profit spreads, which can also be mispriced.

Figure 35: Cumulative Economic Profit Generation Is What Matters Most

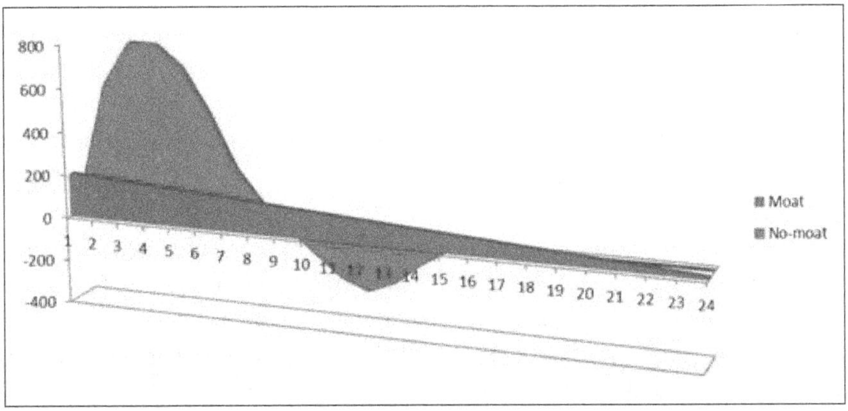

Figure 35 represents a hypothetical future economic value-added curve for a moaty company (slowly fading curve) and a no-moat company (volatile curve), where any area above the x-axis represents economic value added and any area below the x-axis represents economic value destroyed. The hypothetical no-moat firm in this example ceases to generate economic profit or destroy capital at the end of Year 15 due to competitive forces, while the hypothetical moaty firm continues to generate economic profit for significantly longer, through Year 25. As might be hypothesized, a moaty firm never destroys shareholder capital over the time horizon. However, the no-moat company can still generate more cumulative economic profit for shareholders, both in absolute and discounted terms, despite a much more volatile economic value-added curve that includes times of value-destruction.

A moaty company's operations may certainly be more stable, generating economic profits that are more sustainable and durable (slowly fading curve). However, the moaty firm's total economic value creation (net area of slowly fading curve), in absolute and in present value terms, can still be significantly less than that of the no-moat firm (net area of volatile curve), as calculated. In present value terms, in the hypothetical example in Figure 35, the moaty company generates less than half the economic profit of the no-moat company. A no-moat company, as in this example, can generate more value for shareholders than the company with sustainable and durable competitive advantages. The takeaway is that, while moaty firms are durable and sustainable businesses, they may not *always* be the best value-generators for shareholders, as cumulative economic value generation matters most when assessing the value-add to shareholders.

The trajectory of a company's economic value creation (or the areas in Figure 35) is not equivalent to the trajectory of a company's stock price. An estimate of a company's valuation, which is used to identify stock mispricings, already implicitly embeds a forecast of the firm's future economic value creation,[241] as it is a function of EBI (NOPLAT), which itself is the primary driver behind future free cash flows to the firm (enterprise cash flows), or that used in enterprise valuation. Figure 35 shows pure economic value-creation, or in other words, the spread between a company's return on incremental invested capital (RONIC) and its cost of capital. It's possible, though unlikely, that the stock price volatility of the no-moat stock in the example could even be less than that of the moaty stock, despite expectations for the much more volatile economic-value added stream. Stock price volatility, which can be viewed through the lens of expectations revisions[242] within the enterprise valuation context (see Chapter 4), and economic profit volatility, which is based on fundamental business dynamics, are two separate concepts, albeit related ones.

That said, regarding a moaty company's or a no-moat company's stock price, if the company is fairly-valued, the stock price may already largely reflect its respective forecasted economic profit trajectory. As Mauboussin puts it, under a scenario where the equity is fairly-priced, "investors should expect to earn a risk-adjusted market return." Put another way, the value of fairly-priced moaty stocks, which tend to be less risky, may advance at a lower annual pace than the value of

---

[241] Economic value creation occurs when RONIC is greater than WACC within the value construct. RONIC breaks down into the change in EBI divided by net new investment, or the change in Invested Capital. In Chapter 1, I explained how with some massaging, the enterprise valuation framework can be decomposed into residual income or economic-profit models, under a number of somewhat generous assumptions (e.g. clean surplus accounting).

[242] Alfred Rappaport and Michael Mauboussin wrote a book, *Expectations Investing*, that talked about how to use the discounted cash-flow model to "read expectations," or "price-implied expectations." To generate superior returns, they argued, one must correctly anticipate revisions in the market's expectations.

fairly-priced no-moat stocks due in part to the lower risk-adjusted discount rate applied to the moaty company's respective future free cash flow stream. A company's intrinsic value generally advances at the annual pace of its corresponding discount rate less its dividend yield, and since moaty firms generally have lower discount rates and pay dividends, the pace at which their fair values should be expected to increase will trail that of a no-moat firm (assuming the future forecasts are accurate).[243]

What we are after as investors, as Mauboussin states, is anticipating revisions in expectations of financial performance. Is a no-moat's economic value trajectory correctly priced in? Is a wide moat's economic value trajectory overvalued? Is a no-moat company's economic value trajectory undervalued? The economic moat concept alone is less important than an evaluation of how the market has priced a company's future economic value stream, or whether the marketplace is valuing the equity correctly within the enterprise valuation construct. This means that investors should be looking for companies in the global investment universe that have mispriced future economic value streams (i.e. stocks that are underpriced relative to their discounted future free cash flows and net balance sheet), not whether a company has a wide economic moat or a narrow one, per se.

To quote Warren Buffett in his 1992 Letter to Berkshire Hathaway shareholders, "the investment shown by the discounted-flows-of-cash calculation to be the cheapest is the one that the investor should purchase--irrespective of whether the business grows or doesn't, displays volatility or smoothness in its earnings, or carries a high price or low in relation to its current earnings and book value." But don't revenue and earnings have to go up for a stock to advance? In short, no. If a stock is undervalued based on its future enterprise free cash flow stream (its future economic profit stream), price-to-estimated-fair value convergence can occur even if future fundamentals are less-than-desirable and regardless of the trajectory of revenue and earnings in future periods. Within the enterprise valuation framework, undervalued stocks with expectations of declining revenue and earnings can still advance in the context of price-to-estimated-fair value

---

[243] The weighted average cost of capital is a rather subjective measure to begin with, but enterprise value should logically advance at the weighted average cost of capital less the dividend yield. Some models that forecast equity value may advance equity value at the cost of equity less the dividend yield. In any case, for most companies the difference between the weighted average cost of capital and the cost of equity won't be significantly material through the course of the year.

convergence, meaning that the market has priced the stock too low to begin with, even relative to its declining expected revenue and earnings stream.

Magnitude versus Duration and the Economic Castle

The concept of cumulative economic value versus the sustainability and duration of economic value is worth further examination, perhaps with another example. Without question, railroads are fantastic businesses. North American railroads operate as an oligopoly, benefit from substantial barriers to entry, and boast significant pricing power. The group's return on invested capital, however, won't be but a few percentage points greater than their cost of capital at any point in time, given the capital intensity of their operations (it's costly to maintain track), but absent any abnormal shocks to the business, the railroad group will likely add a modest amount of economic value year after year. However, will such a moaty railroad such as Union Pacific generate as much value as perhaps a less-moaty company such as Apple? The answer is probably not.

Apple boasts a significantly larger economic value spread, and it can be reasonably argued that Apple may even generate more economic value in just a few years of peak-level earnings than Union Pacific may generate for the remainder of its corporate life. The duration of Apple's economic value creation or competitive advantage period, which may be much shorter than that of Union Pacific, is less important than the absolute and discounted economic value that a company delivers to shareholders. One could even argue that since the near term is more predictable than the long term that a front-end loaded economic value stream like Apple's may be preferable to a long-duration and slim economic value stream like Union Pacific's. That said, either Apple's or Union Pacific's future economic profit spread can become mispriced, resulting in either company becoming undervalued or overvalued.

Figure 36: Union Pacific's Return on Invested Capital[244]

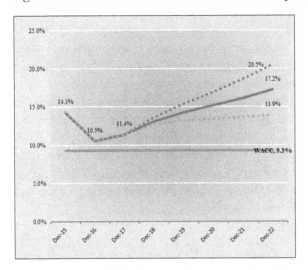

Figure 37: Apple's Return on Invested Capital[245]

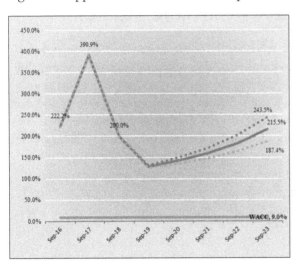

---

[244] Union Pacific's total shareholders' equity was $24.9 billion at the end of 2017, the measure that would form the basis for a capital charge in economic profit models.

[245] Apple's total shareholders' equity was $107.1 billion at the end of fiscal 2018 (ends September). Not only is Apple's shareholders' equity more than four times that of Union Pacific's, but Apple is generating a return on invested capital that is considerably higher than Union Pacific's, too.

The sustainability and duration of a company's economic value creation, or its competitive advantage period, tells us little about a company's Economic Castle, or the magnitude of the value creation that it is expected to deliver to shareholders. Though a focus on economic moats remains an integral part of any competitive-advantage analysis, identifying economic castles, or those businesses that will deliver the most value to shareholders, regardless of the economic-value composition, may be equally important to an investor's process. Whereas an economic moat assessment evaluates a company based on the sustainability and durability of its economic value creation stream, Valuentum's Economic Castle rating evaluates a company based on the magnitude of the economic profit that it will deliver to shareholders. Companies with the best Economic Castle ratings are poised to generate the most economic value for shareholders in the future five-year period, regardless of their competitive positions.

Competitive-Advantage Analysis: Airlines versus Garbage Haulers

Though the structural characteristics of industries can (and do) change as participants enter and leave an industry (and as potential industry earnings shift among participants, both vertically and horizontally, and depending on how they interact), an analysis of the airline industry for much of its history and that of the municipal solid waste industry offers a valuable perspective to compare a poor industry with a strong one. The better the structural characteristics of the industry, the more profits that can be distributed among industry participants. The stronger a company is within its industry, the more profits that accrue to the individual company. Competitive advantage analysis and Porter's 5-forces framework are vital tools to help identify winning and losing companies over the long run.

Airlines

The airline business is a notoriously poor one, but sometimes it attracts even the savviest of investors. In 1989, for example, Warren Buffett purchased $358 million in US Airways' preferred stock, but by 1994, the airline had suspended its dividend and Berkshire Hathaway wrote down the position to $89.5 million. Conditions looked so bleak at that time that Warren Buffett and his partner

Charlie Munger would even decline to stand for reelection to the US Airways board. Much, if not all, seemed lost.

However, in the second half of 1996, US Airways started to turn a profit and pay preferred dividends again, not because of any improvement in the airline's competitive stance, but because of a cyclical upturn and industry tailwind. Berkshire Hathaway would end up fully recouping the value of the preferred investment and eventually receive more than $240 million in preferred dividends thanks to stipulations agreed upon in the event of a deferral of them. Buffett would label this investment as one of his top mistakes, and it's clear that if it weren't for some very good luck, he would have lost big on the endeavor. He had tried unsuccessfully to sell the US Airways' stake at a big loss, not on one occasion but several times during 1995 and into 1996.

In the *Essays of Warren Buffett*, it would read that the Oracle of Omaha "was neither pushed into the (US Airways) investment nor misled by anyone when making it." He would call this an "unforced error." Buffett would add succinctly: "In an unregulated commodity business, a company must lower its cost to competitive levels or face extinction. This principle should have been obvious to your Chairman, but I missed it." In his 2007 Letter to Berkshire Hathaway Shareholders, Warren Buffett would quip that a "if a farsighted capitalist had been present at Kitty Hawk, he would have done his successors a huge favor by shooting Orville down."

Warren Buffett's run-in with the US Airways investment fiasco in the late 1980s and early 1990s is not a one-off event impacting just one airline. Since 1990, there have been over 180 bankruptcies in the airline business, and even more failures since deregulation of the industry in 1978. New airlines seemingly are started every day, and each year dozens of airlines fail, even during the best of times. For example, Island Air, Eastern Airlines, Darwin Airline, Niki, Monarch, and Air Berlin were just a few that closed shop during 2017, a year in which the industry generated approximately $38 billion in net profits, a record high.

The airline industry has undergone meaningful changes since the Financial Crisis. The painful restructuring of labor agreements and balance sheets by most of the legacy carriers via Chapter 11, the significant mega-mergers of Delta/Northwest, UAL/Continental, US Airways/America West, Southwest/AirTran, and US Airways/AMR Corp, the introduction of ancillary revenue streams to combat volatile jet-fuel costs, and continued efforts to right-size domestic capacity to slow the long downward trend in real yields (pricing) are but a few. Though these are steps in the right direction, airline stocks, in my opinion, continue to be speculative bets or hedges on the trajectory of the economy (passenger travel) and the direction of crude oil prices. But why?

Well, let's turn to enterprise valuation. The most enlightening analysis of an airline's business model is to test the sensitivity of its profitability and enterprise free cash flows to changes in the forecasts of a few industry-accepted metrics: revenue per available seat mile (RASM) and cost per available seat mile (CASM). RASM, or unit revenue, is a function of yield (pricing) and capacity utilization (load factor), while CASM, or unit cost, is predominantly driven by jet fuel prices and labor. The difference of the two represents unit profit, or the profit generated by an airline to fly one seat one mile.

Due to the tremendous operating leverage inherent to airline business models non-pursuant to capacity purchase agreements (regional airlines operate on cost-plus arrangements), it becomes apparent that even minor changes in these key forecasted metrics can have large implications on profitability and enterprise free cash flows, and therefore the fair value estimate of an airline's equity and inevitably its share price. Though operating leverage driven by the high fixed cost nature of the airline business may spell considerable profit expansion should these metrics move in favorable directions as they have in more recent years, the wide range of potential profit outcomes as a result of the sensitivity of these metrics suggests that most airline stocks will remain tied to boom-and-bust dynamics.

As many airline executives may attest, both unit revenue (fare prices) and unit cost (jet fuel) are largely out of their control. For one, air travel service is largely commodified and suffers from substantial and intense fare competition driven by severe price transparency and the unavoidable concept of perishable inventory--when a flight takes off, empty seats cannot be filled (the inventory of seats has perished). Such a combination is the weight that keeps real pricing (yield) growth from moving aggressively higher to meaningfully alter the long-term economics of the industry. To this day, network airlines are still forced to match fares offered by low-cost carriers or suffer even greater revenue declines. Fare increases can often only be sustained, and sometimes only temporarily, if they are matched by low-cost peers such as Southwest or JetBlue, for example.

With barriers to entry primarily limited to capital costs (any US carrier deemed fit by the Department of Transportation can operate passenger service in the US), it's safe to assume that we haven't seen the last start up airline in the US, even after the long list of failures that happen every year. There's something about the prestige of running an airline that continues to attract new entrepreneurs, and the mere existence of interested, economically-tied parties (like Boeing, for example) seem to suggest that new entrants will always pose a threat to unleash unwanted capacity (seats) on otherwise healthy routes. One can even tap Boeing's expertise in launching an airline (startup@boeing.com). The poor performance of systemwide--domestic and international--real yields (pricing) across airlines is unlikely to change permanently. Things will look great during upswings, but the nature of the business during difficult times is when most airlines are tested.

As an airline's unit revenue is pressured by intense pricing competition, its unit cost is significantly impacted by the level and volatility of the price of jet fuel. According to the International Air Transport Association, jet fuel represents approximately 25% of industry operating costs, surpassing labor expenses as the largest cost item. Though airlines may hedge fuel to some extent, such a strategic move is financial and should not be viewed as an operational boost or any sort of sustainable competitive advantage. Any airline could hedge prices, and such hedges can cut either way. If an airline hedges at a price that's too high, the airline could end up losing money on those hedged positions. The intrinsic value of an airline rests in the value of its operating assets, and the value of its hedging portfolio is a separate financial consideration.

Elevated jet fuel costs (and the sticky-downward nature of labor costs) coupled with declining industry real yields (fare prices) is the combination that puts airline industry unit profit in a stranglehold. Meanwhile, the capital-intensive nature of the airline business adds operating leverage to an ultra-cyclical demand profile, where even during the best of times, margins are slim (net income margins across the industry come in at 4%-5% during the best of times). Buffett may have had it right when he said that "the worst sort of business is one that grows rapidly, requires significant capital to engender the growth, and then earns little or no money. Think airlines. Here a durable competitive advantage has proven elusive ever since the days of the Wright Brothers."

Since the Financial Crisis, however, the global airline industry has been significantly profitable, and depending on one's estimate of the industry's weighted average cost of capital, it can be argued that the global airline industry might finally be generating economic profits for investors, with the industry posting a return on invested capital of 9% in 2017. However, good companies aren't ones that can only generate economic profits during the best of times, but instead, are ones that can generate economic profits *through the course of the economic cycle*. To make the airline business work for its shareholders, it's taken one of the strongest economies in history, zero and sometimes negative interest rate policy across the globe, and an outright collapse in energy resource prices, not to mention the debt cleansing, cost take-outs, and consolidation that occurred during the prior downturn as a result of the Chapter 11 process.

Buffett said once that he had an 800 number that he would call anytime that he wanted to buy an airline stock again. Maybe that number has been disconnected after all these years, as Berkshire Hathaway is once again an owner of airline equities. Though the structural characteristics of an industry can and do change over time, I'm very skeptical the airline business has changed permanently for the better. Today's airline business may be more oligopolistic in nature and much more profitable thanks to consolidation and the right-sizing of capacity, but it retains a notoriously cyclical passenger-demand profile, ties to the level and volatility of energy resource prices, considerable operating leverage, all the while barriers to entry remain low, exit barriers remain high, and fare pressure endures. The next downturn may not see as many bankruptcies as prior economic cycles due to lower unit-cost profiles, but it may turn out to only be modestly "less bad" for equity holders.

Garbage Haulers

As Benjamin Franklin once said, "nothing is certain but death and taxes." If he had lived during our time, Franklin would probably have added a couple other certainties, and garbage would have been among them. The US non-hazardous solid-waste services industry generates annual revenue of approximately $60 billion, a staggering number just to keep our streets clean. The Big 3 publicly-traded companies, Waste Management, Republic Services, and Waste Connections dominate this market, generating almost half of industry revenue and controlling a large percentage of valuable disposal capacity.

The industry has been built in roll-up fashion, but deals have grown larger in recent years. Republic Services acquired Allied Waste in 2008, Advanced Disposal Services bought Veolia Environnement's US solid waste business in

2012, and Waste Connections bought Progressive Waste in 2016. The top line for the group can be expected to expand at a nominal-GDP rate, with pricing growth in the industry adding an additional tailwind thanks to recent consolidation, a rational focus on return on invested capital, and cost pressures facing independent mom-and-pop trash companies and municipalities.

Within the collection line of a waste hauler's business, residential services provided to municipalities and individual households are on a service-based model (not-volume based) and can largely be viewed as insulated from economic pressures. Such a constant revenue stream helps to mitigate cyclical pressures in a trash taker's commercial collection and industrial roll-off lines, which also fall into the overall waste-collection category. Cell-by-cell landfill build-out provides additional flexibility with respect to capital outlays, as haulers can scale back expenditures during troubled economic times. The Big 3 garbage haulers in the US have free-cash-flow stability, and traditional free cash flow margins have been relatively stable and very healthy.

Transfer-and-disposal is the most lucrative revenue stream in the waste business. Landfill ownership can largely be viewed as the primary competitive advantage for a solid-waste operator. Though anyone that can finance a truck can bid on collection routes (the service is undifferentiated), new entrants are at a significant disadvantage for disposal. For starters, building a landfill is expensive, time-consuming (permits can take 3-7 years to obtain, sometimes longer), and NIMBY (not-in-my-backyard) opposition has only increased with suburban sprawl. Subtitle D of the Resource Conservation and Recovery Act significantly increased the cost and complexity of landfill ownership (composite liners, leachate collection systems, zoning). As a result, many landfills in the US have been closed, and airspace will only become more valuable over time.

Materials recovery (including recycling at about 25% of waste handling disposal) should continue its march upward but landfilling still represents the most prominent form of disposal, at approximately 52.5% of waste handling, declining just 3.5 percentage points during the past decade. Collected waste must go somewhere (direct haul is only practical for 40-50 miles), so the company that controls the disposal assets in a given "wasteshed" (locality) often dictates pricing. According to the Environment Protection Agency, national landfill tipping fees surged from $18.06 per ton in the mid-1980s to nearly $50 per ton in recent years, a 3%+ nominal annual growth clip.

Owning the only disposal facility in town also limits hefty tipping fees paid to other participants, while building pick-up route density and internalizing waste--disposing collected waste into company-owned landfills--helps provide those with local scale higher operating margins relative to privately-held, independent operators. Successful operating strategies target high levels of market share in local wastesheds, elevated route density and well-positioned transfer and disposal assets to maximize operating efficiencies and reduce waste transportation costs. Though many waste haulers are national in scale, the waste business, itself, is very localized.

Comparing and contrasting the US waste business with the US airline business is a valuable analytical exercise. For example, both the waste and airline businesses are oligopolistic, both have largely-commodified products, and both are exposed to energy prices, so why is the waste business so much better? There are a few reasons. For starters, the waste business generally has real pricing power emanating from disposal assets, where the airline business may be among the most competitive businesses around when it comes to fare wars. Second, where garbage collection and disposal are relatively recession-resistant (it's non-discretionary), the airline business and passenger demand can probably be best characterized as ultra-cyclical.

Third, the waste business and the airline business are capital intensive, but waste operators generate strong and predictable traditional free cash flow streams, while this core component of intrinsic value can fluctuate wildly through the course of the economic cycle for the airline industry. Fourth, where airlines have great difficulty in passing along jet fuel costs to customers in the form of higher fares, the garbage business is contractual and sometimes locally exclusive in nature, and diesel fuel surcharges are often easily passed along to customers, who are all too willing to pay them to get their garbage hauled away. Fifth, airlines are exposed to share-hungry new entrants that can cherry-pick their best routes, but when it comes to a local wasteshed, any new entrant must pay the disposal operator tipping fees, should they outbid and win any collection business.

The enterprise valuation process uncovers the unique characteristics of each business model quite well. For example, where small changes in underlying metrics for an airline could cause significant changes in a fair value estimate (a few dollars extra for an average ticket price or an extra passenger per departure could make a huge difference), a modest percentage point change here or there in terms of volumes or pricing won't move the needle too much for a steady-eddy garbage hauler. In valuation parlance, a theoretical range of fair value estimate outcomes for an airline could be significant, to the tune of +/- 50% around the fair value estimate, where such a range may be much more modest for a trash taker. In most cases, attractive P/E ratios for airlines are more reflective of the heightened risk of ultra-cyclical earnings than any attractive investment proposition. Waste-hauler earnings, on the other hand, are backed by robust and consistent enterprise free cash flows.

The Stronger the Competitive Advantage the Lower the Stock Return?

Over a look-back period of ten years ending 2012, research firm Morningstar concluded that companies with wide economic moats underperform stocks with narrow economic moats, and that stocks with no economic moats had the best returns. The relative outperformance of no-moat stocks may be explained in part by the context of enterprise valuation. The values of higher-risk stocks, by definition, should theoretically advance at a higher annual pace than lower-risk stocks over time, all else equal (they have higher discount rates in the enterprise valuation process to reflect their heightened risk profile).

But there may be another dynamic at play. As markets are generally benign during economic upswings, riskier stocks are generally repriced higher using lower discount rates (credit is more readily available). The longer duration cash-flow profile of higher-risk, no-moat companies is then magnified when the cost of borrowing is reduced. This makes no-moat firms very volatile through the credit cycle, but it may also help explain their significant outperformance during good times. Moaty stocks, on the other hand, are less impacted by credit availability, and therefore, their discount rate and intrinsic value should not experience as much volatility.

One might hypothesize that investors may sometimes prefer stocks with moats because they tend to be less volatile, not necessarily because they may be better long-term performers, it seems. Most investors, for example, may not be able to sleep at night if their portfolio experiences wild swings. Investors then accept the lower returns for reduced levels of volatility.

It's important not to misread this takeaway. Investors seeking better long-run returns shouldn't just consider stocks with the worst fundamental qualities either. That's not at all what I'm saying. There's individual bankruptcy risk and potential for considerable price declines in higher-risk small and micro caps under tightening credit cycles, and a concentrated portfolio of fundamentally poor companies is still a bad idea, even if the portfolio might have a good run during the best of times. If not a good business or a bad business, what then makes the best types of investments to consider?

I'd argue that a great company (one with a royal castle!) that is significantly undervalued on an enterprise valuation basis, whose valuation is supported by relative "behavioral" multiples, and one that is experiencing strong share price momentum may be worth a look. In other words, a Valuentum stock! If this company pays a strong and growing dividend, too, all the better.

10

Putting It All Together: Valuentum Investing

Not the Woodstock you're thinking of. Building a hypothesis. Moving mountains to build the infrastructure. Introducing the Valuentum Buying Index. Running a marathon to calculate meaningful data. Forward-looking expected data and walk-forward testing. No data mining, data snooping or data dredging. Putting the logic first. The Valuentum way. Best ideas and dividend growth. The importance of diversification.

W oodstock, Illinois, is known for a few things.

There's the Woodstock Opera House on the Square in the historic downtown area. The city was once home to a young Orson Welles, who may be best known for *War of the Worlds*, and during the early part of the 20th century, Woodstock was called "Typewriter City," home to both the Oliver Typewriter Company and Emerson Typewriter Company. Eugene Debs did some time at the Woodstock Jail for his part in the 1894 Pullman labor strike, and the 1993 movie Groundhog Day, starring Bill Murray, was filmed in the city.

Valuentum would eventually call Woodstock home in 2011.

You may have read many stories of others that learned of stock investing at a really young age, perhaps they bought their first stock before their 8th birthday or their parents had been a part of the finance industry. That wasn't me. I really only became aware of the stock market probably in grade school, with a stock market game we played in either 3rd or 4th grade, and then my interest grew in high school. When I first enrolled in undergraduate studies, however, I actually had plans to major in biology and become a doctor. It wasn't until a week or so into classes where I made the switch to finance.

My professional journey in finance started in the aggressive-growth money-management industry, where I learned to "live" the markets. From my 5am morning coffee and crisp newspaper to anticipating firms "breaking out" in the early afternoon, little did I know that my buyside experience at Driehaus Capital Management was preparing me for this Valuentum journey. After earning an MBA from the University of Chicago Booth School of Business and the Chartered Financial Analyst designation, I then pursued the great satisfaction of helping others achieve their career aspirations.

In my role as Director of Global Equity and Credit Research (Training and Methodology) at Morningstar, one of the largest independent research companies in the world, I dedicated my time to training and mentoring stock and credit analysts on the intricacies of discounted cash-flow and competitive-advantage analysis. Many of these colleagues are now the heads of department at the company. At Morningstar, I truly learned to "live" valuation and competitive analysis.

In early 2011, I realized what I needed to do. It dawned on me that very few investors have ever had the opportunity to use technical and momentum indicators in a money-management setting *and* build an extensive discounted cash-flow valuation infrastructure for one of the largest independent research firms in the world. Though I didn't know what to expect, I knew what I had to do: share with others the tremendous benefits of Valuentum investing.

Origins of Valuentum Thinking

Valuentum thinking must have begun for me in undergrad, 2003 or 2004. I remember reading an article, whether it was in Kiplinger or Money magazine I cannot recall, but it talked about the fantastic track record of consecutive annual relative outperformance by Legg Mason's Bill Miller, a value manager. In the article, it said that he generated a decent part of his outperformance from investing in companies such as Amazon and others like it. Amazon was far from the traditional value stock, so something wasn't quite lining up. Here, one of the best money managers, a value guy, was investing in stocks that were almost surely classified as being more "growthy" in nature than anything else, and he had quite the track record of success.

Aside from an interview question on a test I wrote up for new applicants at Morningstar some years before launching Valuentum, it really wouldn't be until after leaving Morningstar that I started thinking more intensively about this dynamic. By then, I had training in aggressive growth investment management and extensive experience in competitive-advantage analysis, in the spirit of Warren Buffett's economic moat concept, as well as expertise in enterprise valuation analysis and significant background in credit, having worked to develop Morningstar's corporate credit product. It seemed obvious that Warren Buffett's investment style, which has evolved greatly during the past several decades, may at its core be one that captures a combination of an economic moat, or quality consideration, and an enterprise valuation factor (not the traditional quant factor) within individual stocks, the overlap of the two perhaps explaining a significant amount of Berkshire Hathaway's outperformance during the past several decades.

Ever since learning about Bill Miller's success, however, I always believed there was something to this "overlapping styles" thesis, but it wouldn't be until Valuentum's forming where I would try to test it. The hypothesis, itself, was simple: The relative outperformance of some of the most successful investors may in part, or largely, be attributed to a phenomenon where such fund managers and investors, knowingly or unknowingly, have held large "exposures" to several styles *within* individual stocks, forming unique investment approaches commonly undefined (i.e. styles that are outside traditional style boxes). In stocks that have a large overlap of different styles, it would be hypothesized that what transpired to drive outperformance in these equities would be significant buying in such stocks by a larger number of investors, many more investors than otherwise would if such stocks only fit mostly one style, for example.

Stocks that were attractive from a number of investment perspectives--whether it be growth, value, income, momentum, or other--may have the greatest probability of capital appreciation and relative outperformance because the more deep-pocketed institutional investors that are interested in such stocks for reasons based on their respective investment mandates, the more likely they will be bought and the more likely their prices will move higher. It fit nicely into the Keynes' beauty contest analogy. Most outperforming money managers may have been buying what most other investors ended up buying in the future, but instead of consciously "buying what they thought others would," it may quite simply have been less intentional.

Incidentally, prior research seemed to support such a phenomenon, but it's classified under studies related to style drift behavior: "...managers of growth-oriented funds and small funds, and managers having good stock-picking track records, tend to have higher levels of style drift than other managers; these managers also deliver better future portfolio performance as a result of their trades, even after accounting for their higher trading costs." In its traditional definition, style drift may have negative connotations to investors that may rely on advertised styles, but studies that address cross-methodological frameworks *within* individual stocks may explain quite a bit about outperforming stocks. In any case, it became obvious to me that there was something to individual stocks that had qualities common to many different styles within them. There was the incredible success of Bill Miller, Warren Buffett and others[246], where this phenomenon seemed all too apparent, and style drift had been shown to account for better future performance in portfolios, even after accounting for higher trading costs.

Why wasn't anybody going beyond ambiguous and impractical data to study this?

The Valuentum Buying Index (VBI)

I would spend months working on Valuentum's infrastructure. Integrating the inner workings of enterprise valuation into a framework that captured relative valuation considerations and technical/momentum indicators was far from just combining three variables. Enterprise valuation, itself, had thousands of drivers, and the model had to be robust. To capture behavioral valuation, we had to capture expectations across company peers, and then systematically compare

---

[246] Manu Daftary, president of DG Capital Management and portfolio manager of the Quaker Strategic Growth Fund exceeded the S&P 500 Index return for 8 consecutive years, ending in 2006. In Daftary's case, for example, combining other factors with traditional growth within individual stocks, as in moving into sectors in favor (momentum), namely the cyclical and commodity-driven energy sector in 2004, may have helped fuel the strength of certain "growth-oriented" energy holdings, leading to overall outperformance in the fund. At the time both Miller's and Daftary's winning streaks came to an end, there were several other funds that had seven-year winning periods, revealing such streaks of relative outperformance may not be as uncommon as popular opinion may lead one to believe.

those multiples to the company of question. Given the constraints of our new firm, we had to decide which technical and momentum indicators would fit. It was quite the iterative process, but by mid-2011, the Valuentum Buying Index (VBI) had been created.

At the core, the VBI is a fundamentally-based and forward-looking stock-selection methodology that captures an assessment of enterprise valuation, behavioral value (relative value), and technical/momentum qualities within individual stocks at points in time. The VBI combines business valuation analysis with an evaluation of a stock's technical/momentum indicators to derive a single rating between 1 and 10 for each company at each point of measurement (10=best; 1=worst). A VBI rating is generated via a three-step process.

Figure 38: The Valuentum Buying Index

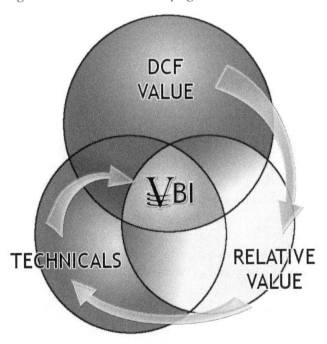

First, the Valuentum Buying Index makes use of a forward-looking enterprise valuation model, enhanced by a fair value range or margin of safety, to determine an analyst-driven assessment of whether a stock is fairly-valued, undervalued or overvalued on an enterprise valuation basis. Second, a stock's forward P/E ratio and forward PEG ratio are assessed to determine whether a stock is unattractive, neutral, or attractive versus peers on a relative value basis (the behavioral valuation component, see Chapter 5). Third, a stock's technical/momentum indicators are assessed to determine whether such indicators are bearish (poor), neutral, or bullish (good) to add additional conviction to the valuation process, and to capture the catalyst that theoretically drives price to estimated intrinsic value.

Depending on how each stock performs with respect to each component (enterprise valuation, behavioral/relative valuation, technical/momentum indicators) and based on the order-of-process as defined by the flow chart on the prior page in Figure 38, a VBI rating is assigned to a stock at a point in time. Though qualitative and subjective considerations are embedded into the process (fair value estimates, for example, are derived by analysts), each VBI rating is systematically generated.

Forward-Looking Expected Data and Walk-Forward Testing

The forward-looking data and simulated nature of the testing would stand in contrast to what many in quantitative research had been doing. There would be no data mining based on historical data and drawing potentially non-causal conclusions. There would be no letting backward-looking "evidence" that could be spurious somehow provide the support for conclusions, instead of what it should be doing, just providing the framework for a hypothesis that can then be tested and/or falsified. There would be no possibility of a Texas Sharpshooter fallacy or drawing the bullseye after firing shots. We'd start with a logical hypothesis first (not one just observed by past data), then we'd test the hypothesis using *walk-forward* data recorded going forward, and then we'd draw our conclusions.

This approach seems like the only way. However, years later, I found out there are many different ways.[247] In Fama and French's three-factor model, published

---

[247] There are a few terms worth getting familiar with. Data snooping is traditionally defined as a method where the statistical inference occurs after looking at the data, without having a pre-planned hypothesis. Data dredging is a closely-related term, in which multiple statistical tests are

in the early 1990s, for example, the three factors were derived based on backward-looking data within a sample,[248] offering a theory of what may be responsible for explaining stock price returns. However, with the first factor, CAPM, shown to have limited real-word implications (despite the logic that risk should be tied to returns), the size factor reconsidered, and "growth" stocks outperforming "value" stocks during the past decade or so, a walk-forward or simulated test of this three-factor model would have simply falsified it. Instead of throwing out the model and its factors, altogether, however, researchers continue to study them, as if they may just be cyclical, moving in and out of favor, instead of spurious or wrong.

In Baum's and Smith's paper, *Great Companies: Looking for Success Secrets in All the Wrong Places*, the duo criticized heavily one of the best-selling books on management, Jim Collins 2001 book, *Good to Great: Why Some Companies Make the Leap*. Mind you – this book was a best-seller, with millions of copies sold. On the list of the 11 companies, however, were Circuit City, which eventually filed for bankruptcy protection in 2008, Fannie Mae, which was bailed out by the government during the Financial Crisis, and Wells Fargo, which is struggling through a public relations nightmare for creating fake customer bank accounts and for aggressive sales practices within its wealth management division. These companies were supposed to be among the select 11 out of 1,435 companies that were supposedly to be followed based on findings in the book? So, what went wrong? Baum and Smith hit the nail on the head:

> The problem with Collins' work is that it is a backward-looking study that is undermined by data mining. Collins wrote that "we developed all of the concepts by making empirical deductions directly from the data.

---

performed on data, with only the ones that come back as statistically-significant being considered. This, again, ignores the scientific process of presenting a hypothesis beforehand, and then conducting a single test for its significance.

[248] In his text *Investment Valuation*, Aswath Damodaran makes a comical reference to situations such as these in what he describes as a cardinal sin in testing for market efficiency, but really it may be applicable to all of quantitative finance, including backward-looking factor development: "*Testing an investment strategy on the same data and time period from which it was extracted.* This is the tool of choice for the unscrupulous investment adviser. An investment scheme is extracted from hundreds through an examination of the data for a particular time period. This investment scheme is then tested on the same time period, with predictable results. (The scheme does miraculously well and makes immense returns.) An investment scheme should always be tested out on a time period different from the one it is extracted from or on a universe different from the one used to derive the scheme."

We did not begin this project with a theory to test of prove. We sought to build a theory from the ground up, derived directly from the evidence."

Collins seemed to think this statement made his study appear unbiased and professional. He did not simply craft his conclusions: He went wherever the data led. In reality, Collins was admitting that he had no idea why some companies do better than others, and he was revealing that he was blissfully unaware of the perils of deriving theories from data. When considering any group of companies at a particular moment in time, whether the companies are the best or worst of the group, commonalities can always be found. For example, every company among the 11 selected by Collins has either a letter *i* or *r* in its name, and several have both an *i* and an *r*. Is ensuring that the company's name has an *i* or *r* in it the key to improving from a good company to a great company? Of course not.

Perhaps a large percentage of statistical work these days may fall into these types of data mining traps, and one in particular known as the Feynman Trap (named after the 1965 Nobel laureate). But what is the Feynman Trap? The story goes that Richard Feynman had asked his Cal Tech students to calculate the probability of his seeing a particular license plate number in the parking lot. The students used all their knowledge of probability and statistics to calculate a chance of one in several million for this particular license plate number, but they were wrong. The professor had already seen the exact license plate in the lot on the way to class, so the probability was actually 1. The point is that once something is observed in a defined set, as in backward-looking data, it may seem likely that it will occur again, as in a high probability of 1 (observing of the license plate in the lot prior to class), but really the chances revert back to one in several million in walk-forward tests (not observing the license plate in the lot prior to class).

This may be a description of the shortcomings of factor-based investing using ambiguous or impractical data at its finest. For example, it may seem more likely that stocks with high B/M ratios will outperform those with low B/M ratios in the future because they have in the past, but in reality, the relationship on a go-forward basis may very well have deteriorated, as more recent data and the relationship between "value" stock performance and "growth" stock performance has indicated. Data mining, data snooping, or data dredging are dirty phrases in the quant community, and most may believe they are not engaging in such practices, which could be more traditionally defined as looking for data to back one's conclusions. But that may not be the most accurate definition. Almost all backtests seem to have some sort of data-mining aspect to them, particularly if conclusions are drawn from "in sample" data or even out-of-sample data, but not in a walk-forward capacity.[249] Even with walk-forward tests with a pre-established hypothesis, however, if the data doesn't include explicit expectations in forward-looking data, the data may still not be casual (or predictive) either. It's not just one of the backward-looking factors, or these backtests and not those backtests. Practically all of them seem to suffer from some misuse of data analysis.

But how does Valuentum thinking differ from research that observes the returns of Warren Buffett and other outperforming investors as some combination of a variety of styles and explains them as such?[250] Second, how does Valuentum thinking differ from just another multi-factor model? Well, regarding the first question, in traditional quant applications, using ambiguous or impractical data in regression models will always result in some sort of answer. After all, there are Bill Miller's and Warren Buffett's stock market returns and there is data, so some output will happen under any statistical endeavor. But is it the correct data to explain the returns? Is the answer the correct answer or just some answer? Worse, does the answer seem to have some "believability" connected to it, as in using B/M ratio as some measure of value, adding further confusion? Most importantly, is the data forward-looking and predictive with respect to walk-forward tests, too?

---

[249] For decades now, researchers have had serious concerns about in-sample results failing, or lacking robustness, in walk-forward tests. More recently, some have argued that its impractical to wait for walk-forward reliability. Genuine walk-forward testing, however, is paramount, and if such a factor is not-forward looking it may still not be causal, or a logical factor explaining returns.

[250] Recent quantitative research has hypothesized, for example, that the track records of Warren Buffett, Bill Gross, George Soros, and Peter Lynch may be viewed as a function of a few factor-based investment styles. After controlling for the factors of value, low-risk, and quality, for example, Warren Buffett's "alpha becomes statistically insignificant (AQR 2016)." Of relevance have been interpretations of the AQR 2016 study on Peter Lynch's eclectic style: "Lynch wasn't value, he wasn't growth, he wasn't size and he wasn't quality. Instead he was all of those things at the same time (Grioli 2017)." One may hypothesize that most stocks that Peter Lynch held in his Magellan Fund, or the ones that contributed most to outperformance, may have had the greatest number of "styles" within them, a phenomenon that may have resulted in the greatest buying interest in such stocks and therefore relative outperformance of the fund. The latter is consistent with Valuentum thinking.

Valuentum thinking seeks to put the logic *first* in the analysis. In developing the hypothesis to test the VBI,[251] there is a reasonable basis for enterprise valuation to be connected to stock prices via the influence of public-to-private arbitrage, unlike for example, the size of the business in the size factor, or the B/M ratio in the quant value factor, which is impacted by the level of its book value, which can be meaningless. Second, through the course of this text, I've argued that the subset of logical data to use to explain stock market returns should be based on forward-looking, expected and causal data, realized or not. Where other multi-factor models may embrace ambiguous or impractical data to try to explain stock returns, the VBI includes the enterprise valuation process, which, in capturing future expectations, realized or not, measures something that is causal and beyond the grasp of traditional backward-looking ambiguous data.

When Valuentum was launched in 2011, our ability to rigorously test the VBI rating system was limited by the lack of available internally-generated data (namely *forward-looking* enterprise-value-derived price-to-estimated-fair value ratios), but preliminary testing of the VBI supported our hypothesis. The performance of the Best Ideas Newsletter portfolio,[252] generated outsize returns, and the sorting efficacy of the VBI among original Best Ideas Newsletter portfolio constituents was notable. In August 2017, we released a more comprehensive study of the nature of future returns of VBI ratings, however. To assess the performance of VBI ratings in identical market conditions, we examined the performance of a cohort of randomly-selected VBI ratings from one distinct point in time to another. To assess timing considerations regardless of market conditions, we assessed the future returns of 20,000+ VBI ratings on stocks based on their individual time series.

Just getting to this point was like moving mountains. To create over 20,000 fair value estimates over the course of more than five years was a tremendous effort by our small research team. 20,000 fully-populated discounted cash-flow models across over 1,000 equities! The conclusions were downright fascinating. The VBI effectively sorted "winners" and "losers," where average returns from the highest

---

[251] Valuentum Buying Index
[252] The Best Ideas Newsletter portfolio, Dividend Growth Newsletter portfolio, and High Yield Dividend Newsletter portfolios are not real money portfolios. Any performance, including that in the Exclusive publication, is hypothetical and does not represent actual trading. Past performance is not a guarantee of future results, and actual results may differ from simulated performance being presented in this book. Valuentum is an investment research publishing company.

VBI ratings significantly outperformed average returns from the lowest VBI ratings over immediate multiple time intervals. The outcome of the years and years of work, and long hours updating thousands of valuation models, supported the view that an increasing overlap of unique styles *within* individual stocks, including but not limited to those of forward-looking enterprise valuation, behavioral valuation, and technical/momentum may be one of the most important drivers behind individual stock outperformance.[253]

Buying Undervalued Stocks on the "Way Up," Selling Overvalued Stocks on the "Way Down"

We are hard-wired as humans to drive a hard bargain. The department stores know it well, perhaps better than most, and in many ways, their business models depend heavily on couponing and big discounts to keep customers coming back. The mad rush during Black Friday to get the very best of deals of the holiday season is yet another example of how humans are drawn to lower prices. How many of us have bought something we may never use, or more of something than we need, just because something was half off the regular price. Even the classic supply and demand curve in economics plainly states that at a lower price, there is more demand for a product.

Where the concept of getting a good deal may make a lot of sense, as in buying a stock that is undervalued, it is not one and the same with a lower price. In the stock market, a lower stock price often means something completely different than a better deal. Prices and estimates of intrinsic value are both dynamic, and a company's intrinsic value could have dropped by even more than the price decline, meaning a falling stock price, unlike that coupon in the mail from Kohl's or those awesome deals on Black Friday at Best Buy, may mean that the stock is more expensive, the opposite of a better deal. The market is not terribly inefficient all the time, so there may be important information that is driving that price lower or higher in most cases.

---

[253] See Notes for an excerpt of the conclusion of the paper "Value and Momentum Within Stocks, Too."

That said, the market can sometimes get things totally wrong, making the value-signaling behind the price moves unclear. This doesn't make evaluating the price moves less important, however. Most investors feel that the only way they can get a bargain is to go against the market, as in when value-conscious investors may look to buy stocks on the way down, when they are out of favor. However, it doesn't have to be this way, as doing so may expose one's portfolio more heavily to "falling knives" and value traps, or stocks that never recover. There's another way. In a buying discipline that considers moaty stocks with strong economic castles that one believes are undervalued, and only on the "way up," there is a greater chance the valuation work backing the idea is right.

The selling discipline of the Valuentum process also has behavioral considerations. We embrace the information contained in prices, meaning that we are sometimes comfortable continuing to "hold" a moaty idea with a strong economic castle at a price above our estimate of its intrinsic value after it has been added to the newsletter portfolio. Quite simply, the market could know more than we do about the true intrinsic value of the company, so we like to "let winners run" in this regard. Enterprise valuation is not a precise science, so it's possible that our fair value estimate may be too conservative, and the market might be right. We only consider removing ideas from the simulated newsletter portfolios when both of the following happen: 1) they are significantly overvalued (above the high end of the fair value estimate range, not just the fair value estimate, itself) and 2) they are showing negative technical and momentum action.

Let's walk through our buying discipline using Apple as an example of the Valuentum process in action. On July 24, 2013, we emailed our members noting that we thought shares of Apple were "significantly undervalued, and we're seeing some re-affirming market action...following its strong quarterly report." Here was a situation involving a fantastic moaty business, one that had an immense "royal" economic castle, whose shares were considerably undervalued on an enterprise valuation basis, whose equity (excluding cash) was trading at an attractive forward earnings multiple, and one that had an enormous excess net cash position to put to work with respect to dividend growth or value-creating buybacks. Almost everything that a Valuentum investor would be looking for in an idea was in Apple at that time. We added the company to the simulated Dividend Growth Newsletter portfolio and added to the position already in the simulated Best Ideas Newsletter portfolio, and the break out was enormous (see Figure 39 on next page).

Figure 39: Apple's Breakout Performance

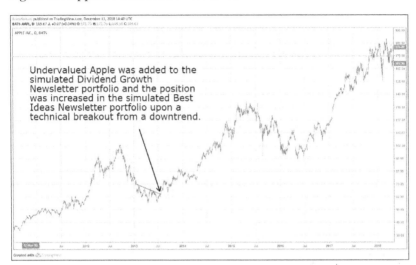

The Valuentum process runs counter in some ways to the natural urge of investors to want to sell a stock *only* because it has risen in price (and buy a stock *only* because it has fallen in price). Even if we think a stock may be getting pricey on an enterprise valuation and relative valuation basis, we won't necessarily consider removing it from the simulated newsletter portfolios until its technical and momentum indicators fade. Even if we think a stock is undervalued on an enterprise valuation and relative valuation basis, we won't necessarily become interested in it until its share price starts to move higher, too. We saw what could happen if one buys stocks that are believed to be undervalued on the way down in the example of General Electric, which turned into the quintessential *value trap* (see the case study of General Electric in Chapter 3).

In the case of Apple, on the other hand, we waited until shares, which we thought were undervalued, to break out of a defined technical downtrend before becoming interested in them. It is more likely that a stock is truly undervalued if both the enterprise-valuation signal and the market point in the same direction (a stock that one believes is undervalued and the market believes is undervalued, too). The most important signal will always be what the market thinks, however, and if we disagree with the market, we generally won't bet against it. Quite simply, if the market doesn't agree with us, we can never be right, but if "everybody" believes the idea is undervalued, the stock is likely to move higher, whether the true intrinsic value is higher than its current price or not (see *Self-fulling Prophecies* in Chapter 4).

Warren Buffett may have said that "the dumbest reason in the world to buy a stock is because it's going up," and this might be true, if it's the *only* reason. But if one is already a huge fan of the "moaty" and valuation characteristics of the company, waiting for the share price to turn first shouldn't matter much for long-term investors. The Oracle of Omaha has been tremendously successful by buying stocks that he believed were undervalued and holding these outperforming stocks with good momentum for long periods of time. In some ways, Buffett's approach may be a variant of the "Valuentum" process, itself. When we find an undervalued idea by our enterprise-valuation specifications, we want to bet in the same direction as the market (wait for the stock to start moving higher, too). In going with the market with an undervalued idea, not against it, we think it helps tilt the odds in investors' favor, not only in uncovering winners but also in avoiding value traps.

Practical VBI Application in the Best Ideas Newsletter Portfolio

The Best Ideas Newsletter portfolio[254] applies Valuentum's research and analytical practices, including its robust valuation processes, derivation of fair value estimates, generation of fair value estimate ranges, as well as a multitude of checks and balances, including a forward relative-value overlay combined with technical and momentum indicators. The application of the Valuentum process is not "quantitative" in the traditional sense (e.g. historical data aggregation and correlation/regression analysis), but instead, it rests on rigorous fundamental analysis of businesses coupled with a forward relative value and

---

[254] I'd like to make an important note regarding survivorship bias, which can best be explained as when a manager may launch several funds, closing the ones that don't do well while only highlighting those that succeed. The simulated portfolio of the Best Ideas Newsletter has been the only one in its category that we broadly define as total return, or capital appreciation. The simulated portfolio of the Dividend Growth Newsletter has been the only one in its category that we broadly define as dividend growth, or dividend opportunity. The same is true with respect to the simulated portfolio in the High Yield Dividend Newsletter and its category, high yield equity.

technical/momentum overlay that serves to augment and refine selections identified first as attractive by the enterprise valuation process.

We believe the price-to-estimated-fair value consideration derived from the enterprise valuation process is the most important component of investing, a key differentiated process from speculative activity that is based on target prices. We believe the future is inherently unpredictable and that nothing is guaranteed when it comes to the stock market, so with respect to idea generation, we focus most on arriving at the "best" fair value estimate ranges for companies than we do in trying to be precise with our forecasts over the next couple years, something that may be largely inconsequential to the long-term value composition of an equity. Precision in forecasting is not our goal. We are less concerned about our forecast for enterprise free cash flow in years one or two of our enterprise valuation models than we are in evaluating whether our fair value estimate range best approximates the true intrinsic value of the equity.

Furthermore, each of the three main components of the Valuentum Buying Index--enterprise valuation estimate --> forward relative value assessment[255] --> technical and momentum indicators--should not be viewed in isolation, but rather as a series of checks and balances embedded in the methodology to further augment and add additional prudence and care to our valuation opinion with respect to the enterprise valuation process. We use forward relative (behavioral) valuation approaches and technical and momentum indicators not by themselves, but instead, apply them to increase the robustness of the enterprise value assessment, itself augmented by a margin of safety (i.e. fair value estimate range).

We wholly embrace technical and momentum indicators and the information contained in prices, and we believe a rising stock price indicates the market believes the fair value estimate of a company should be higher, while we believe a falling stock price indicates the market believes the fair value estimate of a company should be lower. We do not believe a stock is cheaper just because it has fallen in price. We generally prefer stocks that we think are undervalued on both an enterprise value and forward relative value basis that also have strong technical/momentum indicators ("are going up"). We call these stocks that have

---

[255] In addition to the behavioral valuation component, the forward P/E ratio and forward PEG ratio also act as an additional check to ensure that we may not, for example, be overly optimistic or pessimistic within the enterprise valuation process. If the company appears undervalued on both an enterprise value basis and its multiples look enticing, the odds that its true intrinsic value is much higher than where shares are trading theoretically go up.

good value and good momentum characteristics within them "Valuentum stocks."

The Best Ideas Newsletter portfolio seeks to add stocks that are highly-rated on the VBI and seeks to remove stocks when they become lower-rated on the VBI, of which the price-to-estimated-fair value ratio is but one component. *We only view the highest and lowest VBI ratings as material, warranting further consideration of the equity.* Where momentum is traditionally believed to be high turnover, the application of the Valuentum process is low turnover, minimizing trading commissions and tax consequences. Some stocks have been in the Best Ideas Newsletter portfolio since inception in 2011. We may continue to include a stock that has a less desirable price-to-estimated-fair value ratio, provided its technical and momentum indicators remain strong, indicating the possibility we may be too conservative with respect to our fundamental-based valuation estimate.

The Best Ideas Newsletter portfolio is managed qualitatively, and while the research and analysis used to determine portfolio construction is sourced from Valuentum's investment research and methodologies, the portfolio manager ultimately decides which stocks are included or removed and when, as well as their respective weightings in the Best Ideas Newsletter portfolio. The Best Ideas Newsletter portfolio is targeted to comprise anywhere between 15-25 stocks and ETFs at any time and may add put options or hold cash with no limitations, but it doesn't engage in any short-selling measurements due to the reasonableness of the implementation of such activity in the context of members focused primary on long-term wealth creation through capital appreciation.

The Best Ideas Newsletter portfolio targets diversified ideas across all sectors of the economy, but it may not have exposure to all sectors of the economy at any given time. Not all highly-rated stocks on the VBI or undervalued stocks on Valuentum's enterprise valuation process are added to the newsletter portfolio.[256] The Best Ideas Newsletter portfolio is simulated, and performance through

---

[256] Think of it as if you were to imagine a value investor not adding and holding every undervalued stock in their portfolio. He or she wants the very best ones, in his or her opinion-- obviously, that means having to leave some good ideas behind. There are also tactical and sector weighting considerations in any portfolio construction. The VBI rating helps to inform the process, but the portfolio manager makes the allocation decisions based on a number of other firm-specific and portfolio criteria. Sometimes, under certain market conditions, the portfolio manager may even have to relax the VBI criteria entirely in order to target newsletter portfolio goals.

December 2017 was calculated by Valuentum in each monthly newsletter edition, released on the 15th of each month. No matter how it was measured, the simulated Best Ideas Newsletter portfolio was an outperformer during a time period when most of active management was failing.[257]

Dividend Growth Investing

The compounding of reinvested dividends over time is such a powerful dynamic that it may even be more powerful than what Albert Einstein is rumored to have called the "eighth wonder of the world," or compound interest. The reinvestment of growing dividends on an appreciating stock portfolio over time offers the benefit of having more shares of a higher-priced stock, which pays out ever-more dividends per share, a solid combination when it comes to generating long-term capital returns and wealth over decades or longer. It stands to reason that a rigorous methodology that uncovers stocks that not only have strong dividends but also are poised to grow them long into the future may be among the most important tools for long-term dividend growth investors. Most dividend analysis, however, tends to be primarily backward-looking, meaning it rests on what companies have done in the past. Though analyzing historical trends is important, assessing what may happen in the future may be even more important.

The S&P 500 Dividend Aristocrats, or a grouping of companies that have raised their dividends in each of the past 20 or more years, is a great example of why backward-looking analysis can be painful. One only has to look over the past few years to see the removal of well-known companies from this coveted grouping of dividend-growth stocks to learn that backward-looking analysis probably shouldn't take up too much of one's time. The future is what investors should care more about because an evaluation of whether a company may continue to pay a growing dividend is more important than whether the company paid a dividend 10, 15 or even 20 years ago. For dividend growth investors, it is more important to identify stocks that may increase their payouts for 20 years into the future, instead of using a rear-view mirror to build a portfolio of companies that may already be past their prime dividend growth years.

---

[257] See notes for more details regarding the simulated performance of the Best Ideas Newsletter portfolio.

The Dividend Cushion ratio (see Chapter 8) measures how strong a company's dividend payment is today and how much excess capacity the company may have to grow it into the future. The ratio combines information from a company's cash flow statement and the balance sheet to arrive at a helpful measure of dividend health. Specifically, the ratio considers a company's net balance sheet (either net cash or net debt) and adds the net cash (or subtracts the net debt) to a forecast of the company's future free cash flows (cash from operations less capital expenditures) over the next 5 years and divides that sum by an estimate of the company's future expected dividend payments and growth in them over the same time period.

At the core, the Dividend Cushion ratio helps inform investors whether a company has enough cash to pay out its dividends in the future based on reasonable forecasts and in the context of the health of the company's balance sheet. If a company has a Dividend Cushion ratio above 1, it may have an easier time covering its future dividend payments than if the ratio falls below 1 or 0, indicating that there may be trouble on the horizon. Like a credit rating ranks probability of default, the Dividend Cushion ratio can be viewed as a ratio that ranks companies on the probability of a dividend cut (the lower the ratio or more negative the ratio, the higher the probability of a dividend cut).

The Dividend Cushion ratio is also a tool to judge the financial capacity of a company to continue raising its dividend--how much cushion it has--and the analysis can be coupled with an assessment of the company's dividend track record, or management's willingness to raise the dividend. For a company to be considered to have strong *forward-looking* dividend growth prospects, both the financial capacity to raise the dividend and management's willingness to raise the dividend must be present. In addition to other qualitative considerations that speak to the sustainability of its business model, as in competitive-advantage analysis, closely monitoring Dividend Cushion ratios and executive teams' track records could be advantageous to a portfolio targeting long-term dividend growth and wealth expansion.

Dividend growth investing is not independent of value considerations, however, and the application of the enterprise valuation framework may be equally important when it comes to the capital preservation of a diversified, prudently-managed dividend growth portfolio. Even a potentially great dividend growth stock, but one that is purchased at too high of a price relative to an informed intrinsic value estimate, could have a devastating impact on investor capital if shares fall to the fair value estimate, particularly in the event dividend-growth expectations do not materialize or come up short. In assessing the downside risks of the price of dividend-growth equities, an evaluation of their intrinsic worth via an enterprise valuation construct that incorporates a fair value range may be a vital part of the process. Dividend-growth stocks that are trading below an informed fair value estimate range may be considered undervalued, while dividend-growth stocks that are trading above an informed fair value estimate range may be considered overvalued and generally avoided.

Share-price momentum in a dividend-growth equity may offer greater conviction in the valuation assessment of the company, too, as such pricing strength may reveal that the marketplace also believes the equity is underpriced. The information contained in a rising stock price may help the prudent dividend growth investor avoid value traps, or situations where a stock price may never recover to advance to an intrinsic value estimate.[258] The stock price may also inform investors when there may be outsize risk to the dividend, itself. For example, in situations where a company may be yielding 8% or higher in an ultra-low interest rate environment, the high yield may speak more to the heightened risk of it being cut than an opportunity for income.[259]

Share price momentum may not always be present given economic or market conditions, but evaluating the information contained in prices is yet another tool for dividend growth investors to consider. The stock market will always be volatile experiencing ups and downs through the course of the economic cycle as investors build in ever-changing expectations, but a value-focused, dividend growth strategy (which considers the information contained in prices) could potentially meet the needs of a number of different types of investors, assuming

---

[258] See *Price Declines Are Fundamental for High Yield Stocks* in Chapter 8 for more reading on how price momentum can be used within an income setting.

[259] It's important to think logically about this situation. The market is generally not too inefficient, so where it may seem that a high yield may present tremendous opportunity, the lofty yield likely just reflects heightened risk attached to the sustainability of the payout, or a condition where the dividend/distribution is detached from underlying fundamentals. One might also view this outsize yield from a corporate finance standpoint. If an executive team sees that it may not be getting credit for having a yield twice that of its peer average or median, for example, it may be tempted to cut its dividend by half to shore up its finances. The team may decide there may be no need to keep paying an elevated dividend if the company's stock is not being rewarded for it on the marketplace.

such an approach is a good fit for the individual's personal goals and risk tolerances.

Since the inception of the Dividend Growth Newsletter portfolio in 2012, stock ideas within it have never experienced a dividend cut, and the Valuentum process has even issued warnings of potential dividend disappointments of former ideas months in advance of their cuts (e.g. Kinder Morgan, General Electric). When it comes to dividend growth and a strong total return to boot, the simulated Dividend Growth Newsletter portfolio has delivered.

Diversification

I sometimes get the feeling that new investors believe they have to get every idea correct, and every idea should work out immediately. This, unfortunately, is just not how the markets work.[260] If one is a good investor, the winners will outperform the losers, and you'll make money. If one is an excellent investor, there will still be a lot of losers, but you'll end up beating the market's return, or achieving your long-term investing goals, whatever they might be. Even the investment greats such as Warren Buffett have had many disappointing investment propositions over time (e.g. IBM).

The fact of investing is that you, like the very best, will be wrong at times, but that is okay. You will make mistakes, but if you position your portfolio correctly, those mistakes won't be tragic. Some of your investments are destined to lose money. It's inevitable. Remember: Investing is about achieving goals, not being correct all the time. I receive emails every now and then from members that may say they are extremely happy that we picked several winners, for example, but that they were extremely disappointed that one of our ideas didn't work out. For some reason, new investors may not embrace the idea than picking more winners than losers may not only be good, but unbelievably fantastic.

At the very least, I think the equity portion of someone's entire portfolio should consist of *no less* than 15-25 securities. If you're holding less than 15-25 securities that span sectors of the economy, I don't think you're adequately diversified. The

---

[260] I think this is just common sense. Unless you buy a stock at the precise bottom, you're going to be underwater at some point.

work of Surz and Price, *The Truth About Diversification by the Numbers*, talked about how the common view that 90% of diversification is achieved with a 16-stock portfolio and 95% with a 32-stock portfolio may be somewhat imprecise, but they are still good rules of thumb. Surz and Price used r-squared and tracking error, instead of standard deviation, and still found that a 30-stock portfolio achieves approximately 86% of possible diversification.

Adding more companies than 30-60+ in the equity portion of one's portfolio may lead to something that is commonly described as "diworsification.[261]" For example, even a rather large investment team probably can't know the sixty-first best idea in the portfolio as well as the very best idea, and the potential cost of allocating capital to the sixty-first best idea instead of overweighting the top ten ideas may only hurt expected return in the long run, while doing very little to improve overall diversification. An equity portfolio of 30-60+ stocks is probably heavily diversified, or at least sufficiently-diversified. If you're only holding a few stocks in an equity portfolio, however, you're taking on a tremendous amount of risk, and that almost always doesn't end well.

Although there are many components of modern portfolio theory that may fall short, not the least of which is how risk is defined in terms of volatility, one of its core tenets, the concept of diversification is simply wise in practice. It may not necessarily be due to the statistical building blocks of modern portfolio theory that add support for the concept of diversification, but rather that it just makes logical sense to spread one's capital across a meaningful number of good ideas, not in just a handful, and across asset classes, too.

It's all oldie but goodie: "Don't put all your eggs in one basket."

---

[261] The term "diworsification" is reported to have been originally used in Peter Lynch's book, *One Up on Wall Street* (1989). In its current use, the term is connected to Warren Buffett's view that diversification is merely protection against ignorance.

The Threat of Price-Agnostic Trading

Enterprise valuation is typically viewed narrowly.

To many professionals, it is just one aspect of financial modeling to arrive at an estimate of a company's fair value. But it is much more than this. It is my opinion that most of the field of finance rests on the foundation of the enterprise discounted cash flow model. Enterprise valuation is central and inescapable.

It is universal.

Not only can enterprise valuation explain how structural mispricings occur, as in pricing behavior driven by the application of other inadequate valuation processes (e.g. the dividend discount model), but it acts as a behavioral framework in which to interpret stock price movements. In tying enterprise valuation to other commonly-used quantitative metrics (e.g. P/E ratio, the P/DCF ratio), and even to economic-profit models with some massaging, it reveals that value cannot be viewed separately across fundamental or quantitative applications. In doing so, it establishes the Theory of Universal Valuation.

Is believing that enterprise valuation is the bedrock of finance such a radical view? Absolutely not.

All else equal, enterprise valuation explains the upward bias to stock values and stock prices over time via the time value of money, consistent with a submartingale in stock prices, giving credence to the popularity of long-term index investing. Enterprise valuation, as a function of future expectations, realized or not, may be more plausible of a theory explaining stock price behavior than the widely-disseminated efficient markets hypothesis, which also assumes prices are a function of future expectations. A company's competitive advantages are captured within the enterprise valuation framework, as any other qualitative consideration. The public-to-private arbitrage component of the marketplace ties enterprise valuation to real-world applications, *real* cash flow, and because others use enterprise valuation, behavioral methods cannot escape its influence. Enterprise valuation can also be expanded to the context of a market economy, explaining how buybacks can be viewed as a serious threat to wealth preservation.

There are many ways that our financial markets can be improved. We know the insignificance of quarterly EPS to long-term value generation, but yet many hold executives to meeting or beating the numbers, sometimes encouraging them to buy back stock at seemingly any price to do so. We know the dividend is not a driver of intrinsic value, but investors force management to raise the dividend year after year, even if they can't afford to, sometimes leading to disaster. We know that future free cash flows are an important driver behind the value equation, yet there is no mandatory disclosure of free cash flow--cash flow from operations less *all* gross capital spending--in each quarterly press release. We hear so much talk about the P/E ratio, and yet, so little about enterprise valuation. We know the conflicts of interest in advisor models driven by assets under management, but advisor fees seem to be a secondary condition to "best interest" or "fiduciary" responsibilities.

Nobel laureate Richard Thaler wrote in *Misbehaving* that the field of economics appears to be converging to what he described as "evidence-based economics." The same may be true in finance. However, what *should be* the definition of evidence-based? Surely, any empirical observation can be evidence-based, but is it logical, or causal? For example, are we to believe that phases of the moon have predictive ability in the stock market, just because they can be observed and are evidence-based? Of course not. As we've witnessed in finance with the shortcomings of the Fama-French three-factor model, and most notably with B/M, we *must* combine logic with causal evidence. The application of ambiguous data to explain stock returns is insufficient, and as we've witnessed with the failure of CAPM, the application of logic alone is still not enough to make a good model, if the data (i.e. beta) is impractical.

There is nothing wrong with making decisions based on evidence. In fact, you should *always* use evidence. But it is a matter of finding the appropriate evidence. We know stock prices are driven by future expectations, realized or not, something the efficient markets hypothesis even stipulates. So, we shouldn't fear a Copernican shift from backward-looking approaches that use ambiguous or impractical data to forward-looking causal approaches within quantitative finance applications. Surely, such a change may disrupt the ideas of some doctoral theses,[262] but the shift to forward-looking causal data speaks to undeniable logic. Where the CAPM may have failed because of impractical beta, we should not abandon logic in favor of the data mining of ambiguous data.

Backward-looking factor risk premiums and anomalies that are derived by ambiguous or impractical data may be nothing more than transient curiosities in the stock market, and factor return rankings in authentic walk-forward tests only speak to this, since even before the Financial Crisis. This bears repeating: In perhaps the only walk-forward tests that we can perform on some of the most widely-known risk factors (low volatility, income, momentum, size, value), they have not lived up to their in-sample excitement. I make the case in this text that market anomalies that capture differentials between what the market values a company and what the market *should value* a company within the forward-looking enterprise valuation framework (irrespective of true intrinsic value) may be the only market anomalies that can be continuously exploited, assuming, of course, the market structure as we know it today is not challenged.

There is no widespread evidence of an empirical asset pricing model based solely on backward-looking ambiguous or impractical data that has continued to work in real-world, walk-forward testing. Why? Not because the model is mis-specified, but because stock prices are based in part on forward-looking causal data, realized or not. Though "projections" and "forecasts" may be inconvenient to a narrative that may demand backward-looking "empirical" data, it is within the subset of forward-looking causal data, realized or not, where price return behavior can be explained. That is where quantitative researchers should dig. The Staff of Ra is in your hands. All the skills and tools we have, and quantitative methods can just as easily be applied to data that reflects forward-looking causal data as they can with backward-looking ambiguous data.

In June 2017, long-time random walker Burton Malkiel announced that he would be pursuing a new strategy that "aims to exploit market inefficiencies and beat the passive approach." While others remain beholden to past ways of thinking, that some of the most influential investors like Burton Malkiel continue to adapt

---

[262] In *Fooled By Randomness*, Nassim Taleb noted that data scientists may not always be "pure seekers of truth." Doctoral applicants, for example, are forced to "defend" their thesis, and many may be unwilling to change their minds later, even in the face of an abundance of logic and contradictory evidence.

to new market "evidence," even within the backward-looking parameters some researchers, themselves, have established, speaks to the idea that finance is still too young to draw definitive conclusions about what it thinks it might know about stock market prices. Despite the change of heart by Malkiel, the concept of what is quantitatively defined as an inefficiency, as in the development of B/M as a value factor, for example, *should not* mean that such an anomaly should be expected to continue, as this text explains.[263]

The field of finance, too, may fail to recognize the possibility that the upward nature of prices that we've experienced for at least the past century could be the real statistical outlier. We love hearing about how over the past 200 years, stocks have compounded at an annual return of nearly 7% in the US, and we might find comfort in the past. But enterprise valuation offers a framework to understand that, while values *should* advance over time, all else equal, there are variables that can cause values, and therefore prices, to decline over long periods of time, too. Roughly $22 trillion in sovereign U.S. debt and more than $6 trillion in corporate debt means we cannot be sure how the markets will react to a prolonged period of rising interest rates, but we know the markets benefited tremendously from ultra-low interest rate policy since the Federal funds rate hit an all-time high of 20% in March 1980. Falling interest rates have been a boon to both stock and bond values for the past 40 years!

What might be the implications? For starters, what has worked in the past may not work in the next 40 years. Where buy-and-hold and index investing proved to be great strategies while interest rates were in steep decline, one cannot assume that interest rates will remain at ultra-low levels forever. We are already witnessing significantly increased stock return correlations, consistent with index and thematic-ETF proliferation, and that means that individual stock selection, or even widespread diversification within equities, may not completely safeguard one's portfolio against cataclysmic shocks in the equity market. Diversification across various asset classes (bonds and cash, and the like) may be more important in the future than ever before, the Financial Crisis included.

---

[263] This isn't the first time that we've witnessed shifts in opinions by major financial influencers. Nassim Taleb, in *Fooled By Randomness*, talked about how Nobel laureate Robert C. Merton, a staunch defender of "the dogmas of modern finance and efficient markets," co-founded Long-Term Capital Management, which sought to take advantage of market inefficiencies. Long-Term Capital Management eventually failed, almost taking the global economy down with it.

According to some estimates, fundamental traders, or those trading on firm-specific fundamentals, account for just 10% of trading on the exchanges today. Passive and quantitative investing, or price-agnostic trading, accounts for 6 times as much. Prices are set on the marginal trade, not on the amount of assets under management, and if most market participants aren't trading on underlying business value, this in turn, can cause widespread dislocations in prices versus reasonably estimated intrinsic values (dislocations that may never fully be reconciled even over long periods of time). In such a scenario, the capital-raising function of markets could become significantly less attractive. What CEO would want the company's stock price to be driven by quantitative algorithmic trading mechanisms and correlations with unrelated assets instead of on its company's fundamental long-term business outlook, earnings and free cash flow stream?[264]

In recent decades, finance seems to have only pursued more sophisticated methods of data mining to build a seemingly endless supply of new products to sell to investors. There are now more than 70 times as many stock indexes as there are stocks, themselves, and according to research company ETFGI, there are now more than 5,000 ETFs globally, with nearly 1,800 in the US alone, and that doesn't include exchange traded notes (like the one that collapsed in February 2018). Though this sounds like a large number of diverse investing options, less than 1% of US ETFs, for example, receive more than half of fund flows.

What's worse, the core of what equity ETFs are made of is surprisingly shrinking. More than half of all publicly-traded companies have vanished in just the past 20 years.[265] As speculative instruments that are based on targeting price movements in theme-based orientation proliferate (as in the case of many ETFs), the future may simply look nothing at all like the past. *How could it?* The decline in the number of investable stocks has reduced the variety of reasonable investable options for many savers and retirees that need better choices, not more. But fewer listed stocks and more thematic-trading vehicles isn't so bad, right?[266]

---

[264] It might be speculated that wealthy investors that may have no interest in the vicissitudes of ultra-volatile pricing action may take companies private, potentially driving greater global wealth inequality as investment options for the public and savers in which to participate are substantially reduced.

[265] In November 1997, there were more than 7,300 U.S. stocks, but that number has now shrunk to fewer than 3,600. This trend may accelerate if companies are taken private to avoid ultra-volatile market conditions.

[266] Not only is the number of stocks shrinking, but according to Bespoke Investment Group, the total number of shares outstanding on a split-adjusted basis is shrinking, too. For example,

Well, without enough buying and selling based on firm-specific intrinsic value calculations, or value-conscious trading, market prices may simply take on a life of their own, beyond the grasp of even the most advanced computer models that try to forecast them (perhaps the problem is exacerbated by them). That means we could experience even bigger bubbles and even bigger bursts, and they could become even more frequent. There have always been periods of panic in the stock market, of course, but for many decades now, they have always been passing, transient events. What will happen if most market participants are no longer acting on estimates of value, or on expectations of the market's estimate of value? How will prices behave then? Could there be more and more situations like Longfin, but with larger and larger companies as the ranks of passive and quantitative trading continue to swell?

There may be just one other period in history that had more price-agnostic trading than today, and that may be the period pre-dating the publication of John Burr Williams' work *The Theory of Investment Value*, or roughly 1928-1940. This was the most sustainably volatile period in stock market history, as measured by daily percentage changes in the S&P 500. In the 1920s, stocks and bonds were mass marketed to the general public, and many were just speculating on the price behavior of securities they didn't understand. Back then, there may not have been much value-conscious trading activity at all. Today, as index investing and ETFs backed by traditional quantitative theory proliferate, market volatility may once again approach those levels, and if not checked, surpass them.

Indexers and quantitative investors rely on value-conscious active management to set the "correct" prices.[267] Vanguard founder Jack Bogle has said that "if

---

through 2018, split-adjusted shares outstanding of all companies in the Dow Jones Industrial Average has fallen by 15% since 2007. This shouldn't be a big deal, or even a problem if investors are logical. However, index investors generally may not be, meaning that they may keep throwing more and more money at the market regardless of price. If, for example, everyone thinks stock investing is a "good thing" and puts their retirement savings in the market and keeps adding to it no matter what, then the shrinking number of available companies to invest in (and outstanding shares) could drive prices indiscriminately higher (lower supply, more demand). However, when the latter stages of this dynamic approach, the end game could be terrible, especially for those where higher retirement contributions may be occurring at the frothiest part of such a bubble, perhaps leading to a bursting of the bubble. It's important to note, however, that the US has managed to bounce back from every market crash in history to make new highs again, and sometimes experiencing a crash isn't as bad as if one stayed completely out a multi-year bull market just to avoid one (as in the Fed Chairman Alan Greenspan years).

[267] Value-conscious active management in setting stock prices through buying and selling creates a positive externality for society. Indexers and quantitative investors do not pay for this benefit.

everybody indexed, the only word you could use is chaos, catastrophe." The chances of everybody indexing may be zero, but what are the chances of *both* indexers and quantitative investing, or *all* price-agnostic trading, completely overwhelming fundamental value-conscious traders that calculate intrinsic value estimates, causing levels of market volatility we've never seen before? What are the chances that the arbitrage mechanism of the market in setting reasonable prices breaks down? That is a non-zero probability that can have widespread implications, impacting each and every one of our lives.

From Thaler in *Misbehaving*:

> When prices start to move against a money manager and investors start to ask for some of their money back, prices will be driven further against them, which can cause a vicious spiral. The key lesson is that prices can get out of whack, and smart money cannot always set things right.

The Nash equilibrium of the markets today may center on what investors think the market thinks is the best estimate of fair value. But what happens if that Nash equilibrium is disrupted…permanently? Will we take the threat of price-agnostic trading seriously then? To some degree, we've already seen what can happen play out in more modern times, but on a much smaller scale with Long-Term Capital Management. What may have saved the markets during the crisis of the late 1990s, however, was that indexing and quantitative trading was still but a small portion of overall trading.

We may have seen another glimpse of what could happen in August 2007 where just a few bad days in the market caused a rapid unwinding of many quant long-short strategies. Goldman's chief financial officer said at the time that the firm was witnessing "25-standard deviation moves, several days in a row." We may have seen a little bit more when a few "short-vol" products blew up in February 2018 to cause volatility in the stock market not seen since the Financial Crisis. Indexers and quants continue to be a growing part of the Keynesian beauty contest, for better or worse, but what if passive and quantitative trading become

---

This free-riding problem, or the assumption that someone else will do the work in setting prices (bystander effect/apathy), may be the primary reason to expect heightened levels of market volatility as indexing and quantitative trading continues to proliferate. In other words, price-agnostic trading may potentially overwhelm value-conscious active management, which it depends on to set prices in a reasonable manner based on estimates of value.

so large that something truly catastrophic happens the next time around, something that the "smart money," as Thaler puts it, just can't set right?

A lesser-known story about Long-Term Capital Management is that, even though the Federal Reserve orchestrated a bail out of the hedge fund, value-conscious Warren Buffett had also made a bid to save the firm. His bid would be rejected. Years later during the darkest days of the Financial Crisis, Warren Buffett, again, would be there to help bail out the big banks. There's something to be said about this. Value-conscious investing won't save you completely from increasing stock return correlations and heightened systematic risk within equities markets, but if you can identify mispriced enterprise free-cash-flow streams, provided that you have enough liquidity to wait out the storm, it *can* protect you. Even under worst-case scenarios where rational, fundamental price "setters" completely disappear, those free-cash-flow streams can be taken private. Value-conscious investing may very well be the most socially-responsible investing of all.

How should you prepare for what I believe will become one of the most volatile periods in stock market history, set off by the combination of indexing and quant trading proliferation? Within an equity portfolio, consider using enterprise valuation to estimate intrinsic value, and apply behavioral (relative) valuation to assess what others might be thinking. Think about assessing technical/momentum dynamics to evaluate the likelihood of price-to-estimated-fair value convergence, and don't dismiss the valuable information in prices, which could help you avoid value traps. The Valuentum process employs these considerations but consider diversifying your portfolio well beyond stocks, too.

While it is almost certain that asset-return correlations will not act the same way they did during previous crises, the concept of diversification across asset classes may save you big in the event of a systemic crisis driven by price-agnostic investors that hits the equity markets hard. There are rules of thumb about what might be the best asset allocation for your age, but only your personal financial advisor would know best for your individual situation. A good mix of Valuentum stocks (the Best Ideas Newsletter portfolio, or Dividend Growth Newsletter portfolio),[268] high-quality corporate bonds, private real estate or businesses,

---

[268] Not all ideas in the simulated newsletter portfolios will be right for you. Please be sure to do your own due diligence, and where necessary, contact an investment professional that knows what's right for your personal financial goals and risk tolerances.

certificates of deposit, and dry powder in the form of cold-hard cash could make a lot of sense for many.

Integrity and independence remain at the core of everything I do. My experiences with Kinder Morgan and MLPs during 2015 tested me, not only as an analyst, but also challenged me on a very personal level. Even when the analyst crowd was against our small firm, we stood for what we believed was right, and the market eventually proved that we were right. The herding behavior[269] on Wall Street, however, seems to only be getting worse. I see a lot of what I saw with the research in Kinder Morgan and the MLPs during 2015 in quantitative research today. Many indexers and quants are just following the herd, employing questionable data and repeating conclusions that may not make sense. To paraphrase General George S. Patton, if everybody is thinking the same way, then it's likely many aren't thinking.

In spite of all of this, however, there is a reason to be optimistic. The future is not yet written, and it is what we make it.

---

[269] Herding behavior may originate from something called career risk. For example, if you go against the crowd and you're wrong, you might get fired. If you are with the crowd and you're wrong, you probably won't get fired. I let the analyst crowd do its thing, and I focus on what I think is right. This is different from paying attention to the crowd's behavior in the market as in the information contained in prices. The crowd, in that sense, matters greatly.

NOTES

ix   JFK quote: "Address in the Assembly Hall at the Paulskirche in Frankfurt (266)," June 25, 1963, Public Papers of the Presidents: John F. Kennedy, 1963. Documents in the collection prepared by United States officials as part of their official duties are in the public domain.

Preface

Market Inefficiency and Analytical Friction

xii   had cut its dividend 75%: Kinder Morgan Announces 2016 Outlook, December 8, 2015.

xii   most prominently with Barron's.com: Kimelman "The Bear Case," Barron's (2015), June 11, 2015.

xii   Credit Suisse quotes: Credit Suisse Kinder Morgan Research Report, Comment, June 15, 2015.

xix   reference to 2014 Barron's article in the master limited partnership sector totaled $500 billion in market capitalization: Bary (2014), February 22, 2014.

xiv   my counter analysis to Credit Suisse's rebuttal: Stone (2015), June 19, 2015.

xiv   "the timely or untimely resurrection": Seeking Alpha transcript, July 15, 2015.

xiv   Kinder Morgan's executive chairman and director: Surran (a), Seeking Alpha (2015), July 24, 2015.

xiv   would upgrade the MLP sector: Street Insider (2015).

xiv   Goldman Sachs would add the company to its Conviction Buy list: Swanson (2015). August 14, 2015.

xiv   share an extension of our work on MLPs: Kimelman "Why," Barron's (2015). September 28, 2015. See an excerpt of this note below:

> "We now believe the financial operating structure of the MLP may not survive in its current form, even as we say that most businesses using the MLP model are good ones. Our view continues to be that most master limited partnerships including Energy Transfer Partners and most midstream corporate business models including Kinder Morgan are dependent on external capital market assistance to fully fund the current levels of their distributions and dividends, respectively. Their distributions and dividends are not sustainable via internally-generated, traditional free cash flow generation, as measured by cash flow from operations less all capital spending.

However, most traditional brokerage houses have set the price targets of these entities on the faulty belief that their dividends and distributions are a clear and reliable reflection of their underlying operations, as they are with most other corporates. In light of the external capital market assistance that is necessary to support the payouts, however, such dividends and distributions are not; in our view, they are far from it. The industry's definition of "distributable cash flow," which completely ignores the very growth capital that drives future net income, which itself is included in distributable cash flow, further complicates this severe valuation imbalance.

With seemingly infinite support from the external capital markets and investor thirst for income, most master limited partnerships and midstream corporates have been holding on to the belief that their distributions and dividends are invincible, and some may still believe this to be true. After all, they may argue, with unlimited access to incremental external financing via new equity and debt, which entity couldn't grow its dividend or distribution to the moon? This line of thinking comes with a kicker, too. As long as the brokerage houses price such equities on these "financially-engineered" dividends, the price of their stocks would also be propped up, and in turn, the creditworthiness of the entity, its corporate credit rating, would be healthy, too.

But this self-perpetuating, debt-infused "bubble" is coming to an end, in our view, now that bankers are re-evaluating price decks and borrowing capacity and as the energy markets swoon. Most master limited partnerships and midstream corporates may have to make the difficult decision to either cut their distributions/dividends or suspend growth plans in them altogether, a move that would completely negate forever the dividend-based equity pricing framework used by brokerage houses, leading to a further unraveling of equity prices. Falling stock prices would then weaken credit quality, and a bust would truly ensue, as shares finally revert back to traditional, tried-and-true free cash flow valuation processes, as opposed to one based on a financially-engineered payout."

xv rebuttal from CBRE Clarion…: Howard (2015), October 1, 2015.

xv S&P Global Market Intelligence would say: "Janney Montgomery Scott would reportedly say the following…" Mosqueda-Fernandez (2015). October 5, 2015.

xvi revised its dividend growth plans lower: Kinder Morgan Increases Quarterly Dividend. October 21, 2015.

xvi first Credit Suisse downgrade and SunTrust downgrade: Surran (b), Seeking Alpha (2015), "Kinder Morgan -7% on slower…" October 22, 2015.

xvi Argus price target cut: "Surran (c), Seeking Alpha (2015), "Kinder Morgan price target cut to $35 from $50 at Argus." November 10, 2015.

xvi Moody's would downgrade Kinder Morgan's…: Marshall (a), Moody's (2015). December 1, 2015. Moody's would write below:

Rating Action: Moody's changes Kinder Morgan's outlook to negative

Approximately $44 billion of rated debt affected

Toronto, December 01, 2015 -- Moody's Investors Service (Moody's) changed Kinder Morgan Inc.'s (KMI) outlook to negative from stable. Moody's affirmed KMI's Baa3 senior unsecured and Prime-3 commercial paper ratings...

...The negative outlook reflects Kinder Morgan's increased business risk profile and additional pressure on its already high leverage that will result from its agreement to increase ownership in NGPL, a distressed company," said Terry Marshall, Moody's Senior Vice-President. "NGPL is facing potential default on its pending interest payments, suggesting that KMI will need to provide cash injections, which will likely be debt funded initially.

xvii Argus would pull its Buy rating...: Surran (d), Seeking Alpha (2015). December 3, 2015.

xvii Fitch Ratings would say...: Allmendinger (2015), Fitch. December 3, 2015.

xvii On December 4...: Kinder Morgan Announces 2016 Financial Expectations (December 4, 2015); Surran (e), Seeking Alpha (December 4, 2015).

xvii Jefferies would say at the time: Surran (f), Seeking Alpha (2015).

xvii Moody's to rescind the credit outlook downgrade: Marshall (b), Moody's (2015).

xvii Credit Suisse would eventually lower its target price to $18: Surran (g), Seeking Alpha (2015). December 9, 2015.

xviii As of 2018, some 40% of energy infrastructure is comprised of C-Corps...: Reddy, Global X (2018).

xviii we would author another piece that would be shared with Barron's.com: Kimelman "Is Kinder..." Barron's (2016).

xix the entire cryptocurrency market was just $186 billion: Schroeder (2018).

xx footnote, reference to Kinder Morgan's free cash flow coverage: Kinder Morgan, Form 10-K (2017).

xx footnote, reference to CBRE Clarion data regarding distribution cuts: CBRE (2017).

The Data Dilemma and Valuentum Investing

xxv footnote, McKinsey (2010), page 259, reference to Asness quote: Asness (2018).

xxvi For example, a quantitative combination of "value" and momentum in a portfolio...: Asness (2013).

xxvi Another method of portfolio construction might...: Gray (2016), page 145.

Chapter 1: Stock Prices

4   The house had once been used for a funeral business: Driehaus Museum (2013).

What Price Movements Actually Imply

5   Selling losers and letting the winners run: Beattie (2007).

5   since its inception in 1980: Driehaus Small Cap Growth Strategy (2018).

5   An estimated 84%-92%: Soe (2017).

6   Keynes block quote: Keynes (1936).

6   reference to Nash equilibrium: Nash (1950).

7   the measure that was widely-followed by other analysts: Kinder Morgan 10-K (2007).

Getting Lucky

8   reference to Firm-Foundation and Castle-in-the-Air theories: Malkiel (2003).

10   footnote, The first reference to the term "moat" in the investment world…: Loomis (1999).

Factor-Based Investing and Astrologists

11   reference to net current asset value: Graham (1934).

11   quote from *Intelligent Investor*: Graham (2003).

12   "empirical evidence of historical positive risk-adjusted excess returns associated with them": (Pappas, Dickson 2015).

12   reference to five-factor model (Fama 2014).

12   more than 600 factor-based exchange-traded funds: Nielsen (2016)

12   In late 2017, it was estimated: Credit Suisse, Research Institute (2018).

12   "five-factor model can leave lots of the cross-section of expected stock returns unexplained,": Fama (2014).

12   footnote, regarding number of factors identified: Credit Suisse, Research Institute (2018).

13   "do not explain anything about expected or required returns." (Fernandez 2017).

13   footnote, reference to Ibbotson regarding cost of equity data and direct quote: Ibbotson (2009), page 113, 115.

14   "fuzzy thinking": Buffett (1992).

15   Through most of LTCM's existence…: Jorion (2000).

16 According to a study by the Index Industry Association, The PowerShares Multi-Strategy Alternative Portfolio Fund: Beer (2018).

16 footnote, "an index contains histories of returns that…" Chambers (2015), page 416.

17 references to Evangeline Adams (PBS, Crash of 1929).

17 footnote, In *Fooled By Randomness*, Nassim Taleb would joke: Taleb (2005); "US spending on science, space and technology" and other spurious correlations: Vigen (2018).

17 reference to lunar empirical research: (Yuan 2006).

18 reference to misbehaving (Thaler 2015).

Just How Bad Is Data Interpretation?

18 According to a study by J.P. Morgan in 2017: (Cheng 2017).

19 footnote, "Great minds can disagree on the explanation, but nobody can dispute the empirical fact…": (Gray 2016), page 29.

19 footnote, reference to McKinsey study, "virtually indistinguishable from those of value stocks.": Jiang (2007).

20 footnote, reference to percentage of stocks having negative book equity: Brown (2007), reference to 118 companies: Fairchild (2018).

20 reference to Boeing book equity: Boeing (2009 10-K).

20 reference to McDonald's book equity: McDonald's (3Q 2018 10-Q).

21 regarding negative book equity companies: Jan (2012); regarding performance of negative book equity companies: Fairchild (2018).

22 Oakmark quote - "for companies in the S&P 500 today…" Shawal (2018).

22 footnote, reference to B/M in Fama-French model: Fama (2014).

23 "that they did not have any theory to explain why size and value should be risk factors." (Thaler 2015), page 228.

23 footnote, "This finding suggests a predictive model…," reference to Ibbotson: Ibbotson (2009), quote from page 49.

23 "the first systematic collection of stock market prices, was compiled under the auspices of the Alfred Cowles Foundation in the 1930s" (Miller 1999).

23 quote on the criticism of historical stock market data (Zweig 2009).

Notes

How the Market Functions

26   reference to Babson quote: Gravvty (2018).

26   "Babson Break" reference: Thomas (2018). More information provided below:

> A jittery Federal Reserve and what looked like a weakening economy had brought a mini crash in March 1929, but it wasn't until a warning in a speech at the Annual Business Conference in Massachusetts on September 5 from Roger Babson that the market revealed its shaky underpinnings:
>
> > [A] crash is coming, and it may be terrific. .... The vicious circle will get in full swing and the result will be a serious business depression. There may be a stampede for selling which will exceed anything that the Stock Exchange has ever witnessed. Wise are those investors who now get out of debt.
>
> In what is now known as the "Babson Break," the market traded off only a few percentage points that day. The vilification of Babson, however, was widespread on Wall Street and many even questioned his patriotism, but the market action of October 24, 1929 ("Black Thursday"), almost two months later, turned the skeptics, if not their hearts and minds.
>
> At the opening bell that Thursday, the Dow Jones Industrial Average lost more than 10%, and while it had recovered during the trading session, the widespread publicity of the sharp, sudden drop in the market by newspapers over the weekend set the stage for next week. The Dow Jones Industrial Average would fall nearly 13% on Black Monday and another 12% on Black Tuesday. In the years that followed, the market would lose more than 80% of its value from the peak.
>
> Just a week prior to the Crash, on October 17, 1929, Yale University's Irving Fisher would famously say: "Stock prices have reached what looks like to a permanently high plateau." Fisher's reputation would be irreparably harmed.
>
> Babson would later go on to found the Babson College in Massachusetts and author nearly 50 books.

26   Earnings for companies in the Dow Jones Industrial Average: Lundeen (2011).

27   Notes on hidden biases, "best interest," "fiduciary": Freakonomics Asks

> *Freakonomics*, co-authored by Steven D. Levitt and Stephen Dubner, brought attention to the principal-agent problem inherent to the real estate industry. The principal, or the homeowner looking to sell his or her property, believes that the real estate agent is acting completely on his or her behalf, in his or her best interests, but the incentive structure tends to not pass the "sniff" test, or at least as the authors put it, incentives may not be truly aligned. For example, where waiting for a higher offer price on the home would be material to the homeowners' financial well-being, it wouldn't necessarily move the needle with respect to the agents' sales commission, which is but a fraction of the incrementally higher price and must be split several ways. There's

266

therefore a higher incentive for the agent to sell the property as soon as possible to reap the benefits of a whole commission than wait for a higher offer to maximize the sale price for the seller that may not immediately come.

Of course, wrongdoing of any nature is not intended nor can it be proven, nor is there any at all (to my knowledge), as Levitt and Dubner may have noted, but the misaligned incentives within the financial industry may not be too different than those of the real estate industry. Financial industry participants that charge a fee for assets under management, for example, may have a greater incentive to land an incremental client of, let's say $1 million in assets, than they would to prudently reach for an extra percentage point or two in risk-adjusted performance for an existing client, which by comparison, would only translate into maybe a few thousand dollars in additional assets under management when a new client, on the other hand, would bring in much more. The incremental fees generated from slightly better returns might also be absorbed by additional structural costs, thereby wiping out any gain to the agent at all.

But where the compounding dynamics over time of even slightly better annual returns would work wonders on an existing client's retirement portfolio (as in the sale price of the house for the homeowner), the incremental benefit of individual-client portfolio outperformance would be rather muted for the agent when it comes to raking in additional fees tied to assets under management (as in the case of the commission on the house to the realtor), especially when a sizable increase in assets could be just a phone call or an in-person meeting away. For payment structures tied to assets under management, incentives are in place for financial industry participants to spend more time gathering assets from new clients than growing the assets of their existing clients via return-boosting endeavors, whether it is intended or not.

To free up time and resources to recruit new clients, strategies that encourage "buy and hold" investing, "staying in the market" for a long time (no matter what), and minimizing "portfolio drawdowns" during times of weakness have become all-too-convenient study guides for the financial community to inconspicuously hand to clients and prospects. For example, if clients can be baptized or converted to "buy and hold" index investors, all the better. The longer assets are tied up, the more fees that can be generated. The more secure assets are from redemptions during tumultuous times, the more resilient the fee-based revenue model. The less volatile asset returns are, regardless of whether they are optimized over the long haul, the more stable the financial revenue stream for the agent. Though always with good intentions, financial industry participants are human and are motivated by incentives, just like anyone else in any other industry.

When research and studies are readily available that conveniently support the AUM-based revenue models across the financial industry, why would any effort be spent on generating new ideas, research processes, or uncovering conflicting evidence? The financial industry in some respects could be suffering from what can best be described as a confirmation bias. Those that want the "long run" to always work out actively perform and seek out works and studies that support such a line of thinking, just like a reader may prefer a Facebook or Twitter post that supports his or her own political views, or one that highlights his or her favorite brand or celebrity.

In today's society, the risks of confirmation bias are growing exponentially. How many of you have subscribed to a website with a methodology that differs from what you believe to gain further perspective? Do you always actively look for articles on both sides of the issue, or do you stop when you find one that supports your view? Social media sites are so effective today at giving people what they want that many may never even see the other side of the argument. As technologies continue to advance, investors are drifting further and further away from being able to recognize their own biases.

28   reference to "Blue Skies": (PBS, Crash of 1929).

Chapter 2: Once the Mind Is Stretched

The Coup d'etat of Modern Finance

31   Markowitz's mean-variance framework in modern portfolio theory in the early 1950s was followed up by Treynor's development in the early 1960s of the CAPM: Becker (2018), page 5-7.

31   footnote reference to *"Superinvestors of Graham-and-Doddsville"*: Buffett (1984)

32   footnote, "I believe there is no other proposition...," reference to Jensen quote: Jensen (1978), page 95.

32   largely been shown to be less useful even by the late 1970s, but it had become the authoritative 'perceived truth' in the academic community, Becker (2018), "perceived truth" quoted directly from page 8.

32   references to apologetic academic works and quotes (Thaler 2015), page 221.

34   when companies used some "garbled version of the world 'electronics' in their title: Malkiel (2013).

34   or during the dot-com bubble during the late 1990s and early 2000s...: Goldman (2010).

35   "Horses with the first initial 'A' have won..." (Moore 2018).

They're Digging in the Wrong Place

37   The rolling 10-year annualized return of the Fama-French value factor: Hopkins (2018).

37   "if we look at the past 30 years...": Waggoner (2018).

37   assessment of performance of traditional quant value factor: (Hopkins 2018). Graphic in the article used to assess "live" track record.

38   A look at the *walk-forward* performance: Credit Suisse (2018), page 19.

39   footnote, reference to data regarding bull markets: First Trust (2018).

39   In February 2018, the markets: Foerster (2018).

40   some "short-vol" traders didn't stay solvent long: Langlois (2018).

40   Where one may have expected quantitative "value" and momentum to be negatively
      correlated as they have been in some studies: Asness (2013).

41   "Individual factors are likely to experience...": Kalesnik (2018).

Once the Mind Is Stretched

42   footnote, "As more and more factors are added to empirical asset pricing models,
      quantitative finance may inevitably converge to enterprise valuation, eventually incorporating
      forward-looking data that captures the future expectations that drive share prices and
      returns:"

Expected Returns

(1) Rf + factor(1) + factor(2) + factor(3)... = Rf + (estimated fair value/price − 1)

The Theory of Universal Valuation posits that quantitative factor models may
eventually embrace forward-looking criteria to capture the forward-looking dynamics of
price-to-estimated fair value within the enterprise valuation process.

The first series of factors represents the framework of a traditional multi-factor quant
model, while the second series represents the expected return function within
enterprise valuation. By mathematical identity:

(2) Factor(1) + factor(2) + factor(3)... = estimated fair value/price - 1

Historical ambiguous valuation multiples, as those used as factors in traditional quant
applications, cannot theoretically capture this estimated fair-value-to-price mismatch
within enterprise valuation, but only approximate it empirically by adding more
potentially spurious factors.

As more and more factors are added to traditional quant factor models, they may only
grow to approximate enterprise valuation more closely, but with potentially non-causal
data, requiring revisions after revisions. Equation 2 shows how factors should be
forward-looking to capture estimated fair value/price mis-matches.

Rf = risk-free rate

Chapter 3: Lessons from the Financial Crisis

45   reference to Block 37: Crain's Chicago (2005).

45   reference to size of Madoff fraud: (McCool 2009).

Banks and Confidence

48   reference to Washington Mutual run-on-the-bank dynamic: (Zarroli 2008).

48   Morgan Stanley was leveraged 34-to-1 while Goldman Sachs was leveraged 27-to-1: Jackson (2008).

Equity and Credit Analysis Inherently Linked

50   led to the creation of Morningstar's Cash Flow Cushion: (Nelson 2009).

Backward-Looking Data Not the Answer

52   reference to Valuentum research on GE: Nelson, Rosemann (May 2017).

54   According to data from Morningstar, average daily correlation over the trailing six months…: Rawson (2012).

55   A hypothetical portfolio that held 50% US stocks, 40% bonds, and 10% cash only lost 16%: Kaplan (2012).

55   footnote, "markets tend to behave as one during great crashes.": Junior (2010).

Chapter 4: The Right Mental Model

60   "industrial and decorative ability": Buffett (2011)

Establishing Causality: A Critical Framework to View the Markets

61   footnote, reference to Palm and 3Com: Thaler (2015); reference to HNC Software/Retek and other instances of the limits to arbitrage: Nofsinger (2002).

62   footnote, market efficiency does not necessarily require the market price to be equal to true value at every point in time: Damodaran (2002), page 113.

63   reference to Keynes (Keynes 1936).

The End Game for Stock Prices

64   in a 2018 study by the American Investment Council: American Investment Council (2018).

65   footnote, buyout funds represent the largest asset class within the group: McKinsey Global Private Markets Review, page 7.

Value Is Sensitive = Prices Are Volatile

68   footnote, quote from *Intelligent Investor*: Graham (2003).

69   "it is better to be roughly right than exactly wrong," (Read 1878).

Self-Fulfilling Prophecies

70   footnote, quote from Keynes regarding Snap, Old Maid and Musical Chairs: Keynes (1936).

73   footnote, reference to PEG ratio: Lynch (1989).

Notes

The Duration of Value Composition

74   reference to 1992 Berkshire Hathaway Shareholder Letter (Buffett 1992).

76   footnotes that reference McKinsey study, "seldom catastrophic": Koller (2013).

The Long Term Is Elusive

82   footnote, reference to *Stocks for the Long Run*, "a negative real holding period return": Siegel (1998), page 25.

82   footnote, reference to *Future for Investors*: Siegel (2005), page 13.

82   footnote, reference to Sanford Bernstein study: Brown (2007), page 124.

83   footnote, reference to *Fortune*: Brown (2007), page 113.

Chapter 5: The Enterprise Valuation Framework

85   footnote, "anything that doesn't increase cash flows doesn't create value...": McKinsey (2010), page 26.

90   That Millie Bobby Brown's Instagram followers...: (Netflix 2018).

Don't Sweat the WACC

91   footnote, Buffett on required returns: Yahoo Finance (2017).

92   footnote, According to Aswath Damodaran...: Damodaran (2018).

93   "...volatility is almost universally used as a proxy for risk. Though this pedagogic assumption makes for easy teaching, it is dead wrong: Volatility is far from synonymous with risk." (Buffett 2014)

93   footnote, reference to McKinsey cost of equity: McKinsey (2010), page 35.

94   footnote, reference to CRSP data: Ibbotson (2009), page 56.

96   Kinder Morgan, for example, had generally guided...: Kean (2015).

Value Is Not Static

99   footnote, using a 60-month rolling cost of equity measure: Ibbotson (2009), page 113.

Shortcomings of the P/E Ratio

100 footnote, reference to rent expense: Moody's (2006).

Introduction to Behavioral Valuation

103 nearly 79% use a discounted present value approach...: Fabozzi (2017), page 14.

104 according to the same survey by the CFA Institute...: Fabozzi (2017), page 21.

104 Footnote, Thaler's thoughts on money managers: Thaler (2015), page 214.

The Theory of Universal Valuation

109 enterprise valuation is poorly suited for comparative valuations is considered a limitation by some investment professionals: English (2001), page 289.

109 footnote, in an efficient market, stocks with lower P/E ratios should be as likely to be undervalued as overvalued as stocks with high P/E ratios: Damodaran (2002), page 113.

110 There was a study shared by the Enterprising Investor...: Klement (2016).

111 footnote, reference to Enterprising Investor, Klement (2016), and FactSet earnings data: Butters (2018).

111 footnote, reference to Buffett's 1992 Letter to Berkshire Hathaway Shareholders: Buffett (1992).

112 reference to Treynor views and direct quote: Treynor (1973).

112 footnote, reference to Graham-and-Doddsville: Buffett (1984).

112 "required reading": (Thaler 2015), page 209.

Residual Income and Banking Models

114 several of these adjustments...: CFA (2019).

114 footnote, reference to Interbrand: Interbrand (2018).

116 Paulson's "bazooka": Isidore (2008).

Buybacks and Intrinsic Value

117 footnote, reference to Netflix, "momentum-investor-fueled euphoria": Netflix (2013).

118 reference to IBM's buybacks: IBM (2014).

119 the company pulled its operating earnings per share target of $20 by 2015: Seeking Alpha (2014).

120 footnote, reference to McKinsey, "just doesn't matter": Koller (2013).

120 footnote, reference to share issuance, "will need to forecast a price per share": Damodaran (2018).

120 reference to GE's buybacks: General Electric (2017).

122 According to S&P Dow Jones Indices, S&P 500 stock buybacks: (S&P DJI 2018).

122 In 2018, announced buybacks hit $1.1 trillion: Pisani (2018)

Chapter 6: The Greatest Contradiction of All?

124 The stock market in the 1920s, for example, had been openly manipulated: (PBS)

124 During the dot-com bubble of the late 1990s: Sundaram, page 4.

124 "forty million unique sets of eyeballs and growing in time should be worth nicely more than Yahoo's current market value of $10 billion.": Elkind (2001).

125 footnote, reference to Damodaran post regarding user or subscriber-based valuation methods: Damodaran (2017).

126 A 2006 study: Goetzmann (2006).

126 Another poll from Gallup: Fisher (2002)

What Matters in Testing for Efficiency?

127 "security prices at any point in time 'fully reflect' all available information," Fama (1970), page 388.

127 Infospace at $1,305 in March 2000: Heath (2005).

127 footnote, reference to Netscape: McKinsey (2010), page 5.

127 footnote, reference to Yahoo: Penman (2007), page 10.

127 reference to the Arithmetic of Active Management: Sharpe (1991).

128 footnote, reference, In the 1999 book, *The Psychology of Investing*, in Chapter 11," Epstein (1999), page 163.

130 Some say a hypothesis must at least be testable (falsifiable): Popper (1989).

131 there have been intriguing studies on the predictive power of forward-looking fair value estimates: Miller (2013).

131 with Valuentum's efforts in 2017 the only known study: Nelson (Oct 2017). Excerpt from conclusion of paper:

> Though academic research is scarce with respect to measuring the efficacy of discounted enterprise cash-flow-based fair value estimates due to the presence of price targets on Wall Street, the usefulness of a systematically-applied free-cash-flow-to-the-firm method remains intriguing. The study in this paper reveals a higher rate of price-to-estimated-fair value convergence for both undervalued and overvalued stocks, in aggregate (59%), as defined by the discounted enterprise cash flow process, than what otherwise might have been expected under "random walk" or efficient markets theory.

Over the time period studied in this paper, stock prices have experienced a strong advance, and such a dynamic may have been expected to drive a higher frequency of price-to-estimated-fair value convergence in undervalued stocks (FV > P) than in overvalued stocks (FV < P). Such an occurrence was evident in the results. However, a statistically significant difference appeared with respect to undervalued stocks versus "random walk" expectations, and that a 40%+ price-to-estimated-fair value convergence rate for overvalued stocks occurred in a rising-tide-lifts-all-boats market environment was highly encouraging, if not equally intriguing.

In the incidence of fair value estimates that signaled undervaluation, the share price converged to the fair value estimate within eight time periods, or approximately 3 years, in more than 80% of the instances. Share prices of undervalued stocks advanced as much as 20% or 30%, on average, to achieve price-to-estimated-fair value convergence at this elevated cumulative price-to-estimated-fair value convergence rate. We think these statistics with respect to the identification of materially underpriced equities is remarkable under any economic conditions or market environment.

134 footnote, columnist Josh Brown noted in a May 2015 Fortune article: Brown (2015).

134 footnote, the "denominator" effect has shown to have a greater impact than the "numerator" effect: Nissim (2001).

The Logical Inconsistencies of Efficient Markets Theory and Backward-Looking-Derived Factors

135 Random walkers may say that investors may have been pricing in an impending recession prior to the Crash of 1987: Chicago Booth (2016).

135 "most people were saying the Internet was going to revolutionize business, so companies that had a leg up on the Internet were going to be very successful.": Clement (2007).

136 reference to *Great Companies: Looking for Success Secrets in All the Wrong Places.*": Baum (2015). Block quote used with authors' permission.

Rewriting the Arithmetic of Active Management to the Investor Level

138 "...the market prices stocks so efficiently that a blindfolded chimpanzee throwing darts at the *Wall Street Journal* can select a portfolio that performs as well as those managed by the experts." Malkiel (2013).

138 Others have subsequently hypothesized that monkeys might even do better than the experts.: Ferri (2012).

139 According to the Investment Company Institute: Investment Company Institute (2018), page 41-43.

139 reference to Sharpe Arithmetic: Sharpe (1991).

139 reference to Bogle's Syllogism: Bogle (1999).

139 footnote, total stock market capitalization for passive and active mutual funds and ETFs was 29% of the U.S. stock market...: Investment Company Institute (2018), image page 43.

142 "manage a minority share of the actively managed dollars": Sharpe (1991).

142 "self-evident certainty,": Bogle (1999), page 19.

143 footnote, "Famed money-manager Bill Miller...": La Monica (2006).

143 "if you can't lose on purpose, then you can't win on purpose either.": Laughlin (2014).

143 reference to baseball standings: Baseball (2015).

144 reference to Skill Ratio, "by dividing the average excess rolling returns by the standard deviation of excess rolling returns,": Blais (2018).

144 When it comes to long-term returns, fees matter: Kinnel (2016).

144 footnote, Over a 20-year look-back period ending June 1, 2017: Valuentum (2017).

145 with Fidelity introducing zero expense-ratio index mutual funds: Fidelity website.

Bad Math? Finance Does Not Have the Complete Picture

146 "In recent years financial economists have increasingly questioned the efficient market hypothesis...": Malkiel (2005).

146 "households directly own 36% of the $46 trillion U.S. equity market.": Vlastelica (2018).

146 footnote, "the average dollar invested in U.S. stock funds outperformed...": Ptak (2018).

146 footnote, "the market return must equal a weighted average of the returns on the passive and active segments of the market": Sharpe (1991).

147 "after costs, the return of the average actively managed dollar will be less than the return of the average passively managed dollar." Sharpe (1991).

Indexing Moves Markets and Drives Inefficiencies

148 reference to *Economist* article title: Economist (2018).

148 On February 14, 2018, FTSE Russell announced, "pushing the shares up from their February low of $32 to above $71": Smith (2018).

150 A 2010 study by Jeffrey Wurgler of the Stern School of Business..." and corresponding direct quotes in paragraph: Wurgler (2010).

150 reference to *How Index Trading Increases Market Vulnerability*: Sullivan (2012).

Chapter 7: The Latest Bubble to Pop

The More Things Change

156   reference to the origins of Vanguard: Bogle (1997).

157   List of "10 Reasons:"

> 1) The valuation paradigm has changed. 2) Kinder Morgan's dividend growth endeavors will disappoint. 3) The company's net debt load is $40+ billion. 4) The company is trading at 40+ forward earnings. 5) The natural reaction from shareholders will be skepticism and disbelief. 6) Kinder Morgan's dividend is in part organic, in part financially-engineered. 7) The traditional "blind" use of the dividend discount model does not apply to Kinder Morgan. 8) The company's implied leverage is 19 times after considering all cash, debt-like commitments, at least in the eyes of shareholders. 9) Bondholders will start to care. Equity holders will start to care. They will – and then it all unravels. 10) Highly-publicized insider purchases are not a sign of support, in the case of Kinder Morgan, but an admission of vulnerability.

157   reference to first 5 reasons: Nelson (June 11, 2015).

158   reproduction of second 5 reasons: Nelson (June 18, 2015).

166   was invited to give a speech to my fellow CFA charterholders: Nelson (March 2017).

166   using *Moody's Financial Metrics* as a resource: Moody's (2007).

169   "According to work from Global X Funds": Reddy (2018).

The Plea to Retire Distributable Cash Flow

172   reference to Facebook free cash flow: Facebook (2018).

172   reference to Morningstar free cash flow: Morningstar (2018).

172   footnote, reference to Corporate Finance Institute, website.

172   reference to Exxon Mobil free cash flow: Exxon (2018).

174   reference to SEC guidelines regarding free cash flow: SEC (2018).

Maintenance and Growth Capital Expenditures

174   footnote, reference to *Investment Valuation*: Damodaran (2002), page 256.

175   reference to Xilinx's cash flow measures: Xilinx (2018).

175   reference to Energy Transfer Partners' cash flow measures: Energy Transfer Partners (2017).

Introducing Dividend-Adjusted Leverage

178   according to Moody's, RCF/net debt decomposes: Moody's (2007).

Chapter 8: The Dividend Misunderstanding

183 "Dividend Aristocrats" defined as "companies that have consistently increased their dividend for at least 20 consecutive years": State Street Global Advisors website.

185 reference to how prices are adjusted downward by dividends on the exchange: Zacks (2018).

How Dividends Impact Enterprise Valuation

187 reference to Modigliani's and Miller's dividend irrelevance theorem: Miller (1961).

188 reference to Yogi Berra, etc; "Four. I don't think I can eat eight." Abilene (1971).

188 "subsequent to any given year is the (as yet unknown) true fundamental value of the stock market in that year.": (Shiller 2000).

The Importance of "Why"

189 reference to annualized returns, Ned Davis: Hartford Funds (2018), page 6.

190 "Ask 'why' five times about every matter.": Toyota (2006).

191 implied reference to Porter's 5 Forces: Porter (1979).

191 reference to the S&P High Yield Dividend Aristocrats, "have consistently increased their dividend...": S&P Dow Jones Indices (Oct 2018).

192 From December 1960 through December 2017, the growth of $10,000 in the S&P 500...: Hartford (2018).

Understanding Total Return

193 reference to *Common Sense on Mutual Funds* and block quote: Bogle (1999).

194 In a paper, *The Dividend Disconnect*: Hartzmark (2018).

194 as much as 2%-4% less per year: Maiello (2017).

195 at arguably no time..: Nelson (2016).

196 reference to Kimberly-Clark: Kimberly-Clark (2016).

196 reference to Coca-Cola: Coca-Cola (2016).

196 reference to Colgate-Palmolive: Colgate-Palmolive (2016).

196 footnote, in June 2016, we felt the dividend growth "track record" craze: Nelson (June 2016).

196 footnote, with their average P/E ratio of 37 in 1972: Penman (2007), page 7.

197 During the 1990s...: Hartford Funds (2018), page 2.

Time Often Does Not Determine the Time Horizon

199 reference to Buffett's 2012 Letter to Berkshire Hathaway Shareholders: Buffett (2012).

A Financial Construct for Assessing the Capacity for Dividend Growth

199 it has forewarned of the dividend cuts of approximately 50 companies, we estimate that the ratio's efficacy in predicting dividend cuts is just less than 90%: Nelson (Feb 2018).

200 reference to companies being removed from Dividend Aristocrats list: Wikipedia (S&P 500).

Chapter 9: Economic Moats and Economic Castles

208 the five sources of an economic moat: intangibles, cost advantage, switching costs, network effect, and efficient scale.: Brilliant (2014).

ROIC versus RONIC

210 reference to Berkshire Hathaway letter: Buffett (1992).

Warren Buffett's Economic Moat

213 "In business, I look for economic castles protected by unbreachable moats.": Buffett (2009).

213 "leaving the question of price aside." Buffett (1992).

213 direct quotes: "sustainable value creation is rare;" "more rare;" "investors should expect to earn a risk-adjusted market return.": Maubboussin (2002).

214 footnote, study of ROIC decay analysis completed by McKinsey…: McKinsey (2010).

Cumulative Economic Profit Is What Matters Most

216 "investors should expect to earn a risk-adjusted market return.": Maubboussin (2002).

216 footnote, Alfred Rappaport and Michael Mauboussin wrote a book, *Expectations Investing*: Rappaport (2001).

217 is anticipating revisions in expectations of financial performance: Maubboussin (2002).

217 "the investment shown by the discounted-flows-of-cash calculation to be the cheapest is the one": Buffett (1999).

Competitive-Advantage Analysis: Airlines and Garbage Stocks

220 In 1989, for example Warren Buffett purchased $358 million…related direct quotes: Cunningham (2009), pages 143-146.

221 Since 1990, there have been over 180 bankruptcies in the airline business: Hirby (The Law Dictionary).

221 "if a farsighted capitalist…" Buffett (2007).

221 Island Air, Eastern Airlines, Darwin Airline…: Gibbons (2018).

221 a year in which the industry generated approximately $38 billion in net profits: IATA (2018).

223 one can even tap Boeing's expertise in launching an airline (startup@boeing.com): Boeing (2018).

223 jet fuel represents approximately 25% of industry operating costs: IATA (2018).

223 "the worst sort of business is one that grows rapidly": Buffett (2007).

224 with the industry posting a return on invested capital of 9% in 2017: IATA (2018).

224 The US non-hazardous solid-waste services industry generates annual revenue of approximately $60 billion: Republic (2017).

225 Landfilling still represents the most prominent form of disposal: EPA (2018).

225 According to the Environment Protection Agency, national landfill tipping fees: EPA (2018).

The Stronger the Competitive Advantage the Lower the Stock Return?

227 Morningstar concluded that companies with wide economic moats underperform stocks with narrow economic moats…: Miller (Jan 2013).

Chapter 10: Valuentum Investing

229 reference to Woodstock: Wikipedia (Woodstock).

232 "…managers of growth-oriented funds and small funds": Wermers (2010).

232 footnote, "Manu Daftary, president of DG Capital Management" Southall (2006).

Forward-Looking Expected Data and Walk-Forward Testing

235 footnote, "*Testing an investment strategy on the same data and time period from which it was extracted…*": Damodaran (2002), page 122.

235 reference to and block quote selection of Baum and Smith's paper: Baum (2015). Used with authors' permission.

235 and Wells Fargo, which is struggling: McLean (2018).

236 reference to Collins' quote: Collins (2001).

236 reference to the Feynman Trap: Baum (2015).

237 footnote, decades now, researchers have… Credit Suisse (2018), page 18.

237 footnote, references to AQR and direct quote from Alpha Architect, Recent quantitative research has hypothesized…; "Lynch wasn't value, he wasn't growth…": AQR (2016) and Grioli (2017).

238 In August 2017, we released a more comprehensive study: Nelson (Aug 2017). Excerpt of the conclusion of the paper "Value and Momentum Within Stocks, Too:"

> The case for the…Valuentum Buying Index, or the Valuentum Style of Investing remains an excellent one, in our view. The Valuentum Buying Index effectively sorted "winners" and "losers" in both the case-study and time-series studies, where average returns from the highest Valuentum Buying Index ratings (10) (9-10) significantly outperformed average returns from the lowest Valuentum Buying Index ratings (1) (1-2) over immediate multiple time intervals (periods, updates). Negative slope coefficients across Valuentum Buying Index rating cohorts speak to a generalized tendency of higher Valuentum Buying Index ratings outperforming lower Valuentum Buying Index ratings, though varying r-squared values suggest the signal is less-strong in the "big middle" (3-8), as expected and as designed (given the potential for contradicting expected near-term return profiles for certain ratings).

> In the time series study, the Valuentum Buying Index revealed the ability to sort undervalued stocks on the basis of their respective timeliness (9-10 less 8), showcasing the system's potential usefulness as a value-timing indicator in avoiding "value traps…" The outperformance of VBI-rated 10 issues relative to the rest of the universe of stocks (including VBI-rated 9 equities) supports the view that an increasing overlap of relevant, unique styles within individual stocks, even beyond those of enterprise valuation and technical/momentum--namely quality and perhaps value-creating growth and manageable leverage as in 10-rated VBI issues--may be one of the most important drivers behind individual stock outperformance.

Practical VBI Application in the Best Ideas Newsletter Portfolio

245 Simulated performance of Best Ideas Newsletter:

> We believe it is informative to compare the simulated Best Ideas Newsletter portfolio to that of the S&P 500 with the dividends collected and reinvested in the S&P 500, or on a total return basis for the benchmark. Though a true apples-to-apples comparison would also assume to reinvest collected dividends in the Best Ideas Newsletter portfolio, too, we have nonetheless excluded this in the Best Ideas Newsletter portfolio as we might stipulate that such an adjustment may have impacted portfolio management decisions during the study. The imbalanced comparison gives the S&P 500 an inherent dividend-reinvestment advantage over the newsletter portfolio, but it also helps to illustrate just how well the Best Ideas Newsletter portfolio has performed regardless.

> Since inception May 17, 2011, the hypothetical value of the Best Ideas Newsletter portfolio with dividends collected but not reinvested advanced 149.1%, while the S&P 500 with dividends collected and reinvested (its total return) advanced 131.7% over the same time period, revealing 17.4 percentage points of outperformance. On an apples-to-apples basis versus the Best Ideas Newsletter portfolio's declared benchmark, if we assume that dividends are collected but not reinvested for the S&P 500 benchmark, the

hypothetical value of the Best Ideas Newsletter portfolio outperformed the S&P 500 value of $219,322 by 29.7 percentage points since inception.

Since the inaugural edition of the Best Ideas Newsletter, July 13, 2011, the hypothetical value of the Best Ideas Newsletter with dividends collected but not reinvested advanced 134%, while the S&P 500 with dividends collected and reinvested advanced 133% over the same time period, revealing 1 percentage point of outperformance. On an apples-to-apples basis versus the Best Ideas Newsletter portfolio's declared benchmark, if we assume that dividends are collected but not reinvested for the S&P 500 benchmark, the hypothetical value of the Best Ideas Newsletter portfolio outperformed the S&P 500 value of $219,690 by 14.3 percentage points since the inaugural edition of the Best Ideas Newsletter.

Though we feel the latter measures, which illustrate calculations on a dividends-collected but not-reinvested-basis are a more appropriate apples-to-apples comparisons given the capital-appreciation focus of the Best Ideas Newsletter portfolio (and not dividend growth focus), the former comparison is quite insightful as to the potential magnitude of outperformance of the Best Ideas Newsletter, even with dividends reinvested in the benchmark. Had we assumed a full allocation to ideas in the newsletter portfolio (the portfolio held a ~25% cash position, on average) or assumed that dividends had been reinvested for the newsletter portfolio, too, the outperformance gap of the Best Ideas Newsletter portfolio may have been much larger.

The Best Ideas Newsletter portfolio performance was generated in a market where 84%-92% of large-cap managers, mid-cap managers, and small-cap managers lagged their respective benchmarks over a 5-year period ending 2017 and 92%+ of managers lagged their respective benchmarks over a 15-year period ending 2017. The Best Ideas Newsletter portfolio is not a real-money portfolio, but on this comparative basis, the performance puts Valuentum near the very top of the measurement spectrum, in our view. Exceeding the market return with an active process has been a tremendous feat during the past several years.

Though outperformance in the Best Ideas Newsletter portfolio relative to its declared benchmark since inception and since the inaugural edition of the newsletter was evident over the time period measured--on both a dividends-collected-but-not-reinvested basis and on a total-return basis, including reinvested dividends--we think risk-adjusted analysis is key to gaining a better understanding of the proficiency of the Valuentum stock-selection process. Members, in building their own portfolios, for example, could theoretically increase equity exposure of ideas to meet their respective risk profiles, and this decision is beyond the scope of a newsletter publisher.

The average monthly price returns of the Best Ideas Newsletter portfolio and the average monthly price returns for the benchmark, both with dividends collected but not reinvested, were 1.2% and 1.05% respectively, while the monthly standard deviation of the Best Ideas Newsletter portfolio and the monthly standard deviation of the benchmark, both with dividends collected but not reinvested, were 2.68% and 3.3%, respectively, since inception, May 17, 2011.

On a risk-adjusted basis, the Best Ideas Newsletter portfolio did considerably better than that of the benchmark during one of the most difficult periods to do so, where returns for the S&P 500 were high while volatility was low. During 2017, for example, "investors' risk-adjusted returns from the S&P 500 were among the highest in half a century." We believe it may be more important for members to be aware of the return-per-unit-of-risk superiority of the Best Ideas Newsletter portfolio than even its relative outperformance, which is remarkable in and of itself.

Diversification

248 reference to Surz and Price: Surz (2000).

Conclusion – A Call to Action: The Threat of Price-Agnostic Trading

252 "evidence-based economics": Thaler (2015), page 348.

253 footnote, In *Fooled By Randomness*, Nassim Taleb said that…: Taleb (2005).

253 "aims to exploit market inefficiencies and beat the passive approach.": Stewart (2017).

254 We love hearing about how over the past 200 years, stocks have compounded at an annual return of nearly 7% in the US: Siegel (1998).

255 reference to number of stock indexes: Beer (2018)

255 according to research company ETFGI…: Vlastelica (2017)

255 reference to 10% of trading being firm-specific: Cheng (2017).

255 footnote: November 1997, there were more than 7,300 U.S. stocks: Zweig (2017)

255 footnote, not only is the number of stocks shrinking, but according to Bespoke Investment Group…: Racanelli (2018).

256 In the 1920s, stocks and bonds were mass marketed to the general public: (PBS, Crash of 1929).

256 the most sustainably volatile period in stock market history, as measured by daily percentage changes in the S&P 500: Schwert (2018).

256 "if everybody indexed, the only word you could use is chaos, catastrophe.": Udland (2017).

257 block quote from *Misbehaving*. "When prices start to move against a money manager and investors start…": Thaler (2015).

257 "25-standard deviation moves, several days in a row.": Larsen (2007).

258 Warren Buffett had also made a bid to save the firm: Nofsinger (2002), page 209.

BIBLIOGRAPHY

Abilene Reporter, Oak's Pokes by Steve Oakey, Quote Page 9A, Column 2, Abilene, Texas. 5 October 1971.

Allmendinger, Diana, "Fitch Solutions: Kinder Morgan CDS at Widest Level Since 2008." 3 December 2015. https://www.fitchratings.com/site/pr/995907

American Investment Council, "2018 AIC Public Pension Study: Private Equity Delivers Highest Returns for Public Pension Funds." 23 May 2018. https://www.investmentcouncil.org/2018-aic-public-pension-study-private-equity-delivers-highest-returns-for-public-pension-funds/

AQR Alternative Thinking, Fourth-Quarter 2016, "Superstar Investors." https://www.aqr.com/~/media/files/papers/alternative-thinking-superstar-investors.pdf

Asness, Cliff, Tobias J. Moskowitz and Lasse Heje Pedersen, "Value and Momentum Everywhere." The Journal of Finance. http://pages.stern.nyu.edu/~lpederse/papers/ValMomEverywhere.pdf

Asness, Cliff. "It Ain't What You Don't Know That Gets You Into Trouble." 20 June 2018. https://www.aqr.com/Insights/Perspectives/It-Aint-What-You-Dont-Know-That-Gets-You-Into-Trouble

Bary, Andrew, "Kinder Morgan: Trouble in the Pipelines." 22 February 2014. https://www.barrons.com/articles/kinder-morgan-trouble-in-the-pipelines-1393055061

Baseball Reference.com, retrieved October 6, 2015. http://www.baseballreference.com/leagues/MLB/2003-standings.shtml

Baum, Gabrielle and Gary Smith, "Great Companies: *Looking for Success Secrets in All the Wrong Places.*" The Journal of Investing. Fall 2015. http://economics-files.pomona.edu/GarySmith/SuccessSecrets.pdf

Beattie, Andrew. Forbes. "Riding The Momentum Wave." 25 July 2007. https://www.forbes.com/2007/07/25/momentum-volatility-timing-pf-education-in_ab_0725investopedia_inl.html#3f40e020ae69

Becker, Ying L. and Marc R. Reinganum. CFA Institute. "The Current State of Quantitative Investing." https://www.cfainstitute.org/en/research/foundation/2018/current-state-of-quantitative-equity-investing

Beer, Andrew, WealthManagement. "Index Proliferation: Time for SEC Regulation?" 25 June 2018. https://www.wealthmanagement.com/etfs/index-proliferation-time-sec-regulation

Bibliography

Blais, Daniel, CFA Institute, "Skill Ratio: A New Measure for the (Lack of) Persistence in Active Management." https://blogs.cfainstitute.org/investor/2018/03/26/skill-ratio-a-new-metric-for-active-management/

Boeing Company, 2009 Annual Report, page 51. Retrieved November 2, 2018. https://s2.q4cdn.com/661678649/files/doc_financials/annual/2009/2009-annual_report.pdf

Boeing, "StartupBoeing," Retrieved 2018. http://www.boeing.com/company/about-bca/startupboeing.page

Bogle, John C, "The First Index Mutual Fund: A History of Vanguard Index Trust and the Vanguard Index Strategy." 1 April 1997. https://www.vanguard.com/bogle_site/lib/sp19970401.html

Bogle, John C (1999), Common Sense on Mutual Funds: New Imperatives for the Intelligent Investor (John Wiley & Sons).

Brilliant, Heather and Elizabeth Collins (2014). Morningstar, "Why Moats Matter." Wiley.

Brown, Josh, Fortune, "Can your portfolio survive rising interest rates? 26 May 2015. http://fortune.com/2015/05/26/investing-rising-interest-rates/

Brown, Stephen, Paul Lajbcygier, and Bob Li, (2007), "Going Negative: What to Do with Negative Book Equity Stocks. https://core.ac.uk/download/pdf/19481923.pdf

Browne, Christopher H (2007), "The Little Book of Value Investing," John Wiley and Sons.

Buffett, Warren (1984), "The Superinvestors of Graham-and-Doddsville." https://www8.gsb.columbia.edu/articles/columbia-business/superinvestors

Buffett, Warren (1992), Chairman's Letter, Berkshire Hathaway. http://www.berkshirehathaway.com/letters/1992.html

Buffett, Warren (2007), Chairman's Letter, Berkshire Hathaway http://www.berkshirehathaway.com/letters/2007ltr.pdf

Buffett, Warren (2009). "Warren Buffett on Business: Principles from the Sage of Omaha," John Wiley & Sons, p.63.

Buffett, Warren (2011), Chairman's Letter, Berkshire Hathaway, pp. 18-19. http://www.berkshirehathaway.com/letters/2011ltr.pdf

Buffett, Warren (2012), Chairman's Letter, Berkshire Hathaway, pp. 20-21. http://www.berkshirehathaway.com/letters/2012ltr.pdf

Buffett, Warren (2014), Chairman's Letter, Berkshire Hathaway. http://www.berkshirehathaway.com/letters/2014ltr.pdf

Bibliography

Butters, John, FactSet, Earnings Insight. 2 November 2018.
https://www.factset.com/hubfs/Resources%20Section/Research%20Desk/Earnings%20Insight/EarningsInsight_110218.pdf

CBRE Clarion, "MLP Reality Check." October 2017. Retrieved November 6, 2018.
https://www.cbreclarion.com/insights/mlp-reality-check/

CFA Curriculum (2019), "Residual Income Valuation."
https://www.cfainstitute.org/en/membership/professional-development/refresher-readings/2019/residual-income-valuation

Chambers, Donald R and Mark J. P. Anson, Keith H. Black, Hossein Kazemi (2015), CAIA Association. Alternative Investments. John Wiley & Sons.

Cheng, Evelyn (2017), "Just 10% of trading is regular stock picking, JPMorgan estimates."
https://www.cnbc.com/2017/06/13/death-of-the-human-investor-just-10-percent-of-trading-is-regular-stockpicking-jpmorgan-estimates.html

Chicago Booth Review (2016), YouTube. "Are Markets Efficient?,"
https://www.youtube.com/watch?v=bM9bYOBuKF4

Clement, Douglas (2007). "Interview with Eugene Fama. Federal Reserve Bank of Minneapolis.
https://www.minneapolisfed.org/publications/the-region/interview-with-eugene-fama

Coca-Cola (2016), "The Coca-Cola Company Reports Second Quarter 2016 Results" http://coca-cola-ir.prod-use1.investis.com/~/media/Files/C/Coca-Cola-IR/documents/2016-Q2-Earnings-Release.pdf

Colgate-Palmolive (2016), Form 10-Q, Three Months Ended June 30, 2016.
http://investor.colgatepalmolive.com/static-files/7579e24b-982e-4161-bb1b-64b4e4b825b0

Collins, Jim. Good to Great: Why Some Companies Make the Leap…And Others Don't. New York, NY: HarperCollins, 2001.

Corporate Finance Institute, "The Ultimate Cash Flow Guide (EBITDA, CF, FCF, FCFE, FCFF)." https://corporatefinanceinstitute.com/resources/knowledge/valuation/cash-flow-guide-ebitda-cf-fcf-fcff/

Crain's Chicago Business (2005). "Morningstar to move to Block 37." 1 September 2005.
https://www.chicagobusiness.com/article/20050901/NEWS12/200017650/morningstar-to-move-to-block-37

Credit Suisse. Securities Research and Analysis. Kinder Morgan. "Reiterate Outperform, $52 Target Price, 15 June 2015.

Credit Suisse, Research Institute, Global Investment Returns Yearbook 2018. Summary Edition.
https://www.credit-suisse.com/media/assets/corporate/docs/about-us/media/media-release/2018/02/giry-summary-2018.pdf

Bibliography

Cunningham, Lawrence A (2009), "The Essays of Warren Buffett: Lessons for Investors and Managers." John Wiley & Sons. Third Edition.

Damodaran, Aswath, Damodaran Online. http://pages.stern.nyu.edu/~adamodar/. Retrieved November 7, 2018.

Damodaran, Aswath, "User/Subscriber Economics: An Alternative View of Uber's Value." 28 June 2017. http://aswathdamodaran.blogspot.com/2017/06/usersubscriber-economics-alternative.html

Damodaran, Aswath, "Share Count Confusion: Dilution, Employee Options and Multiple Share Classes!" 25 July 2018. https://aswathdamodaran.blogspot.com/2018/07/share-count-confusion-dilution-employee.html

Damodaran, Aswath (2002), "Investment Valuation." John Wiley & Sons.

Driehaus Museum. "[You Asked] What is That Other Mansion?" 20 April 2013. http://driehausmuseum.org/blog/view/you-asked-what-is-that-other-mansion

Driehaus Small Cap Growth Strategy. Retrieved November 2, 2018. https://www.driehaus.com/Strategy-SmallCap.php

Economist. "The growth of index investing has not made markets less efficient." 5 July 2018. https://www.economist.com/finance-and-economics/2018/07/05/the-growth-of-index-investing-has-not-made-markets-less-efficient

Elkind, Peter Report Associates, et al. Fortune, "Where Mary Meeker Went Wrong." 14 May 2001. http://archive.fortune.com/magazines/fortune/fortune_archive/2001/05/14/302981/index.ht

Energy Transfer Partners, "Form 10-K, 2017." Retrieved November 3, 2018.

English James (2001), Applied Equity Analysis: Stock Valuation Techniques for Wall Street Professionals. McGraw-Hill Companies.

EPA, "Advancing Sustainable Materials Management: 2015 Fact Sheet." July 2018. https://www.epa.gov/sites/production/files/2018-07/documents/2015_smm_msw_factsheet_07242018_fnl_508_002.pdf

Epstein, Ira and David Garfield, M.D. (1999), "The Psychology of Smart Investing, Meeting the 6 Mental Challenges."

Exxon Mobil, Slide Deck Presentation, "2018 Investor Information." 2 February 2018. https://cdn.exxonmobil.com/~/media/global/files/investor-reports/2018/2018-investor-information.pdf, Supplemental Information.

Fabozzi, Frank J, Sergio M. Focardi, and Caroline Jonas (2017). CFA Institute. "Equity Valuation: Science, Art, or Craft." https://www.cfainstitute.org/en/research/foundation/2017/equity-valuation-science-art-or-craft

Bibliography

Facebook, Earnings Slide Deck, "Q3 2018 Results." 30 October 2018, page 17. https://s21.q4cdn.com/399680738/files/doc_financials/2018/Q3/Q3-2018-Earnings-Presentation.pdf

Fairchild, Travis. O'Shaughnessy Asset Management, "Negative Equity, Veiled Value, and the Erosion of Price-to-Book." April 2018. https://www.osam.com/Commentary/negative-equity-veiled-value-and-the-erosion-of-price-to-book

Fama, Eugene F., The Journal of Finance, Vol. 25, No. 2, Papers and Proceedings of the Twenty-Eighth Annual Meeting of the American Finance Association New York, N.Y. December, 28-30, 1969 (May, 1970), pp. 383-417.

Fama, Eugene F. and Kenneth R. French (2014), "A Five-Factor Asset Pricing Model." https://www8.gsb.columbia.edu/programs/sites/programs/files/finance/Finance%20Seminar/spring%202014/ken%20french.pdf

Fernandez, Pablo (2017), "Is It Ethical to Teach That Beta and CAPM Explain Something?" https://ssrn.com/abstract=2980847

Ferri, Rick (2012), "Any Monkey Can Beat the Market." December 20, 2012. https://www.forbes.com/sites/rickferri/2012/12/20/any-monkey-can-beat-themarket/#70ba5b92630a

Fidelity website. https://www.fidelity.com/mutual-funds/investing-ideas/index-funds. Retrieved November 3, 2018.

First Trust, "History of U.S. Bear & Bull Markets Since 1926." Retrieved November 23, 2018. https://www.ftportfolios.com/Common/ContentFileLoader.aspx?ContentGUID=4ecfa978-d0bb-4924-92c8-628ff9bfe12d

Fisher, Kenneth L and Meir Statman. "Bubble Expectations." The Journal of Wealth Management. Fall 2002. http://www.simonemariotti.com/downloads/Papers%20finanziari/Fisher-Statman.pdf

Foerster, Jan-Henrik and Rachel Evans, Bloomberg, "Credit Suisse Fund Liquidated, ETFs Halted as Short-Vol Bets Die." 6 February 2018. https://www.bloomberg.com/news/articles/2018-02-06/credit-suisse-is-said-to-consider-redemption-of-volatility-note

Freakonomics Asks: Does your real estate agent have your best interest in mind? YouTube. Retrieved November 11, 2018. https://www.youtube.com/watch?v=n0rV3ydBhUw

General Electric, Form 10-K, page 105. Retrieved November 3, 2018. https://www.ge.com/investor-relations/sites/default/files/GE_AR17.pdf

Gibbons, Ryan, Airways, "In Memoriam: The Airlines We Lost in 2017." 1 January 2018. https://airwaysmag.com/airlines/memoriam-airlines-lost-2017/

Goetzmann, William N. Yale International Center for Finance. "Bubble Investors: What Were They Thinking? 17 August 2006.
http://depot.som.yale.edu/icf/papers/fileuploads/2494/original/06-22.pdf

Goldman, David, CNN Money, "10 big dot.com flops." 10 March 2010.
https://money.cnn.com/galleries/2010/technology/1003/gallery.dot_com_busts/index.html

Graham, Benjamin and David Dodd (1934), "Security Analysis," New York, McGraw-Hill.

Graham, Benjamin (2003), "The Intelligent Investor," revised edition, updated with new commentary by Jason Zweig. HarperCollins.

Gravyty, webpage retrieved November 2, 2018. http://info.gravyty.com/blog/the-harmonious-origin. (The Investing and Trading Experiences of Roger Babson).

Gray, Wesley R, and Jack R. Vogel (2016), "Quantitative Momentum: A Practitioner's Guide to Building a Momentum-Based Stock Selection System." John Wiley & Sons.

Grioli, Dan, Alpha Architect, "Greatest Stock Picker of All Time: Buffett or Lynch? 8 February 2017. https://alphaarchitect.com/2017/02/08/greatest-stock-picker-of-all-time-buffett-or-lynch/

Hartford Funds, "The Power of Dividends, Past, Present, and Future."
https://www.hartfordfunds.com/dam/en/docs/pub/whitepapers/WP106.pdf.

Hartzmark, Samuel M. and Solomon, David H., The Dividend Disconnect (March 22, 2018). 7th Miami Behavioral Finance Conference 2016. https://ssrn.com/abstract=2876373 or http://dx.doi.org/10.2139/ssrn.2876373

Heath, David and Sharon Pian Chan (2005), The Seattle Times, "Dot-con job: How InfoSpace took its investors for a ride."
http://old.seattletimes.com/html/businesstechnology/2002198103_dotcon1main06.html

Hirby, James, The Law Dictionary, "List of airlines that are currently bankrupt?"
https://thelawdictionary.org/article/list-of-airlines-that-are-currently-bankrupt/

Hopkins, Johnny. The Acquirer's Multiple. "Schroders: Why Value Investing May Be Primed To Bounce Back." 27 June 2018. https://acquirersmultiple.com/2018/06/schroders-why-value-investing-may-be-primed-to-bounce-back/

Howard, Hinds. Barron's. "MLPs for the Long Run." 1 October 2015.
https://www.barrons.com/articles/mlps-for-the-long-run-1443716955

IATA, "Solid Profits Despite Rising Costs." 4 June 2018.
https://www.iata.org/pressroom/pr/Pages/2018-06-04-01.aspx

Ibbotson (2009), Morningstar. Ibbotson 2009 Valuation Handbook.

IBM, "IBM Reports 2014 First-Quarter Results." 12 April 2014. https://www-03.ibm.com/press/us/en/pressrelease/43696.wss

Bibliography

Interbrand, "Interbrand Releases 2018 Best Global Brands Report." 4 October 2018.
https://www.businesswire.com/news/home/20181003005944/en/Interbrand-Releases-2018-Global-Brands-Report

Investment Company Institute, "2018 Investment Company Fact Book."
https://www.ici.org/pdf/2018_factbook.pdf

Isidore, Chris, CNN Money. Paulson in hot seat over Fannie, Freddie. 15 July 2008.
https://money.cnn.com/2008/07/15/news/economy/Freddie_Fannie_Senate/

Jackson, Paul, Housingwire. "The Death of Wall Street." 22 September 2008.
https://www.housingwire.com/articles/death-wall-street

Jan, Ching-Lih and Jane A. Ou (2012) Negative-Book-Value Firms and Their Valuation.
Accounting Horizons: March 2012, Vol. 26, No. 1, pp. 91-110.
http://aaapubs.org/doi/abs/10.2308/acch-50094?journalCode=acch

Jensen, Michael C (1978) "Some Anomalous Evidence Regarding Market Efficiency." Journal of
Financial Economics, page 95.

Jiang, Bin and Timothy Koller, McKinsey on Finance, "The truth about growth and value
stocks." Perspectives on Corporate Finance and Strategy. Number 22, Winter 2007.

Jorion, Philippe, "Risk Management Lessons from Long-Term Capital Management." European
Financial Management. September 2000. https://merage.uci.edu/~jorion/papers/ltcm.pdf

Junior, Leonidas Sandoval and Italo De Paula Franca. Insper, Instituto de Ensino e Pesquisa,
Correlation of Financial Markets in Times of Crisis. 31 August 2010.
http://www.phys.sinica.edu.tw/~socioecono/econophysics2010/pdfs/SandovalPaper.pdf

Kalesnik, Vitali and Juhani Linnainmaa (Research Affiliates), Advisor Perspectives, "Ignored
Risks of Factor Investing." 11 October 2018.
https://www.advisorperspectives.com/commentaries/2018/10/11/ignored-risks-of-factor-investing

Kaplan, Paul, Morningstar. "5 Myths of the Post-Financial Crisis World. 19 March 2012.
http://www.morningstar.co.uk/uk/news/69450/5-myths-of-the-post-financial-crisis-world.aspx

Kean, Steve, Slide Deck Presentation. "Kinder Morgan, Run By Shareholders, For Shareholders."
4 February 2015.
https://ir.kindermorgan.com/sites/kindermorgan.investorhq.businesswire.com/files/event/additional/0204_investor_pres_vF.pdf

Kennedy, John. F. Address in the Assembly Hall at the Paulskirche, Frankfurt, 25 June 1963.
https://www.jfklibrary.org/asset-viewer/archives/JFKPOF/045/JFKPOF-045-023

Keynes, John Maynard (1936). "The General Theory of Employment, Interest and Money.
London: Macmillan.

Bibliography

Kimberly Clark (2016). "Kimberly-Clark Announces Second Quarter 2016 Results" https://investor.kimberly-clark.com/news-releases/news-release-details/kimberly-clark-announces-second-quarter-2016-results

Kimelman, John. Barron's, "Is Kinder Morgan on Road to Recovery?" 21 January 2016. https://www.barrons.com/articles/is-kinder-morgan-on-road-to-recovery-1453421112?mod=BOLFeed&tesla=y

Kimelman, John. Barron's, "The Bear Case Against Kinder Morgan, 11 June 2015. https://www.barrons.com/articles/the-bear-case-against-mlp-kinder-morgan-1434062853

Kimelman, John. Barron's, "Why the MLP Business Model May Be a Goner." 28 September 2015. https://www.barrons.com/articles/why-the-mlp-business-model-may-be-a-goner-1443476002

Kinder Morgan Announces 2016 Financial Expectations, 4 December 2015. https://ir.kindermorgan.com/press-release/kindermorgan/kinder-morgan-announces-2016-financial-expectations

Kinder Morgan Announces 2016 Outlook, 8 December 2015. https://ir.kindermorgan.com/press-release/kinder-morgan-announces-2016-outlook

Kinder Morgan Increases Quarterly Dividend to $0.51 Per Share, up 16%. 21 October 2015. https://ir.kindermorgan.com/press-release/kinder-morgan-increases-quarterly-dividend-051-share-16

Kinder Morgan, Form 10-K, page 45. Retrieved November 2, 2018. https://ir.kindermorgan.com/sites/kindermorgan.investorhq.businesswire.com/files/report/additional/KMI-2016-10K_Final_with_Exhibits.pdf

Kinnel, Russel, Morningstar, "Fund Fees Predict Future Success or Failure." 5 May 2016. When it comes to long-term returns, fees matter.

Klement, Joachim, "Dumb Alpha: Trailing or Forward Earnings?" 12 July 2016. https://blogs.cfainstitute.org/investor/2016/07/12/dumb-alpha-trailing-or-forward-earnings/

Kohler, Time and Rishi Raj and Abhishek Saxena, McKinsey, "Avoiding the Consensus Earnings Trap." January 2013. https://www.mckinsey.com/business-functions/strategy-and-corporate-finance/our-insights/avoiding-the-consensus-earnings-trap

La Monica, Paul R, CNN Money, "Bill Miller's streak nears an end," 11 December 2016. http://money.cnn.com/2006/12/11/pf/funds/miller/index.htm

Langlois, Shawn, Marketwatch, "XIV trader: 'I've lost $4 million, 3 years of work and other people's money," 7 February 2018. https://www.marketwatch.com/story/xiv-trader-ive-lost-4-million-3-years-of-work-and-other-peoples-money-2018-02-06

Larsen, Peter Thal, Financial Times, "Goldman pays the price of being big," 13 August 2007. https://www.ft.com/content/d2121cb6-49cb-11dc-9ffe-0000779fd2ac

Laughlin, Lauren Silva (2014), "Luck vs. skill: What Bill Gross and Bill Miller have in common. Fortune. http://fortune.com/2014/03/18/luck-vs-skill-what-bill-gross-and-bill-miller-have-in-common/

Loomis, Carol. Fortune. "Mr. Buffett on the Stock Market." 22 November 1999. https://archive.fortune.com/magazines/fortune/fortune_archive/1999/11/22/269071/index.htm

Lundeen, Mark J. "Dow Jones Industrials And Its Earnings: 1929-2011." 30 April 2011. http://www.gold-eagle.com/article/dow-jones-industrials-and-its-earnings-1929-2011-nyse-composite-financial-indexes

Lynch, Peter (1989). "One Up on Wall Street: How To Use What You Already Know To Make Money In The Market," Simon & Schuster.

Maiello, Michael, Chicago Booth Review. "Dividends are not free money (though lots of investors seem to think they are)." 6 March 2017. http://review.chicagobooth.edu/finance/2017/article/dividends-are-not-free-money-though-lots-investors-seem-think-they-are

Malkiel, Burton G (2003), "A Random Walk Down Wall Street," (eighth edition).

Malkiel, Burton G. "Reflections on the Efficient Market Hypothesis: 30 Years Later. The Financial Review 40 (2005) 1-9.

Marshall, Terry, et al (a). Moody's. "Moody's changes Kinder Morgan's outlook to negative." 1 December 2015. https://www.moodys.com/research/Moodys-changes-Kinder-Morgans-outlook-to-negative--PR_339913

Marshall, Terry, et al (b). Moody's. "Moody's changes Kinder Morgan's outlook to stable." 8 December 2015. https://www.moodys.com/research/Moodys-changes-Kinder-Morgans-outlook-to-stable--PR_340835

Mauboussin, Michael J. and Kristen Bartholdson. Credit Suisse. "Measuring the Moat: Assessing the Magnitude and Sustainability of Value Creation." http://www.valuewalk.com/wp-content/uploads/2014/07/measuringthemoat.pdf

McCool, Grant and Martha Graybow. Reuters. "Madoff pleads guilty, is jailed for $65 billion fraud." 12 March 2009. https://www.reuters.com/article/us-madoff/madoff-pleads-guilty-is-jailed-for-65-billion-fraud-idUSTRE52A5JK20090313

McDonald's Corporation, 3Q 2018 Form 10-Q. Retrieved November 2, 2018. http://d18rn0p25nwr6d.cloudfront.net/CIK-0000063908/ff117d66-8327-42a6-8063-dda6552d9c36.pdf

McKinsey Global Private Markets Review, "A routinely exceptional year." February 2017. https://www.mckinsey.com/industries/private-equity-and-principal-investors/our-insights/a-routinely-exceptional-year-for-private-equity

Bibliography

McKinsey & Company (2010), "Valuation: Measuring and Managing the Value of Companies." Fifth Edition. John Wiley & Sons.

McLean, Bethany and Ethan Wolff-Mann. Yahoo Finance. "Exclusive: Wells Fargo automated high-net-worth wealth management as advisors faced sales pressure." 18 July 2018. https://finance.yahoo.com/news/wells-fargo-automated-high-net-worth-wealth-management-advisors-faced-sales-pressure-151535558.html

Miller, Merton H (1999), "The History of Finance," The Journal of Portfolio Management.

Miller, Merton H and Franco Modigliani, "Dividend Policy, Growth, and the Valuation of Shares." The Journal of Business, Vol 34, No. 4 (Oct., 1961). https://www2.bc.edu/thomas-chemmanur/phdfincorp/MF891%20papers/MM%20dividend.pdf

Miller, Warren. Morningstar. "How our stock star ratings have performed." 14 January 2013. http://cawidgets.morningstar.ca/ArticleTemplate/ArticleGL.aspx?id=580860. Retrieved November 4, 2018.

Miller, Warren, James X. Xiong, and Thomas Idzorek (2013), "The Predictive Power of Fair Value Estimates." http://www.nxtbook.com/nxtbooks/morningstar/advisor_20131011/index.php?startid=58#/64

Moody's Financial Metrics™ Key Ratios by Rating and Industry for Global Non-Financial Corporations, December 2007.

Moody's, Guideline Rent Expense Multiples for Use with Moody's Global Standard Adjustment to Capitalize Operating Leases. Revised March 2006. https://www.elfaonline.org/cvweb_elfa/product_downloads/mlac06rtngagen.pdf

Moore, Christina. The Sport. "Twelve Things You Should Know About the 2018 Kentucky Derby." 24 April 2018. https://www.americasbestracing.net/the-sport/2018-twelve-things-you-should-know-about-the-2018-kentucky-derby

Morningstar, "Morningstar, Inc. Reports Third-Quarter 2018 Financial Results." 24 October 2018. https://newsroom.morningstar.com/newsroom/news-archive/press-release-details/2018/Morningstar-Inc-Reports-Third-Quarter-2018-Financial-Results/default.aspx

Mosqueda-Fernandez, Ximena, "Analysts rebuke article predicting the demise of MLPs, argue some may be oversold." 5 October 2015. https://www.americasbestracing.net/the-sport/2018-twelve-things-you-should-know-about-the-2018-kentucky-derby

Nash, John Forbes (1950). "Equilibrium Points in N-person Games". Proceedings of the National Academy of Sciences of the United States of America.

Nelson, Brian. Morningstar. "Morningstar's Cash Flow Cushion." Introducing Morningstar's Forward-looking Measure of Financial Health. 1 December 2009. https://select.morningstar.com/welcome/credit/pdfs/Morningstar_CashFlowCushion.pdf

Bibliography

Nelson, Brian (2015). Valuentum. "5 Reasons Why We Think Kinder Morgan's Shares Will Collapse." 11 June 2015. https://www.valuentum.com/articles/20150611

Nelson, Brian (2015). Valuentum. "5 More Reasons Why We Think Kinder Morgan's Shares Will Collapse." 18 June 2015. https://www.valuentum.com/articles/20150618

Nelson, Brian (2015), Valuentum, "5 Years Strong!" 15 June 2016. https://www.valuentum.com/articles/20160615

Nelson, Brian (2016), Valuentum, "A Kleenex? Consumer Staples Trading At Nosebleed Levels," 3 August 2016. https://www.valuentum.com/articles/20160804

Nelson, Brian (March 2017), CFA Society of Houston, "Trust the Numbers, Not Just Management. "How Simple Financial Statement Analysis Can Save You Big." https://www.valuentum.com/downloads/20170312_2/download

Nelson, Brian, Tatiana Dmitrieva, and Kris Rosemann (2017), "Value and Momentum Within Stocks, Too." Study of Individual Time Series of 20,000+ Valuentum Buying Ratings. https://www.valuentum.com/articles/Value_and_Momentum_Within_Stocks_Too

Nelson, Brian and Kris Rosemann. Valuentum. "Newsletter Alert: Title Withheld – Members Only". 15 May 2017. https://www.valuentum.com/articles/20170515

Nelson, Brian, Tatiana Dmitrieva, and Kris Rosemann (Oct 2017), "How Well Do Enterprise-Cash-Flow-Derived Fair Value Estimates Predict Future Stock Prices? https://www.valuentum.com/articles/How_Well_Do_Enterprise_Cash_Flow_Derived_Fair_Value_Estimates_Predict_Future_Stock_Prices_And_Thoughts_on_Behavioral_Valuation

Nelson, Brian. Valuentum, "Efficacy of the Dividend Cushion Ratio." 9 February 2018. https://www.valuentum.com/articles/20130528

Netflix, Shareholder Letter. 21 October 2013. https://s22.q4cdn.com/959853165/files/doc_financials/quarterly_reports/2013/q3/Q313-Earnings-Letter-10.21.13-10.30am.pdf

Netflix, Shareholder Letter. 16 October 2018. https://s22.q4cdn.com/959853165/files/doc_financials/quarterly_reports/2018/q3/FINAL-Q3-18-Shareholder-Letter.pdf

Nielsen, Frank and Darby Nielson, Michael Boucher, Andrew Wilson, Fidelity. "How to Evaluate Factor-Based Investment Strategies." September 2016. https://institutional.fidelity.com/app/proxy/content?literatureURL=/9878907.PDF

Nissim, Doron and Stephen H. Penman (2001), "An Empirical Analysis of the Effect of Changes in Interest Rates on Accounting Rates of Return, Growth, and Equity Values." http://citeseerx.ist.psu.edu/viewdoc/download?doi=10.1.1.199.2214&rep=rep1&type=pdf

Nofsinger, John R (2002), "Investment Blunders of the Rich and Famous and What You Can Learn from Them," Financial Times Prentice Hall.

Bibliography

Pappas, Scott N, and Joel M. Dickson (2015), "Factor-based investing," Vanguard Research.

PBS, "American Experience: The Crash of 1929." Video documentary. Transcript: http://fliphtml5.com/kyye/lwxt/basic

Penman, Stephen H (2007), "Financial Statement Analysis and Security Valuation. McGraw-Hill.

Pisani, Bob, CNBC, "Stock buybacks hit a record $1.1 trillion, and the year's not over," 18 December 2018. https://www.cnbc.com/2018/12/18/stock-buybacks-hit-a-record-1point1-trillion-and-the-years-not-over.html

Popper, Karl (1989). "Zwei Bedeutungen von Falsifizierbarkeit [Two meanings of falsifiability]". In Seiffert, H.; Radnitzky, G. Handlexikon der Wissenschaftstheorie [Dictionary of epistemology] (in German) (1992 ed.).

Porter, Michael E. (March–April 1979), How Competitive Forces Shape Strategy, Harvard Business Review.

Ptak, Jeff, Morningstar, "Why Active Funds Have Outperformed in Theory But Fallen Short in Practice." 19 November 2018. https://www.morningstar.com/articles/901361/why-active-funds-have-outperformed-in-theory-but-f.html

Racanelli, Vito J, Barron's, Number of Dow Jones Shares Is Shrinking." 13 August 2018. https://www.barrons.com/articles/number-of-dow-jones-shares-is-shrinking-1534194995

Rappaport, Alfred and Michael J. Mauboussin (2001), "Expectations Investing: Reading Stock Prices for Better Returns." Harvard Business School Press. http://www.expectationsinvesting.com/chapter3.shtml

Rawson, Michael, Morningstar, "The Correlation Conundrum and What to Do About It." 3 May 2012. http://www.morningstar.co.uk/uk/news/69640/the-correlation-conundrum-and-what-to-do-about-it.aspx/

Read, Carveth (1898), "Logic: Deductive and Inductive (first edition), chapter 22.

Reddy, Rohan. Global X. "MLP Insights: Q2 2018. 5 June 2018. https://www.globalxfunds.com/mlp-insights-q2-2018/

Republic Services, 2017 Form 10-K, page 2. Retrieved December 3, 2018.

S&P DJI, "S&P 500 Q4 2017 Buybacks Rose 6.0% to $137.0 Billion; Full-Year 2017 Fell 3.2% to $519.4 Billion." 21 March 2018. https://www.prnewswire.com/news-releases/sp-500-q4-2017-buybacks-rose-60-to-1370-billion-full-year-2017-fell-32-to-5194-billion-300617373.html

S&P DJI, Factsheet. "S&P Dow Jones Indices," S&P High Yield Dividend Aristocrats." 31 October 2018. https://us.spindices.com/idsenhancedfactsheet/file.pdf?calcFrequency=M&force_download=true&hostIdentifier=48190c8c-42c4-46af-8d1a-0cd5db894797&indexId=2325

Bibliography

Schwert, G. William, Daily Percent Changes in the Standard & Poor's Index, 1928-2018. Retrieved December 19, 2018. http://schwert.ssb.rochester.edu/spret.pdf

SEC, "Non-GAAP Financial Measures." 4 April 2018. https://www.sec.gov/divisions/corpfin/guidance/nongaapinterp.htm

Seeking Alpha, "International Business Machines' (IBM) CEO Ginni Rometty on Q3 2014 Results - Earnings Call Transcript." 20 October 2014. https://seekingalpha.com/article/2575975-international-business-machines-ibm-ceo-ginni-rometty-on-q3-2014-results-earnings-call-transcript?part=single

Seeking Alpha, "Kinder Morgan's (KMI) CEO Steve Kean on Q2 2015 Results - Earnings Call Transcript." 15 July 2015. https://seekingalpha.com/article/3329175-kinder-morgans-kmi-ceo-steve-kean-on-q2-2015-results-earnings-call-transcript?part=single

Sharpe, William F (1991), "The Arithmetic of Active Management." http://www.cfapubs.org/doi/pdf/10.2469/faj.v47.n1.7

Shawal, David (2018). Twitter. https://twitter.com/DavidSchawel/status/1026270679967182849. Retrieved October 31, 2018.

Shiller, Robert (2000). Irrational Exuberance, page 185. http://www.library.fa.ru/files/Shiller2.pdf

Shroeder, Stan, Mashable. "Total cryptocurrency market cap shrinks to $186 billion." 12 September 2018. https://mashable.com/article/crypto-market-cap-lowest-2018/#k_qV4NBJmsqX

Siegel, Jeremy (1998), Stocks for the Long Run: The Definitive Guide to Financial Market Returns and Long-Term Investment Strategies." McGraw-Hill.

Siegel, Jeremy (2005), The Future for Investors: Why the Tried and the True Triumph Over the Bold and the New." Crown Publishing Group.

Smith, Peter, Financial Times. "Investors nurse $10m losses on LongFin index mistake." 3 April 2018. https://www.ft.com/content/acb5ddb6-3341-11e8-ac48-10c6fdc22f03

Soe, Aye M. and Ryan Poirier, FRM (2017), "SPIVA US Scorecard." S&P Dow Jones Indices. https://us.spindices.com/documents/spiva/spiva-us-year-end-2017.pdf

Southall, Brooke, Investment News, "With Manu Daftary of DG Capital Management, Inc," 22 May 2006. http://www.investmentnews.com/article/20060522/SUB/605220712/with-manu-daftaryof-dg-capital-management-inc

State Street Global Advisors. "SPDR S&P Dividend ETF. https://us.spdrs.com/en/etf/spdr-sp-dividend-etf-SDY

Bibliography

Stewart, James B (2017), "An Index-Fund Evangelist Is Straying From His Gospel, 22 June 2017. https://www.nytimes.com/2017/06/22/business/burton-malkiel-investment-stock-indexfunds.html

Stone, Amey, "Kinder Morgan Bear: 5 More Reasons to Worry." 19 June 2015. https://www.barrons.com/articles/kinder-morgan-bear-5-more-reasons-to-worry-1434744809

Street Insider, "Credit Suisse Upgrades MLPs to Overweight." 11 August 2015. https://www.streetinsider.com/Analyst+Comments/Credit+Suisse+Upgrades+MLPs+to+Overweight%3B+Sees+Over+40%25+Upside+on+Revision+to+the+Mean+Yield+Ranges/108010 15.html

Sullivan, Rodney and James X Xiong, (2012). "How Index Trading Increases Market Vulnerability." Financial Analysts Journal. https://www.cfapubs.org/doi/abs/10.2469/faj.v68.n2.7

Sundaram, Kailash, "Faulty Ratings: How Analysts Fueled the Internet Bubble." https://projects.iq.harvard.edu/files/lead/files/faulty_ratings_-_how_analysts_fueled_the_internet_bubble.pdf

Surran, Carl (a), Seeking Alpha. "Richard Kinder buys 100K KMI shares, stock bounces higher." 24 July 2015. https://seekingalpha.com/news/2656165-richard-kinder-buys-100k-kmi-shares-stock-bounces-higher

Surran, Carl (b), Seeking Alpha. "Kinder Morgan -7% on slower dividend growth view, uncertain funding needs." 22 October 2015. https://seekingalpha.com/news/2849046-kinder-morgan-minus-7-percent-slower-dividend-growth-view-uncertain-funding-needs

Surran, Carl (c), Seeking Alpha. "Kinder Morgan price target cut to $25 from $50 at Argus." https://seekingalpha.com/news/2918096-kinder-morgan-price-target-cut-35-50-argus

Surran, Carl (d), Seeking Alpha. "Kinder Morgan extends losses, now -15% this week." 3 December 2015. https://seekingalpha.com/news/2964106-kinder-morgan-extends-losses-now-minus-15-percent-week

Surran, Carl (e), Seeking Alpha. "Kinder Morgan expects 2016 DCF OK to support dividend growth guidance." 4 December 2015. https://seekingalpha.com/news/2966596-kinder-morgan-expects-2016-dcf-ok-support-dividend-growth-guidance

Surran, Carl (f), Seeking Alpha. "Kinder Morgan should cut dividend to $0.01, analyst says." 7 December 2018. https://seekingalpha.com/news/2968586-kinder-morgan-cut-dividend-0_01-analyst-says

Surran, Carl (g), Seeking Alpha. "Kinder Morgan higher after 'clearing the deck' with dividend cut. 9 December 2015. https://seekingalpha.com/news/2974536-kinder-morgan-higher-clearing-deck-dividend-cut

Surz, Ronald J. and Mitchell Price. The Journal of Investing. "The Truth About Diversification by the Numbers." Winter 2000. http://ppca-inc.com/Articles/DiversByNumbers.pdf

Bibliography

Swanson, Jim. "Goldman Sachs: Kinder Morgan Has 45% Upside." 14 August 2015. https://www.benzinga.com/analyst-ratings/analyst-color/15/08/5766600/goldman-sachs-kinder-morgan-has-45-upside

Taleb, Nassim (2005), "Fooled by Randomness: The Hidden Role of Chance in Life and in the Markets." Random House Trade Paperbacks.

Thaler, Richard (2016), "Misbehaving: The Making of Behavioral Economics." W. W. Norton & Company.

Thomas, Jeff, Babson's Warning, Casey Research International Man. Retrieved November 5, 2018. http://www.internationalman.com/articles/babsons-warning

Toyota (2006), Toyota Traditions, "Ask 'why' five times about every matter." https://www.toyota-global.com/company/toyota_traditions/quality/mar_apr_2006.html

Treynor, Jack and Fischer Black (1973), "How to Use Security Analysis to Improve Portfolio Selection," Journal of Business, vol. 46.

Udland, Myles, Yahoo Finance. "Jack Bogle envisions 'chaos, catastrophe' in markets if everyone were to index." https://finance.yahoo.com/news/jack-bogle-envisions-chaos-catastrophe-markets-everyone-indexed-194610197.html

Valuentum, "Adviser Fees on Indexed Assets Can Eat Up Your Nest Egg." 7 September 2017. https://www.valuentum.com/articles/Adviser_Fees_on_Indexed_Assets_Can_Eat_Up_Your_N est_Egg

Vigen, Tyler, "TylerVigen.com," Spurious Correlations. Retrieved November 25, 2018. http://www.tylervigen.com/spurious-correlations

Vlastelica, Ryan, "Less than 1% of ETFs getting half of all inflows in 2017." 20 July 2017. https://www.marketwatch.com/story/less-than-1-of-etfs-getting-half-of-all-inflows-in-2017-2017-07-19

Vlastelica, Ryan (2018). "Goldman blames mom-and-pop investors for volatility in stocks." https://www.marketwatch.com/amp/story/guid/76120B14-52F3-11E8-8AA1-3C71A5012970

Waggoner, John. "Warren Buffett be damned, case for value wanes." http://www.investmentnews.com/article/20180510/FREE/180519994/warren-buffett-be-damned-case-for-value-investing-wanes. 10 May 2018.

Wermers, Russ (2010), "A Matter of Style: The Causes and Consequences of Style Drift in Institutional Portfolios." https://papers.ssrn.com/sol3/papers.cfm?abstract_id=2024259

Wikipedia. S&P 500 Dividend Aristocrats. Retrieved November 4, 2011. https://en.wikipedia.org/wiki/S%26P_500_Dividend_Aristocrats

Wikipedia. Woodstock, Illinois. Retrieved November 4, 2018. https://en.wikipedia.org/wiki/Woodstock,_Illinois

Wurgler, Jeffrey, (2010). "On the Economic Consequences of Index-Linked Investing." In Challenges to Business in the Twenty-First Century: The Way Forward. Edited by W.T. Allen, R. Khurana, J. Lorsch, and G. Rosenfeld. Cambridge, MA: American Academy of Arts and Sciences.

Xilinx, "Form 10-K, Fiscal 2018." http://investor.xilinx.com/static-files/13e52459-fd4c-44da-adee-19e463d02ae8. Retrieved November 3, 2018.

Yahoo Finance Video, "Buffett on intrinsic value." 6 May 2017. https://finance.yahoo.com/video/buffett-intrinsic-value-160028095.html

Yuan, Kathy, Lu Zheng and Qiaoqiao Zhu (2006), "Are investors moonstruck? Lunar phases and stock returns." Journal of Empirical Finance. https://www.sciencedirect.com/science/article/abs/pii/S0927539805000691

Zacks, "How Does the Stock Price Change When a Dividend Is Paid?" 14 May 2018. https://finance.zacks.com/stock-price-change-dividend-paid-3571.html. Retrieved November 3. 2018.

Zarooli, Jim. NPR, "Washington Mutual Collapses." 26 September 2008. https://www.npr.org/templates/story/story.php?storyId=95105112

Zweig, Jason (2009), "Does Stock-Market Data Really Go Back 200 Years?," July 11, 2009. https://www.wsj.com/articles/SB124725925791924871

Zweig, Jason, (2017) "Stock Picking Is Dying Because There Are No More Stocks to Pick." https://blogs.wsj.com/moneybeat/2017/06/23/stockpicking-is-dying-because-there-are-no-more-stocks-topick/

LIST OF FIGURES

List of Figures

ACKNOWLEDGEMENTS

W e did it. buddy.

My son Nathan has been with me since the beginning of Valuentum, born just a month or so after we published the company's very first newsletter. He's spent so many hours with his daddy while I was at home working, not only the time spent launching the business but also the time that went into writing this manuscript. We'd spend so many hours together at home, but never quite be together. He deserves as much credit as anybody for this text. He is "my everything."

This is you for, Nate. I love you so much.

Head of Data at Valuentum, Kris Rosemann has worked tirelessly to build Valuentum into the independent research publishing company it has become. Kris has been with me through almost every critical decision made about the future of Valuentum, and I am very much indebted to him. His thoughts and edits through the course of writing this book have been invaluable. Stock and Dividend Analyst Chris Araos not only read this text, but also the first financial history book I tried to write, which went incomplete and unpublished. Boy that book would have been dead on arrival, and he was so polite about it! Thank you, Chris.

I'd like to thank my wife Elizabeth, my brother Leonard, my parents Leonard and Marilyn, and my parents-in-law David and Gail. My wife has spent countless hours answering member questions, and she's been a pillar of strength through the entrepreneurial journey called Valuentum. She has read through this book at least twice, and I hope not to let her down. I feel like the book should be much better given all the help I've received.

My brother Leonard helped so much with the infrastructure behind Valuentum's company reports that without him, I don't think the company would have much to stand on. To my parents Leonard and Marilyn, and to my parents-in-law David and Gail, thank you for always being there for us. To my father especially, I don't think Valuentum would have sustained, yet alone thrived, without your positive influence on my life.

I'd like to thank TradingView for the use of their charts in this text, and the dozens of analysts at Morningstar and Driehaus Capital Management that I've worked with for many years. Special thanks go to Benedictine University and the University of Chicago Booth School of Business, but also Northern Illinois University, which is overflowing with talented interns, and DePaul University, where our good friends at the Chicago Chapter of the American Association of Individual Investors meet.

What is a company without its supporters? Our dear Valuentum subscribers are so very important. Without them, this book would definitely not be possible. They pushed the Valuentum team every day to deliver something of value, and in doing so, have made our investment research organization one of the best around. We give you our best, always, and your loyalty is appreciated more than you could ever imagine. We did all of this for you. Thank you, thank you, and thank you!

I'd like to mention some key influences in this work. For starters, I'd like to thank Richard Driehaus for giving me my first real job in this business, and for all my supervisors at Morningstar who gave me opportunity after opportunity. The thoughts in the book stand on the shoulders of giants, the list of which can never be comprehensive, from John Burr Williams, Benjamin Graham, John Maynard Keynes to Warren Buffett, Richard Thaler and beyond.

Finally, thank you for reading! I feel like I could have spent years writing this text, but I only had a couple months. I sincerely hope you have enjoyed it.

INDEX

The number following *n* refers to the number of the footnote in the text.

Index

Index

Index

CPSIA information can be obtained
at www.ICGtesting.com
Printed in the USA
LVHW091713120819
627348LV00004B/872/P